PLUTARCH'S LIVES

VOLUME THREE

FEAST OF LUCULLUS

PLUTARCH'S LIVES

The Translation Called Dryden's

Corrected from the Greek and Revised by

A. H. CLOUGH

Sometime Fellow and Tutor of the Oriel College, Oxford, and Late Professor of the English Language and Literature at University College, London

With
Dr. William Smith's Historical Notes

IN FIVE VOLUMES

VOLUME THREE

Illustrated

WILDSIDE PRESS

CONTENTS

Vol. III

	PAGE
Pyrrhus	1
Caius Marius	52
Lysander	113
Sylla	152
Comparison of Lysander with Sylla	207
Cimon	213
Lucullus	243
Comparison of Lucullus with Cimon	302
Nicias	307
Crassus	351
Comparison of Crassus with Nicias	398
Sertorius	405
Eumenes	441
Comparison of Sertorius with Eumenes	467

ILLUSTRATIONS

Vol. III

Feast of Lucullus	*Frontispiece*
	FACING PAGE
The Battle of Issus	8
Marius on the Ruins of Carthage	102
Hercules	340
The Catilinian Conspiracy	368
Alexander the Great	442

PLUTARCH'S LIVES

PYRRHUS[1]

Translated by William Croune, M. D.,
Fellow of the College of Physicians.

Of the Thesprotians and Molossians after the great inundation, the first king, according to some historians, was Phaethon, one of those who came into Epirus with Pelasgus. Others tell us that Deucalion and Pyrrha, having set up the worship of Jupiter at Dodona, settled there among the Molossians. In after time, Neoptolemus, Achilles's son, planting a colony, possessed these parts himself, and left a succession of kings, who, after him, were named Pyrrhidæ; as he in his youth was called Pyrrhus, and of his legitimate children, one born of Lanassa, daughter of Cleodæus, Hyllus's son, had also that name. From him, Achilles came to have divine honors in Epirus, under the name of Aspetus, in the language of the country. After these first kings, those of the following intervening times becoming barbarous, and insignificant both in their power and their lives, Tharrhypas is said to have been the first, who by introducing Greek manners and learning, and humane laws into his cities, left any fame of himself. Alcetas was the son of Tharrhypas, Arybas of Alcetas, and of Arybas and Troas his queen, Æacides: he married Phthia, the daughter of Menon, the Thessalian, a man of note at the time of the Lamiac war, and of

[1] He was the greatest warrior and one of the best princes of his time. He was born 318 B. C., killed at Argos, Greece, about 272 B. C.—Dr. William Smith.

highest command in the confederate army next to
Leosthenes. To Æacides were born of Phthia, Deidamia and Troas daughters, and Pyrrhus a son.

The Molossians, afterwards falling into factions,
and expelling Æacides, brought in the sons of Neoptolemus, and such friends of Æacides as they could
take were all cut off; Pyrrhus, yet an infant, and
searched for by the enemy, had been stolen away and
carried off by Androclides and Angelus; who, however, being obliged to take with them a few servants, and women to nurse the child, were much impeded and retarded in their flight, and when they
were now overtaken, they delivered the infant to
Androcleon, Hippias, and Neander, faithful and able
young fellows, giving them in charge to make for
Megara, a town of Macedon, with all their might,
while they themselves, partly by entreaty, and partly
by force, stopped the course of the pursuers till late
in the evening. At last, having hardly forced them
back, they joined those who had the care of Pyrrhus;
but the sun being already set, at the point of attaining their object they suddenly found themselves cut
off from it. For on reaching the river that runs by
the city they found it looking formidable and rough,
and endeavoring to pass over, they discovered it was
not fordable; late rains having heightened the water,
and made the current violent. The darkness of the
night added to the horror of all, so that they durst
not venture of themselves to carry over the child and
the women that attended it; but, perceiving some of
the country people on the other side, they desired
them to assist their passage, and showed them Pyrrhus, calling out aloud, and importuning them. They,
however, could not hear for the noise and roaring
of the water. Thus time was spent while those called

out, and the others did not understand what was said, till one recollecting himself, stripped off a piece of bark from an oak, and wrote on it with a tongue of a buckle, stating the necessities and the fortunes of the child, and then rolling it about a stone, which was made use of to give force to the motion, threw it over to the other side, or, as some say, fastened it to the end of a javelin, and darted it over. When the men on the other shore read what was on the bark, and saw how time pressed, without delay they cut down some trees, and lashing them together, came over to them. And it so fell out, that he who first got ashore, and took Pyrrhus in his arms, was named Achilles, the rest being helped over by others as they came to hand.

Thus being safe, and out of the reach of pursuit, they addressed themselves to Glaucias, then king of the Illyrians, and finding him sitting at home with his wife, they laid down the child before them. The king began to weigh the matter, fearing Cassander, who was a mortal enemy of Æacides, and, being in deep consideration, said nothing for a long time; while Pyrrhus, crawling about on the ground, gradually got near and laid hold with his hand upon the king's robe, and so helping himself upon his feet against the knees of Glaucias, first moved laughter, and then pity, as a little humble, crying petitioner. Some say he did not throw himself before Glaucias, but catching hold of an altar of the gods, and spreading his hands about it, raised himself up by that; and that Glaucias took the act as an omen. At present, therefore, he gave Pyrrhus into the charge of his wife, commanding he should be brought up with his own children; and a little after, the enemies sending to demand him, and Cassander himself offering two

hundred talents, he would not deliver him up; but
when he was twelve years old, bringing him with an
army into Epirus, made him king. Pyrrhus in the
air of his face had something more of the terrors,
than of the augustness of kingly power, he had not
a regular set of upper teeth, but in the place of them
one continued bone, with small lines marked on it,
resembling the divisions of a row of teeth. It was a
general belief he could cure the spleen, by sacrificing
a white cock, and gently pressing with his right foot
on the spleen of the persons as they lay down on their
backs, nor was any one so poor or inconsiderable as
not to be welcome if he desired it, to the benefit of
his touch. He accepted the cock for the sacrifice as
a reward, and was always much pleased with the present.
The large toe of that foot was said to have a
divine virtue; for after his death, the rest of the body
being consumed, this was found unhurt and untouched
by the fire. But of these things hereafter.

Being now about seventeen years old, and the
government in appearance well settled, he took a
journey out of the kingdom to attend the marriage of
one of Glaucias's sons, with whom he was brought
up; upon which opportunity the Molossians again
rebelling, turned out all of his party, plundered his
property, and gave themselves up to Neoptolemus.
Pyrrhus, having thus lost the kingdom, and being in
want of all things, applied to Demetrius the son of
Antigonus, the husband of his sister Deidamia, who,
while she was but a child, had been in name the wife
of Alexander,[2] son of Roxana, but their affairs after-

---

[2] The *affairs of Alexander,* called Ægus, son by Roxana, and
lawful heir of Alexander the Great, *proved unfortunate,* as did
those of all the blood royal of the old Macedonian family, in the
time of Cassander. Alexander and Roxana were both put to

wards proving unfortunate, when she came to age, Demetrius married her. At the great battle of Ipsus, where so many kings were engaged, Pyrrhus, taking part with Demetrius, though yet but a youth, routed those that encountered him, and highly signalized himself among all the soldiery; and afterwards, when Demetrius's fortunes were low, he did not forsake him then, but secured for him the cities of Greece with which he was intrusted; and upon articles of agreement being made between Demetrius and Ptolemy, he went over as an hostage for him into Egypt, where both in hunting and other exercises, he gave Ptolemy an ample proof of his courage and strength. Here observing Berenice in greatest power, and of all Ptolemy's wives highest in esteem for virtue and understanding, he made his court principally to her. He had a particular art of gaining over the great to his own interest, as on the other hand he readily overlooked such as were below him; and being also well-behaved and temperate in his life, among all the young princes then at court, he was thought most fit to have Antigone for his wife, one of the daughters of Berenice by Philip, before she married Ptolemy.

After this match, advancing in honor, and Antigone being a very good wife to him, having procured a sum of money, and raised an army, he so ordered matters as to be sent into his kingdom of Epirus, and arrived there to the great satisfaction of many, from their hate to Neoptolemus, who was governing in a violent and arbitrary way. But fearing lest Neoptolemus should enter into alliance with some

death by his orders. Olympias, with whom they had acted, was cousin to Pyrrhus's father, Æacides. For *the great battle of Ipsus where* all the kings, or as one reading has it, all the kings of the earth *were engaged,* see the life of Demetrius in Volume V.

neighboring princes, he came to terms and friendship with him, agreeing that they should share the government between them. There were people, however, who, as time went, on secretly exasperated them, and fomented jealousies between them. The cause chiefly moving Pyrrhus is said to have had this beginning. It was customary for the kings to offer sacrifice to Mars, at Passaro, a place in the Molossian country, and that done to enter into a solemn covenant with the Epirots; they to govern according to law, these to preserve the government as by law established. This was performed in the presence of both kings, who were there with their immediate friends, giving and receiving many presents; here Gelo, one of the friends of Neoptolemus, taking Pyrrhus by the hand, presented him with two pair of draught oxen. Myrtilus, his cup-bearer, being then by, begged these of Pyrrhus, who not giving them to him, but to another, Myrtilus extremely resented it, which Gelo took notice of, and, inviting him to a banquet, (amidst drinking and other excesses, as some relate, Myrtilus being then in the flower of his youth,) he entered into discourse, persuading him to adhere to Neoptolemus, and destroy Pyrrhus by poison. Myrtilus received the design, appearing to approve and consent to it, but privately discovered it to Pyrrhus, by whose command he recommended Alexicrates, his chief cup-bearer, to Gelo, as a fit instrument for their design, Pyrrhus being very desirous to have proof of the plot by several evidences. So Gelo being deceived, Neoptolemus, who was no less deceived, imagining the design went prosperously on, could not forbear, but in his joy spoke of it among his friends, and once at an entertainment at his sister Cadmea's, talked openly of it, thinking none heard but themselves.

PYRRHUS 7

Nor was any one there but Phænarete the wife of Samon, who had the care of Neoptolemus's flocks and herds. She, turning her face towards the wall upon a couch, seemed fast asleep, and having heard all that passed, unsuspected, next day came to Antigone, Pyrrhus's wife, and told her what she had heard Neoptolemus say to his sister. On understanding which Pyrrhus for the present said little, but on a sacrifice day, making an invitation for Neoptolemus, killed him; being satisfied before that the great men of the Epirots were his friends, and that they were eager for him to rid himself of Neoptolemus, and not to content himself with a mere petty share of the government, but to follow his own natural vocation to great designs, and now when a just ground of suspicion appeared, to anticipate Neoptolemus by taking him off first.

In memory of Berenice and Ptolemy, he named his son by Antigone, Ptolemy, and having built a city in the peninsula of Epirus,[3] called it Berenicis. From this time he began to revolve many and vast projects in his thoughts; but his first special hope and design lay near home, and he found means to engage himself in the Macedonian affairs under the following pretext. Of Cassander's sons, Antipater, the eldest, killed Thessalonica his mother, and expelled his brother Alexander, who sent to Demetrius entreating his assistance, and also called in Pyrrhus; but De-

[3] The only peninsula or *chersonese* of Epirus that appears to be mentioned, is that on which Buthrotum stands. Niebuhr suggests the peninsula in the lake of Janina. *Tymphœa and Parauœa* are corrections of Niebuhr's for Nymphæa and Paralia. They are districts commanding the passage from Macedonia to the Greek city, Ambracia, which Strabo tells us became Pyrrhus's capital.

metrius being retarded by multitude of business, Pyrrhus, coming first, demanded in reward of his service the districts called Tymphæa and Parauæa in Macedon itself, and, of their new conquests, Ambracia, Acarnania, and Amphilochia. The young prince giving way, he took possession of these countries, and secured them with good garrisons, and proceeded to reduce for Alexander himself other parts of the kingdom which he gained from Antipater. Lysimachus, designing to send aid to Antipater, was involved in much other business, but knowing Pyrrhus would not disoblige Ptolemy, or deny him any thing, sent pretended letters to him as from Ptolemy, desiring him to give up his expedition, upon the payment of three hundred talents to him by Antipater. Pyrrhus, opening the letter, quickly discovered the fraud of Lysimachus; for it had not the accustomed style of salutation, "The father to the son, health," but "King Ptolemy to Pyrrhus, the king, health;" and reproaching Lysimachus, he notwithstanding made a peace, and they all met to confirm it by a solemn oath upon sacrifice. A goat, a bull, and a ram being brought out, the ram on a sudden fell dead. The others laughed, but Theodotus the prophet forbade Pyrrhus to swear, declaring that Heaven by that portended the death of one of the three kings, upon which he refused to ratify the peace.

The affairs of Alexander being now in some kind of settlement, Demetrius arrived, contrary, as soon appeared, to the desire and indeed not without the alarm of Alexander. After they had been a few days together, their mutual jealousy led them to conspire against each other; and Demetrius taking advantage of the first occasion, was beforehand with the young king, and slew him, and proclaimed himself king of

THE BATTLE OF ISSUS (FROM A FRESCO IN POMPEII)

Macedon. There had been formerly no very good understanding between him and Pyrrhus; for besides the inroads he made into Thessaly, the innate disease of princes, ambition of greater empire, had rendered them formidable and suspected neighbors to each other, especially since Deidamia's death; and both having seized Macedon, they came into conflict for the same object, and the difference between them had the stronger motives. Demetrius having first attacked the Ætolians and subdued them, left Pantauchus there with a considerable army, and marched direct against Pyrrhus, and Pyrrhus, as he thought, against him; but by mistake of the ways they passed by one another, and Demetrius falling into Epirus wasted the country, and Pyrrhus, meeting with Pantauchus, prepared for an engagement. The soldiers fell to, and there was a sharp and terrible conflict, especially where the generals were. Pantauchus, in courage, dexterity, and strength of body, being confessedly the best of all Demetrius's captains, and having both resolution and high spirit, challenged Pyrrhus to fight hand to hand; on the other side Pyrrhus, professing not to yield to any king in valor and glory, and esteeming the fame of Achilles more truly to belong to him for his courage than for his blood, advanced against Pantauchus through the front of the army. First they used their lances, then came to a close fight, and managed their swords both with art and force; Pyrrhus receiving one wound, but returning two for it, one in the thigh, the other near the neck, repulsed and overthrew Pantauchus, but did not kill him outright, as he was rescued by his friends. But the Epirots exulting in the victory of their king, and admiring his courage, forced through and cut in pieces the phalanx of the Macedonians, and pursuing those that fled, killed many, and took five thousand prisoners.

This fight did not so much exasperate the Macedonians with anger for their loss, or with hatred to Pyrrhus, as it caused esteem, and admiration of his valor, and great discourse of him among those that saw what he did, and were engaged against him in the action. They thought his countenance, his swiftness, and his motions expressed those of the great Alexander, and that they beheld here an image and resemblance of his rapidity and strength in fight; other kings merely by their purple and their guards, by the formal bending of their necks, and lofty tone of speech, Pyrrhus only by arms, and in action, represented Alexander. Of his knowledge of military tactics and the art of a general, and his great ability that way, we have the best information from the commentaries he left behind him. Antigonus, also, we are told, being asked who was the greatest soldier, said, "Pyrrhus, if he lives to be old," referring only to those of his own time; but Hannibal of all great commanders esteemed Pyrrhus for skill and conduct the first, Scipio the second, and himself the third, as is related in the life of Scipio. In a word, he seemed ever to make this all his thought and philosophy, as the most kingly part of learning; other curiosities he held in no account. He is reported, when asked at a feast whether he thought Python or Caphisias the best musician, to have said, Polysperchon was the best soldier, as though it became a king to examine and understand only such things. Towards his familiars he was mild, and not easily incensed; zealous, and even vehement in returning kindnesses. Thus when Aeropus was dead, he could not bear it with moderation, saying, he indeed had suffered what was common to human nature, but condemning and blaming himself, that by puttings off and delays he had not returned his kindness in time. For our debts may be satisfied to the creditor's heirs, but not to have made the acknowledgment of received favors, while they to whom it is due can be sensible of it, afflicts a good and a worthy nature. Some thinking it fit that Pyrrhus should banish a certain ill-tongued fellow in Ambracia, who had spoken very indecently of him, "Let him rather," said he, "speak against us here to a few, than rambling about to a great many." And others who in their wine had made reflections upon him, being afterward questioned for it, and asked by him whether they had said such words, on one of the young fellows answering, "Yes, all that, king; and should have said more if we had had more wine;" he laughed and discharged them. After Antigone's death, he married several wives to enlarge his interest and power. He had the daughter of Autoleon, king of the Pæonians, Bircenna, Bardyllis the Illyrian's daughter, Lanassa, daughter of Agathocles the Syracusan, who brought with her in dower the city of Corcyra which had been taken by Agathocles. By Antigone he had Ptolemy, Alexander by Lanassa, and Helenus, his youngest son, by Bircenna; he brought them up all in arms, hot and eager youths, and by him sharpened and whetted to war from their very infancy. It is said, when one of them, while yet a child, asked him to which he would leave the kingdom, he replied, to him that had the sharpest sword, which indeed was much like that tragical curse of Oedipus to his sons:—

Not by the lot decide,
But with the sword the heritage divide.[4]

[4] *Not by the lot decide, But with the sword the heritage divide,* is from the Phœnissæ of Euripides, (66).

So unsocial and wild-beast-like is the nature of ambition and cupidity.

After this battle Pyrrhus, returning gloriously home, enjoyed his fame and reputation, and being called "Eagle" by the Epirots, "By you," said he, "I am an eagle; for how should I not be such, while I have your arms as wings to sustain me?" A little after, having intelligence that Demetrius was dangerously sick, he entered on a sudden into Macedonia, intending only an incursion, and to harass the country; but was very near seizing upon all, and taking the kingdom without a blow. He marched as far as Edessa unresisted, great numbers deserting, and coming in to him. This danger excited Demetrius beyond his strength, and his friends and commanders in a short time got a considerable army together, and with all their forces briskly attacked Pyrrhus, who, coming only to pillage, would not stand a fight, but retreating lost part of his army, as he went off, by the close pursuit of the Macedonians. Demetrius, however, although he had easily and quickly forced Pyrrhus out of the country, yet did not slight him, but having resolved upon great designs, and to recover his father's kingdom with an army of one hundred thousand men, and a fleet of five hundred ships, would neither embroil himself with Pyrrhus, nor leave the Macedonians so active and troublesome a neighbor; and since he had no leisure to continue the war with him, he was willing to treat and conclude a peace, and to turn his forces upon the other kings. Articles being agreed upon, the designs of Demetrius quickly discovered themselves by the greatness of his preparation. And the other kings being alarmed, sent to Pyrrhus ambassadors and letters, expressing their wonder that he should choose to let his own opportunity pass by, and wait till Demetrius could use his; and whereas he was now able to chase him out of Macedon, involved in designs and disturbed, he should expect till Demetrius at leisure, and grown great, should bring the war home to his own door, and make him fight for his temples and sepulchres in Molossia; especially having so lately, by his means, lost Corcyra and his wife together. For Lanassa had taken offence at Pyrrhus for too great an inclination to those wives of his that were barbarians, and so withdrew to Corcyra, and desiring to marry some king, invited Demetrius, knowing of all the kings he was most ready to entertain offers of marriage; so he sailed thither, married Lanassa, and placed a garrison in the city. The kings having written thus to Pyrrhus, themselves likewise contrived to find Demetrius work, while he was delaying and making his preparations. Ptolemy, setting out with a great fleet, drew off many of the Greek cities. Lysimachus out of Thrace wasted the upper Macedon; and Pyrrhus, also, taking arms at the same time, marched to Berœa, expecting, as it fell out, that Demetrius, collecting his forces against Lysimachus, would leave the lower country undefended. That very night he seemed in his sleep to be called by Alexander the Great, and approaching saw him sick abed, but was received with very kind words and much respect, and promised zealous assistance. He making bold to reply: "How, Sir, can you, being sick, assist me?" "With my name," said he, and mounting a Nisæan horse, seemed to lead the way. At the sight of this vision he was much assured, and with swift marches overrunning all the interjacent places, takes Berœa, and making his headquarters there, reduced the rest of the country by his commanders. When Demetrius received intelligence of this, and perceived likewise the Macedonians ready to mutiny in the army, he was afraid to advance further, lest coming near Lysimachus, a Macedonian king, and of great fame, they should revolt to him. So returning, he marched directly against Pyrrhus, as a stranger, and hated by the Macedonians. But while he lay encamped there near him, many who came out of Berœa infinitely praised Pyrrhus as invincible in arms, a glorious warrior, who treated those he had taken kindly and humanely. Several of these Pyrrhus himself sent privately, pretending to be Macedonians, and saying, now was the time to be delivered from the severe government of Demetrius, by coming over to Pyrrhus, a gracious prince, and a lover of soldiers. By this artifice a great part of the army was in a state of excitement, and the soldiers began to look every way about, inquiring for Pyrrhus. It happened he was without his helmet, till understanding they did not know him, he put it on again, and so was quickly recognized by his lofty crest, and the goat's horns he wore upon it. Then the Macedonians, running to him, desired to be told his password, and some put oaken boughs upon their heads, because they saw them worn by the soldiers about him. Some persons even took the confidence to say to Demetrius himself, that he would be well advised to withdraw, and lay down the government. And he, indeed, seeing the mutinous movements of the army to be only too consistent with what they said, privately got away, disguised in a broad hat, and a common soldier's coat. So Pyrrhus became master of the army without fighting, and was declared king of the Macedonians.

But Lysimachus now arriving, and claiming the defeat of Demetrius as the joint exploit of them both, and that therefore the kingdom should be shared between them, Pyrrhus, not as yet quite assured of the Macedonians, and in doubt of their faith, consented to the proposition of Lysimachus, and divided the country and cities between them accordingly. This was for the present useful, and prevented a war; but shortly after they found the partition not so much a peaceful settlement, as an occasion of further complaint and difference. For men whose ambition neither seas nor mountains, nor unpeopled deserts can limit, nor the bounds dividing Europe from Asia confine their vast desires, it would be hard to expect to forbear from injuring one another when they touch, and are close together. These are ever naturally at war, envying and seeking advantages of one another, and merely make use of those two words, peace and war, like current coin, to serve their occasions, not as justice but as expediency suggests, and are really better men when they openly enter on a war, than when they give to the mere forbearance from doing wrong, for want of opportunity, the sacred names of justice and friendship. Pyrrhus was an instance of this; for setting himself against the rise of Demetrius again, and endeavoring to hinder the recovery of his power, as it were from a kind of sickness, he assisted the Greeks, and came to Athens, where, having ascended the Acropolis, he offered sacrifice to the goddess, and the same day came down again, and told the Athenians he was much gratified by the good-will and the confidence they had shown to him; but if they were wise, he advised them never to let any king come thither again, or open their city gates to him. He concluded also a peace with Demetrius, but shortly after he was gone into Asia, at the persuasion of Lysimachus, he tampered with the Thessalians to revolt, and besieged his cities in Greece; finding he could better preserve the attachment of the Macedonians in war than in peace, and being of his own inclination not much given to rest.

At last, after Demetrius had been over thrown in Syria, Lysimachus, who had secured his affairs, and had nothing to do, immediately turned his whole forces upon Pyrrhus, who was in quarters at Edessa, and falling upon and seizing his convoy of provisions, brought first a great scarcity into the army; then partly by letters, partly by spreading rumors abroad, he corrupted the principal officers of the Macedonians, reproaching them that they had made one their master who was both a stranger and descended from those who had ever been servants to the Macedonians, and that they had thrust the old friends and familiars of Alexander out of the country. The Macedonian soldiers being much prevailed upon, Pyrrhus withdrew himself with his Epirots and auxiliary forces, relinquishing Macedon just after the same manner he took it. So little reason have kings to condemn popular governments for changing sides as suits their interests, as in this they do but imitate them who are the great instructors of unfaithfulness and treachery; holding him the wisest that makes the least account of being an honest man.

Pyrrhus having thus retired into Epirus, and left Macedon, fortune gave him a fair occasion of enjoying himself in quiet, and peaceably governing his own subjects; but he who thought it a nauseous course of life not to be doing mischief to others, or receiving some from them, like Achilles, could not endure repose,

―――――But sat and languished far,
Desiring battle and the shout of war,[5]

and gratified his inclination by the following pretext for new troubles. The Romans were at war with the Tarentines, who, not being able to go on with the war,

[5] *Iliad*, I. 491, 492.

PYRRHUS 17

nor yet, through the foolhardiness, and the viciousness of their popular speakers, to come to terms and give it up, proposed now to make Pyrrhus their general, and engage him in it, as of all the neighboring kings the most at leisure, and the most skilful as a commander. The more grave and discreet citizens opposing these counsels, were partly overborne by the noise and violence of the multitude; while others, seeing this, absented themselves from the assemblies; only one Meton, a very sober man, on the day this public decree was to be ratified, when the people were now seating themselves, came dancing into the assembly like one quite drunk, with a withered garland and a small lamp in his hand, and a woman playing on a flute before him. And as in great multitudes met at such popular assemblies, no decorum can be well observed, some clapped him, others laughed, none forbade him, but called to the woman to play, and to him to sing to the company, and when they thought he was going to do so, " 'T is only right of you, O men of Tarentum," he said, "not to hinder any from making themselves merry, that have a mind to it, while it is yet in their power; and if you are wise, you will take out your pleasure of your freedom while you can, for you must change your course of life, and follow other diet when Pyrrhus comes to town." These words made a great impression upon many of the Tarentines, and a confused murmur went about, that he had spoken much to the purpose; but some who feared they should be sacrificed if a peace were made with the Romans, reviled the whole assembly for so tamely suffering themselves to be abused by a drunken sot, and crowding together upon Meton, thrust him out. So the public order was passed, and ambassadors sent into Epirus, not only in their own names, but in those of all the Italian

Greeks, carrying presents to Pyrrhus, and letting him know they wanted a general of reputation and experience; and that they could furnish him with large forces of Lucanians, Messapians, Samnites, and Tarentines, amounting to twenty thousand horse, and three hundred and fifty thousand foot. This did not only quicken Pyrrhus, but raised an eager desire for the expedition in the Epirots.

There was one Cineas, a Thessalian, considered to be a man of very good sense, a disciple of the great orator Demosthenes, who of all that were famous at that time for speaking well, most seemed, as in a picture, to revive in the minds of the audience the memory of his force and vigor of eloquence; and being always about Pyrrhus, and sent about in his service to several cities, verified the saying of Euripides, that

───── the force of words
Can do whate'er is done by conquering swords.[6]

And Pyrrhus was used to say, that Cineas had taken more towns with his words, than he with his arms, and always did him the honor to employ him in his most important occasions. This person, seeing Pyrrhus eagerly preparing for Italy, led him one day when he was at leisure into the following reasonings: "The Romans, sir, are reported to be great warriors and conquerors of many war-like nations; if God permit us to overcome them, how should we use our victory?" "You ask," said Pyrrhus, "a thing evident of itself. The Romans once conquered, there is neither Greek nor barbarian city that will resist us, but we shall presently be masters of all Italy, the extent and resources and strength of which any one should rather profess to be ignorant of, than yourself." Cineas,

[6] Euripides, Phoenissae, 516, 517.

PYRRHUS

after a little pause, "And having subdued Italy, what shall we do next?" Pyrrhus not yet discovering his intention, "Sicily," he replied, "next holds out her arms to receive us, a wealthy and populous island, and easy to be gained; for since Agathocles left it, only faction and anarchy, and the licentious violence of the demagogues prevail." "You speak," said Cineas, "what is perfectly probable, but will the possession of Sicily put an end to the war?" "God grants us," answered Pyrrhus, "victory and success in that, and we will use these as forerunners of greater things; who could forbear from Libya and Carthage then within reach, which Agathocles, even when forced to fly from Syracuse, and passing the sea only with a few ships, had all but surprised? These conquests once perfected, will any assert that of the enemies who now pretend to despise us, any one will dare to make further resistance?" "None," replied Cineas, "for then it is manifest we may with such mighty forces regain Macedon, and make an absolute conquest of Greece; and when all these are in our power, what shall we do then?" Said Pyrrhus, smiling, "we will live at our ease, my dear friend, and drink all day, and divert ourselves with pleasant conversation." When Cineas had led Pyrrhus with his argument to this point: "And what hinders us now, sir, if we have a mind to be merry, and entertain one another, since we have at hand without trouble all those necessary things, to which through much blood and great labor, and infinite hazards and mischief done to ourselves and to others, we design at last to arrive?" Such reasonings rather troubled Pyrrhus with the thought of the happiness he was quitting than any way altered his purpose, being unable to abandon the hopes of what he so much desired.

And first, he sent away Cineas to the Tarentines

with three thousand men; presently after, many vessels for transport of horse, and galleys, and flat-bottomed boats of all sorts arriving from Tarentum, he shipped upon them twenty elephants, three thousand horse, twenty thousand foot, two thousand archers, and five hundred slingers. All being thus in readiness, he set sail, and being half way over, was driven by the wind, blowing, contrary to the season of the year, violently from the north, and carried from his course, but by the great skill and resolution of his pilots and seamen, he made the land with infinite labor, and beyond expectation. The rest of the fleet could not get up, and some of the dispersed ships, losing the coast of Italy, were driven into the Libyan and Sicilian Sea; others not able to double the Cape of Japygium, were overtaken by the night; and with a boisterous and heavy sea, throwing them upon a dangerous and rocky shore, they were all very much disabled except the royal galley. She, while the sea bore upon her sides, resisted with her bulk and strength, and avoided the force of it, till the wind coming about, blew directly in their teeth from the shore, and the vessel keeping up with her head against it, was in danger of going to pieces; yet on the other hand, to suffer themselves to be driven off to sea again, which was thus raging and tempestuous, with the wind shifting about every way, seemed to them the most dreadful of all their present evils. Pyrrhus, rising up, threw himself overboard. His friends and guards strove eagerly who should be most ready to help him, but night and the sea with its noise and violent surge, made it extremely difficult to do this; so that hardly, when with the morning the wind began to subside, he got ashore, breathless, and weakened in body, but with high courage and strength of mind resisting his hard fortune. The Messapians, upon whose shore they were thrown by the tempest, came up eagerly to help them in the best manner they could; and some of the straggling vessels that had escaped the storm arrived; in which were a very few horse, and not quite two thousand foot, and two elephants.

With these Pyrrhus marched straight to Tarentum, where Cineas, being informed of his arrival, led out the troops to meet him. Entering the town, he did nothing unpleasing to the Tarentines, nor put any force upon them, till his ships were all in harbor, and the greatest part of the army got together; but then perceiving that the people, unless some strong compulsion was used to them, were not capable either of saving others or being saved themselves, and were rather intending, while he engaged for them in the field, to remain at home bathing and feasting themselves, he first shut up the places of public exercise, and the walks where, in their idle way, they fought their country's battles and conducted her campaigns in their talk; he prohibited likewise all festivals, revels, and drinking-places, as unseasonable, and summoning them to arms, showed himself rigorous and inflexible in carrying out the conscription for service in the war. So that many, not understanding what it was to be commanded, left the town, calling it mere slavery not to do as they pleased. He now received intelligence that Lævinus, the Roman consul, was upon his march with a great army, and plundering Lucania as he went. The confederate forces were not come up to him, yet he thought it impossible to suffer so near an approach of an enemy, and drew out with his army, but first sent an herald to the Romans to know if before the war they would decide the differences between them and the Italian Greeks by his arbitrament and mediation. But Lævinus returning answer, that the Romans neither accepted him as arbitrator, nor feared him as an enemy, Pyrrhus advanced, and encamped in the plain between the cities of Pandosia and Heraclea, and having notice the Romans were near, and lay on the other side of the river Siris, he rode up to take a view of them, and seeing their order, the appointment of the watches, their method and the general form of their encampment, he was amazed, and addressing one of his friends next to him: "This order," said he, "Megacles, of the barbarians, is not at all barbarian in character; we shall see presently what they can do;" and, growing a little more thoughtful of the event, resolved to expect the arriving of the confederate troops. And to hinder the Romans, if in the mean time they should endeavor to pass the river, he planted men all along the bank to oppose them. But they, hastening to anticipate the coming up of the same forces which he had determined to wait for, attempted the passage with their infantry, where it was fordable, and with the horse in several places, so that the Greeks, fearing to be surrounded, were obliged to retreat, and Pyrrhus, perceiving this and being much surprised, bade his foot officers draw their men up in line of battle, and continue in arms, while he himself, with three thousand horse, advanced, hoping to attack the Romans as they were coming over, scattered and disordered. But when he saw a vast number of shields appearing above the water, and the horse following them in good order, gathering his men in a closer body, himself at the head of them, he began the charge, conspicuous by his rich and beautiful armor, and letting it be seen that his reputation had not outgone what he was able effectually to perform. While exposing his hands and body in the fight, and bravely repelling all that engaged him, he still guided the battle with a steady and undisturbed reason, and such presence of mind, as if he had been out of the action and watching it from a distance, passing still from point to point, and assisting those whom he thought most pressed by the enemy. Here Leonnatus the Macedonian, observing one of the Italians very intent upon Pyrrhus, riding up towards him, and changing places as he did, and moving as he moved: "Do you see, sir," said he, "that barbarian on the black horse with white feet? he seems to me one that designs some great and dangerous thing, for he looks constantly at you, and fixes his whole attention, full of vehement purpose, on you alone, taking no notice of others. Be on your guard, sir, against him." "Leonnatus," said Pyrrhus, "it is impossible for any man to avoid his fate; but neither he nor any other Italian shall have much satisfaction in engaging with me." While they were in this discourse, the Italian, lowering his spear and quickening his horse, rode furiously at Pyrrhus, and run his horse through with his lance; at the same instant Leonnatus ran his through. Both horses falling, Pyrrhus's friends surrounded him and brought him off safe, and killed the Italian, bravely defending himself. He was by birth a Frentanian, captain of a troop, and named Oplacus.

This made Pyrrhus use greater caution, and now seeing his horse give ground, he brought up the infantry against the enemy, and changing his scarf and his arms with Megacles, one of his friends, and obscuring himself, as it were, in his, charged upon the Romans, who received and engaged him, and a great while the success of the battle remained undetermined; and it is said there were seven turns of fortune both of pursuing and being pursued. And the change of his arms was very opportune for the safety

of his person, but had like to have overthrown his
cause and lost him the victory; for several falling
upon Megacles, the first that gave him his mortal
wound was one Dexous,⁷ who, snatching away his
helmet and his robe, rode at once to Lævinus, holding
them up, and saying aloud he had killed Pyrrhus.
These spoils being carried about and shown among
the ranks, the Romans were transported with joy, and
shouted aloud; while equal discouragement and terror prevailed among the Greeks, until Pyrrhus understanding what had happened, rode about the
army with his face bare, stretching out his hand to his
soldiers, and telling them aloud it was he. At last,
the elephants more particularly began to distress the
Romans, whose horses, before they came near, not
enduring them went back with their riders; and upon
this, he commanded the Thessalian cavalry to charge
them in their disorder, and routed them with great
loss. Dionysius affirms near fifteen thousand of the
Romans fell; Hieronymus, no more than seven thousand. On Pyrrhus's side, the same Dionysius makes
thirteen thousand slain, the other under four thousand; but they were the flower of his men, and
amongst them his particular friends as well as officers
whom he most trusted and made use of. However,
he possessed himself of the Romans' camp which they
deserted, and gained over several confederate cities,
and wasted the country round about, and advanced
so far that he was within about thirty-seven miles of
Rome itself. After the fight many of the Lucanians
and Samnites came in and joined him, whom he chid

---

[7] Thus written in the manuscripts. Dexius, or Dexter, is one
form that has, since Amyot's translation, been received; and Decius
is a recent conjecture. For Lævinus also, which is the correct name
in the manuscripts we have with scarcely any exception Albinus,
which Niebuhr inclines to think was Plutarch's own writing.

for their delay, but yet he was evidently well pleased and raised in his thoughts, that he had defeated so great an army of the Romans with the assistance of the Tarentines alone.

The Romans did not remove Lævinus from the consulship; though it is told that Caius Fabricius said, that the Epirots had not beaten the Romans, but only Pyrrhus, Lævinus; insinuating that their loss was not through want of valor but of conduct; but filled up their legions, and enlisted fresh men with all speed, talking high and boldly of war, which struck Pyrrhus with amazement. He thought it advisable by sending first to make an experiment whether they had any inclination to treat, thinking that to take the city and make an absolute conquest was no work for such an army as his was at that time, but to settle a friendship, and bring them to terms, would be highly honorable after his victory. Cineas was despatched away, and applied himself to several of the great ones, with presents for themselves and their ladies from the king; but not a person would receive any, and answered, as well men as women, that if an agreement were publicly concluded, they also should be ready, for their parts, to express their regard to the king. And Cineas, discoursing with the senate in the most persuasive and obliging manner in the world, yet was not heard with kindness or inclination, although Pyrrhus offered also to return all the prisoners he had taken in the fight without ransom, and promised his assistance for the entire conquest of all Italy, asking only their friendship for himself, and security for the Tarentines, and nothing further. Nevertheless, most were well-inclined to a peace, having already received one great defeat, and fearing another from an additional force of the native Italians, now joining with Pyrrhus. At this point Appius Claudius, a man of great distinction, but who, because of his great age and loss of sight, had declined the fatigue of public business, after these propositions had been made by the king, hearing a report that the senate was ready to vote the conditions of peace, could not forbear, but commanding his servants to take him up, was carried in his chair through the forum to the senate house. When he was set down at the door, his sons and sons-in-law took him up in their arms, and, walking close round about him, brought him into the senate. Out of reverence for so worthy a man, the whole assembly was respectfully silent.

And a little after raising up himself: "I bore," said he, "until this time, the misfortune of my eyes with some impatience, but now while I hear of these dishonorable motions and resolves of yours, destructive to the glory of Rome, it is my affliction, that being already blind, I am not deaf, too. Where is now that discourse of yours that became famous in all the world, that if he, the great Alexander, had come into Italy, and dared to attack us when we were young men, and our fathers, who were then in their prime, he had not now been celebrated as invincible, but either flying hence, or falling here, had left Rome more glorious? You demonstrate now that all that was but foolish arrogance and vanity by fearing Molossians and Chaonians, ever the Macedonian's prey, and by trembling at Pyrrhus who was himself but an humble servant to one of Alexander's life-guard, and comes here, not so much to assist the Greeks that inhabit among us, as to escape from his enemies at home, a wanderer about Italy, and yet dares to promise you the conquest of it all by that army which has not been able to preserve for him a little part of Macedon. Do not persuade yourselves that making him your friend is the way to

PYRRHUS

send him back, it is the way rather to bring over other invaders from thence, contemning you as easy to be reduced, if Pyrrhus goes off without punishment for his outrages on you, but, on the contrary, with the reward of having enabled the Tarentines and Samnites to laugh at the Romans." When Appius had done, eagerness for the war seized on every man, and Cineas was dismissed with this answer, that when Pyrrhus had withdrawn his forces out of Italy, then, if he pleased, they would treat with him about friendship and alliance, but while he stayed there in arms, they were resolved to prosecute the war against him with all their force, though he should have defeated a thousand Lævinuses. It is said that Cineas, while he was managing this affair, made it his business carefully to inspect the manners of the Romans, and to understand their methods of government, and having conversed with their noblest citizens, he afterwards told Pyrrhus, among other things, that the senate seemed to him an assembly of kings, and as for the people, he feared lest it might prove that they were fighting with a Lernæan hydra, for the consul had already raised twice as large an army as the former, and there were many times over the same number of Romans able to bear arms.

Then Caius Fabricius came in embassy from the Romans to treat about the prisoners that were taken, one whom Cineas had reported to be a man of highest consideration among them as an honest man and a good soldier, but extremely poor. Pyrrhus received him with much kindness, and privately would have persuaded him to accept of his gold, not for any evil purpose, but calling it a mark of respect and hospitable kindness. Upon Fabricius's refusal, he pressed him no further, but the next day, having a mind to discompose him, as he had never seen an elephant before, he commanded one of the largest, completely armed, to be placed behind the hangings, as they were talking together. Which being done, upon a sign given the hanging was drawn aside, and the elephant, raising his trunk over the head of Fabricius, made an horrid and ugly noise. He, gently turning about and smiling, said to Pyrrhus, "neither your money yesterday nor this beast to-day make any impression upon me." At supper, amongst all sorts of things that were discoursed of, but more particularly Greece and the philosophers there, Cineas, by accident, had occasion to speak of Epicurus, and explained the opinions his followers hold about the gods and the commonwealth, and the object of life, placing the chief happiness of man in pleasure, and declining public affairs as an injury and disturbance of a happy life, removing the gods afar off both from kindness or anger, or any concern for us at all, to a life wholly without business and flowing in pleasures. Before he had done speaking, "O Hercules!" Fabricius cried out to Pyrrhus, "may Pyrrhus and the Samnites entertain themselves with this sort of opinions as long as they are in war with us." Pyrrhus, admiring the wisdom and gravity of the man, was the more transported with desire of making friendship instead of war with the city, and entreated him, personally, after the peace should be concluded, to accept of living with him as the chief of his ministers and generals. Fabricius answered quietly, "Sir, this will not be for your advantage, for they who now honor and admire you, when they have had experience of me, will rather choose to be governed by me, than by you." Such was Fabricius. And Pyrrhus received his answer without any resentment or tyrannic passion; nay, among his friends he highly commended the great mind of Fabricius, and intrusted the prisoners to him alone, on condition that if the senate should not vote a peace, after they had conversed with their friends and celebrated the festival of Saturn, they should be remanded. And, accordingly, they were sent back after the holidays; it being decreed pain of death for any that stayed behind.

After this, Fabricius taking the consulate, a person came with a letter to the camp written by the king's principal physician, offering to take off Pyrrhus by poison, and so end the war without further hazard to the Romans, if he might have a reward proportionable to his service. Fabricius, hating the villany of the man, and disposing the other consul to the same opinion, sent despatches immediately to Pyrrhus to caution him against the treason. His letter was to this effect: "Caius Fabricius and Quintus Æmilius, consuls of the Romans, to Pyrrhus the king, health. You seem to have made an ill judgment both of your friends and enemies; you will understand by reading this letter sent to us, that you are at war with honest men, and trust villains and knaves. Nor do we disclose this to you out of any favor to you, but lest your ruin might bring a reproach upon us, as if we had ended the war by treachery, as not able to do it by force." When Pyrrhus had read the letter, and made inquiry into the treason, he punished the physician, and as an acknowledgment to the Romans sent to Rome the prisoners without ransom, and again employed Cineas to negotiate a peace for him. But they, regarding it as at once too great a kindness from an enemy, and too great a reward of not doing an ill thing to accept their prisoners so, released in return an equal number of the Tarentines and Samnites, but would admit of no debate of alliance or peace until he had removed his arms and forces out of Italy, and sailed back to Epirus with the same ships that brought him over. Afterwards, his affairs demanding a second fight, when he had refreshed his men, he decamped, and met the Romans about the city Asculum, where, however, he was much incommoded by a woody country unfit for his horse, and a swift river, so that the elephants, for want of sure treading, could not get up with the infantry. After many wounded and many killed, night put an end to the engagement. Next day, designing to make the fight on even ground, and have the elephants among the thickest of the enemy, he caused a detachment to possess themselves of those incommodious grounds, and, mixing slingers and archers among the elephants, with full strength and courage, he advanced in a close and well-ordered body. The Romans, not having those advantages of retreating and falling on as they pleased, which they had before, were obliged to fight man to man upon plain ground, and, being anxious to drive back the infantry before the elephants could get up, they fought fiercely with their swords among the Macedonian spears, not sparing themselves, thinking only to wound and kill, without regard of what they suffered. After a long and obstinate fight, the first giving ground is reported to have been where Pyrrhus himself engaged with extraordinary courage; but they were most carried away by the overwhelming force of the elephants, not being able to make use of their valor, but overthrown as it were by the irruption of a sea or an earthquake, before which it seemed better to give way than to die without doing any thing, and not gain the least advantage by suffering the utmost extremity, the retreat to their camp not being far. Hieronymus says, there fell six thousand of the Romans, and of Pyrrhus's men, the king's own commentaries reported three thousand five hundred and fifty lost in this action. Dionysius, however, neither gives any account of two engagements at Asculum, nor allows the Romans to have been certainly beaten, stating that once only, after they had fought till sunset, both armies were unwillingly separated by the night, Pyrrhus being wounded by a javelin in the arm, and his baggage plundered by the Samnites, that in all there died of Pyrrhus's men and the Romans above fifteen thousand. The armies separated; and, it is said, Pyrrhus replied to one that gave him joy of his victory, that one other such would utterly undo him. For he had lost a great part of the forces he brought with him, and almost all his particular friends and principal commanders; there were no others there to make recruits, and he found the confederates in Italy backward. On the other hand, as from a fountain continually flowing out of the city, the Roman camp was quickly and plentifully filled up with fresh men, not at all abating in courage for the losses they sustained, but even from their very anger gaining new force and resolution to go on with the war.

Among these difficulties he fell again into new hopes and projects distracting his purposes. For at the same time some persons arrived from Sicily, offering into his hands the cities of Agrigentum, Syracuse, and Leontini, and begging his assistance to drive out the Carthaginians, and rid the island of tyrants; and others brought him news out of Greece that Ptolemy, called Ceraunus, was slain in a fight, and his army cut in pieces by the Gauls, and that now, above all others, was his time to offer himself to the Macedonians, in great need of a king. Complaining much of fortune for bringing him so many occasions of great things all together at a time, and thinking that to have both offered to him, was to lose one of them, he was doubtful, balancing in his thoughts. But the affairs of Sicily seeming to hold out the greater prospects, Africa lying so near, he turned himself to them, and presently despatched away Cineas, as he used to do, to make terms beforehand with the cities. Then he placed a garrison in Tarentum, much to the Tarentines' discontent, who required him either to perform what he came for, and continue with them in a war against the Romans, or leave the city as he found it. He returned no pleasing answer, but commanded them to be quiet and attend his time, and so sailed away. Being arrived in Sicily, what he had designed in his hopes was confirmed effectually, and the cities frankly surrendered to him; and wherever his arms and force were necessary, nothing at first made any considerable resistance. For advancing with thirty thousand foot, and twenty-five hundred horse, and two hundred ships, he totally routed the Phœnicians, and overran their whole province, and Eryx being the strongest town they held, and having a great garrison in it, he resolved to take it by storm. The army being in readiness to give the assault, he put on his arms, and coming to the head of his men, made a vow of plays and sacrifices in honor to Hercules, if he signalized himself in that day's action before the Greeks that dwelt in Sicily, as became his great descent and his fortunes. The sign being given by sound of trumpet, he first scattered the barbarians with his shot, and then brought his ladders to the wall, and was the first that mounted upon it himself, and, the enemy appearing in great numbers, he beat them back; some he threw down from the walls on each side, others he laid dead in a heap round about him with his sword, nor did he receive the least wound, but by his very aspect inspired terror in the enemy;

PYRRHUS

and gave a clear demonstration that Homer[8] was in the right, and pronounced according to the truth of fact, that fortitude alone, of all the virtues, is wont to display itself in divine transports and frenzies. The city being taken, he offered to Hercules most magnificently, and exhibited all varieties of shows and plays.

A sort of barbarous people about Messena, called Mamertines, gave much trouble to the Greeks, and put several of them under contribution. These being numerous and valiant (from whence they had their name, equivalent in the Latin tongue to *warlike*[9]), he first intercepted the collectors of the contribution money, and cut them off, then beat them in open fight, and destroyed many of their places of strength. The Carthaginians being now inclined to composition, and offering him a round sum of money, and to furnish him with shipping, if a peace were concluded, he told them plainly, aspiring still to greater

---

[8] Page 30.—*Homer* uses such words as madness or *frenzy*, for example, of Hector, *who rages beyond all further withstanding, and bold in Zeus, is possessed with a terrible frenzy*. Fortitude, through the Latin, has become the cardinal name of the virtue, which in the Greek has not chiefly to do with the endurance of pain, but is exercised in the encounter of all danger, and is more properly *bravery, courage*, or *intrepidity*, etymologically *manliness*. It is in the Greek ethics the virtue or excellence of the active part, as temperance is of the passive, and wisdom in its two divisions, practical and scientific, of the intellectual part, of the human soul. This classification of the elements of our nature into the active impulses, the sensibilities or appetites, and the reason or mind, occurs everywhere in Greek. It is the basis, for example, of the whole system of Plato's republic with its triple division, corresponding to this, of soldiers, artisans, and governors.

[9] *Mamers* being another and older form for *Mars*. The Mamertines were the descendants of Campanian or Oscan mercenaries, speaking a language almost identical with Latin.

things, there was but one way for a friendship and
right understanding between them, if they, wholly
abandoning Sicily, would consent to make the African
sea the limit between them and the Greeks. And
being elevated with his good fortune, and the strength
of his forces, and pursuing those hopes in prospect of
which he first sailed thither, his immediate aim was
at Africa; and as he had abundance of shipping, but
very ill equipped, he collected seamen, not by fair and
gentle dealing with the cities, but by force in a
haughty and insolent way, and menacing them with
punishments. And as at first he had not acted thus,
but had been unusually indulgent and kind, ready to
believe, and uneasy to none; now of a popular leader
becoming a tyrant by these severe proceedings, he got
the name of an ungrateful and a faithless man. However,
they gave way to these things as necessary, although
they took them very ill from him; and especially
when he began to show suspicion of Thœnon
and Sosistratus, men of the first position in Syracuse,
who invited him over into Sicily, and when he was
come, put the cities into his power, and were most instrumental
in all he had done there since his arrival,
whom he now would neither suffer to be about his
person, nor leave at home; and when Sosistratus out
of fear withdrew himself, and then he charged
Thœnon, as in a conspiracy with the other, and put
him to death, with this all his prospects changed, not
by little and little, nor in a single place only, but a
mortal hatred being raised in the cities against him,
some fell off to the Carthaginians, others called in the
Mamertines. And seeing revolts in all places, and
desires of alterations, and a potent faction against
him, at the same time he received letters from the
Samnites and Tarentines, who were beaten quite out
of the field, and scarce able to secure their towns

against the war, earnestly begging his help. This served as a color to make his relinquishing Sicily no flight, nor a despair of good success; but in truth not being able to manage Sicily, which was as a ship laboring in a storm, and willing to be out of her, he suddenly threw himself over into Italy. It is reported that at his going off he looked back upon the island, and said to those about him, "How brave a field of war do we leave, my friends, for the Romans and Carthaginians to fight in," which, as he then conjectured, fell out indeed not long after.

When he was sailing off, the barbarians having conspired together, he was forced to a fight with the Carthaginians in the very road, and lost many of his ships; with the rest he fled into Italy. There, about one thousand Mamertines, who had crossed the sea a little before, though afraid to engage him in open field, setting upon him where the passages were difficult, put the whole army in confusion. Two elephants fell and a great part of his rear was cut off. He, therefore, coming up in person, repulsed the enemy, but ran into great danger among men long trained and bold in war. His being wounded in the head with a sword, and retiring a little out of the fight, much increased their confidence, and one of them advancing a good way before the rest, large of body and in bright armor, with an haughty voice challenged him to come forth if he were alive. Pyrrhus, in great anger, broke away violently from his guards, and, in his fury, besmeared with blood, terrible to look upon, made his way through his own men, and struck the barbarian on the head with his sword such a blow, as with the strength of his arm, and the excellent temper of the weapon, passed downward so far that his body being cut asunder fell in two pieces. This stopped the course of the barbarians, amazed and confounded at Pyrrhus, as one more than man; so that continuing his march all the rest of the way undisturbed, he arrived at Tarentum with twenty thousand foot and three thousand horse, where, reinforcing himself with the choicest troops of the Tarentines, he advanced immediately against the Romans, who then lay encamped in the territories of the Samnites, whose affairs were extremely shattered, and their counsels broken, having been in many fights beaten by the Romans. There was also a discontent amongst them at Pyrrhus for his expedition into Sicily, so that not many came in to join him.

He divided his army into two parts, and despatched the first into Lucania to oppose one of the consuls there, so that he should not come in to assist the other; the rest he led against Manius Curius, who had posted himself very advantageously near Beneventum, and expected the other consul's forces, and partly because the priests had dissuaded him by unfavorable omens, was resolved to remain inactive. Pyrrhus, hastening to attack these before the other could arrive, with his best men, and the most serviceable elephants, marched in the night toward their camp. But being forced to go round about, and through a very woody country, their lights failed them, and the soldiers lost their way. A council of war being called, while they were in debate, the night was spent, and, at the break of day, his approach, as he came down the hills, was discovered by the enemy, and put the whole camp into disorder and tumult. But the sacrifices being auspicious, and the time absolutely obliging them to fight, Manius drew his troops out of the trenches, and attacked the vanguard, and, having routed them all, put the whole army into consternation, so that many were cut off, and some of the elephants taken. This success drew on Manius into the level plain, and here, in open battle, he defeated part of the enemy; but, in other quarters, finding himself overpowered by the elephants and forced back to his trenches, he commanded out those who were left to guard them, a numerous body, standing thick at the ramparts, all in arms and fresh. These coming down from their strong position, and charging the elephants, forced them to retire; and they in the flight turning back upon their own men, caused great disorder and confusion, and gave into the hands of the Romans the victory, and the future supremacy. Having obtained from these efforts and these contests the feeling, as well as the fame of invincible strength, they at once reduced Italy under their power, and not long after Sicily too.

Thus fell Pyrrhus from his Italian and Sicilian hopes, after he had consumed six years in these wars, and though unsuccessful in his affairs, yet preserved his courage unconquerable among all these misfortunes, and was held, for military experience, and personal valor and enterprise much the bravest of all the princes of his time, only what he got by great actions he lost again by vain hopes, and by new desires of what he had not, kept nothing of what he had. So that Antigonus used to compare him to a player with dice, who had excellent throws, but knew not how to use them. He returned into Epirus with eight thousand foot and five hundred horse, and for want of money to pay them, was fain to look out for a new war to maintain the army. Some of the Gauls joining him, he invaded Macedonia, where Antigonus, son of Demetrius, governed, designing merely to plunder and waste the country. But after he had made himself master of several towns, and two thousand men came over to him, he began to hope for something greater, and adventured upon Antigonus him-

self, and meeting him at a narrow passage, put the
whole army in disorder. The Gauls, who brought up
Antigonus's rear, were very numerous and stood firm,
but after a sharp encounter, the greatest part of them
were cut off, and they who had the charge of the elephants being surrounded every way, delivered up
both themselves and the beasts. Pyrrhus, taking this
advantage, and advising more with his good fortune
than his reason, boldly set upon the main body of the
Macedonian foot, already surprised with fear, and
troubled at the former loss. They declined any action
or engagement with him; and he, holding out his hand
and calling aloud both to the superior and under officers by name, brought over the foot from Antigonus,
who, flying away secretly, was only able to retain
some of the seaport towns. Pyrrhus, among all these
kindnesses of fortune, thinking what he had effected
against the Gauls the most advantageous for his
glory, hung up their richest and goodliest spoils in
the temple of Minerva Itonis, with this inscription:—

> Pyrrhus, descendant of Molossian kings,
> These shields to thee, Itonian goddess, brings,
> Won from the valiant Gauls when in the fight
> Antigonus and all his host took flight;
> 'T is not to-day nor yesterday alone
> That for brave deeds the Æacidæ are known.

After this victory in the field, he proceeded to secure
the cities, and having possessed himself of Aegæ, beside other hardships put upon the people there, he left
in the town a garrison of Gauls, some of those in his
own army, who, being insatiably desirous of wealth,
instantly dug up the tombs of the kings that lay buried there, and took away the riches, and insolently
scattered about their bones. Pyrrhus, in appearance,
made no great matter of it, either deferring it on
account of the pressure of other business, or wholly

passing it by, out of a fear of punishing those barbarians; but this made him very ill spoken of among the Macedonians, and his affairs being yet unsettled and brought to no firm consistence, he began to entertain new hopes and projects, and in raillery called Antigonus a shameless man, for still wearing his purple and not changing it for an ordinary dress; but upon Cleonymus, the Spartan, arriving and inviting him to Lacedæmon, he frankly embraced the overture. Cleonymus was of royal descent, but seeming too arbitrary and absolute, had no great respect nor credit at home; and Areus was king there. This was the occasion of an old and public grudge between him and the citizens; but, beside that, Cleonymus, in his old age, had married a young lady of great beauty and royal blood, Chilonis, daughter of Leotychides, who, falling desperately in love with Acrotatus, Areus's son, a youth in the flower of manhood, rendered this match both uneasy and dishonorable to Cleonymus, as there was none of the Spartans who did not very well know how much his wife slighted him; so these domestic troubles added to his public discontent. He brought Pyrrhus to Sparta with an army of twenty-five thousand foot, two thousand horse, and twenty-four elephants. So great a preparation made it evident to the whole world, that he came not so much to gain Sparta for Cleonymus, as to take all Peloponnesus for himself, although he expressly denied this to the Lacedæmonian ambassadors that came to him at Megalopolis, affirming he came to deliver the cities from the slavery of Antigonus, and declaring he would send his younger sons to Sparta, if he might, to be brought up in Spartan habits, that so they might be better bred than all other kings. With these pretensions amusing those who came to meet him in his march, as soon as ever

he entered Laconia, he began to plunder and waste
the country, and on the ambassadors complaining
that he began the war upon them before it was proclaimed: "We know," said he, "very well, that
neither do you Spartans, when you design any thing,
talk of it beforehand." One Mandroclidas, then
present, told him, in the broad Spartan dialect: "If
you are a god, you will do us no harm, we are wrong-
ing no man; but if you are a man, there may be another stronger than you."

He now marched away directly for Lacedæmon,
and being advised by Cleonymus to give the assault
as soon as he arrived, fearing, as it is said, lest the soldiers, entering by night, should plunder the city, he
answered, they might do it as well next morning, because there were but few soldiers in town, and those
unprovided against his sudden approach, as Areus
was not there in person, but gone to aid the Gorty-
nians in Crete. And it was this alone that saved the
town, because he despised it as not tenable, and so
imagining no defence would be made, he sat down
before it that night. Cleonymus's friends, and the
Helots, his domestic servants, had made great preparation at his house, as expecting Pyrrhus there at
supper. In the night the Lacedæmonians held a consultation to ship over all the women into Crete, but
they unanimously refused, and Archidamia came into
the senate with a sword in her hand, in the name of
them all, asking if the men expected the women to
survive the ruins of Sparta. It was next resolved to
draw a trench in a line directly over against the
enemy's camp, and, here and there in it, to sink wagons in the ground, as deep as the naves of the wheels,
that, so being firmly fixed, they might obstruct the
passage of the elephants. When they had just begun the work, both maids and women came to them,

the married women with their robes tied like girdles round their underfrocks, and the unmarried girls in their single frocks only,[10] to assist the elder men at the work. As for the youth that were next day to engage, they left them to their rest, and undertaking their proportion, they themselves finished a third part of the trench, which was in breadth six cubits, four in depth, and eight hundred feet long,[11] as Phylarchus says; Hieronymus makes it somewhat less. The enemy beginning to move by break of day, they brought their arms to the young men, and giving them also in charge the trench, exhorted them to defend and keep it bravely, as it would be happy for them to conquer in the view of their whole country, and glorious to die in the arms of their mothers and wives, falling as became Spartans. As for Chilonis, she retired with a halter about her neck, resolving to die so rather than fall into the hands of Cleonymus, if the city were taken.

Pyrrhus himself, in person, advanced with his foot to force through the shields of the Spartans ranged against him, and to get over the trench, which was scarce passable, because the looseness of the fresh earth afforded no firm footing for the soldiers. Ptolemy, his son, with two thousand Gauls, and some choice men of the Chaonians, went around the trench, and endeavored to get over where the wagons were. But they, being so deep in the ground, and placed close together, not only made his passage, but also the defence of the Lacedæmonians very troublesome. Yet

[10] The married women wearing two pieces of dress, the unmarried, one only; see the description in the life of Lycurgus, vol. i. p. 163.

[11] Cubits of eighteen inches; and Greek feet, 101 to 100 English.

now the Gauls had got the wheels out of the ground, and were drawing off the wagons toward the river, when young Acrotatus, seeing the danger, passing through the town with three hundred men, surrounded Ptolemy undiscerned, taking the advantage of some slopes of the ground, until he fell upon his rear, and forced him to wheel about. And thrusting one another into the ditch, and falling among the wagons, at last with much loss, not without difficulty, they withdrew. The elderly men and all the women saw this brave action of Acrotatus, and when he returned back into the town to his first post, all covered with blood, and fierce and elate with victory, he seemed to the Spartan women to have become taller and more beautiful than before, and they envied Chilonis so worthy a lover. And some of the old men followed him, crying aloud, "Go on, Acrotatus, be happy with Chilonis, and beget brave sons for Sparta." Where Pyrrhus himself fought was the hottest of the action, and many of the Spartans did gallantly, but in particular one Phyllius signalized himself, made the best resistance, and killed most assailants; and when he found himself ready to sink with the many wounds he had received, retiring a little out of his place behind another, he fell down among his fellow-soldiers, that the enemy might not carry off his body. The fight ended with the day, and Pyrrhus, in his sleep, dreamed that he threw thunderbolts upon Lacedæmon, and set it all on fire, and rejoiced at the sight; and waking, in this transport of joy, he commanded his officers to get all things ready for a second assault, and relating his dream among his friends, supposing it to mean that he should take the town by storm, the rest assented to it with admiration, but Lysimachus was not pleased with the dream, and told him he feared, lest as places struck with lightning are held sacred, and not to be trodden upon, so the gods might by this let him know the city should not be taken. Pyrrhus replied, that all these things were but idle talk, full of uncertainty, and only fit to amuse the vulgar; their thought, with their swords in their hands, should always be

> The one good omen is king Pyrrhus' cause,[12]

and so got up, and drew out his army to the walls by break of day. The Lacedæmonians, in resolution and courage, made a defence even beyond their power; the women were all by, helping them to arms, and bringing bread and drink to those that desired it, and taking care of the wounded. The Macedonians attempted to fill up the trench, bringing huge quantities of materials and throwing them upon the arms and dead bodies, that lay there and were covered over. While the Lacedæmonians opposed this with all their force, Pyrrhus, in person, appeared on their side of the trench and the wagons, pressing on horseback toward the city, at which the men who had that post calling out, and the women shrieking and running about, while Pyrrhus violently pushed on, and beat down all that disputed his way, his horse received a shot in the belly from a Cretan arrow, and, in his convulsions as he died, threw off Pyrrhus on slippery and steep ground. And all about him being in con-

---

[12] Parodying, by the change of a word, the famous line of the Iliad, xii. 243, "You bid me," says Hector to Polydamas, "be guided by the flight of birds. I heed them not, whether they pass to the right hand towards the morning and the sun, or to the left hand to the vapor and the darkness. The one only best omen is to be defending one's country.

"The one good omen is one's country's cause."

fusion at this, the Spartans came boldly up, and making good use of their missiles, forced them off again. After this Pyrrhus, in other quarters also, put an end to the combat, imagining the Lacedæmonians would be inclined to yield, as almost all of them were wounded, and very great numbers killed outright; but the good fortune of the city either satisfied with the experiment upon the bravery of the citizens, or willing to prove how much even in the last extremities such interposition may effect, brought when the Lacedæmonians had now but very slender hopes left, Aminias, the Phocian, one of Antigonus's commanders, from Corinth to their assistance, with a force of mercenaries; and they were no sooner received into the town, but Areus, their king, arrived there himself, too, from Crete, with two thousand men more. The women upon this went all home to their houses, finding it no longer necessary for them to meddle with the business of the war; and they also were sent back, who, though not of military age, were by necessity forced to take arms, while the rest prepared to fight Pyrrhus.

He, upon the coming of these additional forces, was indeed possessed with a more eager desire and ambition than before, to make himself master of the town; but his designs not succeeding, and receiving fresh losses every day, he gave over the siege, and fell to plundering the country, determining to winter thereabout. But fate is unavoidable, and a great feud happening at Argos between Aristeas and Aristippus, two principal citizens, after Aristippus had resolved to make use of the friendship of Antigonus, Aristeas, to anticipate him, invited Pyrrhus thither. And he always revolving hopes upon hopes, and treating all his successes as occasions of more, and his reverses as defects to be amended by new enterprises, allowed neither losses nor victories to limit him in his receiving or giving trouble, and so presently went for Argos. Areus, by frequent ambushes, and seizing positions where the ways were most unpracticable, harassed the Gauls and Molossians that brought up the rear. It had been told Pyrrhus by one of the priests that found the liver of the sacrificed beast imperfect, that some of his near relations would be lost; in this tumult and disorder of his rear, forgetting the prediction, he commanded out his son Ptolemy with some of his guards to their assistance, while he himself led on the main body rapidly out of the pass. And the fight being very warm where Ptolemy was, (for the most select men of the Lacedæmonians, commanded by Evalcus, were there engaged,) one Oryssus of Aptera in Crete, a stout man and swift of foot, running on one side of the young prince, as he was fighting bravely, gave him a mortal wound and slew him. On his fall those about him turned their backs, and the Lacedæmonian horse, pursuing and cutting off many, got into the open plain, and found themselves engaged with the enemy before they were aware, without their infantry; Pyrrhus, who had received the ill news of his son, and was in great affliction, drew out his Molossian horse against them, and charging at the head of his men, satiated himself with the blood and slaughter of the Lacedæmonians, as indeed he always showed himself a terrible and invincible hero in actual fight, but now he exceeded all he had ever done before in courage and force. On his riding his horse up to Evalcus, he, by declining a little to one side, had almost cut off Pyrrhus's hand in which he held the reins, but lighting on the reins, only cut them; at the same instant Pyrrhus, running him through with his spear, fell from his horse, and there on foot as he was, proceeded to slaughter all those choice men that fought about the body of Evalcus; a

severe additional loss to Sparta, incurred after the
war itself was now at an end, by the mere animosity
of the commanders. Pyrrhus having thus offered, as
it were, a sacrifice to the ghost of his son, and fought
a glorious battle in honor of his obsequies, and having
vented much of his pain in action against the enemy,
marched away to Argos. And having intelligence
that Antigonus was already in possession of the high
grounds, he encamped about Nauplia, and the next
day despatched a herald to Antigonus, calling him a
villain, and challenging him to descend into the plain
field and fight with him for the kingdom. He answered, that his conduct should be measured by times
as well as by arms, and that if Pyrrhus had no leisure
to live, there were ways enough open to death. To
both the kings, also, came ambassadors from Argos,
desiring each party to retreat, and to allow the city
to remain in friendship with both, without falling into
the hands of either. Antigonus was persuaded, and
sent his son as a hostage to the Argives; but Pyrrhus,
although he consented to retire, yet, as he sent no
hostage, was suspected. A remarkable portent happened at this time to Pyrrhus; the heads of the sacrificed oxen, lying apart from the bodies, were seen
to thrust out their tongues and lick up their own gore.
And in the city of Argos, the priestess of Apollo Lycius rushed out of the temple, crying she saw the city
full of carcasses and slaughter, and an eagle coming
out to fight, and presently vanishing again.

In the dead of the night, Pyrrhus, approaching
the walls, and finding the gate called Diamperes set
open for them by Aristeas, was undiscovered long
enough to allow all his Gauls to enter and take possession of the market-place. But the gate being too
low to let in the elephants, they were obliged to take
down the towers which they carried on their backs,

and put them on again in the dark and in disorder, so that time being lost, the city took the alarm, and the people ran, some to Aspis the chief citadel, and others to other places of defence, and sent away to Antigonus to assist them. He, advancing within a short distance, made an halt, but sent in some of his principal commanders, and his son with a considerable force. Areus came thither, too, with one thousand Cretans, and some of the most active men among the Spartans, and all falling on at once upon the Gauls, put them in great disorder. Pyrrhus, entering in with noise and shouting near the Cylarabis,[13] when the Gauls returned the cry, noticed that it did not express courage and assurance, but was the voice of men distressed, and that had their hands full. He, therefore, pushed forward in haste the van of his horse that marched but slowly and dangerously, by reason of the drains and sinks of which the city is full. In this night engagement, there was infinite uncertainty as to what was being done, or what orders were given; there was much mistaking and straggling in the narrow streets; all generalship was useless in that darkness and noise and pressure; so both sides continued without doing any thing, expecting daylight. At the first dawn, Pyrrhus, seeing the great citadel

---

[13] This was an exercise ground, a gymnasium, near one of the city gates; the tomb of Licymnius, mentioned presently, was also near it. "As you follow a straight road towards the gymnasium of Cylarabes, so called from the son of Sthenelus, stands the tomb of Licymnius, the son of Electryon. . . . In the gymnasium, there is a statue of Athena called Pania, and they show a tomb of Sthenelus, and one of Cylarabes himself; and not far off, there is a monument in memory of the Argives, who sailed with the Athenians on the expedition for subjugating Syracuse and Sicily." *Pausanias,* ii. 22. Cylarabes, son of the Homeric hero Sthenelus, ruled in Argos, while Orestes did in Mycenæ.

Aspis full of enemies, was disturbed, and remarking, among a variety of figures dedicated in the marketplace, a wolf and bull of brass, as it were ready to attack one another, he was struck with alarm, recollecting an oracle that formerly predicted fate had determined his death when he should see a wolf fighting with a bull. The Argives say, these figures were set up in record of a thing that long ago had happened there. For Danaus, at his first landing in the country, near the Pyramia in Thyreatis, as he was on his way towards Argos, espied a wolf fighting with a bull, and conceiving the wolf to represent him, (for this stranger fell upon a native, as he designed to do,) stayed to see the issue of the fight, and the wolf [14] prevailing, he offered vows to Apollo Lycius, and thus made his attempt upon the town, and succeeded; Gelanor, who was then king, being displaced by a faction. And this was the cause of dedicating those figures.

Pyrrhus, quite out of heart at this sight, and seeing none of his designs succeed, thought best to retreat, but fearing the narrow passage at the gate, sent to his son Helenus, who was left without the town with a great part of his forces, commanding him to break down part of the wall, and assist the retreat if the enemy pressed hard upon them. But what with haste and confusion, the person that was sent delivered nothing clearly; so that quite mistaking, the young prince with the best of his men and the remain-

---

[14] *Lukos* or *Lycus*, in Greek, is a *wolf*, and *Lukeios*, or *Lycius*, a common epithet of Apollo, who as the archer-god was conceived of as the slayer of wolves, and who was also the tutelar deity of *Lycia*. The word *lukē*, however, is found in Greek vocabularies, corresponding to *lux*, *light*, and this, it is very possible, was the original significance of *lukeios*, though in after times more obvious meanings were attached to it.

ing elephants marched straight through the gates into the town to assist his father. Pyrrhus was now making good his retreat, and while the market-place afforded them ground enough both to retreat and fight, frequently repulsed the enemy that bore upon him. But when he was forced out of that broad place into the narrow street leading to the gate, and fell in with those who came the other way to his assistance, some did not hear him call out to them to give back, and those who did, however eager to obey him, were pushed forward by others behind, who poured in at the gate. Besides, the largest of his elephants falling down on his side in the very gate, and lying roaring on the ground, was in the way of those that would have got out. Another of the elephants already in the town, called Nicon, striving to take up his rider, who, after many wounds received, was fallen off his back, bore forward upon those that were retreating, and, thrusting upon friends as well as enemies, tumbled them all confusedly upon one another, till having found the body, and taken it up with his trunk, he carried it on his tusks, and, returning in a fury, trod down all before him. Being thus pressed and crowded together, not a man could do any thing for himself, but being wedged, as it were, together into one mass, the whole multitude rolled and swayed this way and that all together, and did very little execution either upon the enemy in their rear, or on any of them who were intercepted in the mass, but very much harm to one another. For he who had either drawn his sword or directed his lance, could neither restore it again, nor put his sword up; with these weapons they wounded their own men, as they happened to come in the way, and they were dying by mere contact with each other.

Pyrrhus, seeing this storm and confusion of

things, took off the crown he wore upon his helmet, by which he was distinguished, and gave it to one nearest his person, and trusting to the goodness of his horse, rode in among the thickest of the enemy, and being wounded with a lance through his breastplate, but not dangerously, nor indeed very much, he turned about upon the man who struck him, who was an Argive, not of any illustrious birth, but the son of a poor old woman; she was looking upon the fight among other women from the top of a house, and perceiving her son engaged with Pyrrhus, and affrighted at the danger he was in, took up a tile with both hands, and threw it at Pyrrhus. This falling on his head below the helmet, and bruising the vertebræ of the lower part of the neck, stunned and blinded him; his hands let go the reins, and sinking down from his horse, he fell just by the tomb of Licymnius. The common soldiers knew not who it was; but one Zopyrus, who served under Antigonus, and two or three others running thither, and knowing it was Pyrrhus, dragged him to a door way hard by, just as he was recovering a little from the blow. But when Zopyrus drew out an Illyrian sword, ready to cut off his head, Pyrrhus gave him so fierce a look, that confounded with terror, and sometimes his hands trembling, and then again endeavoring to do it, full of fear and confusion, he could not strike him right, but cutting over his mouth and chin, it was a long time before he got off the head. By this time what had happened was known to a great many, and Alcyoneus hastening to the place, desired to look upon the head, and see whether he knew it, and taking it in his hand rode away to his father, and threw it at his feet, while he was sitting with some of his particular favorites. Antigonus, looking upon it, and knowing it, thrust his son from him, and struck him with his staff, calling him wicked and barbarous, and covering his eyes with his robe, shed tears, thinking of his own father and grandfather, instances in his own family of the changefulness of fortune, and caused the head and body of Pyrrhus to be burned with all due solemnity. After this, Alcyoneus, discovering Helenus under a mean disguise in a threadbare coat, used him very respectfully, and brought him to his father. When Antigonus saw him, "This, my son," said he, "is better; and yet even now you have not done wholly well in allowing these clothes to remain, to the disgrace of those who it seems now are the victors." And treating Helenus with great kindness, and as became a prince, he restored him to his kingdom of Epirus, and gave the same obliging reception to all Pyrrhus's principal commanders, his camp and whole army having fallen into his hands.

CAIUS MARIUS[1]

TRANSLATED BY MILES STAPLETON, FELLOW OF ALL-SOULS COLLEGE, OXFORD.

WE are altogether ignorant of any third name of Caius Marius; as also of Quintus Sertorius, that possessed himself of Spain; or of Lucius Mummius that destroyed Corinth, though this last was surnamed Achaicus from his conquests, as Scipio was called Africanus, and Metellus, Macedonicus. Hence Posidonius draws his chief argument to confute those that hold the third to be the Roman proper name, as Camillus, Marcellus, Cato; as in this case, those that had but two names would have no proper name at all. He did not, however, observe that by his own reasoning he must rob the women absolutely of their names; for none of them have the first, which Posidonius imagines the proper name with the Romans. Of the other two, one was common to the whole family, Pompeii, Manlii, Cornelii, (as with us Greeks, the Heraclidæ, and Pelopidæ,) the other titular, and personal, taken either from their natures, or actions, or bodily characteristics, as Macrinus, Torquatus, Sylla; such as are Mnemon, Grypus, or Callinicus among the Greeks. On the subject of

---

[1] Born, of an obscure family, 157 B. C., elected consul for the fifth time 101 B. C., and up to this time his career was a glorious one; the remainder of his life is full of horrors, and brings out the worst features of his character. He showed, in later years, his incapacity for politics and died as Plutarch relates in his 71st year, 86 B. C.—Dr. William Smith.

names, however, the irregularity of custom, would we insist upon it, might furnish us with discourse enough.

There is a likeness of Marius in stone at Ravenna, in Gaul,[2] which I myself saw, quite corresponding with that roughness and harshness of character that is ascribed to him. Being naturally valiant and warlike, and more acquainted also with the discipline of the camp than of the city, he could not moderate his passion when in authority. He is said never to have either studied Greek, or to have made use of that language in any matter of consequence; thinking it ridiculous to bestow time in that learning, the teachers of which were little better than slaves. So after his second trimph, when at the dedication of a temple he presented some shows after the Greek fashion, coming into the theatre, he only sat down and immediately departed. And, accordingly, as Plato often used to say to Xenocrates the philosopher, who was thought to show more than ordinary harshness of disposition, "I pray you, good Xenoncrates, sacrifice to the Graces"; so if any could have persuaded Marius to pay his devotions to the Greek Muses and Graces, he had never brought his incomparable actions, both in war and peace, to so unworthy a conclusion, or wrecked himself, so to say, upon an old age of cruelty and vindictiveness, through passion, ill-timed ambition, and insatiable cupidity. But this will further appear by and by from the facts.

He was born of parents altogether obscure and indigent, who supported themselves by their daily labor; his father of the same name with himself, his

[2] Cisalpine Gaul.—The name of Italy, originally belonging only to the southernmost districts, was but slowly extended northwards.

mother called Fulcinia. He had spent a considerable part of his life before he saw and tasted the pleasures of the city; having passed previously in Cirrhæaton,[3] a village of the territory of Arpinum, a life, compared with city delicacies, rude and unrefined, yet temperate, and conformable to the ancient Roman severity. He first served as a soldier in the war against the Celtiberians, when Scipio Africanus besieged Numantia where he signalized himself to his general by courage far above his comrades, and, particularly, by his cheerfully complying with Scipio's reformation of his army, before almost ruined by pleasures and luxury. It is stated, too, that he encountered and vanquished an enemy in single combat, in his general's sight. In consequence of all this he had several honors conferred upon him; and once when at an entertainment a question arose about commanders, and one of the company (whether really desirous to know, or only in complaisance) asked Scipio where the Romans, after him, should obtain such another general, Scipio, gently clapping Marius on the shoulder as he sat next him, replied, "Here, perhaps." So promising was his early youth of his future greatness, and so discerning was Scipio to detect the distant future in the present first beginnings. It was this speech of Scipio, we are told, which, like a divine, admonition, chiefly emboldened Marius to aspire to a political career. He sought, and by the assistance of Cæcilius Metellus, of whose family he as well as his father were dependents, ob-

[3] *Cirrhœaton* is simply a corruption for Cirrhæatæ, equivalent to Cereatæ or Cereate, a little town in the district of Arpinum, which in Pliny's time was a municipality whose people, the Cereatini Mariani, still bore Marius's name; of which, if the site be correctly identified with the monastery of Casa Mara or Casamari, some traces may be thought to remain even now.

tained the office of tribune of the people. In which place, when he brought forward a bill for the regulation of voting,[4] which seemed likely to lessen the authority of the great men in the courts of justice, the consul Cotta opposed him, and persuaded the senate to declare against the law, and call Marius to account for it. He, however, when this decree was prepared, coming into the senate, did not behave like a young man newly and undeservedly advanced to authority, but, assuming all the courage that his future actions would have warranted, threatened Cotta, unless he recalled the decree, to throw him into prison. And on his turning to Metellus, and asking his vote, and Metellus rising up to concur with the consul, Marius, calling for the officer outside, commanded him to take Metellus into custody. He appealed to the other tribunes, but not one of them assisted him; so that the senate, immediately complying, withdrew the decree. Marius came forth with glory to the people and confirmed his law, and was henceforth esteemed a man of undaunted courage and assurance, as well as a vigorous opposer of the senate in favor of the commons. But he immediately lost their opinion of him by a contrary action; for when a law for the distribution of corn was proposed, he vigorously and successfully resisted it, making himself equally honored by both parties, in gratifying neither, contrary to the public interest.

After his tribuneship, he was candidate for the office of chief ædile; there being two orders of them,

[4] *The bill for the regulation of voting* had no natural connection with *the courts of justice*. A very slight correction of a single word would change *courts of justice* into *elections;* but it is of course always possible for Plutarch to make a mistake about Roman matters, or a slip of a word in copying from his authorities.

one the curules, from the stool with crooked feet on
which they sat when they performed their duty; the
other and inferior, called ædiles of the people. As
soon as they have chosen the former, they give their
voices again for the latter. Marius, finding he was
likely to be put by for the greater, immediately
changed and stood for the less; but because he seemed
too forward and hot, he was disappointed of that also.
And yet though he was in one day twice frustrated of
his desired preferment, (which never happened to any
before,) yet he was not at all discouraged, but a
little while after sought for the prætorship, and was
nearly suffering a repulse, and then, too, though he
was returned last of all, was nevertheless accused of
bribery.

Cassius Sabaco's servant, who was observed
within the rails among those that voted, chiefly occasioned the suspicion, as Sabaco was an intimate
friend of Marius; but on being called to appear before the judges, he alleged, that being thirsty by
reason of the heat, he called for cold water, and that
his servant brought him a cup, and as soon as he had
drunk, departed; he was, however, excluded from the
senate by the succeeding censors, and not undeservedly either, as was thought, whether it might be for
his false evidence, or his want of temperance. Caius
Herennius was also cited to appear as evidence, but
pleaded that it was not customary for a patron, (the
Roman word for *protector,*) to witness against his
clients, and that the law excused them from that
harsh duty; and both Marius and his parents had
always been clients to the family of the Herennii.
And when the judges would have accepted of this
plea, Marius himself opposed it, and told Herennius,
that when he was first created magistrate he ceased
to be his client; which was not altogether true. For

CAIUS MARIUS

it is not every office that frees clients and their posterity from the observance due to their patrons, but only those to which the law has assigned a curule chair. Notwithstanding, though at the beginning of the suit it went somewhat hard with Marius, and he found the judges no way favorable to him; yet, at last, their voices being equal, contrary to all expectation, he was acquitted.

In his prætorship he did not get much honor, yet after it he obtained the further Spain; which province he is said to have cleared of robbers, with which it was much infested, the old barbarous habits still prevailing, and the Spaniards, in those days, still regarding robbery as a piece of valor. In the city he had neither riches nor eloquence to trust to, with which the leading men of the time obtained power with the people, but his vehement disposition, his indefatigable labors, and his plain way of living, of themselves gained him esteem and influence; so that he made an honorable match with Julia, of the distinguished family of the Cæsars, to whom that Cæsar was nephew who was afterwards so great among the Romans, and, in some degree, from his relationship, made Marius his example, as in his life we have observed.

Marius is praised for both temperance and endurance, of which latter he gave a decided instance in an operation of surgery. For having, as it seems, both his legs full of great tumors,[5] and disliking the

---

[5] For the *tumors,* or swellings, with which Marius was troubled in his legs, Mr. Long in his translation has *varicose veins,* on the authority of Cicero, who in his Tusculan Disputations (*II.,* 15 *and* 22) uses the word *varices.* Cicero adduces the story in elucidation of the question as to the nature of pain. Of the fortitude of Marius there could be no doubt; others had followed the example after him; but he had been the first who ever had sub-

deformity, he determined to put himself into the hands of an operator; when, without being tied, he stretched out one of his legs, and silently, without changing countenance, endured most excessive torments in the cutting, never either flinching or complaining; but when the surgeon went to the other, he declined to have it done, saying, "I see the cure is not worth the pain."

The consul Cæcilius Metellus, being declared general in the war against Jugurtha in Africa, took with him Marius for lieutenant; where, eager himself to do great deeds and services that would get him distinction, he did not, like others, consult Metellus's glory and the serving his interest, and attributing his honor of lieutenancy not to Metellus, but to fortune, which had presented him with a proper opportunity and theatre of great actions, he exerted his utmost courage. That war, too, affording several difficulties, he neither declined the greatest, nor disdained undertaking the least of them; but surpassing his equals in counsel and conduct, and matching the very common soldiers in labor and abstemiousness, he gained great popularity with them; as indeed any voluntary partaking with people in their labor is felt as an easing of that labor, as it seems to take away the constraint and necessity of it. It is the most obliging sight in the world to the Roman soldier to see a commander eat the same bread as himself, or lie upon an ordinary bed, or assist the work in the drawing a trench and raising a bulwark. For they do not so much admire

mitted to the operation without being tied down. Yet that with him pain was not simply indifferent, (neither an evil nor a good, as the Stoics taught,) appeared by his declining to let the surgeon have his other leg to cut.

those that confer honors and riches upon them, as those that partake of the same labor and danger with themselves; but love them better that will vouchsafe to join in their work, than those that encourage their idleness.

Marius thus employed, and thus winning the affections of the soldiers, before long filled both Africa and Rome with his fame, and some, too, wrote home from the army that the war with Africa would never be brought to a conclusion, unless they chose Caius Marius consul. All which was evidently unpleasing to Metellus; but what more especially grieved him was the calamity of Turpillius. This Turpillius had from his ancestors, been a friend of Metellus, and kept up constant hospitality with him; and was now serving in the war, in command of the smiths and carpenters of the army.[6] Having the charge of a garrison in Vaga, a considerable city, and trusting too much to the inhabitants, because he treated them civilly and kindly, he unawares fell into the enemy's hands. They received Jugurtha into the city; yet, nevertheless, at their request, Turpillius was dismissed safe and without receiving any injury; whereupon he was accused of betraying it to the enemy. Marius, being one of the council of war, was not only violent against him himself, but also incensed most of the others, so that Metellus was forced, much against his will, to put him to death. Not long after the accusation proved false, and when others were comforting Metellus, who took heavily the loss of his friend, Marius, rather insulting and arrogating it to himself, boasted in all companies that he had involved

[6] The Fabri, or corps of engineers, who accompanied a Roman army.

Metellus in the guilt of putting his friend to death.[7]

Henceforward they were at open variance; and it is reported that Metellus once, when Marius was present, said, insultingly, "You, sir, design to leave us to go home and stand for the consulship, and will not be content to wait and be consul with this boy of mine?" Metellus's son being a mere boy at the time. Yet for all this Marius being very importunate to be gone, after several delays, he was dismissed about twelve days before the election of consuls; and performed that long journey from the camp to the seaport of Utica, in two days and a night, and there doing sacrifice before he went on shipboard, it is said the augur told him, that heaven promised him some incredible good fortune, and such as was beyond all expectation. Marius, not a little elated with this good omen, began his voyage, and in four days, with a favorable wind, passed the sea; he was welcomed with great joy by the people, and being brought into the assembly by one of the tribunes, sued for the consulship, inveighing in all ways against Metellus, and promising either to slay Jugurtha or take him alive.

He was elected triumphantly, and at once proceeded to levy soldiers, contrary both to law and custom, enlisting slaves and poor people; whereas former commanders never accepted of such, but bestowed arms, like other favors, as a matter of distinction, on persons who had the proper qualification, a man's property being thus a sort of security for his good behavior. These were not the only occasions of ill-

---

[7] More literally, "had brought upon him an avenging deity or genius," an *alastor;* had put him, as it were, within the range of the punishment divinely attaching to particular acts, however committed.

will against Marius; some haughty speeches, uttered with great arrogance and contempt, gave great offence to the nobility; as, for example, his saying that he had carried off the consulship as a spoil from the effeminacy of the wealthy and high-born citizens, and telling the people that he gloried in wounds he had himself received for them, as much as others did in the monuments of dead men and images of their ancestors.[8] Often speaking of the commanders that had been unfortunate in Africa, naming Bestia, for example, and Albinus, men of very good families, but unfit for war, and who had miscarried through want of experience, he asked the people about him, if they did not think that the ancestors of these nobles had much rather have left a descendant like him, since they themselves grew famous not by nobility, but by their valor and great actions? This he did not say merely out of vanity and arrogance, or that he were willing, without any advantage, to offend the nobility; but the people always delighting in affronts and scurrilous contumelies against the senate, making boldness of speech their measure of greatness of spirit, continually encouraged him in it, and strengthened his inclination not to spare persons of repute, so he might gratify the multitude.

As soon as he arrived again in Africa, Metellus, no longer able to control his feelings of jealousy, and his indignation that now when he had really finished the war, and nothing was left but to secure the person of Jugurtha, Marius, grown great merely through his ingratitude to him, should come to bereave him

[8] The *images of ancestors* are emphatically the *imagines*, the busts, in wax or other material, of those of their ancestry who had borne office and gained distinction, which it was the pride of a Roman family to accumulate in the hall (the *atrium*), and to display on great occasions.

both of his victory and triumph, could not bear to
have any interview with him; but retired himself,
whilst Rutilius, his lieutenant, surrendered up the
army to Marius, whose conduct, however, in the end
of the war, met with some sort of retribution, as Sylla
deprived him of the glory of the action, as he had
done Metellus. I shall state the circumstances
briefly here, as they are given at large in the life of
Sylla. Bocchus was king of the more distant barbarians, and was father-in-law to Jugurtha, yet sent
him little or no assistance in his war, professing fears
of his unfaithfulness, and really jealous of his growing power; but after Jugurtha fled, and in his distress came to him as his last hope, he received him
as a suppliant, rather because ashamed to do otherwise, than out of real kindness; and when he had him
in his power, he openly entreated Marius on his behalf, and interceded for him with bold words, giving
out that he would by no means deliver him. Yet privately designing to betray him, he sent for Lucius
Sylla, quæstor to Marius, and who had on a previous
occasion befriended Bocchus in the war. When Sylla,
relying on his word, came to him, the African began
to doubt and repent of his purpose, and for several
days was unresolved with himself, whether he should
deliver Jugurtha or retain Sylla; at length he fixed
upon his former treachery, and put Jugurtha alive
into Sylla's possession. Thus was the first occasion
given of that fierce and implacable hostility which so
nearly ruined the whole Roman empire. For many
that envied Marius, attributed the success wholly to
Sylla; and Sylla himself got a seal made on which
was engraved Bocchus betraying Jugurtha to him,
and constantly used it, irritating the hot and jealous
temper of Marius, who was naturally greedy of distinction, and quick to resent any claim to share in

his glory, and whose enemies took care to promote the quarrel, ascribing the beginning and chief business of the war to Metellus, and its conclusion to Sylla; that so the people might give over admiring and esteeming Marius as the worthiest person.

But these envying and calumnies were soon dispersed and cleared away from Marius, by the danger that threatened Italy from the west; when the city, in great need of a good commander, sought about whom she might set at the helm, to meet the tempest of so great a war, no one would have any thing to say to any members of noble or potent families who offered themselves for the consulship, and Marius, though then absent, was elected.

Jugurtha's apprehension was only just known, when the news of the invasion of the Teutones and Cimbri began. The accounts at first exceeded all credit, as to the number and strength of the approaching army; but in the end, report proved much inferior to the truth, as they were three hundred thousand effective fighting men, besides a far greater number of women and children. They professed to be seeking new countries to sustain these great multitudes, and cities where they might settle and inhabit, in the same way as they had heard the Celti before them had driven out the Tyrrhenians, and possessed themselves of the best part of Italy. Having had no commerce with the southern nations, and travelling over a wide extent of country, no man knew what people they were, or whence they came, that thus like a cloud burst over Gaul and Italy; yet by their gray eyes and the largeness of their stature, they were conjectured to be some of the German races dwelling by the northern sea; besides that, the Germans call plunderers Cimbri.

There are some that say, that the country of the

Celti, in its vast size and extent, reaches from the
furthest sea and the arctic regions to the lake Mæotis
eastward, and to that part of Scythia which is near
Pontus, and that there the nations mingle together;
that they did not swarm out of their country all at
once, or on a sudden, but advancing by force of arms,
in the summer season, every year, in the course of
time they crossed the whole continent. And thus,
though each party had several appellations, yet the
whole army was called by the common name of Celto-
Scythians. Others say that the Cimmerii, anciently
known to the Greeks, were only a small part of the
nation, who were driven out upon some quarrel
among the Scythians, and passed all along from the
lake Mæotis to Asia, under the conduct of one
Lygdamis; and that the greater and more warlike
part of them still inhabit the remotest regions lying
upon the outer ocean. These, they say, live in a dark
and woody country hardly penetrable by the sun-
beams, the trees are so close and thick, extending into
the interior as far as the Hercynian forest; and their
position on the earth is under that part of heaven,
where the pole is so elevated, that by the declination
of the parallels, the zenith of the inhabitants seems
to be but little distant from it; and that their days
and nights being almost of an equal length, they divide their year into one of each. This was Homer's
occasion for the story of Ulysses calling up the dead,[9]

[9] When Ulysses bade Circe fulfil her promise, and send him on
his way, she told him he must first visit the home of the dead and
consult Tiresias; crossing the ocean, he would come to a shore
and to the woods of Persephone. Accordingly, "through the
whole day the sails of the ship, travelling through the seas, were
stretched; and the sun set and all ways were darkening, and she
came to the ends of the deep-flowing ocean; there is the people
and town of the Cimmerians, hidden in mist and cloud; the shin-

and from this region the people, anciently called Cimmerii, and afterwards, by an easy change, Cimbri, came into Italy. All this, however, is rather conjecture than an authentic history.

Their numbers, most writers agree, were not less, but rather greater than was reported. They were of invincible strength and fierceness in their wars, and hurried into battle with the violence of a devouring flame; none could withstand them; all they assaulted became their prey. Several of the greatest Roman commanders with their whole armies, that advanced for the defence of Transalpine Gaul, were ingloriously overthrown, and, indeed, by their faint resistance, chiefly gave them the impulse of marching towards Rome. Having vanquished all they had met, and found abundance of plunder, they resolved to settle themselves nowhere till they should have razed the city, and wasted all Italy. The Romans, being from all parts alarmed with this news, sent for Marius to undertake the war, and nominated him the second time consul, though the law did not permit any one that was absent, or that had not waited a certain time after his first consulship to be again created. But the people rejected all opposers; for they considered this was not the first time that the law gave place to the common interest; nor the present occasion less urgent than that when, contrary to law, they made Scipio consul, not in fear for the destruction of their own city, but desiring the ruin of that of the Carthaginians.

Thus it was decided; and Marius, bringing over

ing sun never looks on them with his rays, either when he climbs the starry heaven, or when he turns again from heaven to the earth; darkness is spread over unhappy mortals. There we brought our ship to shore."

his legions out of Africa on the very first day of January, which the Romans count the beginning of the year, received the consulship, and then, also, entered in triumph, showing Jugurtha a prisoner to the people, a sight they had despaired of ever beholding, nor could any, so long as he lived, hope to reduce the enemy in Africa; so fertile in expedients was he to adapt himself to every turn of fortune, and so bold as well as subtle. When, however, he was led in triumph, it is said that he fell distracted, and when he was afterwards thrown into prison, where some tore off his clothes by force, and others, whilst they struggled for his golden ear-ring, with it pulled off the tip of his ear, and when he was, after this, cast naked into the dungeon, in his amazement and confusion, with a ghastly laugh, he cried out, "O Hercules! how cold your bath is!" Here for six days struggling with hunger, and to the very last minute desirous of life, he was overtaken by the just reward of his villanies. In this triumph was brought, as is stated, of gold three thousand and seven pounds weight, of silver bullion five thousand seven hundred and seventy-five, of money in gold and silver coin two hundred and eighty-seven thousand drachmas. After the solemnity, Marius called together the senate in the capitol, and entered, whether through inadvertency or unbecoming exultation with his good fortune, in his triumphal habit; but presently observing the senate offended at it, went out, and returned in his ordinary purple-bordered robe.

On the expedition he carefully disciplined and trained his army whilst on their way, giving them practice in long marches, and running of every sort, and compelling every man to carry his own baggage and prepare his own victuals; insomuch that thenceforward laborious soldiers, who did their work silently without grumbling, had the name of "Marius's mules." Some, however, think the proverb had a different occasion; that when Scipio besieged Numantia, and was careful to inspect not only their horses and arms, but their mules and carriages too, and see how well equipped and in what readiness each one's was, Marius brought forth his horse which he had fed extremely well, and a mule in better case, stronger and gentler than those of others; that the general was very well pleased, and often afterwards mentioned Marius's beasts; and that hence the soldiers, when speaking jestingly in the praise of a drudging, laborious fellow, called him Marius's mule.

But to proceed; very great good fortune seemed to attend Marius, for by the enemy in a manner changing their course, and falling first upon Spain, he had time to exercise his soldiers, and confirm their courage, and, which was most important, to show them what he himself was. For that fierce manner of his in command, and inexorableness in punishing, when his men became used not to do amiss or disobey, was felt to be wholesome and advantageous, as well as just, and his violent spirit, stern voice, and harsh aspect, which in a little while grew familiar to them, they esteemed terrible not to themselves, but only to their enemies. But his uprightness in judging more specially pleased the soldiers, one remarkable instance of which is as follows. One Caius Lusius, his own nephew, had a command under him in the army, a man not in other respects of bad character, but shamefully licentious with young men. He had one young man under his command called Trebonius, with whom notwithstanding many solicitations he could never prevail. At length one night, he sent a messenger for him, and Trebonius came, as it was not lawful for him to refuse when he was sent for, and being brought into his tent, when Lusius began to use violence with him, he drew his sword and ran him through. This was done whilst Marius was absent. When he returned, he appointed Trebonius a time for his trial, where, whilst many accused him, and not any one appeared in his defence, he himself boldly related the whole matter, and brought witness of his previous conduct to Lusius, who had frequently offered him considerable presents. Mairus, admiring his conduct and much pleased, commanded the garland, the usual Roman reward of valor, to be brought, and himself crowned Trebonius with it, as having performed an excellent action, at a time that very much wanted such good examples.

This being told at Rome, proved no small help to Marius towards his third consulship; to which also conduced the expectation of the barbarians at the summer season, the people being unwilling to trust their fortunes with any other general but him. However, their arrival was not so early as was imagined, and the time of Marius's consulship was again expired. The election coming on, and his colleague being dead, he left the command of the army to Manius Aquilius, and hastened to Rome, where, several eminent persons being candidates for the consulship, Lucius Saturninus, who more than any of the other tribunes swayed the populace, and of whom Marius himself was very observant, exerted his eloquence with the people, advising them to choose Marius consul. He playing the modest part, and professing to decline the office, Saturninus, called him traitor to his country, if, in such apparent danger, he would avoid command. And though it was not difficult to discover that he was merely helping Marius in putting this pretence upon the people, yet, considering that the present juncture much required his skill, and his good fortune too, they voted him the fourth time consul, and made Catulus Lutatius his colleague, a man very much esteemed by the nobility, and not unagreeable to the commons.

Marius, having notice of the enemy's approach, with all expedition passed the Alps, and pitching his camp by the river Rhone, took care first for plentiful supplies of victuals; lest at any time he should be forced to fight at a disadvantage for want of necessaries. The carriage of provision for the army from the sea, which was formerly long and expensive, he made speedy and easy. For the mouth of the Rhone, by the influx of the sea, being barred and almost filled up with sand and mud mixed with clay, the passage there became narrow, difficult, and dangerous for the ships that brought their provisions. Hither, therefore, bringing his army, then at leisure, he drew a great trench;[10] and by turning the course of a great part of the river, brought it to a convenient point on the shore where the water was deep enough to receive ships of considerable burden, and where there was a calm and easy opening to the sea. And this still retains the name it took from him.

The enemy dividing themselves into two parts, the Cimbri arranged to go against Catulus higher up through the country of the Norici, and to force that passage; the Teutones and Ambrones to march against Marius by the sea-side through Liguria. The Cimbri were a considerable time in doing their part. But the Teutones and Ambrones with all expedition

[10] The *great trench* or canal bore the name of Fossa Mariana. The phrase just below, *to march against Marius by the seaside through Liguria,* is an incorrect one, but the incorrectness seems to be Plutarch's. Marius was on the Rhone, to oppose any march into Liguria. What the Teutones and Ambrones proposed to do was to beat him, and so enter Italy by Liguria.

passing over the interjacent country, soon came in sight, in numbers beyond belief, of a terrible aspect, and uttering strange cries and shouts. Taking up a great part of the plain with their camp, they challenged Marius to battle; he seemed to take no notice of them, but kept his soldiers within their fortifications, and sharply reprehended those that were too forward and eager to show their courage, and who, out of passion, would needs be fighting, calling them traitors to their country, and telling them they were not now to think of the glory of triumphs and trophies, but rather how they might repel such an impetuous tempest of war, and save Italy.

Thus he discoursed privately with his officers and equals, but placed the soldiers by turns upon the bulwarks to survey the enemy, and so made them familiar with their shape and voice, which were indeed altogether extravagant and barbarous, and he caused them to observe their arms, and way of using them, so that in a little time what at first appeared terrible to their apprehensions, by often viewing became familiar. For he very rationally supposed, that the strangeness of things often makes them seem formidable when they are not so; and that by our better acquaintance, even things which are really terrible, lose much of their frightfulness. This daily converse not only diminished some of the soldiers' fear, but their indignation warmed and inflamed their courage, when they heard the threats and insupportable insolence of their enemies; who not only plundered and depopulated all the country round, but would even contemptuously and confidently attack the ramparts.

Complaints of the soldiers now began to come to Marius's ears. "What effeminacy does Marius see in us, that he should thus like women lock us up from encountering our enemies? Come on, let us show ourselves men, and ask him if he expects others to fight for Italy; and means merely to employ us in servile offices, when he would dig trenches, cleanse places of mud and dirt, and turn the course of rivers? It was to do such works as these, it seems, that he gave us all our long training; he will return home, and boast of these great performances of his consulships to the people. Does the defeat of Carbo and Cæpio, who were vanquished by the enemy, affright him? Surely they were much inferior to Marius both in glory and valor, and commanded a much weaker army; at the worst, it is better to be in action, though we suffer for it like them, than to sit idle spectators of the destruction of our allies and companions." Marius, not a little pleased to hear this, gently appeased them, pretending that he did not distrust their valor, but that he took his measures as to the time and place of victory from some certain oracles.

And, in fact, he used solemnly to carry about in a litter, a Syrian woman, called Martha, a supposed prophetess, and to do sacrifice by her directions. She had formerly been driven away by the senate, to whom she addressed herself, offering to inform them about these affairs, and to foretell future events; and after this betook herself to the women, and gave them proofs of her skill, especially Marius's wife, at whose feet she sat when she was viewing a contest of gladiators, and correctly foretold which of them should overcome. She was for this and the like predictings sent by her to Marius and the army, where she was very much looked up to, and, for the most part, carried about in a litter. When she went to sacrifice, she wore a purple robe lined and buckled up, and had in her hand a little spear trimmed with ribbons and garlands. This theatrical show made many question, whether Marius really gave any credit to her himself, or only played the counterfeit, when he showed her publicly, to impose upon the soldiers.

What, however, Alexander the Myndian relates about the vultures, does really deserve admiration; that always before Marius's victories there appeared two of them, and accompanied the army, which were known by their brazen collars, (the soldiers having caught them and put these about their necks, and so let them go, from which time they in a manner knew and saluted the soldiers,)[11] and whenever these appeared in their marches, they used to rejoice at it, and thought themselves sure of some success. Of the many other prodigies that then were taken notice of, the greater part were but of the ordinary stamp; it was, however, reported that at Ameria and Tuder, two cities in Italy, there were seen at nights in the sky, flaming darts and shields, now waved about, and then again clashing against one another, all in accordance with the postures and motions soldiers use in fighting; that at length one party retreating, and the other pursuing, they all disappeared westward. Much about the same time came Bataces, one of Cybele's priests, from Pessinus,[12] and reported how the goddess had declared to him out of her oracle, that the Romans should obtain the victory. The senate giving credit to him, and voting the goddess a temple to be built in hopes of the victory, Aulus Pompeius, a tribune, prevented Bataces, when he would have gone and told the people this same story,

---

[11] In the sixth line, *the soldiers* might be omitted and *them* substituted. The text is as the translation, but it must be corrected. It was certainly the soldiers who recognized the birds, not the birds who saluted the soldiers.

[12] In Galatia of Asia Minor, the chief seat of the worship of the Great Mother, the goddess Cybele.

calling him impostor, and ignominously pulling him off the hustings; which action in the end was the main thing that gained credit for the man's story, for Aulus had scarce dissolved the assembly, and returned home, when a violent fever seized him, and it was matter of universal remark, and in everybody's mouth, that he died within a week after.

Now the Teutones, whilst Marius lay quiet, ventured to attack his camp; from whence, however, being encountered with showers of darts, and losing several of their men, they determined to march forward hoping to reach the other side of the Alps without opposition, and, packing up their baggage, passed securely by the Roman camp, where the greatness of their number was especially made evident by the long time they took in their march, for they were said to be six days continually going on in passing Marius's fortifications; they marched pretty near, and revilingly asked the Romans if they would send any commands by them to their wives, for they would shortly be with them. As soon as they were passed and had gone on a little distance ahead, Marius began to move, and follow them at his leisure, always encamping at some small distance from them; choosing also strong positions, and carefully fortifying them, that he might quarter with safety. Thus they marched till they came to the place called Sextilius's Waters,[13] from whence it was but a short way before being amidst the Alps, and here Marius put himself in readiness for the encounter.

He chose a place for his camp of considerable strength, but where there was a scarcity of water; designing, it is said, by this means, also, to put an

---

[13] Aquæ Sextiliæ, more correctly Aquæ Sextiæ, the modern Aix of Provence, a little north of Marseilles.

edge on his soldiers' courage; and when several were not a little distressed, and complained of thirst, pointing to a river that ran near the enemy's camp: "There," said he, "you may have drink, if you will buy it with your blood." "Why, then," replied they, "do you not lead us to them, before our blood is dried up in us?" He answered, in a softer tone, "let us first fortify our camp," and the soldiers, though not without repining, proceeded to obey. Now a great company of their boys and camp-followers, having neither drink for themselves nor for their horses, went down to that river; some taking axes and hatchets, and some, too, swords and darts with their pitchers, resolving to have water though they fought for it. These were first encountered by a small party of the enemies; for most of them had just finished bathing, and were eating and drinking, and several were still bathing, the country thereabouts abounding in hot springs; so that the Romans partly fell upon them whilst they were enjoying themselves, and occupied with the novel sights and pleasantness of the place. Upon hearing the shouts, greater numbers still joining in the fight, it was not a little difficult for Marius to contain his soldiers, who were afraid of losing the camp-servants; and the more warlike part of the enemies, who had overthrown Manlius and Cæpio, (they were called Ambrones, and were in number, one with another, above thirty thousand,) taking the alarm, leaped up and hurried to arms.

These, though they had just been gorging themselves with food, and were excited and disordered with drink, nevertheless did not advance with an unruly step, or in mere senseless fury, nor were their shouts mere inarticulate cries; but clashing their arms in concert, and keeping time as they leapt and bounded onward, they continually repeated their own name, "Ambrones!" either to encourage one another, or to strike the greater terror into their enemies. Of all the Italians in Marius's army, the Ligurians were the first that charged; and when they caught the word of the enemy's confused shout, they, too, returned the same, as it was an ancient name also in their country, the Ligurians always using it when speaking of their descent. This acclamation, bandied from one army to the other before they joined, served to rouse and heighten their fury, while the men on either side strove, with all possible vehemence, the one to overshout the other.

The river disordered the Ambrones; before they could draw up all their army on the other side of it, the Ligurians presently fell upon the van, and began to charge them hand to hand. The Romans, too, coming to their assistance, and from the higher ground pouring upon the enemy, forcibly repelled them, and the most of them (one thrusting another into the river) were there slain, and filled it with their blood and dead bodies. Those that got safe over, not daring to make head, were slain by the Romans, as they fled to their camp and wagons; where the women meeting them with swords and hatchets, and making a hideous outcry, set upon those that fled as well as those that pursued, the one as traitors, the other as enemies; and, mixing themselves with the combatants, with their bare arms pulling away the Romans' shields, and laying hold on their swords, endured the wounds and slashing of their bodies to the very last, with undaunted resolution. Thus the battle seems to have happened at that river rather by accident than by the design of the general.

After the Romans were retired from the great slaughter of the Ambrones, night came on; but the army was not indulged, as was the usual custom, with songs of victory, drinking in their tents, and mutual entertainments, and (what is most welcome to soldiers after successful fighting) quiet sleep, but they passed that night, above all others, in fears and alarm. For their camp was without either rampart or palisade, and there remained thousands upon thousands of their enemies yet unconquered; to whom were joined as many of the Ambrones as escaped. There were heard from these, all through the night, wild bewailings, nothing like the sighs and groans of men, but a sort of wild-beastlike howling and roaring, joined with threats and lamentations rising from the vast multitude, and echoed among the neighboring hills and hollow banks of the river. The whole plain was filled with hideous noise, insomuch that the Romans were not a little afraid, and Marius himself was apprehensive of a confused tumultuous night engagement. But the enemy did not stir either this night or the next day, but were employed in disposing and drawing themselves up to the greatest advantage.

Of this occasion Marius made good use; for there were beyond the enemies some wooded ascents and deep valleys thickly set with trees, whither he sent Claudius Marcellus, secretly, with three thousand regular soldiers, giving him orders to post them in ambush there, and show themselves at the rear of the enemies, when the fight was begun. The others, refreshed with victuals [14] and sleep, as soon as it was day he drew up before the camp, and commanded the horse to sally out into the plain, at the sight of which the Teutones could not contain themselves till the

[14] *The others refreshed with victuals and sleep* is more correctly translated, *the others who got their supper in good time and went to bed.*

Romans should come down and fight them on equal terms, but hastily arming themselves, charged in their fury up the hill-side. Marius, sending officers to all parts, commanded his men to stand still and keep their ground; when they came within reach, to throw their javelins, then use their swords, and, joining their shields, force them back; pointing out to them them that the steepness of the ground would render the enemy's blows inefficient, nor could their shields be kept close together, the inequality of the ground hindering the stability of their footing.

This counsel he gave them, and was the first that followed it; for he was inferior to none in the use of his body, and far excelled all in resolution. The Romans accordingly stood for their approach, and, checking them in their advance upwards, forced them little by little to give way and yield down the hill, and here, on the level ground, no sooner had the Ambrones begun to restore their van into a posture of resistance, but they found their rear disordered. For Marcellus had not let slip the opportunity; but as soon as the shout was raised among the Romans on the hills, he, setting his men in motion, fell in upon the enemy behind, at full speed, and with loud cries, and routed those nearest him, and they, breaking the ranks of those that were before them, filled the whole army with confusion. They made no long resistance after they were thus broke in upon, but having lost all order, fled.

The Romans, pursuing them, slew and took prisoners above one hundred thousand, and possessing themselves of their spoil, tents, and carriages, voted all that was not purloined to Marius's share, which, though so magnificent a present, yet was generally thought less than his conduct deserved in so great a danger. Other authors give a different account, both about the division of the plunder and the number of the slain. They say, however, that the inhabitants of Massilia made fences round their vineyards with the bones, and that the ground, enriched by the moisture of the putrefied bodies, (which soaked in with the rain of the following winter,) yielded at the season a prodigious crop, and fully justified Archilochus, who said, that the fallows thus are fattened. It is an observation, also, that extraordinary rains pretty generally fall after great battles; whether it be that some divine power thus washes and cleanses the polluted earth with showers from above, or that moist and heavy evaporations, steaming forth from the blood and corruption, thicken the air, which naturally is subject to alteration from the smallest causes.

After the battle, Marius chose out from amongst the barbarians' spoils and arms, those that were whole and handsome, and that would make the greatest show in his triumph; the rest he heaped upon a large pile, and offered a very splendid sacrifice. Whilst the army stood round about with their arms and garlands, himself attired (as the fashion is on such occasions) in the purple-bordered robe,[15] taking a lighted torch, and with both hands lifting it up towards heaven, he was then going to put it to the pile, when some friends were espied with all haste coming towards him on horseback. Upon which every one remained in silence and expectation. They, upon

[15] Plutarch's words, *attired in the purple-bordered robe* (which might be more closely rendered, *girding himself, and taking up,* or *wearing the purple-bordered robe*), are meant to describe the *cinctus Gabinus* or Gabine cincture, used by officiating persons on great occasions; when the purple-bordered or purple-striped robe, the *prætexta* or *trabea*, was gathered up, and tied like a girdle round the body. As in Virgil: "Ipse Quirinali trabea cinctuque Gabino Insignis reserat stridentia limina consul."

their coming up, leapt off and saluted Marius, bringing him the news of his fifth consulship, and delivered him letters to that effect. This gave the addition of no small joy to the solemnity; and while the soldiers clashed their arms and shouted, the officers again crowned Marius with a laurel-wreath, and he thus set fire to the pile, and finished his sacrifice.

But whatever it be, which interferes to prevent the enjoyment of prosperity ever being pure and sincere, and still diversifies human affairs with the mixture of good and bad, whether fortune or divine displeasure, or the necessity of the nature of things, within a few days Marius received an account of his colleague, Catulus, which as a cloud in serenity and calm, terrified Rome with the apprehension of another imminent storm. Catulus, who marched against the Cimbri, despairing of being able to defend the passes of the Alps, lest, being compelled to divide his forces into several parties, he should weaken himself, descended again into Italy, and posted his army behind the river Adige; where he occupied the passages with strong fortifications on both sides the river, and made a bridge, that so he might cross to the assistance of his men on the other side, if so be the enemy, having forced their way through the mountain passes, should storm the fortresses. The barbarians, however, came on with such insolence and contempt of their enemies, that to show their strength and courage, rather than out of any necessity, they went naked in the showers of snow, and through the ice and deep snow climbed up to the tops of the hills, and from thence, placing their broad shields under their bodies, let themselves slide from the precipices along their vast slippery descents.

When they had pitched their camp at a little distance from the river, and surveyed the passage, they began to pile it up, giant-like, tearing down the neighboring hills; and brought trees pulled up by the roots, and heaps of earth to the river, damming up its course; and with great heavy materials which they rolled down the stream and dashed against the bridge, they forced away the beams which supported it; in consequence of which the greatest part of the Roman soldiers, much affrighted, left the large camp and fled. Here Catulus showed himself a generous and noble general, in preferring the glory of his people before his own; for when he could not prevail with his soldiers to stand to their colors, but saw how they all deserted them, he commanded his own standard to be taken up, and running to the foremost of those that fled, he led them forward, choosing rather that the disgrace should fall upon himself than upon his country, and that they should not seem to fly, but, following their captain, to make a retreat. The barbarians assaulted and took the fortress on the other side the Adige; where much admiring the few Romans there left, who had shown extreme courage, and had fought worthily of their country, they dismissed them upon terms, swearing them upon their brazen bull, which was afterwards taken in the battle, and carried, they say, to Catulus's house, as the chief trophy of victory.

Thus falling in upon the country destitute of defence, they wasted it on all sides. Marius was presently sent for to the city; where, when he arrived, every one supposing he would triumph, the senate, too, unanimously voting it, he himself did not think it convenient; whether that he were not willing to deprive his soldiers and officers of their share of the glory, or that to encourage the people in this juncture, he would leave the honor due to his past victory on trust, as it were, in the hands of the city and its future fortune; deferring it now, to receive it afterwards with the greater splendor. Having left such orders as the occasion required, he hastened to Catulus, whose drooping spirits he much raised, and sent for his own army from Gaul: and as soon as it came, passing the river Po, he endeavored to keep the barbarians out of that part of Italy which lies south of it.

They professed they were in expectation of the Teutones, and, saying they wondered they were so long in coming, deferred the battle; either that they were really ignorant of their defeat, or were willing to seem so. For they certainly much maltreated those that brought them such news, and, sending to Marius, required some part of the country for themselves and their brethren, and cities fit for them to inhabit. When Marius inquired of the ambassadors who their brethren were, upon their saying, the Teutones, all that were present began to laugh; and Marius scoffingly answered them, "Do not trouble yourselves for your brethren, for we have already provided lands for them, which they shall possess forever." The ambassadors, understanding the mockery, broke into insults, and threatened that the Cimbri would make him pay for this, and the Teutones, too, when they came. "They are not far off," replied Marius, "and it will be unkindly done of you to go away before greeting your brethren." Saying so, he commanded the kings of the Teutones to be brought out, as they were, in chains; for they were taken by the Sequani among the Alps, before they could make their escape. This was no sooner made known to the Cimbri, but they with all expedition came against Marius, who then lay still and guarded his camp.

It is said, that against this battle, Marius first altered the construction of the Roman javelins. For before, at the place where the wood was joined to the iron, it was made fast with two iron pins; but now Marius let one of them alone as it was, and pulling

out the other, put a weak wooden peg in its place,
thus contriving, that when it was driven into the
enemy's shield, it should not stand right out, but the
wooden peg breaking, the iron should bend, and so
the javelin should hold fast by its crooked point, and
drag. Bœorix, king of the Cimbri, came with a small
party of horse to the Roman camp, and challenged
Marius to appoint the time and place, where they
might meet and fight for the country. Marius answered, that the Romans never consulted their enemies when to fight; however, he would gratify the
Cimbri so far; and so they fixed upon the third day
after, and for the place, the plain near Vercellæ,
which was convenient enough for the Roman horse,
and afforded room for the enemy to display their
numbers.

They observed the time appointed, and drew out
their forces against each other. Catulus commanded
twenty thousand three hundred, and Marius thirty-
two thousand, who were placed in the two wings,
leaving Catulus the centre. Sylla, who was present
at the fight, gives this account; saying, also, that
Marius drew up his army in this order, because he
expected that the armies would meet on the wings,
since it generally happens that in such extensive fronts
the centre falls back, and thus he would have the
whole victory to himself and his soldiers, and Catulus
would not be even engaged. They tell us, also, that
Catulus himself alleged this in vindication of his honor,
accusing, in various ways, the enviousness of Marius.
The infantry of the Cimbri marched quietly out of
their fortifications, having their flanks equal to their
front; every side of the army taking up thirty furlongs. Their horse, that were in number fifteen thousand, made a very splendid appearance. They wore
helmets, made to resemble the heads and jaws of wild

beasts, and other strange shapes, and heightening these with plumes of feathers, they made themselves appear taller than they were. They had breastplates of iron, and white glittering shields; and for their offensive arms, every one had two darts, and when they came to hand to hand, they used large and heavy swords.

The cavalry did not fall directly upon the front of the Romans, but, turning to the right, they endeavored to draw them on in that direction by little and little, so as to get them between themselves and their infantry, who were placed in the left wing. The Roman commanders soon perceived the design, but could not contain the soldiers; for one happening to shout out that the enemy fled, they all rushed to pursue them, while the whole barbarian foot came on, moving like a great ocean. Here Marius, having washed his hands, and lifting them up towards heaven, vowed an hecatomb to the gods; and Catulus, too, in the same posture, solemnly promised to consecrate a temple to the "Fortune of that day." They say, too, that Marius, having the victim showed to him as he was sacrificing, cried out with a loud voice, "the victory is mine."

However, in the engagement, according to the accounts of Sylla and his friends, Marius met with what might be called a mark of divine displeasure. For a great dust being raised, which (as it might very probably happen) almost covered both the armies, he, leading on his forces to the pursuit, missed the enemy, and having passed by their array, moved, for a good space, up and down the field; meanwhile the enemy, by chance, engaged with Catulus, and the heat of the battle was chiefly with him and his men, among whom Sylla says he was; adding, that the Romans had great advantage of the heat and sun that shone in the faces of the Cimbri. For they, well able to endure cold, and having been bred up, (as we observed before,) in cold and shady countries, were overcome with the excessive heat; they sweated extremely, and were much out of breath, being forced to hold their shields before their faces; for the battle was fought not long after the summer solstice, or, as the Romans reckon, upon the third day before the new moon of the month now called August, and then Sextilis. The dust, too, gave the Romans no small addition to their courage, inasmuch as it hid the enemy. For afar off they could not discover their number; but every one advancing to encounter those that were nearest to them, they came to fight hand to hand, before the sight of so vast a multitude had struck terror into them. They were so much used to labor, and so well exercised, that in all the heat and toil of the encounter, not one of them was observed either to sweat, or to be out of breath; so much so, that Catulus himself, they say, recorded it in commendation of his soldiers.

Here the greatest part and most valiant of the enemies were cut in pieces; for those that fought in the front, that they might not break their ranks, were fast tied to one another, with long chains put through their belts. But as they pursued those that fled to their camp, they witnessed a most fearful tragedy; the women, standing in black clothes on their wagons, slew all that fled, some their husbands, some their brethren, others their fathers; and strangling their little children with their own hands, threw them under the wheels, and the feet of the cattle, and then killed themselves. They tell of one who hung herself from the end of the pole of a wagon, with her children tied dangling at her heels. The men, for want of trees, tied themselves, some to the horns of the oxen, others by the neck to their legs, that so pricking them on, by the starting and springing of the beasts, they might be torn and trodden to pieces. Yet for all they thus massacred themselves, above sixty thousand were taken prisoners, and those that were slain were said to be twice as many.

The ordinary plunder was taken by Marius's soldiers, but the other spoils, as ensigns, trumpets, and the like, they say, were brought to Catulus's camp; which he used for the best argument that the victory was obtained by himself and his army. Some dissensions arising, as was natural, among the soldiers, the deputies from Parma being then present, were made judges of the controversy; whom Catulus's men carried about among their slain enemies, and manifestly showed them that they were slain by their javelins, which were known by the inscription, having Catulus's name cut in the wood. Nevertheless, the whole glory of the action was ascribed to Marius, on account of his former victory, and under color of his present authority; the populace more especially styling him the third founder of their city, as having diverted a danger no less threatening than was that when the Gauls sacked Rome; and every one, in their feasts and rejoicings at home with their wives and children, made offerings and libations in honor of *"The Gods and Marius;"* and would have had him solely have the honor of both the triumphs. However, he did not do so, but triumphed together with Catulus, being desirous to show his moderation even in such great circumstances of good fortune; besides, he was not a little afraid of the soldiers in Catulus's army, lest, if he should wholly bereave their general of the honor, they should endeavor to hinder him of his triumph.

Marius was now in his fifth consulship, and he sued for his sixth in such a manner as never any man before him had done, even for his first; he courted the people's favor and ingratiated himself with the multitude by every sort of complaisance; not only derogating from the state and dignity of his office, but also belying his own character, by attempting to seem popular and obliging, for which nature had never designed him. His passion for distinction did, indeed, they say, make him exceedingly timorous in any political matters, or in confronting public assemblies; and that undaunted presence of mind he always showed in battle against the enemy, forsook him when he was to address the people; he was easily upset by the most ordinary commendation or dispraise. It is told of him, that having at one time given the freedom of the city to one thousand men of Camerinum who had behaved valiantly in this war, and this seeming to be illegally done, upon some one or other calling him to an account for it, he answered, that the law spoke too softly to be heard in such a noise of war; yet he himself appeared to be more disconcerted and overcome by the clamor made in the assemblies. The need they had of him in time of war procured him power and dignity; but in civil affairs, when he despaired of getting the first place, he was forced to betake himself to the favor of the people, never caring to be a good man, so that he were but a great one.

He thus became very odious to all the nobility; and, above all, he feared Metellus, who had been so ungratefully used by him, and whose true virtue made him naturally an enemy to those that sought influence with the people, not by the honorable course, but by subservience and complaisance. Marius, therefore, endeavored to banish him from the city, and for this purpose he contracted a close alliance with Glaucia and Saturninus, a couple of daring fellows, who had the great mass of the indigent and seditious multitude at their control; and by their assistance he enacted various laws, and bringing the soldiers, also, to attend the assembly, he was enabled to overpower Metellus. And as Rutilius relates, (in all other respects a fair and faithful authority, but, indeed, privately an enemy to Marius,) he obtained his sixth consulship by distributing vast sums of money among the tribes, and by this bribery kept out Metellus, and had Valerius Flaccus given him as his instrument, rather than his colleague, in the consulship. The people had never before bestowed so many consulships on any one man, except on Valerius Corvinus only, and he, too, they say, was forty-five years between his first and last; but Marius, from his first ran through five more, with one current of good fortune.

In the last, especially, he contracted a great deal of hatred, by committing several gross misdemeanors in compliance with the desires of Saturninus; among which was the murder of Nonius, whom Saturinus slew, because he stood in competition with him for the tribuneship. And when, afterwards, Saturninus, on becoming tribune, brought forward his law for the division of lands, with a clause enacting that the senate should publicly swear to confirm whatever the people should vote, and not to oppose them in any thing, Marius, in the senate, cunningly feigned to be against this provision, and said that he would not take any such oath, nor would any man, he thought, who was wise; for it there were no ill design in the law, still it would be an affront to the senate, to be compelled to give their approbation, and not to do it willingly and upon persuasion. This he said, not that it was agreeable to his own sentiments, but that he might entrap Metellus beyond any possibility of escape. For Marius, in whose ideas virtue and capacity consisted largely in deceit, made very little account of what he had openly professed

to the senate; and knowing that Metellus was one of
a fixed resolution, and, as Pindar has it, esteemed
"Truth the first principle of heroic virtue,"[16] he
hoped to ensnare him into a declaration before the
senate, and on his refusing, as he was sure to do,
afterwards to take the oath, he expected to bring
him into such odium with the people, as should never
be wiped off. The design succeeded to his wish. As
soon as Metellus had declared that he would not
swear to it, the senate adjourned. A few days after,
on Saturninus citing the senators to make their appearance,
and take the oath before the people, Marius
stepped forth, amidst a profound silence, every
one being intent to hear him, and bidding farewell
to those fine speeches he had before made in the senate,
said, that his back was not so broad that he
should think himself bound, once for all, by any
opinion once given on so important a matter; he
would willingly swear and submit to the law, if so
be it were one, a proviso which he added as a mere
cover for his effrontery. The people, in great joy
at his taking the oath, loudly clapped and applauded
him, while the nobility stood by ashamed and vexed
at his inconstancy; but they submitted out of fear
of the people, and all in order took the oath, till it
came to Metellus's turn. But he, though his friends
begged and entreated him to take it, and not to
plunge himself irrecoverably into the penalties which
Saturninus had provided for those that should refuse

[16] The passage in which Pindar calls *Truth the first principle
of heroic virtue* is a fragment of a lost and unknown composition,
found, however, at a little greater length elsewhere. "First beginning
of great virtue, queen Truth, shipwreck not my faith on any
rock of falsehood; *i. e.* let not my promise ever come to be broken
by me; keep me ever faithful to my engagements. (*Boeckh,
Fragm. Incerta*, 118.)

it, would not flinch from his resolution, nor swear; but, according to his fixed custom, being ready to suffer any thing rather than do a base, unworthy action, he left the forum, telling those that were with him, that to do a wrong thing is base, and to do well where there is no danger, common; the good man's characteristic is to do so, where there is danger.

Hereupon Saturninus put it to the vote, that the consuls should place Metellus under their interdict, and forbid him fire, water, and lodging. There were enough, too, of the basest of people ready to kill him. Nevertheless, when many of the better sort were extremely concerned, and gathered about Metellus, he would not suffer them to raise a sedition upon his account, but with this calm reflection left the city, "Either when the posture of affairs is mended and the people repent, I shall be recalled, or if things remain in their present condition, it will be best to be absent." But what great favor and honor Metellus received in his banishment, and in what manner he spent his time at Rhodes, in philosophy, will be more fitly our subject, when we write his life.

Marius, in return for this piece of service, was forced to connive at Saturninus, now proceeding to the very height of insolence and violence, and was, without knowing it, the instrument of mischief beyond endurance, the only course of which was through outrages and massacres to tyranny and the subversion of the government. Standing in some awe of the nobility, and, at the same time, eager to court the commonalty, he was guilty of a most mean and dishonest action. When some of the great men came to him at night to stir him up against Saturninus, at the other door, unknown to them, he let him in; then making the same pretence of some disorder of body to both, he ran from one party to the other, and staying at one time with them and another with him, he instigated and exasperated them one against another. At length when the senate and equestrian order concerted measures together, and openly manifested their resentment, he did bring his soldiers into the forum, and driving the insurgents into the capitol, and then cutting off the conduits, forced them to surrender by want of water. They, in this distress, addressing themselves to him, surrendered, as it is termed, on the *public faith*. He did his utmost to save their lives, but so wholly in vain, that when they came down into the forum, they were all basely murdered. Thus he had made himself equally odious both to the nobility and commons, and when the time was come to create censors, though he was the most obvious man, yet he did not petition for it; but fearing the disgrace of being repulsed, permitted others, his inferiors, to be elected, though he pleased himself by giving out, that he was not willing to disoblige too many by undertaking a severe inspection into their lives and conduct.

There was now an edict preferred to recall Metellus from banishment; thus he vigorously, but in vain, opposed, both by word and deed, and was at length obliged to desist. The people unanimously voted for it; and he, not able to endure the sight of Metellus's return, made a voyage to Cappadocia and Galatia; giving out that he had to perform the sacrifices, which he had vowed to Cybele; but actuated really by other less apparent reasons. For, in fact, being a man altogether ignorant of civil life and ordinary politics, he received all his advancement from war; and supposing his power and glory would by little and little decrease by his lying quietly out of action, he was eager by every means to excite some new commotions, and hoped that by setting at variance some of the kings, and by exasperating Mithridates, especially, who was then apparently making preparations for war, he himself should be chosen general against him, and so furnish the city with new matter of triumph, and his own house with the plunder of Pontus, and the riches of its king. Therefore, though Mithridates entertained him with all imaginable attention and respect, yet he was not at all wrought upon or softened by it; but said, "O king, either endeavor to be stronger than the Romans, or else quietly submit to their commands." With which he left Mithridates astonished, as he indeed had often heard the fame of the bold speaking of the Romans, but now for the first time experienced it.

When Marius returned again to Rome, he built a house close by the forum, either, as he himself gave out, that he was not willing his clients should be tired with going far, or that he imagined distance was the reason why more did not come. This, however, was not so; the real reason was, that being inferior to others in agreeableness of conversation and the arts of political life, like a mere tool and implement of war, he was thrown aside in time of peace. Amongst all those whose brightness eclipsed his glory, he was most incensed against Sylla, who had owed his rise to the hatred which the nobility bore Marius; and had made his disagreement with him the one principle of his political life. When Bocchus, king of Numidia, who was styled the associate of the Romans' dedicated some figures of Victory in the capitol, and with them a representation in gold, of himself delivering Jugurtha to Sylla, Marius upon this was almost distracted with rage and ambition, as though Sylla had arrogated this honor to himself, and endeavored forcibly to pull down these presents; Sylla, on the other side, as vigorously resisted him;

but the Social War then on a sudden threatening the city, put a stop to this sedition, when just ready to break out. For the most warlike and best-peopled countries of all Italy formed a confederacy together against Rome, and were within a little of subverting the empire; as they were indeed strong, not only in their weapons and the valor of their soldiers, but stood nearly upon equal terms with the Romans, as to the skill and daring of their commanders.

As much glory and power as this war, so various in its events and so uncertain as to its success, conferred upon Sylla, so much it took away from Marius, who was thought tardy, unenterprising, and timid, whether it were that his age was now quenching his former heat and vigor, (for he was above sixty-five years old,) or that having, as he himself said, some distemper that affected his muscles, and his body being unfit for action, he did service above his strength. Yet, for all this, he came off victor in a considerable battle, wherein he slew six thousand of the enemies, and never once gave them any advantage over him; and when he was surrounded by the works of the enemy, he contained himself, and though insulted over, and challenged, did not yield to the provocation. The story is told that when Publius [17] Silo, a man of the greatest repute and authority among the enemies, said to him, "If you are indeed a great general, Marius, leave your camp and fight a battle," he replied, "If you are one, make me do so." And another time, when the enemy gave them a good opportunity of a battle, and the Romans through fear durst not charge, so that both parties retreated, he called an assembly of his soldiers and said, "It is no small question whether I should call

---

[17] More correctly Pompædius.

CAIUS MARIUS 93

the enemies, or you, the greater cowards, for neither did they dare to face your backs, nor you to confront theirs." At length, professing to be worn out with the infirmity of his body, he laid down his command.

Afterwards, when the Italians were worsted, there were several candidates suing, with the aid of the popular leaders, for the chief command in the war with Mithridates. Sulpicius, tribune of the people, a bold and confident man, contrary to everybody's expectation, brought forward Marius, and proposed him as proconsul and general in that war. The people were divided; some were on Marius's side, others voted for Sylla, and jeeringly bade Marius go to his baths at Baiæ, to cure his body, worn out, as himself confessed, with age and catarrhs. Marius had, indeed, there, about Misenum, a villa more effeminately and luxuriously furnished than seemed to become one that had seen service in so many and great wars and expeditions. This same house Cornelia bought for seventy-five thousand drachmas, and not long after Lucius Lucullus, for two million five hundred thousand; so rapid and so great was the growth of Roman sumptuosity. Yet, in spite of all this, out of a mere boyish passion for distinction, affecting to shake off his age and weakness, he went down daily to the Campus Martius, and exercising himself with the youth, showed himself still nimble in his armor, and expert in riding; though he was undoubtedly grown bulky in his old age, and inclining to excessive fatness and corpulency.

Some people were pleased with this, and went continually to see him competing and displaying himself in these exercises; but the better sort that saw him, pitied the cupidity and ambition that made one who had risen from utter poverty to extreme wealth, and out of nothing into greatness, unwilling to admit any limit to his high fortune, or to be content with being admired, and quietly enjoying what he had already got: why, as if he still were indigent, should he at so great an age leave his glory and his triumphs to go into Cappadocia and the Euxine Sea, to fight Archelaus and Neoptolemus, Mithridates's generals? Marius's pretences for this action of his seemed very ridiculous; for he said he wanted to go and teach his son to be a general.

The condition of the city, which had long been unsound and diseased, became hopeless now that Marius found so opportune an instrument for the public destruction as Sulpicius's insolence. This man professed, in all other respects, to admire and imitate Saturninus; only he found fault with him for backwardness and want of spirit in his designs. He, therefore, to avoid this fault, got six hundred of the equestrian order about him as his guard, whom he named anti-senators; and with these confederates he set upon the consuls, whilst they were at the assembly, and took the son of one of them, who fled from the forum, and slew him. Sylla, being hotly pursued, took refuge in Marius's house, which none could suspect, by that means escaping those that sought him, who hastily passed by there, and, it is said, was safely conveyed by Marius himself out at the other door, and came to the camp. Yet Sylla, in his memoirs, positively denies that he fled to Marius, saying he was carried thither to consult upon the matters to which Sulpicius would have forced him, against his will, to consent; that he, surrounding him with drawn swords, hurried him to Marius, and constrained him thus, till he went thence to the forum and removed, as they required him to do, the interdict on business.[18]

Sulpicius, having thus obtained the mastery, decreed the command of the army to Marius, who proceeded to make preparations for his march, and sent two tribunes to receive the charge of the army from Sylla. Sylla hereupon exasperating his soldiers, who were about thirty-five thousand full-armed men, led them towards Rome. First falling upon the tribunes Marius had sent, they slew them; Marius having done as much for several of Sylla's friends in Rome, and now offering their freedom to the slaves on condition of their assistance in the war; of whom, however, they say, there were but three who accepted his proposal. For some small time he made head against Sylla's assault, but was soon overpowered and fled; those that were with him, as soon as he had escaped out of the city, were dispersed, and night coming on, he hastened to a country-house of his, called Solonium. Hence he sent his son to some neighboring farms of his father-in-law, Mucius, to provide necessaries; he went himself to Ostia, where his friend Numerius had prepared him a ship, and hence, not staying for his son, he took with him his son-in-law Granius, and weighed anchor.

Young Marius, coming to Mucius's farms, made his preparations; and the day breaking, was almost discovered by the enemy. For there came thither a party of horse that suspected some such matter; but the farm steward, foreseeing their approach, hid Marius in a cart full of beans, then yoking in his team and driving toward the city, met those that were in search of him. Marius, thus conveyed home to his

---

[18] The Roman Justitium, during which no public proceedings could be lawfully carried on. Such is the meaning of the probable text.

wife, took with him some necessaries, and came at
night to the sea-side; where, going on board a ship
that was bound for Africa, he went away thither.
Marius, the father, when he had put to sea, with a
strong gale passing along the coast of Italy, was in
no small apprehension of one Geminius, a great man
at Terracina, and his enemy; and therefore bade the
seamen hold off from that place. They were, indeed,
willing to gratify him, but the wind now blowing in
from the sea, and making the waves swell to a great
height, they were afraid the ship would not be able
to weather out the storm, and Marius, too, being in-
disposed and seasick, they made for land, and not
without some difficulty reached the shore near Cir-
ceium.

The storm now increasing and their victuals failing, they left their ship and wandered up and down
without any certain purpose, simply as in great dis-
tresses people shun the present as the greatest evil,
and rely upon the hopes of uncertainties. For the
land and sea were both equally unsafe for them; it
was dangerous to meet with people, and it was no
less so to meet with none, on account of their want
of necessaries. At length, though late, they lighted
upon a few poor shepherds, that had not any thing
to relieve them; but knowing Marius, advised him to
depart as soon as might be, for they had seen a little
beyond that place a party of horse that were gone in
search of him. Finding himself in a great straight,
especially because those that attended him were not
able to go further, being spent with their long fasting, for the present he turned aside out of the road,
and hid himself in a thick wood, where he passed the
night in great wretchedness. The next day, pinched
with hunger, and willing to make use of the little
strength he had, before it were all exhausted, he

travelled by the sea-side, encouraging his companions not to fall away from him before the fulfilment of his final hopes, for which, in reliance on some old predictions, he professed to be sustaining himself. For when he was yet but very young, and lived in the country, he caught in the skirt of his garment an eagle's nest, as it was falling, in which were seven young ones, which his parents seeing and much admiring, consulted the augurs about it, who told them that he should become the greatest man in the world, and that the fates had decreed he should seven times be possessed of the supreme power and authority. Some are of opinion that this really happened to Marius, as we have related it; others say, that those who then and through the rest of his exile heard him tell these stories, and believed him, have merely repeated a story that is altogether fabulous; for an eagle never hatches more than two; and even Musæus was deceived, who, speaking of the eagle, says that,—

"She lays three eggs, hatches two, and rears one." [19]

However this be, it is certain Marius, in his exile and greatest extremities, would often say, that he should attain a seventh consulship.

When Marius and his company were now about twenty furlongs distant from Minturnæ, a city in Italy, they espied a troop of horse making up toward them with all speed, and by chance, also, at the same time, two ships under sail. Accordingly they ran every one with what speed and strength they could to the sea, and plunging into it, swam to the ships. Those that were with Granius, reaching one of them, passed over to an island opposite, called Ænaria; Marius

[19] The line about the eagle's young, ascribed to Musæus, is cited also by Aristotle in his History of Animals.

himself whose body was heavy and unwieldy, was with great pains and difficulty kept above the water by two servants, and put into the other ship. The soldiers were by this time come to the sea-side, and from thence called out to the seamen to put to shore, or else to throw out Marius, and then they might go whither they would. Marius besought them with tears to the contrary, and the masters of the ship, after frequent changes, in a short space of time, of their purpose, inclining, first to one, then to the other side, resolved at length to answer the soldiers, that they would not give up Marius. As soon as they had ridden off in a rage, the seamen, again changing their resolution, came to land, and casting anchor at the mouth of the river Liris, where it overflows and makes a great marsh, they advised him to land, refresh himself on shore, and take some care of his discomposed body, till the wind came fairer; which, said they, will happen at such an hour, when the wind from the sea will calm, and that from the marshes rise, Marius, following their advice, did so, and when the seamen had set him on shore, he laid him down in an adjacent field, suspecting nothing less than what was to befall him. They, as soon as they had got into the ship, weighed anchor and departed, as thinking it neither honorable to deliver Marius into the hands of those that sought him, nor safe to protect him.

He thus, deserted by all, lay a good while silently on the shore; at length collecting himself, he advanced with pain and difficulty, without any path, till, wading through deep bogs and ditches full of water and mud, he came upon the hut of an old man that worked in the fens, and falling at his feet besought him to assist and preserve one who, if he escaped the present danger, would make him returns beyond his expectation. The poor man, whether he had formerly known him, or were then moved with his superior aspect, told him that if he wanted only rest, his cottage would be convenient; but if he were flying from anybody's search, he would hide him in a more retired place. Marius desiring him to do so, he carried him into the fens and bade him hide himself in an hollow place by the river side, where he laid upon him a great many reeds, and other things that were light, and would cover, but not oppress him. But within a very short time he was disturbed with a noise and tumult from the cottage, for Geminius had sent several from Terracina in pursuit of him; some of whom, happening to come that way, frightened and threatened the old man for having entertained and hid an enemy of the Romans. Wherefore Marius, arising and stripping himself, plunged into a puddle full of thick muddy water; and even there he could not escape their search, but was pulled out covered with mire, and carried away naked to Minturnæ, and delivered to the magistrates. For there had been orders sent through all the towns, to make public search for Marius, and if they found him to kill him; however, the magistrates thought convenient to consider a little better of it first, and sent him prisoner to the house of one Fannia.

This woman was supposed not very well affected towards him upon an old account. One Tinnius had formerly married this Fannia; from whom she afterwards being divorced, demanded her portion, which was considerable, but her husband accused her of adultery; so the controversy was brought before Marius in his sixth consulship. When the cause was examined thoroughly, it appeared both that Fannia had been incontinent, and that her husband knowing her to be so, had married and lived a considerable time with her. So that Marius was severe enough with

both, commanding him to restore her portion, and
laying a fine of four copper coins upon her by way
of disgrace. But Fannia did not then behave like a
woman that had been injured, but as soon as she
saw Marius, remembered nothing less than old affronts; took care of him according to her ability, and
comforted him. He made her his returns and told her
he did not despair, for he had met with a lucky omen,
which was thus. When he was brought to Fannia's
house, as soon as the gate was open, an ass came running out to drink at a spring hard by, and giving a
bold and encouraging look, first stood still before him,
then brayed aloud and pranced by him. From which
Marius drew his conclusion, and said, that the fates
designed him safety, rather by sea than land, because
the ass neglected his dry fodder, and turned from it
to the water. Having told Fannia this story, he bade
the chamber door to be shut and went to rest.

Meanwhile the magistrates and councillors of Minturnæ consulted together and determined not to delay
any longer, but immediately to kill Marius; and when
none of their citizens durst undertake the business, a
certain soldier, a Gaulish or Cimbrian horseman,
(the story is told both ways,) went in with his sword
drawn to him. The room itself was not very light,
that part of it especially where he then lay was dark,
from whence Marius's eyes, they say, seemed to the
fellow to dart out flames at him, and a loud voice to
say, out of the dark, "Fellow, darest thou kill Caius
Marius?" The barbarian hereupon immediately fled,
and leaving his sword in the place rushed out of doors,
crying only this, "I cannot kill Caius Marius." At
which they were all at first astonished, and presently
began to feel pity, and remorse, and anger at themselves for making so unjust and ungrateful a decree
against one who had preserved Italy, and whom it

was bad enough not to assist. "Let him go," said they, "where he please to banishment, and find his fate somewhere else; we only entreat pardon of the gods for thrusting Marius distressed and deserted out of our city."

Impelled by thoughts of this kind, they went in a body into the room, and taking him amongst them, conducted him towards the sea-side; on his way to which, though every one was very officious to him, and all made what haste they could, yet a considerable time was likely to be lost. For the grove of Marica, (as she is called,) which the people hold sacred, and make it a point of religion not to let any thing that is once carried into it be taken out, lay just in their road to the sea, and if they should go round about, they must needs come very late thither. At length one of the old men cried out and said, there was no place so sacred, but they might pass through it for Marius's preservation; and thereupon, first of all, he himself, taking up some of the baggage that was carried for his accommodation to the ship, passed through the grove, all the rest immediately, with the same readiness, accompanying him. And one Belæus, (who afterwards had a picture of these things drawn, and put it in a temple at the place of embarkation), having by this time provided him a ship, Marius went on board, and, hoisting sail, was by fortune thrown upon the island Ænaria, where meeting with Granius, and his other friends, he sailed with them for Africa. But their water failing them in the way, they were forced to put in near Eryx, in Sicily, where was a Roman quæstor on the watch, who all but captured Marius himself on his landing, and did kill sixteen of his retinue that went to fetch water. Marius, with all expedition loosing thence, crossed the sea to the isle of Meninx, where he first heard the news of his son's escape with Cethegus, and of his going to implore the assistance of Hiempsal, king of Numidia.

With this news, being somewhat comforted, he ventured to pass from that isle towards Carthage. Sextilius, a Roman, was then governor in Africa; one that had never received either any injury or any kindness from Marius; but who from compassion, it was hoped, might lend him some help. But he was scarce got ashore with a small retinue, when an officer met him, and said, "Sextilius, the governor, forbids you, Marius, to set foot in Africa; if you do, he says, he will put the decree of the senate in execution, and treat you as an enemy to the Romans." When Marius heard this, he wanted words to express his grief and resentment, and for a good while held his peace, looking sternly upon the messenger, who asked him what he should say, or what answer he should return to the governor? Marius answered him with a deep sigh: "Go tell him that you have seen Caius Marius sitting in exile among the ruins of Carthage;" appositely applying the example of the fortune of that city to the change of his own condition.

In the interim, Hiempsal, king of Numidia, dubious of what he should determine to do, treated young Marius and those that were with him very honorably; but when they had a mind to depart, he still had some pretence or other to detain them, and it was manifest he made these delays upon no good design. However, there happened an accident that made well for their preservation. The hard fortune which attended young Marius, who was of a comely aspect, touched one of the king's concubines, and this pity of hers, was the beginning and occasion of love for him. At first he declined the woman's solicitations, but when he perceived that there was no other way of escaping, and that her offers were more seri-

MARIUS ON THE RUINS OF CARTHAGE

ous than for the gratification of intemperate passion, he accepted her kindness, and she finding means to convey them away, he escaped with his friends and fled to his father. As soon as they had saluted each other, and were going by the sea-side, they saw some scorpions fighting, which Marius took for an ill omen, whereupon they immediately went on board a little fisher-boat, and made toward Cercina, an island not far distant from the continent. They had scarce put off from shore when they espied some horse, sent after them by the king, with all speed making toward that very place from which they were just retired. And Marius thus escaped a danger, it might be said, as great as any he ever incurred.

At Rome news came that Sylla was engaged with Mithridates's generals in Bœotia; the consuls, from factious opposition, were fallen to downright fighting, wherein Octavius prevailing, drove Cinna out of the city for attempting despotic government, and made Cornelius Merula consul in his stead; while Cinna, raising forces in other parts of Italy, carried the war against them. As soon as Marius heard of this, he resolved, with all expedition, to put to sea again, and taking with him from Africa some Mauritanian horse, and a few of the refugees out of Italy, all together not above one thousand, he, with this handful, began his voyage. Arriving at Telamon, in Etruria, and coming ashore, he proclaimed freedom for the slaves; and many of the countrymen, also, and shepherds thereabouts, who were already freemen, at the hearing his name flocked to him to the sea-side. He persuaded the youngest and strongest to join him, and in a small time got together a competent force with which he filled forty ships. Knowing Octavius to be a good man and willing to execute his office with the greatest justice imaginable, and Cinna to be suspected by

Sylla, and in actual warfare against the established government, he determined to join himself and his forces with the latter. He, therefore, sent a message to him, to let him know that he was ready to obey him as consul.

When Cinna had joyfully received his offer, naming him proconsul, and sending him the fasces and other ensigns of authority, he said, that grandeur did not become his present fortune; but wearing an ordinary habit, and still letting his hair grow as it had done, from that very day he first went into banishment, and being now above threescore and ten years old, he came slowly on foot, designing to move people's compassion; which did not prevent, however, his natural fierceness of expression from still predominating, and his humiliation still let it appear that he was not so much dejected as exasperated, by the change of his condition. Having saluted Cinna and the soldiers, he immediately prepared for action, and soon made a considerable alteration in the posture of affairs. He first cut off the provision ships, and plundering all the merchants, made himself master of the supplies of corn; then bringing his navy to the seaport towns, he took them, and at last, becoming master of Ostia by treachery, he pillaged that town, and slew a multitude of the inhabitants, and, blocking up the river, took from the enemy all hopes of supply by the sea; then marched with his army toward the city, and posted himself upon the hill called Janiculum.

The public interest did not receive so great damage from Octavius's unskilfulness in his management of affairs, as from his omitting needful measures, through too strict observance of the law. As when several advised him to make the slaves free, he said that the would not give slaves the privilege of the country from which he then, in defence of the laws, was driving away Marius. When Metellus, son to that Metellus who was general in the war in Africa, and afterwards banished through Marius's means, came to Rome, being thought a much better commander than Octavius, the soldiers, deserting the consul, came to him and desired him to take the command of them and preserve the city; that they, when they had got an experienced valiant commander, should fight courageously, and come off conquerors. But when Metellus, offended at it, commanded them angrily to return to the consul, they revolted to the enemy. Metellus, too, seeing the city in a desperate condition, left it; but a company of Chaldæans, sacrificers, and interpreters of the Sibyl's books, persuaded Octavius that things would turn out happily, and kept him at Rome. He was, indeed, of all the Romans the most upright and just, and maintained the honor of the consulate, without cringing or compliance, as strictly in accordance with ancient laws and usages, as though they had been immutable mathematical truths; and yet fell, I know not how, into some weaknesses, giving more observance to fortune-tellers and diviners, than to men skilled in civil and military affairs. He therefore, before Marius entered the city, was pulled down from the rostra, and murdered by those that were sent before by Marius; and it is reported there was a Chaldæan writing found in his gown, when he was slain. And it seemed a thing very unaccountable, that of two famous generals, Marius should be often successful by the observing divinations, and Octavius ruined by the same means.

When affairs were in this posture, the senate assembled, and sent a deputation to Cinna and Marius, desiring them to come into the city peaceably and spare the citizens. Cinna, as consul, received the

embassy, sitting in the curule chair, and returned a
kind answer to the messengers; Marius stood by him
and said nothing, but gave sufficient testimony by the
gloominess of his countenance, and the sternness of
his looks, that he would in a short time fill the city
with blood. As soon as the council arose, they went
toward the city, where Cinna entered with his guards,
but Marius stayed at the gates, and, dissembling his
rage, professed that he was then an exile and banished his country by course of law; that if his presence were necessary, they must, by a new decree,
repeal the former act by which he was banished; as
though he were, indeed, a religious observer of the
laws, and as if he were returning to a city free from
fear or oppression. Hereupon the people were assembled, but before three or four tribes had given
their votes, throwing up his pretences and his legal
scruples about his banishment, he came into the city
with a select guard of the slaves who had joined him,
whom he called Bardyæi. These proceeded to murder
a number of citizens, as he gave command, partly
by word of mouth, partly by the signal of his nod.
At length Ancharius, a senator, and one that had been
prætor, coming to Marius, and not being resaluted by
him, they with their drawn swords slew him before
Marius's face; and henceforth this was their token,
immediately to kill all those who met Marius and
saluting him were taken no notice of, nor answered
with the like courtesy; so that his very friends were
not without dreadful apprehensions and horror,
whensoever they came to speak with him.

When they had now butchered a great number,
Cinna grew more remiss and cloyed with murders;
but Marius's rage continued still fresh and unsatisfied,
and he daily sought for all that were any way suspected by him. Now was every road and every town

filled with those that pursued and hunted them that fled and hid themselves; and it was remarkable that there was no more confidence to be placed, as things stood, either in hospitality or friendship; for there were found but a very few that did not betray those that fled to them for shelter. And thus the servants of Cornutus deserve the greater praise and admiration, who, having concealed their master in the house, took the body of one of the slain, cut off the head, put a gold ring on the finger, and showed it to Marius's guards, and buried it with the same solemnity as if it had been their own master. This trick was perceived by nobody, and so Cornutus escaped, and was conveyed by his domestics into Gaul.

Marcus Antonius, the orator, though he, too, found a true friend, had ill-fortune. The man was but poor and a plebeian, and as he was entertaining a man of the greatest rank in Rome, trying to provide for him with the best he could, he sent his servant to get some wine of a neighboring vintner. The servant carefully tasting it and bidding him to draw better, the fellow asked him what was the matter, that he did not buy new and ordinary wine as he used to do, but richer and of a greater price; he, without any design, told him as his old friend and acquaintance, that his master entertained Marcus Antonius, who was concealed with him. The villanous vintner, as soon as the servant was gone, went himself to Marius, then at supper, and being brought into his presence, told him, he would deliver Antonius into his hands. As soon as he heard it, it is said he gave a great shout, and clapped his hands for joy, and had very nearly risen up and gone to the place himself; but being detained by his friends, he sent Annius, and some soldiers with him, and commanded him to bring Antonius's head to him with all speed. When they came to the house,

Annius stayed at the door, and the soldiers went up stairs into the chamber; where, seeing Antonius, they endeavored to shuffle off the murder from one to another; for so great it seems were the graces and charms of his oratory, that as soon as he began to speak and beg his life, none of them durst touch or so much as look upon him; but hanging down their heads, every one fell a weeping. When their stay seemed something tedious, Annius came up himself and found Antonius discoursing, and the soldiers astonished and quite softened by it, and calling them cowards, went himself and cut off his head.

Catulus Lutatius, who was colleague with Marius, and his partner in the triumph over the Cimbri, when Marius replied to those that interceded for him and begged his life, merely with the words, "he must die," shut himself up in a room, and making a great fire, smothered himself. When maimed and headless carcasses were now frequently thrown about and trampled upon in the streets, people were not so much moved with compassion at the sight, as struck into a kind of horror and consternation. The outrages of those that were called Bardyæi, was the greatest grievance. These murdered the masters of families in their own houses, abused their children and ravished their wives, and were uncontrollable in their rapine and murders, till those of Cinna's and Sertorius's party, taking counsel together, fell upon them in the camp and killed them every man.

In the interim, as if a change of wind was coming on, there came news from all parts that Sylla, having put an end to the war with Mithridates, and taken possession of the provinces, was returning into Italy with a great army. This gave some small respite and intermission to these unspeakable calamities. Marius

CAIUS MARIUS

and his friends believing war to be close at hand, Marius was chosen consul the seventh time, and appearing [20] on the very calends of January, the beginning of the year, threw one Sextus Lucinius,[21] from the Tarpeian precipice; an omen, as it seemed, portending the renewed misfortunes both of their party and of the city. Marius, himself now worn out with labor and sinking under the burden of anxieties, could not sustain his spirits, which shook within him with the apprehension of a new war and fresh encounters and dangers, the formidable character of which he knew by his own experience. He was not now to hazard the war with Octavius or Merula, commanding an inexperienced multitude or seditious rabble; but Sylla himself was approaching, the same who had formerly banished him, and since that, had driven Mithridates as far as the Euxine Sea.

Perplexed with such thoughts as these, and calling to mind his banishment, and the tedious wanderings and dangers he underwent, both by sea and land, he fell into despondency, nocturnal frights, and unquiet

[20] A part of the ceremonial of the consul's *appearing* on his first assuming office *on the calends of January* was to go up and offer sacrifice in the Capitoline Temple, attended apparently by the senate, a full meeting of which took place immediately after. The words, a little above, *as if a change of wind were coming on,* are more expressive in the original; it is, *as if the wind, which had been blowing steadily from the one quarter, were setting in from the opposite.* The word *tropaia* (the *turn* or *return* wind), according to a passage of Aristotle (quoted by Coray), was specially applied to the wind which set from the sea after it had blown for its regular time from the shore; the sea breeze, succeeding the land breeze.

[21] Thus it stands in all the manuscripts but one, and it may very likely have thus been written by Plutarch. The true name is undoubtedly Licinius.

sleep, still fancying that he heard some one telling him, that

——— the lion's lair
Is dangerous, though the lion be not there.

Above all things fearing to lie awake, he gave himself up to drinking deep and besotting himself at night in a way most unsuitable to his age; by all means provoking sleep, as a diversion to his thoughts. At length, on the arrival of a messenger from the sea, he was seized with new alarms, and so what with his fear for the future, and what with the burden and satiety of the present, on some slight predisposing cause, he fell into a pleurisy, as Posidonius the philosopher relates, who says he visited and conversed with him when he was sick, about some business relating to his embassy. Caius Piso, an historian, tells us, that Marius, walking after supper with his friends, fell into a conversation with them about his past life, and after reckoning up the several changes of his condition, that from the beginning had happened to him, said, that it did not become a prudent man to trust himself any longer with fortune; and, thereupon, taking leave of those that were with him, he kept his bed seven days, and then died.

Some say his ambition betrayed itself openly in his sickness, and that he ran into an extravagant frenzy, fancying himself to be general in the war against Mithridates, throwing himself into such postures and motions of his body as he had formerly used when he was in battle, with frequent shouts and loud cries. With so strong and invincible a desire of being employed in that business had he been possessed through his pride and emulation. Though he had now lived seventy years, and was the first man that ever was chosen seven times consul, and had an establishment and riches sufficient for many kings, he yet complained of his ill fortune, that he must now die before he had attained what he desired. Plato, when he saw his death approaching, thanked the guiding providence and fortune of his life,[22] first, that he was born a man and a Grecian, not a barbarian or a brute, and next, that he happened to live in Socrates's age. And so, indeed, they say Antipater of Tarsus, in like manner, at his death, calling to mind the happiness that he had enjoyed, did not so much as omit his prosperous voyage to Athens; thus recognizing every favor of his indulgent fortune with the greatest acknowledgements, and carefully saving all to the last in that safest of human treasure-chambers, the memory. Unmindful and thoughtless persons, on the contrary, let all that occurs to them slip away from them as time passes on. Retaining and preserving nothing, they lose the enjoyment of their present prosperity by fancying something better to come; whereas by fortune we may be prevented of this, but that cannot be taken from us. Yet they reject their present success, as though it did not concern them, and do nothing but dream of future uncertainties; not indeed unnaturally; as till men have by reason and education laid a good foundation for external superstructures, in the seeking after and gathering them they can never satisfy the unlimited desires of their mind.

Thus died Marius on the seventeenth day of his

---

[22] The story of *Plato's thanks to the providence and fortune of his life* is told a little more fully by Lactantius (*Instit. III.*, 19). "Plato returned thanks," he says, "that he had been born, first, a human and not a brute creature; secondly, a man and not a woman; thirdly, a Greek and not a barbarian; lastly, an Athenian, and in the age of Socrates;" *as if,* adds Lactantius, scornfully, *had he been born a barbarian, a woman, or an ass, he would still have been the same Plato.*

seventh consulship, to the great joy and content of
Rome, which thereby was in good hopes to be delivered from the calamity of a cruel tyranny; but in
a small time they found, that they had only changed
their old and wornout master for another young and
vigorous; so much cruelty and savageness did his son
Marius show in murdering the noblest and most approved citizens. At first, being esteemed resolute
and daring against his enemies, he was named the son
of Mars, but afterwards, his actions betraying his
contrary disposition, he was called the son of Venus.
At last, besieged by Sylla in Præneste, where he endeavored in many ways, but in vain, to save his life,
when on the capture of the city there was no hope of
escape, he killed himself with his own hand.

LYSANDER[1]

TRANSLATED BY THE HONORABLE CHARLES BOYLE OF CHRIST'S CHURCH, (THE ONCE FAMOUS EDITOR OF THE EPISTLES OF PHALARIS, AND UNEQUAL OPPONENT OF BENTLEY.)

The treasure-chamber of the Acanthians at Delphi has this inscription: "The spoils which Brasidas and the Acanthians took from the Athenians." And, accordingly, many take the marble statue, which stands within the building by the gates, to be Brasidas's; but, indeed, it is Lysander's, representing him [2] with his hair at full length, after the old fashion, and with an ample beard. Neither is it true, as some give out, that because the Argives, after their great defeat, shaved themselves for sorrow, that the Spartans contrarywise triumphing in their achievements, suffered their hair to grow; neither did the Spartans come to be ambitious of wearing long hair, because the Bac-

---

[1] Lysander, a Spartan of servile origin, became a distinguished general and by far the most powerful man in Greece about 400 B. C. He displayed unusual pride and haughtiness. Died in battle, 395 B. C.—Dr. William Smith.

[2] In the description of the statue, the phrase, *but indeed it is Lysander's, representing him,* is in the original a good deal more precise; *but indeed it is an iconic figure of Lysander.* Iconic (from the Greek *icon* or *eikon*, the word that is used in the title *Ikon basilike,* and forms part of the compound *iconoclast,* and means an image or likeness) was a technical term applied in Latin, as well as Greek, to real portraitures from the life as distinguished from ideal representations.

chiadæ, who fled from Corinth to Lacedæmon, looked mean and unsightly, having their heads all close cut. But this, also, is indeed one of the ordinances of Lycurgus, who, as it is reported, was used to say, that long hair made good-looking men more beautiful, and ill-looking men more terrible.

Lysander's father is said to have been Aristoclitus, who was not indeed of the royal family, but yet of the stock of the Heraclidæ. He was brought up in poverty, and showed himself obedient and conformable, as ever any one did, to the customs of his country; of a manly spirit, also, and superior to all pleasures, excepting only that which their good actions bring to those who are honored and successful; and it is accounted no base thing in Sparta for their young men to be overcome with this kind of pleasure. For they are desirous, from the very first, to have their youth susceptible to good and bad repute, to feel pain at disgrace, and exultation at being commended; and any one who is insensible and unaffected in these respects is thought poor spirited and of no capacity for virtue. Ambition and the passion for distinction were thus implanted in his character by his Laconian education, nor, if they continued there, must we blame his natural disposition much for this. But he was submissive to great men, beyond what seems agreeable to the Spartan temper, and could easily bear the haughtiness of those who were in power, when it was any way for his advantage, which some are of opinion is no small part of political discretion. Aristotle,[3] who says all great characters are

---

[3] *Aristotle* has a long chapter in his Problemata (*XXX.*, 1) on this subject. *Why is it*, he asks, *that all remarkable men that have ever lived, in philosophy, politics, poetry, or the arts, have been atrabilious* (melan-cholic)? *some so much so as to be subject*

more or less atrabilious, as Socrates and Plato and Hercules were, writes, that Lysander, not indeed early in life, but when he was old, became thus affected. What is singular in his character is that he endured poverty very well, and that he was not at all enslaved or corrupted by wealth, and yet he filled his country with riches and the love of them, and took away from them the glory of not admiring money; importing amongst them an abundance of gold and silver after the Athenian war, though keeping not one drachma for himself. When Dionysius, the tyrant, sent his daughters some costly gowns of Sicilian manufacture, he would not receive them, saying he was afraid they would make them look more unhandsome. But a while after, being sent ambassador from the same city to the same tyrant, when he had sent him a couple of robes, and bade him choose which of them he would, and carry to his daughter: "She," said he, "will be able to choose best for herself," and taking both of them, went his way.

The Peloponnesian war having now been carried on a long time, and it being expected, after the disaster of the Athenians in Sicily, that they would at once lose the mastery of the sea, and erelong be routed everywhere, Alcibiades, returning from banishment, and taking the command, produced a great

---

to maladies occasioned by black bile, as we are told Hercules was, from whom epileptic fits have received a name, and who also suffered before his death on Œta from an eruption of boils on his skin, a thing often caused by black bile. Lysander, the Lacedæmonian, before his death, suffered from them. Ajax and Bellerophon among the heroes are other instances. In later times, Empedocles, Plato, Socrates, and many other famous men. So, too, the great majority of the Poets. He proceeds to compare the vaporous effects of this temperament to those of wine, which he says is so *creative of character and moral dispositions.*

change, and made the Athenians again a match for their opponents by sea; and the Lacedæmonians, in great alarm at this, and calling up fresh courage and zeal for the conflict, feeling the want of an able commander and of a powerful armament, sent out Lysander to be admiral of the seas. Being at Ephesus, and finding the city well affected towards him, and favorable to the Lacedæmonian party, but in ill condition, and in danger to become barbarized by adopting the manners of the Persians, who were much mingled among them, the country of Lydia bordering upon them, and the king's generals being quartered there a long time, he pitched his camp there, and commanded the merchant ships all about to put in thither, and proceeded to build ships of war there; and thus restored their ports by the traffic he created, and their market by the employment he gave, and filled their private houses and their workshops with wealth, so that from that time, the city began, first of all, by Lysander's means, to have some hopes of growing to that stateliness and grandeur which now it is at.

Understanding that Cyrus, the king's son, was come to Sardis, he went up to talk with him, and to accuse Tisaphernes, who, receiving a command to help the Lacedæmonians, and to drive the Athenians from the sea, was thought, on account of Alcibiades, to have become remiss and unwilling, and by paying the seamen slenderly to be ruining the fleet. Now Cyrus was willing that Tisaphernes might be found in blame, and be ill reported of, as being, indeed, a dishonest man, and privately at feud with himself. By these means, and by their daily intercouse together, Lysander, especially by the submissiveness of his conversation, won the affections of the young prince, and greatly roused him to carry on the war;

LYSANDER 117

and when he would depart, Cyrus gave him a banquet, and desired him not to refuse his good-will, but to speak and ask whatever he had a mind to, and that he should not be refused any thing whatsoever: "Since you are so very kind," replied Lysander, "I earnestly request you to add one penny to the seamen's pay, that instead of three pence, they may now receive four pence."[4] Cyrus, delighted with his public spirit, gave him ten thousand darics, out of which he added the penny to the seamen's pay, and by the renown of this in a short time emptied the ships of the enemies, as many would come over to that side which gave the most pay, and those who remained, being disheartened and mutinous, daily created trouble to the captains. Yet for all Lysander had so distracted and weakened his enemies, he was afraid to engage by sea, Alcibiades being an energetic commander, and having the superior number of ships, and having been hitherto, in all battles, unconquered both by sea and land.

But afterwards, when Alcibiades sailed from Samos to Phocæa, leaving Antiochus, the pilot, in command of all his forces, this Antiochus, to insult Lysander, sailed with two galleys into the port of the Ephesians, and with mocking and laughter proudly rowed along before the place where the ships lay drawn up. Lysander, in indignation, launched at first a few ships only and pursued him, but as soon as he saw the Athenians come to his help, he added some other ships, and, at last, they fell to a set battle together; and Lysander won the victory, and taking fifteen of their ships, erected a trophy. For this,

[4] The obolus, six to the drachma, may not unfairly be called the Greek penny, though in actual value worth three half-pence; exactly like the Swiss batz.

the people in the city being angry, put Alcibiades out of command, and finding himself despised by the soldiers in Samos, and ill spoken of, he sailed from the army into the Chersonese. And this battle, although not important in itself, was made remarkable by its consequences to Alcibiades.

Lysander, meanwhile, inviting to Ephesus such persons in the various cities as he saw to be bolder and haughtier-spirited than the rest, proceeded to lay the foundations of that government by bodies of ten, and those revolutions which afterwards came to pass, stirring up and urging them to unite in clubs; and apply themselves to public affairs, since as soon as ever the Athenians should be put down, the popular governments, he said, should be suppressed, and they should become supreme in the several countries. And he made them believe these things by present deeds, promoting those who were his friends already to great employments, honors, and offices, and, to gratify their covetousness, making himself a partner in injustice and wickedness. So much so, that all flocked to him, and courted and desired him, hoping, if he remained in power, that the highest wishes they could form would all be gratified. And therefore, from the very beginning, they could not look pleasantly upon Callicratidas, when he came to succeed Lysander as admiral; nor, afterwards, when he had given them experience that he was a most noble and just person, were they pleased with the manner of his government, and its straightforward, Dorian, honest character. They did, indeed, admire his virtue, as they might the beauty of some hero's image; but their wishes were for Lysander's zealous and profitable support of the interests of his friends and partisans, and they shed tears, and were much disheartened when he sailed from them. He himself made

LYSANDER 119

them yet more disaffected to Callicratidas; for what remained of the money which had been given him to pay the navy, he sent back again to Sardis, bidding them, if they would, apply to Callicratidas himself, and see how he was able to maintain the soldiers. And, at the last, sailing away, he declared to him that he delivered up the fleet in possession and command of the sea. But Callicratidas, to expose the emptiness of these high pretensions, said, "In that case, leave Samos on the left hand, and, sailing to Miletus, there deliver up the ships to me; for if we are masters of the sea, we need not fear sailing by our enemies in Samos." To which Lysander answering, that not himself, but he, commanded the ships, sailed to Peloponnesus, leaving Callicratidas in great perplexity. For neither had he brought any money from home with him, nor could he endure to tax the towns or force them, being in hardship enough. Therefore, the only course that was to be taken was to go and beg at the doors of the king's commanders, as Lysander had done; for which he was most unfit of any man, being of a generous and great spirit, and one who thought it more becoming for the Greeks to suffer any damage from one another, than to flatter and wait at the gates of barbarians, who, indeed, had gold enough, but nothing else that was commendable. But being compelled by necessity, he proceeded to Lydia, and went at once to Cyrus's house, and sent in word, that Callicratidas, the admiral, was there to speak with him; one of those who kept the gates replied, "Cyrus, O stranger, is not now at leisure, for he is drinking." To which Callicratidas answered, most innocently, "Very well, I will wait till he has done his draught." This time, therefore, they took him for some clownish fellow, and he withdrew, merely laughed at by the barbarians; but when, after-

wards, he came a second time to the gate, and was
not admitted, he took it hardly and set off for Ephesus, wishing a great many evils to those who first let
themselves be insulted over by these barbarians, and
taught them to be insolent because of their riches;
and added vows to those who were present, that as
soon as ever he came back to Sparta, he would do
all he could to reconcile the Greeks, that they might
be formidable to barbarians, and that they should
cease henceforth to need their aid against one another. But Callicratidas, who entertained purposes
worthy a Lacedæmonian, and showed himself worthy
to compete with the very best of Greece, for his justice, his greatness of mind and courage, not long
after, having been beaten in a sea-fight at Arginusæ,
died.

And now affairs going backwards, the associates
in the war sent an embassy to Sparta, requiring Lysander to be their admiral, professing themselves
ready to undertake the business much more zealously,
if he was commander; and Cyrus, also, sent to request
the same thing. But because they had a law which
would not suffer any one to be admiral twice, and
wished, nevertheless, to gratify their allies, they gave
the title of admiral to one Aracus, and sent Lysander
nominally as vice-admiral, but, indeed, with full powers. So he came out, long wished for by the greatest
part of the chief persons and leaders in the towns,
who hoped to grow to greater power still by his
means, when the popular governments should be
everywhere destroyed.

But to those who loved honest and noble behavior
in their commanders, Lysander, compared with Callicratidas, seemed cunning and subtle, managing most
things in the war by deceit, extolling what was just
when it was profitable, and when it was not, using

that which was convenient, instead of that which was good; and not judging truth to be in nature better than falsehood, but setting a value upon both according to interest. He would laugh at those who thought that Hercules's posterity ought not to use deceit in war: "For where the lion's skin will not reach, you must patch it out with the fox's." Such is the conduct recorded of him in the business about Miletus; for when his friends and connections, whom he had promised to assist in suppressing popular government and expelling their political opponents, had altered their minds, and were reconciled to their enemies, he pretended openly as if he was pleased with it, and was desirous to further the reconciliation, but privately he railed at and abused them, and provoked them to set upon the multitude. And as soon as ever he perceived a new attempt to be commencing, he at once came up and entered into the city, and the first of the conspirators he lit upon, he pretended to rebuke, and spoke roughly, as if he would punish them; but the others, meantime, he bade be courageous, and to fear nothing now he was with them. And all this acting and dissembling was with the object that the most considerable men of the popular party might not fly away, but might stay in the city and be killed; which so fell out, for all who believed him were put to death.

There is a saying, also, recorded by Androclides, which makes him guilty of great indifference to the obligations of an oath. His recommendation, according to this account, was to "cheat boys with dice, and men with oaths," an imitation of Polycrates of Samos, not very honorable to a lawful commander, to take example, namely, from a tyrant; nor in character with Laconian usages, to treat gods as ill as enemies, or, indeed, even more injuriously; since he who overreaches by an oath admits that he fears his enemy, while he despises his God.

    Cyrus now sent for Lysander to Sardis, and gave him some money, and promised him some more, youthfully protesting in favor to him, that if his father gave him nothing, he would supply him of his own; and if he himself should be destitute of all, he would cut up, he said, to make money, the very throne upon which he sat to do justice, it being made of gold and silver; and, at last, on going up into Media to his father, he ordered that he should receive the tribute of the towns, and committed his government to him, and so taking his leave, and desiring him not to fight by sea before he returned, for he would come back with a great many ships out of Phœnicia and Cilicia, departed to visit the king.

    Lysander's ships were too few for him to venture to fight, and yet too many to allow of his remaining idle; he set out, therefore, and reduced some of the islands, and wasted Ægina and Salamis; and from thence landing in Attica, and saluting Agis, who came from Decelea to meet him, he made a display to the land-forces of the strength of the fleet, as though he could sail where he pleased, and were absolute master by sea. But hearing the Athenians pursued him, he fled another way through the islands into Asia. And finding the Hellespont without any defence he attacked Lampsacus with his ships by sea; while Thorax, acting in concert with him with the land army, made an assault on the walls; and so, having taken the city by storm, he gave it up to his soldiers to plunder. The fleet of the Athenians, a hundred and eighty ships, had just arrived at Elæus in the Chersonese; and hearing the news, that Lampsacus was destroyed, they presently sailed to Sestos; where, taking in victuals, they advanced to Ægos

Potami, over against their enemies, who were still stationed about Lampsacus. Amongst other Athenian captains who were now in command was Philocles, he who persuaded the people to pass a decree to cut off the right thumb of the captives in the war, that they should not be able to hold the spear, though they might the oar.

Then they all rested themselves, hoping they should have battle the next morning. But Lysander had other things in his head; he commanded the mariners and pilots to go on board at dawn, as if there should be a battle as soon as it was day, and to sit there in order, and without any noise, expecting what should be commanded, and in like manner that the land army should remain quietly in their ranks by the sea. But the sun rising, and the Athenians sailing up with their whole fleet in line, and challenging them to battle, he, though he had had his ships all drawn up and manned before daybreak, nevertheless did not stir. He merely sent some small boats to those who lay foremost, and bade them keep still and stay in their order; not to be disturbed, and none of them to sail out and offer battle. So about evening, the Athenians sailing back, he would not let the seamen go out of the ships before two or three, which he had sent to espy, were returned, after seeing the enemies disembark. And thus they did the next day, and the third, and so to the fourth. So that the Athenians grew extremely confident, and disdained their enemies, as if they had been afraid and daunted. At this time, Alcibiades, who was in his castle in the Chersonese, came on horseback to the Athenian army, and found fault with their captains, first of all that they had pitched their camp neither well nor safely, on an exposed and open beach, a very bad landing for the ships, and, secondly, that where they were, they had to fetch all they wanted from Sestos, some considerable way off; whereas if they sailed round a little way to the town and harbor of Sestos, they would be at a safer distance from an enemy, who lay watching their movements, at the command of a single general, terror of whom made every order rapidly executed. This advice, however, they would not listen to; and Tydeus answered disdainfully, that not he, but others, were in office now. So Alcibiades, who even suspected there must be treachery, departed.

But on the fifth day, the Athenians having sailed towards them, and gone back again as they were used to do, very proudly and full of contempt, Lysander sending some ships, as usual, to look out, commanded the masters of them that when they saw the Athenians go to land, they should row back again with all their speed, and that when they were about halfway across, they should lift up a brazen shield from the foredeck, as the sign of battle. And he himself sailing round, encouraged the pilots and masters of the ships, and exhorted them to keep all their men to their places, seamen and soldiers alike, and as soon as ever the sign should be given, to row up boldly to their enemies. Accordingly when the shield had been lifted up from the ships, and the trumpet from the admiral's vessel had sounded for battle, the ships rowed up, and the foot-soldiers strove to get along by the shore to the promontory. The distance there between the two continents is fifteen furlongs, which, by the zeal and eagerness of the rowers, was quickly traversed. Conon, one of the Athenian commanders, was the first who saw from the land the fleet advancing, and shouted out to embark, and in the greatest distress bade some and entreated others, and some he forced to man the ships. But all his diligence signified nothing, because the men were scattered about; for as soon as they came out of the ships, expecting no such matter, some went to market, others walked about the country, or went to sleep in their tents, or got their dinners ready, being, through their commanders' want of skill, as far as possible from any thought of what was to happen; and the enemy now coming up with shouts and noise, Conon, with eight ships, sailed out, and making his escape, passed from thence to Cyprus, to Evagoras. The Peloponnesians falling upon the rest, some they took quite empty, and some they destroyed while they were filling; the men, meantime, coming unarmed and scattered to help, died at their ships, or, flying by land, were slain, their enemies disembarking and pursuing them. Lysander took three thousand prisoners, with the generals, and the whole fleet, excepting the sacred ship Paralus, and those which fled with Conon. So taking their ships in tow, and having plundered their tents, with pipe and songs of victory, he sailed back to Lampsacus, having accomplished a great work with small pains, and having finished in one hour, a war which had been protracted in its continuance, and diversified in its incidents and its fortunes to a degree exceeding belief, compared with all before it. After altering its shape and character a thousand times, and after having been the destruction of more commanders than all the previous wars of Greece put together, it was now put an end to by the good counsel and ready conduct of one man.

Some, therefore, looked upon the result as a divine intervention, and there were certain who affirmed that the stars of Castor and Pollux were seen on each side of Lysander's ship, when he first set sail from the haven toward his enemies, shining about the helm; and some say the stone which fell down was a sign of this slaughter. For a stone of a great size did fall, according to the common belief, from heaven, at Ægos Potami, which is shown to this day, and had in great esteem by the Chersonites. And it is said that Anaxagoras foretold, that the occurrence of a slip or shake among the bodies fixed in the heavens, dislodging any one of them, would be followed by the fall of the whole of them. For no one of the stars is now in the same place in which it was at first; for they, being, according to him, like stones and heavy, shine by the refraction of the upper air round about them, and are carried along forcibly by the violence of the circular motion by which they were originally withheld from falling, when cold and heavy bodies were first separated from the general universe. But there is a more probable opinion than this maintained by some, who say that falling stars are no effluxes, nor discharges of ethereal fire, extinguished almost at the instant of its igniting by the lower air; neither are they the sudden combustion and blazing up of a quantity of the lower air let loose in great abundance into the upper region; but the heavenly bodies, by a relaxation of the force of their circular movement, are carried by an irregular course, not in general into the inhabited part of the earth, but for the most part into the wide sea; which is the cause of their not being observed. Daimachus, in his treatise on Religion, supports the view of Anaxagoras. He says, that before this stone fell, for seventy-five days continually, there was seen in the heavens a vast fiery body, as if it had been a flaming cloud, not resting, but carried about with several intricate and broken movements, so that the flaming pieces, which were broken off by this commotion and running about, were carried in all directions, shining as falling stars do. But when it afterwards came

LYSANDER

down to the ground in this district, and the people of the place recovering from their fear and astonishment came together; there was no fire to be seen, neither any sign of it; there was only a stone lying, big indeed, but which bore no proportion, to speak of, to that fiery compass. It is manifest that Daimachus needs to have indulgent hearers; but if what he says be true, he altogether proves those to be wrong who say that a rock broken off from the top of some mountain, by winds and tempests, and caught and whirled about like a top, as soon as this impetus began to slacken and cease, was precipitated and fell to the ground. Unless, indeed, we choose to say that the phenomenon which was observed for so many days was really fire, and that the change in the atmosphere ensuing on its extinction was attended with violent winds and agitations, which might be the cause of this stone being carried off. The exacter treatment of this subject belongs, however, to a different kind of writing.

Lysander, after the three thousand Athenians whom he had taken prisoners were condemned by the commissioners to die, called Philocles the general, and asked him what punishment he considered himself to deserve, for having advised the citizens as he had done, against the Greeks; but he, being nothing cast down at his calamity, bade him not accuse him of matters of which nobody was a judge, but to do to him, now he was a conqueror, as he would have suffered, had he been overcome. Then washing himself, and putting on a fine cloak, he led the citizens the way to the slaughter, as Theophrastus writes in his history.[5] After this Lysander, sailing about to the various cities, bade all the Athenians he met go

[5] *As Theophratus writes in his history* should be rather. *as Theophratus the historian* or *historical inquirer writes.*

into Athens, declaring that he would spare none, but kill every man whom he found out of the city, intending thus to cause immediate famine and scarcity there, that they might not make the siege laborious to him, having provisions sufficient to endure it. And suppressing the popular governments and all other constitutions, he left one Lacedæmonian chief officer in every city, with ten rulers to act with him, selected out of the societies which he had previously formed in the different towns. And doing thus as well in the cities of his enemies, as of his associates, he sailed leisurely on, establishing, in a manner, for himself supremacy over the whole of Greece. Neither did he make choice of rulers by birth or by wealth, but bestowed the offices on his own friends and partisans, doing every thing to please them, and putting absolute power of reward and punishment into their hands. And thus, personally appearing on many occasions of bloodshed and massacre, and aiding his friends to expel their opponents, he did not give the Greeks a favorable specimen of the Lacedæmonian government; and the expression of Theopompus, the comic poet, seemed but poor, when he compared the Lacedæmonians to tavern women, because when the Greeks had first tasted the sweet wine of liberty, they then poured vinegar into the cup; for from the very first it had a rough and bitter taste, all government by the people being suppressed by Lysander, and the boldest and least scrupulous of the oligarchical party selected to rule the cities.

Having spent some little time about these things, and sent some before to Lacedæmon to tell them he was arriving with two hundred ships, he united his forces in Attica with those of the two kings Agis and Pausanias, hoping to take the city without delay. But when the Athenians defended themselves, he with his fleet passed again to Asia, and in like manner destroyed the forms of government in all the other cities, and placed them under the rule of ten chief persons, many in every one being killed, and many driven into exile; and in Samos, he expelled the whole people, and gave their cities to the exiles whom he brought back. And the Athenians still possessing Sestos, he took it from them, and suffered not the Sestians themselves to dwell in it, but gave the city and country to be divided out among the pilots and masters of the ships under him; which was his first act that was disallowed by the Lacedæmonians, who brought the Sestians back again into their country. All Greece, however, rejoiced to see the Æginetans, by Lysander's aid, now again, after a long time, receiving back their cities, and the Melians and Scionæans restored, while the Athenians were driven out, and delivered up the cities.

But when he now understood they were in a bad case in the city because of the famine, he sailed to Piræus, and reduced the city, which was compelled to surrender on what conditions he demanded. One hears it said by Lacedæmonians that Lysander wrote to the Ephors thus: "Athens is taken;" and that these magistrates wrote back to Lysander, "Taken is enough." But this saying was invented for its neatness' sake; for the true decree of the magistrates was on this manner: "The government of the Lacedæmonians has made these orders; pull down the Piræus and the long walls; quit all the towns, and keep to your own land; if you do these things, you shall have peace, if you wish it, restoring also your exiles. As concerning the number of the ships, whatsoever there be judged necessary to appoint, that do." This scroll of conditions the Athenians accepted. Theramenes, son of Hagnon, supporting it.

At which time, too, they say that when Cleomences, one of the young orators, asked him how he durst act and speak contrary to Themistocles, delivering up the walls to the Lacedæmonians, which he had built against the will of the Lacedæmonians, he said, "O young men, I do nothing contrary to Themistocles; for he raised these walls for the safety of the citizens, and we pull them down for their safety; and if walls make a city happy, then Sparta must be the most wretched of all, as it has none."

Lysander, as soon as he had taken all the ships except twelve, and the walls of the Athenians, on the sixteenth day of the month Munychion, the same on which they had overcome the barbarians at Salamis, then proceeded to take measures for altering the government. But the Athenians taking that very unwillingly, and resisting, he sent to the people and informed them, that he found that the city had broken the terms, for the walls were standing when the days were past within which they should have been pulled down. He should, therefore, consider their case anew, they having broken their first articles. And some state, in fact, the proposal was made in the congress of the allies, that the Athenians should all be sold as slaves; on which occasion, Erianthus, the Theban, gave his vote to pull down the city, and turn the country into sheep-pasture; yet afterwards, when there was a meeting of the captains together, a man of Phocis, singing the first chorus in Euripides's Electra,[6] which begins,

> Electra, Agamemnon's child, I come
> Unto thy desert home,

they were all melted with compassion, and it seemed to be a cruel deed to destroy and pull down a city which had been so famous, and produced such men.

[6] Begins at the 167th line.

Accordingly Lysander, the Athenians yielding up every thing, sent for a number of flute-women out of the city and collected together all that were in the camp, and pulled down the walls, and burnt the ships to the sound of the flute, the allies being crowned with garlands, and making merry together, as counting that day the beginning of their liberty. He proceeded also at once to alter the government, placing thirty rulers in the city, and ten in the Piræus; he put, also, a garrison into the Acropolis, and made Callibius, a Spartan, the governor of it; who afterwards taking up his staff to strike Autolycus, the athlete, about whom Xenophon wrote his "Banquet," on his tripping up his heels and throwing him to the ground, Lysander was not vexed at it, but chid Callibius, telling him he did not know how to govern freemen. The thirty rulers, however, to gain Callibius's favor, a little after killed Autolycus.

Lysander, after this, sails out to Thrace, and what remained of the public money, and the gifts and crowns which he had himself received, numbers of people, as might be expected, being anxious to make presents to a man of such great power, who was, in a manner, the lord of Greece, he sends to Lacedæmon by Gylippus, who had commanded formerly in Sicily. But he, it is reported, unsewed the sacks at the bottom, took a considerable amount of silver out of every one of them, and sewed them up again, not knowing there was a writing in every one stating how much there was. And coming into Sparta, what he had thus stolen away he hid under the tiles of his house, and delivered up the sacks to the magistrates, and showed the seals were upon them. But afterwards, on their opening the sacks and counting it, the quantity of the silver differed from what the writing expressed; and the matter causing some perplexity to the magistrates, Gylippus's servant tells them in a riddle, that under the tiles lay many owls; for, as it seems, the greatest part of the money then current, bore the Athenian stamp of the owl. Gylippus having committed so foul and base a deed, after such great and distinguished exploits before, removed himself from Lacedæmon.

But the wisest of the Spartans, very much on account of this occurrence, dreading the influence of money, as being what had corrupted the greatest citizens, exclaimed against Lysander's conduct, and declared to the Ephors, that all the silver and gold should be sent away, as mere "alien mischiefs." These consulted about it; and Theopompus says, it was Sciraphidas, but Ephorus, that it was Phlogidas, who declared they ought not to receive any gold or silver into the city; but to use their own country coin which was iron, and was first of all dipped in vinegar when it was red hot, that it might not be worked up anew, but because of the dipping might be hard and unpliable. It was also, of course, very heavy and troublesome to carry, and a great deal of it in quantity and weight was but a little in value. And perhaps all the old money was so, coin consisting of iron, or in some countries, copper skewers, whence it comes that we still find a great number of small pieces of money retain the name of *obolus*,[7] and the drachma is six of these, because so much may be grasped in one's hand.

---

[7] *Obelus*, a small spit or skewer, is probably the same word with *obolus*, the Greek penny, the sixth part of a drachma: *drachma*, a handful, comes from *drassomai*, to grasp in the hand; thus in Homer, *dragma*, of the stalks of corn in the reaper's hands. "As when reapers, facing each other, cut a swathe in a rich man's field, of wheat or of barley, and the *handfuls* fall thickly, so stood the Trojans and Achæans, fighting:" and again of the gleaners, in the shield of Achilles.

But Lysander's friends being against it, and endeavoring to keep the money in the city, it was resolved to bring in this sort of money to be used publicly, enacting, at the same time, that if any one was found in possession of any privately, he should be put to death, as if Lycurgus had feared the coin, and not the covetousness resulting from it, which they did not repress by letting no private man keep any, so much as they encouraged it, by allowing the state to possess it; attaching thereby a sort of dignity to it, over as they encouraged it, by allowing the state to possible, that what they saw was so much esteemed publicly, they should privately despise as unprofitable; and that every one should think that thing could be nothing worth for his own personal use, which was so extremely valued and desired for the use of the state. And moral habits, induced by public practices, are far quicker in making their way into men's private lives, than the failings and faults of individuals are in infecting the city at large. For it is probable that the parts will be rather corrupted by the whole if that grows bad; while the vices which flow from a part into the whole, find many correctives and remedies from that which remains sound. Terror and the law were now to keep guard over the citizens' houses, to prevent any money entering into them; but their minds could no longer be expected to remain superior to the desire of it, when wealth in general was thus set up to be striven after, as a high and noble object. On this point, however, we have given our censure of the Lacedæmonians in one of our other writings.

Lysander erected out of the spoils brazen statues at Delphi of himself, and of every one of the masters of the ships, as also figures of the golden stars of Castor and Pollux, which vanished before the battle at Leuctra. In the treasury of Brasidas and the Acanthians, there was a trireme made of gold and ivory, of two cubits, which Cyrus sent Lysander in honor of his victory. But Alexandrides of Delphi writes in his history, that there was also a deposit of Lysander's, a talent of silver, and fifty-two minas, besides eleven staters; a statement not consistent with the generally received account of his poverty. And at that time, Lysander, being in fact of greater power than any Greek before, was yet thought to show a pride, and to affect a superiority greater even than his power warranted. He was the first, as Duris says in his history, among the Greeks, to whom the cities reared altars as to a god, and sacrificed; to him were songs of triumph first sung, the beginning of one of which still remains recorded:—

> Great Greece's general from spacious Sparta we
> Will celebrate with songs of victory.

And the Samians decreed that their solemnities of Juno should be called the Lysandria; and out of the poets he had Chœrilus always with him, to extol his achievements in verse; and to Antilochus, who had made some verses in his commendation, being pleased with them, he gave a hat full of silver; and when Antimachus of Colophon, and one Niceratus of Heraclea, competed with each other in a poem on the deeds of Lysander, he gave the garland to Niceratus; at which Antimachus, in vexation, suppressed his poem; but Plato, being then a young man, and admiring Antimachus for his poetry, consoled him for his defeat by telling him that it is the ignorant who are the sufferers by ignorance, as truly as the blind by want of sight. Afterwards, when Aristonus, the musician, who had been a conqueror six times at the Pythian games, told him as a piece of flattery, that if he

LYSANDER

were successful again, he would proclaim himself in the name of Lysander, "that is," he answered, "as his slave?"

This ambitious temper was indeed only burdensome to the highest personages and to his equals, but through having so many people devoted to serve him, an extreme haughtiness and contemptuousness grew up, together with ambition, in his character. He observed no sort of moderation, such as befitted a private man, either in rewarding or in punishing; the recompense of his friends and guests was absolute power over cities, and irresponsible authority, and the only satisfaction of his wrath was the destruction of his enemy; banishment would not suffice. As for example, at a later period, fearing lest the popular leaders of the Milesians should fly, and desiring also to discover those who lay hid, he swore he would do them no harm, and on their believing him and coming forth, he delivered them up to the oligarchical leaders to be slain, being in all no less than eight hundred. And, indeed, the slaughter in general of those of the popular party in the towns exceeded all computation; as he did not kill only for offences against himself, but granted these favors without sparing, and joined in the execution of them, to gratify the many hatreds, and the much cupidity of his friends everywhere round about him. From whence the saying of Eteocles, the Lacedæmonian, came to be famous, that "Greece could not have borne two Lysanders." Theophrastus says, that Archestratus said the same thing concerning Alcibiades. But in his case what had given most offence was a certain licentious and wanton self-will; Lysander's power was feared and hated because of his unmerciful disposition. The Lacedæmonians did not at all concern themselves for any other accusers; but afterwards, when Pharnabazus, having been injured by him, he having pillaged and wasted his country, sent some to Sparta to inform against him, the Ephors taking it very ill, put one of his friends and fellow-captains, Thorax, to death, taking him with some silver privately in his possession; and they sent him a scroll, commanding him to return home. This scroll is made up thus; when the Ephors send an admiral or general on his way, they take two round pieces of wood, both exactly of a length and thickness, and cut even to one another; they keep one themselves, and the other they give to the person they send forth; and these pieces of wood they call Scytales. When, therefore, they have occasion to communicate any secret or important matter, making a scroll of parchment long and narrow like a leathern thong, they roll it about their own staff of wood, leaving no space void between, but covering the surface of the staff with the scroll all over. When they have done this, they write what they please on the scroll, as it is wrapped about the staff; and when they have written, they take off the scroll, and send it to the general without the wood. He, when he has received it, can read nothing of the writing, because the words and letters are not connected, but all broken up; but taking his own staff, he winds the slip of the scroll about it, so that this folding, restoring all the parts into the same order that they were in before, and putting what comes first into connection with what follows, brings the whole consecutive contents to view round the outside. And this scroll is called a *staff,* after the name of the wood, as a thing measured is by the name of the measure.

But Lysander, when the staff came to him to the Hellespont, was troubled, and fearing Pharnabazus's accusations most, made haste to confer with him, hoping to end the difference by a meeting to-

gether. When they met, he desired him to write another letter to the magistrates, stating that he had not been wronged, and had no complaint to prefer. But he was ignorant that Pharnabazus, as it is in the proverb, played Cretan against Cretan;[8] for pretending to do all that was desired, openly he wrote such a letter as Lysander wanted, but kept by him another, written privately; and when they came to put on the seals, changed the tablets, which differed not at all to look upon, and gave him the letter which had been written privately. Lysander, accordingly, coming to Lacedæmon, and going, as the custom is, to the magistrates' office, gave Pharnabazus's letter to the Ephors, being persuaded that the greatest accusation against him was now withdrawn; for Pharnabazus was beloved by the Lacedæmonians, having been the most zealous on their side in the war of all the king's captains. But after the magistrates had read the letter they showed it him, and he understanding now that
> Others besides Ulysses deep can be,
> Not the one wise man of the world is he,[9]

in extreme confusion, left them at the time. But a few days after, meeting the Ephors, he said he must go to the temple of Ammon, and offer the god the sacrifices which he had vowed in war. For some state it as a truth, that when he was besieging the city of Aphytæ in Thrace, Ammon stood by him in his sleep; whereupon raising the siege, supposing the god had commanded it, he bade the Aphytæans sacrifice to Ammon, and resolved to make a journey into

---

[8] Or "cheat against cheat," the mendacity. "The Cretans are Cretans being famous for their always liars."

[9] *Others besides Ulysses deep can be* is thought by some critics to be a fragment of the lost Palamedes of Euripides.

Libya to propitiate the god. But most were of opinion that the god was but the pretence, and that in reality he was afraid of the Ephors, and that impatience of the yoke at home, and dislike of living under authority, made him long for some travel and wandering, like a horse just brought in from open feeding and pasture to the stable, and put again to his ordinary work. For that which Ephorus states to have been the cause of this travelling about, I shall relate by and by.

And having hardly and with difficulty obtained leave of the magistrates to depart, he set sail. But the kings, while he was on his voyage, considering that keeping, as he did, the cities in possession by his own friends and partisans, he was in fact their sovereign and the lord of Greece, took measures for restoring the power to the people, and for throwing his friends out. Disturbances commencing again about these things, and, first of all, the Athenians from Phyle setting upon their thirty rulers and overpowering them, Lysander, coming home in haste, persuaded the Lacedæmonians to support the oligarchies and to put down the popular governments, and to the thirty in Athens, first of all, they sent a hundred talents for the war, and Lysander himself, as general, to assist them. But the kings envying him, and fearing lest he should take Athens again, resolved that one of themselves should take the command. Accordingly Pausanias went, and in words, indeed, professed as if he had been for the tyrants against the people, but in reality exerted himself for peace, that Lysander might not by the means of his friends become lord of Athens again. This he brought easily to pass; for, reconciling the Athenians, and quieting the tumults, he defeated the ambitious hopes of Lysander, though shortly after, on the Athenians rebelling again, he was censured for having thus taken, as it were, the bit out of the mouth of the people, which, being freed from the oligarchy, would now break out against into affronts and insolence; and Lysander regained the reputation of a person who employed his command not in gratification of others, nor for applause, but strictly for the good of Sparta.

His speech, also, was bold and daunting to such as opposed him. The Argives, for example, contended about the bounds of their land, and thought they brought juster pleas than the Lacedæmonians; holding out his sword, "He," said Lysander, "that is master of this, brings the best argument about the bounds of territory." A man of Megara, at some conference, taking freedom with him, "This language, my friend," said he, "should come from a city."[10] To the Bœotians, who were acting a doubtful part, he put the question, whether he should pass through their country with spears upright, or levelled. After the revolt of the Corinthians, when, on coming to their walls, he perceived the Lacedæmonians hesitating to make the assault, and a hare was seen to leap through the ditch: "Are you not ashamed," he said, "to fear an enemy, for whose laziness, the very hares sleep up their walls?"

When king Agis died, leaving a brother Agesilaus, and Leotychides, who was supposed his son, Lysander, being attached to Agesilaus, persuaded him to lay claim to the kingdom, as being a true descendant of Hercules; Leotychides lying under the suspicion of being the son of Alcibiades, who lived priv-

---

[10] Literally, "Your words require a city," ought, that is, to proceed from one who represents some place of political importance. "You speak as if any one cared about Megara's opinion."

ately in familiarity with Timæa, the wife of Agis, at the time he was a fugitive in Sparta. Agis, they say, computing the time, satisfied himself that she could not have conceived by him, and had hitherto always neglected and manifestly disowned Leotychides; but now when he was carried sick to Heræa, being ready to die, what by the importunities of the young man himself, and of his friends, in the presence of many he declared Leotychides to be his; and desiring those who were present to bear witness of this to the Lacedæmonians, died. They accordingly did so testify in favor of Leotychides. And Agesilaus, being otherwise highly reputed of, and strong in the support of Lysander, was, on the other hand, prejudiced by Diopithes, a man famous for his knowledge of oracles, who adduced this prophecy in reference to Agesilaus's lameness:—

> Beware, great Sparta, lest there come of thee,
> Though sound thyself, an halting sovereignty;
> Troubles, both long and unexpected too,
> And storms of deadly warfare shall ensue.

When many, therefore, yielded to the oracle, and inclined to Leotychides, Lysander said that Diopithes did not take the prophecy rightly; for it was not that the god would be offended if any lame person ruled over the Lacedæmonians, but that the kingdom would be a lame one, if bastards and false-born should govern with the posterity of Hercules. By this argument, and by his great influence among them, he prevailed, and Agesilaus was made king.

Immediately, therefore, Lysander spurred him on to make an expedition into Asia, putting him in hopes that he might destroy the Persians, and attain the height of greatness. And he wrote to his friends in Asia, bidding them request to have Agesilaus appointed to command them in the war against the barbarians; which they were persuaded to, and sent ambassadors to Lacedæmon to entreat it. And this would seem to be a second favor done Agesilaus by Lysander, not inferior to his first in obtaining him the kingdom. But with ambitious natures, otherwise not ill qualified for command, the feeling of jealousy of those near them in reputation continually stands in the way of the performance of noble actions; they make those their rivals in virtue, whom they ought to use as their helpers to it. Agesilaus took Lysander, among the thirty counsellors that accompanied him, with intentions of using him as his especial friend; but when they were come into Asia, the inhabitants there, to whom he was but little known, addressed themselves to him but little and seldom; whereas Lysander, because of their frequent previous intercourse, was visited and attended by large numbers, by his friends out of observance, and by others out of fear; and just as in tragedies it not uncommonly is the case with the actors, the person who represents a messenger or servant is much taken notice of, and plays the chief part, while he who wears the crown and sceptre is hardly heard to speak, even so was it about the counsellor, he had all the real honors of the government, and to the king was left the empty name of power. This disproportionate ambition ought very likely to have been in some way softened down, and Lysander should have been reduced to his proper second place, but wholly to cast off and to insult and affront for glory's sake, one who was his benefactor and friend, was not worthy Agesilaus to allow in himself. For, first of all, he gave him no opportunity for any action, and never set him in any place of command; then, for whomsoever he perceived him exerting his interest, these persons he always sent away with a refusal, and with less attention than any ordinary suitors, thus silently undoing and weakening his influence.

Lysander, miscarrying in every thing, and perceiving that his diligence for his friends was but a hinderance to them, forbore to help them, entreating them that they would not address themselves to, nor observe him, but that they would speak to the king, and to those who could be of more service to friends than at present he could; most, on hearing this, forbore to trouble him about their concerns; but continued their observances to him, waiting upon him in the walks and places of exercise; at which Agesilaus was more annoyed than ever, envying him the honor; and, finally, when he gave many of the officers places of command and the governments of cities, he appointed Lysander carver at his table, adding, by way of insult to the Ionians, "Let them go now, and pay their court to my carver." Upon this, Lysander thought fit to come and speak with him; and a brief laconic dialogue passed between them as follows: "Truly, you know very well, O Agesilaus, how to depress your friends;" "Those friends," replied he, "who would be greater than myself; but those who increase my power, it is just should share in it." "Possibly, O Agesilaus," answered Lysander, "in all this there may be more said on your part than done on mine, but I request you, for the sake of observers from without, to place me in any command under you where you may judge I shall be the least offensive, and most useful."

Upon this he was sent ambassador to the Hellespont; and though angry with Agesilaus, yet did not neglect to perform his duty, and having induced Spithridates the Persian, being offended with Pharnabazus, a gallant man, and in command of some forces, to revolt, he brought him to Agesilaus. He was not, however, employed in any other service, but having completed his time, returned to Sparta, without honor, angry with Agesilaus, and hating more than ever the whole Spartan government, and resolved to delay no longer, but while there was yet time, to put into execution the plans which he appears some time before to have concerted for a revolution and change in the constitution. These were as follows. The Heraclidæ who joined with the Dorians, and came into Peloponnesus, became a numerous and glorious race in Sparta, but not every family belonging to it had the right of succession in the kingdom, but the kings were chosen out of two only, called the Eurypontidæ and the Agiadæ; the rest had no privilege in the government by their nobility of birth, and the honors which followed from merit lay open to all who could obtain them. Lysander, who was born of one of these families, when he had risen into great renown for his exploits, and had gained great friends and power, was vexed to see the city which had increased to what it was by him, ruled by others not at all better descended than himself, and formed a design to remove the government from the two families, and to give it in common to all the Heraclidæ; or, as same say, not to the Heraclidæ only, but to all the Spartans; that the reward might not belong to the posterity of Hercules, but to those who were like Hercules, judging by that personal merit which raised even him to the honor of the Godhead; and he hoped that when the kingdom was thus to be competed for, no Spartan would be chosen before himself.

Accordingly he first attempted and prepared to persuade the citizens privately, and studied an oration composed to this purpose by Cleon, the Halicarnassian. Afterwards perceiving so unexpected and great an innovation required bolder means of support, he proceeded as it might be on the stage, to avail himself of machinery,[11] and to try the effects of divine agency upon his countrymen. He collected and arranged for his purpose, answers and oracles from Apollo, not expecting to get any benefit from Cleon's rhetoric, unless he should first alarm and overpower the minds of his fellow-citizens by religious and superstitious terrors, before bringing them to the consideration of his arguments. Ephorus relates, after he had endeavored to corrupt the oracle of Apollo, and had again failed to persuade the priestesses of Dodona by means of Pherecles, that he went to Ammon, and discoursed with the guardians of the oracle there, proffering them a great deal of gold, and that they, taking this ill, sent some to Sparta to accuse Lysander; and on his acquittal the Libyans, going away, said, "You will find us, O Spartans, better judges when you come to dwell with us in Libya," there being a certain ancient oracle, that the Lacedæmonians should dwell in Libya. But as the whole intrigue and the course of the contrivance was no ordinary one, nor lightly undertaken, but depended as it went on, like some mathematical proposition, on a variety of important admissions, and proceeded through a series of intricate and difficult steps to its conclusion, we will go into it at length, following the account of one who was at once an historian and a philosopher.

There was a woman in Pontus, who professed to be pregnant by Apollo, which many, as was nat-

[11] Machinery, that is, in the sense of supernatural intervention, derived from the actual machines by which actors personating gods were introduced on, or rather above the stage. Lysander, finding ordinary agencies insufficient, resolves to introduce a *Deus ex machina* for the solution of the difficulty of his position.

ural, disbelieved, and many also gave credit to, and when she had brought forth a man-child, several, not unimportant persons, took an interest in its rearing and bringing up. The name given the boy was Silenus, for some reason or other. Lysander, taking this for the groundwork, frames and devises the rest himself, making use of not a few, nor these insignificant champions of his story, who brought the report of the child's birth into credit without any suspicion. Another report, also, was procured from Delphi and circulated in Sparta, that there were some very old oracles which were kept by the priests in private writings; and they were not to be meddled with, neither was it lawful to read them, till one in after times should come, descended from Apollo, and, on giving some known token to the keepers, should take the books in which the oracles were. Things being thus ordered beforehand, Silenus, it was intended, should come and ask for the oracles, as being the child of Apollo, and those priests who were privy to the design, were to profess to search narrowly into all particulars, and to question him concerning his birth; and, finally, were to be convinced, and, as to Apollo's son, to deliver up to him the writings. Then he, in the presence of many witnesses, should read amongst other prophecies, that which was the object of the whole contrivance, relating to the office of the kings, that it would be better and more desirable to the Spartans to choose their kings out of the best citizens. And now, Silenus being grown up to a youth, and being ready for the action, Lysander miscarried in his drama through the timidity of one of his actors, or assistants, who just as he came to the point lost heart and drew back. Yet nothing was found out while Lysander lived, but only after his death.

He died before Agesilaus came back from Asia,

being involved, or perhaps more truly having himself involved Greece, in the Bœotian war. For it is stated both ways; and the cause of it some make to be himself, others the Thebans, and some both together; the Thebans, on the one hand, being charged with casting away the sacrifices at Aulis, and that being bribed with the king's money brought by Androclides and Amphitheus, they had with the object of entangling the Lacedæmonians in a Grecian war, set upon the Phocians, and wasted their country; it being said, on the other hand, that Lysander was angry that the Thebans had preferred a claim to the tenth part of the spoils of the war, while the rest of the confederates submitted without complaint; and because they expressed indignation about the money which Lysander sent to Sparta, but most especially, because from them the Athenians had obtained the first opportunity of freeing themselves from the thirty tyrants, whom Lysander had made, and to support whom the Lacedæmonians issued a decree that political refugees from Athens might be arrested in whatever country they were found, and that those who impeded their arrest should be excluded from the confederacy. In reply to this the Thebans issued counter decrees of their own, truly in the spirit and temper of the actions of Hercules and Bacchus,[12] that every house and city in Bœotia should be opened to the Athenians who required it, and that he who did not help a fugitive who was seized, should be fined a talent for damages, and if any one should bear arms through Bœotia to Attica against the tyrants, that none of the Thebans should either see or hear of it. Nor did they pass these humane and truly Greek de-

---

[12] Their countrymen, so to say, of old, the Theban Hercules and the Theban Bacchus, Hercules to whom Alcmena gave birth in Thebes, and Bacchus the child of the Theban princess.

crees, without at the same time making their acts conformable to their words. For Thrasybulus and those who with him occupied Phyle, set out upon that enterprise from Thebes, with arms and money, and secresy and a point to start from, provided for them by the Thebans. Such were the causes of complaint Lysander had against Thebes. And being now grown violent in his temper through the atrabilious tendency which increased upon him in his old age, he urged the Ephors and persuaded them to place a garrison in Thebes, and taking the commander's place, he marched forth with a body of troops. Pausanias, also, the king, was sent shortly after with an army. Now Pausanias, going round by Cithæron, was to invade Bœotia; Lysander, meantime, advanced through Phocis to meet him, with a numerous body of soldiers. He took the city of the Orchomenians, who came over to him of their own accord, and plundered Lebadea. He despatched also letters to Pausanias, ordering him to move from Platæa to meet him at Haliartus, and that himself would be at the walls of Haliartus by break of day. These letters were brought to the Thebans, the carrier of them falling into the hands of some Thebans scouts. They, having received aid from Athens, committed their city to the charge of the Athenian troops, and sallying out about the first sleep, succeeded in reaching Haliartus [13] a little before

[13] The localities about Haliartus, the spring of Cissusa, the rivulet Hoplites, and the hill Orchalides or Alopecus (p. 138), are identified by Col. Leake in his Travels in Northern Greece (*Chap. XIII., Vol. II., pages* 206 *to* 211). Haliartus is on a low hill terminating in cliffs on the edge of the lake Copais, and, "though not fifty feet higher than the water," the "rocky point projecting into the marsh is remarkable from every part of the plain." Hoplites is "the rivulet under the western wall," and Cissusa, "the fountain below the cliffs." In Plutarch's time, the town was extinct; one of the few remaining objects when Pau-

Lysander, and part of them entered into the city. He, upon this, first of all resolved, posting his army upon a hill, to stay for Pausanias; then as the day advanced, not being able to rest, he bade his men take up their arms, and encouraging the allies, led them in a column along the road to the walls. But those Thebans who had remained outside, taking the city on the left hand, advanced against the rear of their enemies, by the fountain which is called Cissusa; here they tell the story that the nurses washed the infant Bacchus after his birth; the water of it is of a bright wine color, clear, and most pleasant to drink; and not far off the Cretan storax grows all about, which the Haliartians adduce in token of Rhadamanthus having dwelt there, and they show his sepulchre, calling it Alea. And the monument also of Alcmena is hard by; for there, as they say, she was buried, having married Rhadamanthus after Amphitryon's death. But the Thebans inside the city forming in order of battle with the Haliartians stood still for some time, but on seeing Lysander with a party of those who were foremost approaching, on a sudden opening the gates and falling on, they killed him with the soothsayer at his side, and a few others; for the greater part immediately fled back to the main force. But the Thebans not slackening, but closely pursuing them, the whole body turned to fly towards the hills. There were one thousand of them slain; there died, also, of the Thebans three hundred, who were killed with their enemies, while chasing them into craggy and difficult places. These had been under suspicion of favoring

sanias went there, was a monument of Lysander. *Alea,* the name of the tomb ascribed to Rhadamanthus, should in correctness be *Aleës* or *Aleäs*. There is no reason for supposing Cissusa to be a corruption for Tilphussa or Tilphossa, the spring beside which Tiresias died; this is in a different place.

the Lacedæmonians, and in their eagerness to clear themselves in the eyes of their fellow-citizens, exposed themselves in the pursuit, and so met their death. News of the disaster reached Pausanias as he was on the way from Platæa to Thespiæ, and having set his army in order he came to Haliartus; Thrasybulus, also, came from Thebes, leading the Athenians.

Pausanias proposing to request the bodies of the dead under truce, the elders of the Spartans took it ill, and were angry among themselves, and coming to the king, declared that Lysander should not be taken away upon any conditions; if they fought it out by arms about his body, and conquered, then they might bury him; if they were overcome, it was glorious to die upon the spot with their commander. When the elders had spoken these things, Pausanias saw it would be a difficult business to vanquish the Thebans, who had but just been conquerors; that Lysander's body also lay near the walls, so that it would be hard for them, though they overcame, to take it away without a truce; he therefore sent a herald, obtained a truce, and withdrew his forces, and carrying away the body of Lysander, they buried it in the first friendly soil they reached on crossing the Bœotian frontier, in the country of the Panopæans; where the monument still stands as you go on the road from Delphi to Chæronæ. Now the army quartering there, it is said that a person of Phocis, relating the battle to one who was not in it, said, the enemies fell upon them just after Lysander had passed over the Hoplites; surprised at which a Spartan, a friend of Lysander, asked what Hoplites he meant, for he did not know the name. "It was there," answered the Phocian, "that the enemy killed the first of us; the rivulet by the city is called Hoplites." On hearing which the Spartan shed tears and observed, how impossible it is for any man to avoid his appointed lot; Lysander, it appears, having received an oracle, as follows:—

> Sounding Hoplites see thou bear in mind,
> And the earthborn dragon following behind.

Some, however, say that Hoplites does not run by Haliartus, but is a watercourse near Coronea, falling into the river Philarus, not far from the town in former times called Hoplias, and now Isomantus.

The man of Haliartus who killed Lysander, by name Neochorus, bore on his shield the device of a dragon; and this, it was supposed, the oracle signified. It is said, also, that at the time of the Peloponnesian war, the Thebans received an oracle from the sanctuary of Ismenus,[14] referring at once to the battle at Delium, and to this which thirty years after took place at Haliartus. It ran thus:—

> Hunting the wolf, observe the utmost bound,
> And the hill Orchalides where foxes most are found.

By the words, "the utmost bound," Delium being intended, where Bœotia touches Attica, and by Orchalides, the hill now called Alopecus,[15] which lies in the parts of Haliartus towards Helicon.

But such a death befalling Lysander, the Spartans took it so grievously at the time, that they put the king to a trial for his life, which he not daring to await, fled to Tegea, and there lived out his life in the sanctuary of Minerva. The poverty also of Lysander being discovered by his death, made his merit

---

[14] *The sanctuary of Ismenus*, or the Ismenian sanctuary, is the temple of the Ismenian Apollo.

[15] Alōpĕcus, derived from *alōpex*, a fox. *Hoplites*, it may also be noticed, in explanation of the surprise of Lysander's friend, would be an unusual name for a stream, being the ordinary word for a heavy-armed soldier, a man-at-arms.

more manifest, since from so much wealth and power, from all the homage of the cities, and of the Persian kingdom, he had not in the least degree, so far as money goes, sought any private aggrandizement, as Theopompus in his history relates, whom any one may rather give credit to when he commends, than when he finds fault, as it is more agreeable to him to blame than to praise. But subsequently, Ephorus says, some controversy arising among the allies at Sparta, which made it necessary to consult the writing which Lysander had kept by him, Agesilaus came to his house, and finding the book in which the oration on the Spartan constitution was written at length, to the effect that the kingdom ought to be taken from the Eurypontidæ and Agiadæ, and to be offered in common, and a choice made out of the best citizens, at first he was eager to make it public, and to show his countrymen the real character of Lysander. But Lacratidas, a wise man, and at that time chief of the Ephors, hindered Agesilaus, and said, they ought not to dig up Lysander again, but rather to bury with him a discourse, composed so plausibly and subtilly. Other honors, also, were paid him after his death; and amongst these they imposed a fine upon those who had engaged themselves to marry his daughters, and then when Lysander was found to be poor, after his decease, refused them; because when they thought him rich they had been observant of him, but now his poverty had proved him just and good, they forsook him. For there was, it seems, in Sparta, a punishment for not marrying, for a late, and for a bad marriage; and to the last penalty those were most especially liable, who sought alliances with the rich instead of with the good and with their friends. Such is the account we have found given of Lysander.

SYLLA[1]

TRANSLATED BY WILLIAM DAVIES, FELLOW
OF TRINITY COLLEGE, CAMBRIDGE.

LUCIUS CORNELIUS SYLLA was descended of a patrician or noble family. Of his ancestors, Rufinus, it is said, had been consul, and incurred a disgrace more signal than his distinction. For being found possessed of more than ten pounds of silver plate, contrary to the law, he was for this reason put out of the senate. His posterity continued ever after in obscurity, nor had Sylla himself any opulent parentage. In his younger days he lived in hired lodgings, at a low rate, which in after-times was adduced against him as proof that he had been fortunate above his quality. When he was boasting and magnifying himself for his exploits in Libya, a person of noble station made answer, "And how can you be an honest man, who, since the death of a father who left you nothing, have become so rich?" The time in which he lived was no longer an age of pure and upright manners, but had

---

[1] Lucius Sulla (there is no authority for writing the word Sylla, as is done by many modern writers) surnamed Felix the Dictator, was born 138 B. C., and early imbibed that love for literature and art by which he was distinguished throughout life, yet his youth as well as manhood was disgraced by the most sensual vices. Nevertheless no Roman, during the latter days of the republic, with the exception of Julius Cæsar, had a clearer judgment, a keener discrimination of character, or a firmer will. He died in 78 B. C. Plutarch's Life of Sulla is specially recommended.—Dr. William Smith.

already declined, and yielded to the appetite for riches and luxury; yet still, in the general opinion, they who deserted the hereditary poverty of their family, were as much blamed as those who had run out a fair patrimonial estate. And afterwards, when he had seized the power into his hands, and was putting many to death, a freedman suspected of having concealed one of the proscribed, and for that reason sentenced to be thrown down the Tarpeian rock, in a reproachful way recounted, how they had lived long together under the same roof, himself for the upper rooms paying two thousand sesterces, and Sylla for the lower three thousand; so that the difference between their fortunes then was no more than one thousand sesterces, equivalent in Attic coin to two hundred and fifty drachmas. And thus much of his early fortune.

His general personal appearance may be known by his statues; only his blue eyes, of themselves extremely keen and glaring, were rendered all the more forbidding and terrible by the complexion of his face, in which white was mixed with rough blotches of fiery red. Hence, it is said, he was surnamed Sylla, and in allusion to it one of the scurrilous jesters at Athens made the verse upon him,

> Sylla is a mulberry sprinkled o'er with meal.

Nor is it out of place to make use of marks of character like these, in the case of one who was by nature so addicted to raillery, that in his youthful obscurer years he would converse freely with players and professed jesters, and join them in all their low pleasures. And when supreme master of all, he was often wont to muster together the most impudent players and stage-followers of the town, and to drink and bandy jests with them without regard to his age or the dignity of his place, and to the prejudice of important affairs that required his attention. When he was once at table, it was not in Sylla's nature to admit of any thing that was serious, and whereas at other times he was a man of business, and austere of countenance, he underwent all of a sudden, at his first entrance upon wine and good-fellowship, a total revolution, and was gentle and tractable with common singers and dancers, and ready to oblige any one that spoke with him. It seems to have been a sort of diseased result of this laxity, that he was so prone to amorous pleasures, and yielded without resistance to any temptations of voluptuousness, from which even in his old age he could not refrain. He had a long attachment for Metrobius,[2] a player. In his first amours it happened, that he made court to a common but rich lady, Nicopolis by name, and, what by the air of his youth, and what by long intimacy, won so far on her affections, that she rather than he was the lover, and at her death she bequeathed him her whole property. He likewise inherited the estate of a step-mother who loved him as her own son. By these means he had pretty well advanced his fortunes.

He was chosen quæstor to Marius in his first consulship, and set sail with him for Libya, to war upon Jugurtha. Here, in general, he gained approbation; and more especially, by closing in dexterously with an accidental occasion, made a friend of Bocchus, king of Numidia. He hospitably entertained the king's ambassadors, on their escape from some Numidian robbers, and after showing them much kindness, sent them on their journey with presents, and an escort to pro-

---

[2] The *long attachment for Metrobius the player* has very likely been brought in here by some copyist from the passage in the closing scene of the life. The text is various and uncertain.

tect them. Bocchus had long hated and dreaded his son-in-law, Jugurtha, who had now been worsted in the field and had fled to him for shelter; and it so happened, he was at this time entertaining a design to betray him. He accordingly invited Sylla to come to him, wishing the seizure and surrender of Jugurtha to be effected rather through him, than directly by himself. Sylla, when he had communicated the business to Marius, and received from him a small detachment, voluntarily put himself into this imminent danger; and confiding in a barbarian, who had been unfaithful to his own relations, to apprehend another man's person, made surrender of his own. Bocchus, having both of them now in his power, was necessitated to betray one or other, and after long debate with himself, at last resolved on his first design, and gave up Jugurtha into the hands of Sylla.

For this Marius triumphed, but the glory of the enterprise, which through people's envy of Marius was ascribed to Sylla, secretly grieved him. And the truth is, Sylla himself was by nature vainglorious, and this being the first time that from a low and private condition he had risen to esteem amongst the citizens and tasted of honor, his appetite for distinction carried him to such a pitch of ostentation, that he had a representation of this action engraved on a signet ring; which he carried about with him, and made use of ever after. The impress was, Bocchus delivering, and Sylla receiving, Jugurtha. This touched Marius to the quick; however, judging Sylla to be beneath his rivalry, he made use of him as lieutenant, in his second consulship, and in his third, as tribune; and many considerable services were effected by his means. When acting as lieutenant he took Copillus, chief of the Tectosages, prisoner, and compelled the Marsians,[3] a great and populous nation, to become friends and confederates of the Romans.

Henceforward, however, Sylla perceiving that Marius bore a jealous eye over him, and would no longer afford him opportunities of action, but rather opposed his advance, attached himself to Catulus, Marius's colleague, a worthy man, but not energetic enough as a general. And under this commander, who intrusted him with the highest and most important commissions, he rose at once to reputation and to power. He subdued by arms most part of the Alpine barbarians; and when there was a scarcity in the armies, he took that care upon himself, and brought in such a store of provisions, as not only to furnish the soldiers of Catulus with abundance, but likewise to supply Marius. This, as he writes himself, wounded Marius to the very heart. So slight and childish were the first occasions and motives of that emnity between them, which, passing afterwards through a long course of civil bloodshed and incurable divisions to find its end in tyranny, and the confusion of the whole State, proved Euripides to have been truly wise and thoroughly acquainted with the causes of disorders in the body politic, when he forewarned all men to beware of Ambition,[4] as of all the higher Powers, the most destructive and pernicious to her votaries.

Sylla, by this time thinking that the reputation of his arms abroad was sufficient to entitle him to a

[3] It is not likely that these were the Marsians of central Italy, the kinsmen and allies of the Samnites. It has been supposed that they were a German tribe.

[4] Euripides's warning against Ambition is in the Phœnissæ (532). Cæsar, just below, is of course not the great Cæsar, but a Cæsar of the previous generation; probably Sextus Cæsar, his uncle.

part in the civil administration, betook himself immediately from the camp to the assembly, and offered himself as a candidate for a prætorship, but failed. The fault of this disappointment he wholly ascribes to the populace, who, knowing his intimacy with king Bocchus, and for that reason expecting, that if he was made ædile before his prætorship, he would then show them magnificent hunting-shows and combats between Libyan wild beasts, chose other prætors, on purpose to force him into the ædileship. The vanity of this pretext is sufficiently disproved by matter-of-fact. For the year following, partly by flatteries to the people, and partly by money, he got himself elected prætor. Accordingly, once while he was in office, on his angrily telling Cæsar that he should make use of his authority against him, Cæsar answered him with a smile, "You do well to call it your own, as you bought it." At the end of his prætorship he was sent over into Cappadocia, under the pretence of reëstablishing Ariobarzanes in his kingdom, but in reality to keep in check the restless movements of Mithridates, who was gradually procuring himself as vast a new acquired power and dominion, as was that of his ancient inheritance. He carried over with him no great forces of his own, but making use of the cheerful aid of the confederates, succeeded, with considerable slaughter of the Cappadocians, and yet greater of the Armenian succors, in expelling Gordius and establishing Ariobarzanes as king.

During his stay on the banks of the Euphrates, there came to him Orobazus, a Parthian, ambassador from king Arsaces, as yet there having been no correspondence between the two nations. And this also we may lay to the account of Sylla's felicity, that he should be the first Roman, to whom the Parthians made address for alliance and friendship. At the time of which reception, the story is, that having ordered three chairs of state to be set, one for Ariobarzanes, one for Orobazus, and a third for himself, he placed himself in the middle, and so gave audience. For this the king of Parthia afterwards put Orobazus to death. Some people commended Sylla for his lofty carriage towards the barbarians; others again accused him of arrogance and unseasonable display. It is reported, that a certain Chaldæan, of Orobazus's retinue, looking Sylla wistfully in the face, and observing carefully the motions of his mind and body, and forming a judgment of his nature, according to the rules of his art, said that it was impossible for him not to become the greatest of men; it was rather a wonder how he could even then abstain from being head of all.

At his return, Censorinus impeached him of extortion, for having exacted a vast sum of money from a well-affected and associate kingdom. However, Censorinus did not appear at the trial, but dropped his accusation. His quarrel, meantime, with Marius began to break out afresh, receiving new material from the ambition of Bocchus, who, to please the people of Rome, and gratify Sylla, set up in the temple of Jupiter Capitolinus images bearing trophies, and a representation in gold of the surrender of Jugurtha to Sylla. When Marius, in great anger, attempted to pull them down, and others aided Sylla, the whole city would have been in tumult and commotion with this dispute, had not the Social War, which had long lain smouldering, blazed forth at last, and for the present put an end to the quarrel.

In the course of this war, which had many great changes of fortune, and which, more than any afflicted the Romans, and, indeed, endangered the very being of the Commonwealth, Marius was not able to signalize his valor in any action, but left behind him a clear proof, that warlike excellence requires a strong and still vigorous body. Sylla, on the other hand, by his many achievements, gained himself, with his fellow-citizens, the name of a great commander, while his friends thought him the greatest of all commanders, and his enemies called him the most fortunate. Nor did this make the same sort of impression on him, as it made on Timotheus the son of Conon, the Athenian; who, when his adversaries ascribed his successes to his good luck, and had a painting made, representing him asleep and Fortune by his side, casting her nets over the cities, was rough and violent in his indignation at those who did it, as if by attributing all to Fortune, they had robbed him of his just honors; and said to the people on one occasion at his return from war, "In this, ye men of Athens, Fortune had no part." A piece of boyish petulance, which the deity, we are told, played back upon Timotheus; who from that time was never able to achieve any thing that was great, but proving altogether unfortunate in his attempts, and falling into discredit with the people, was at last banished the city. Sylla, on the contrary, not only accepted with pleasure the credit of such divine felicities and favors, but joining himself in extolling and glorifying what was done, gave the honor of all to Fortune, whether it were out of boastfulness, or a real feeling of divine agency. He remarks, in his Memoirs, that of all his well-advised actions, none proved so lucky in the execution, as what he had boldly enterprised, not by calculation, but upon the moment. And in the character which he gives of himself, that he was born for fortune rather than war, he seems to give Fortune a higher place than merit, and in short, makes himself entirely the creature of a superior power, accounting even his concord with Metellus, his equal in office, and his connection by marriage, a piece of preternatural felicity. For expecting to have met in him a most troublesome, he found him a most accommodating colleague. Moreover, in the Memoirs which he dedicated to Lucullus, he admonishes him to esteem nothing more trustworthy, than what the divine powers advise him by night. And when he was leaving the city with an army, to fight in the Social War, he relates, that the earth near the Laverna [5] opened, and a quantity of fire came rushing out of it, shooting up with a bright flame into the heavens. The soothsayers upon this foretold, that a person of great qualities, and of a rare and singular aspect, should take the government in hand, and quiet the present troubles of the city. Sylla affirms he was the man, for his golden head of hair made him an extraordinary-looking man, nor had he any shame, after the great actions he had done, in testifying to his own great qualities. And thus much of his opinion as to divine agency.

In general he would seem to have been of a very irregular character, full of inconsistencies with himself; much given to rapine, to prodigality yet more; in promoting or disgracing whom he pleased, alike unaccountable; cringing to those he stood in need of, and domineering over others who stood in need of him, so that it was hard to tell, whether his nature had more in it of pride or of servility. As to his unequal distribution of punishments, as, for example, that

[5] Laverna was the goddess of thieves, and the patroness of dishonesty in general,—"Grant me, sweet Laverna, to be thought just and upright," is the hypocrite's prayer in Horace. The place here mentioned may probably be the neighborhood of some chapel or altar dedicated to her. An altar near the Porta Lavernalis is mentioned.

upon slight grounds he would put to the torture, and again would bear patiently with the greatest wrongs; would readily forgive and be reconciled after the most heinous acts of enmity, and yet would visit small and inconsiderable offences with death, and confiscation of goods; one might judge, that in himself he was really of a violent and revengeful nature, which, however he could qualify, upon reflection, for his interest. In this very Social War, when the soldiers with stones and clubs had killed an officer of prætorian rank, his own lieutenant, Albinus by name, he passed by this flagrant crime without any inquiry, giving it out moreover in a boast, that the soldiers would behave all the better now, to make amends, by some special bravery, for their breach of discipline. He took no notice of the clamors of those that cried for justice, but designing already to supplant Marius, now that he saw the Social War near its end, he made much of his army, in hopes to get himself declared general of the forces against Mithridates.

At his return to Rome, he was chosen Consul with Quintus Pompeius, in the fiftieth year of his age, and made a most distinguished marriage with Cæcilia, daughter of Metellus, the chief priest. The common people made a variety of verses in ridicule of the marriage, and many of the nobility also were disgusted at it, esteeming him, as Livy writes, unworthy of this connection, whom before they thought worthy of a consulship. This was not his only wife, for first, in his younger days, he was married to Ilia, by whom he had a daughter; after her to Ælia; and thirdly to Clœlia, whom he dismissed as barren, but honorably, and with professions of respect, adding, moreover, presents. But the match between him and Metella, falling out a few days after, occasioned suspicions that he had complained of Clœlia without due cause. To Metella he always showed great deference, so much so that the people, when anxious for the recall of the exiles of Marius's party, upon his refusal, entreated the intercession of Metella. And the Athenians, it is thought, had harder measure, at the capture of their town, because they used insulting language to Metella in their jests from the walls during the siege. But of this hereafter.

At present esteeming the consulship but a small matter in comparison of things to come, he was impatiently carried away in thought to the Mithridatic War. Here he was withstood by Marius; who out of mad affectation of glory and thirst for distinction, those never dying passions, though he were now unwieldy in body, and had given up service, on account of his age, during the late campaigns, still coveted after command in a distant war beyond the seas. And whilst Sylla was departed for the camp, to order the rest of his affairs there, he sate brooding at home, and at last hatched that execrable sedition, which wrought Rome more mischief than all her enemies together had done, as was indeed foreshown by the gods. For a flame broke forth of its own accord, from under the staves of the ensigns, and was with difficulty extinguished. Three ravens brought their young into the open road, and ate them, carrying the relics into the nest again. Mice having gnawed the consecrated gold in one of the temples, the keepers caught one of them, a female, in a trap; and she bringing forth five young ones in the very trap, devoured three of them. But what was greatest of all, in a calm and clear sky there was heard the sound of a trumpet, with such a loud and dismal blast, as struck terror and amazement into the hearts of the people. The Etruscan sages affirmed, that this prodigy betokened the mutation of the age, and a general revolution in the world. For according to them there are in all eight ages, differing one from another in the lives and the characters of men, and to each of these God has allotted a certain measure of time, determined by the circuit of the great year. And when one age is run out, at the approach of another, there appears some wonderful sign from earth or heaven, such as makes it manifest at once to those who have made it their business to study such things, that there has succeeded in the world a new race of men, differing in customs and institutes of life, and more or less regarded by the gods, than the preceding. Amongst other great changes that happen, as they say, at the turn of ages, the art of divination, also, at one time rises in esteem, and is more successful in its predictions, clearer and surer tokens being sent from God, and then again, in another generation declines as low, becoming mere guesswork for the most part, and discerning future events by dim and uncertain intimations. This was the mythology of the wisest of the Tuscan sages, who were thought to possess a knowledge beyond other men. Whilst the Senate sat in consultation with the soothsayers, concerning these prodigies, in the temple of Bellona, a sparrow came flying in, before them all, with a grasshopper in its mouth, and letting fall one part of it, flew away with the remainder. The diviners foreboded commotions and dissension between the great landed proprietors and the common city populace; the latter, like the grasshopper, being loud and talkative; while the sparrow might represent the "dwellers in the field."

Marius had taken into alliance Sulpicius, the tribune, a man second to none in any villanies, so that it was less the question what others he surpassed, but rather in what respects he most surpassed himself in wickedness. He was cruel, bold, rapacious, and in all these points utterly shameless and unscrupulous; not hesitating to offer Roman citizenship by public sale to freed slaves and aliens, and to count out the price on public money-tables in the forum. He maintained three thousand swordsmen, and had always about him a company of young men of the equestrian class ready for all occasions, whom he styled his Anti-Senate. Having had a law enacted, that no senator should contract a debt above two thousand drachmas, he himself, after death, was found indebted three millions. This was the man whom Marius let in upon the Commonwealth, and who, confounding all things by force and the sword, made several ordinances of dangerous consequence, and amongst the rest, one giving Marius the conduct of the Mithridatic war. Upon this the consuls proclaimed a public cessation of business, but as they were holding an assembly near the temple of Castor and Pollux, he let loose the rabble upon them, and amongst many others slew the consul Pompeius's young son in the forum, Pompeius himself hardly escaping in the crowd. Sylla being closely pursued into the house of Marius, was forced to come forth and dissolve the cessation; and for his doing this, Sulpicius, having deposed Pompeius, allowed Sylla to continue his consulship, only transferring the Mithridatic expedition to Marius.

There were immediately despatched to Nola tribunes, to receive the army, and bring it to Marius; but Sylla having got first to the camp, and the soldiers, upon hearing of the news, having stoned the tribunes, Marius, in requital, proceeded to put the friends of Sylla in the city to the sword, and rifled their goods. Every kind of removal and flight went on, some hastening from the camp to the city, others from the city to the camp. The senate, no more in its own power, but wholly governed by the dictates of Marius and

Sulpicius, alarmed at the report of Sylla's advancing with his troops towards the city, sent forth two of the prætors, Brutus and Servilius, to forbid his nearer approach. The soldiers would have slain these prætors in a fury, for their bold language to Sylla; contenting themselves, however, with breaking their rods, and tearing off their purple-edged robes, after much contumelious usage they sent them back, to the sad dejection of the citizens, who beheld their magistrates despoiled of their badges of office, and announcing to them, that things were now manifestly come to a rupture past all cure. Marius put himself in readiness, and Sylla with his colleague moved from Nola, at the head of six complete legions, all of them willing to march up directly against the city, though he himself as yet was doubtful in thought, and apprehensive of the danger. As he was sacrificing, Postumius the soothsayer, having inspected the entrails, stretching forth both hands to Sylla, required to be bound and kept in custody till the battle was over, as willing, if they had not speedy and complete success, to suffer the utmost punishment. It is said, also, that there appeared to Sylla himself in a dream, a certain goddess, whom the Romans learnt to worship from the Cappadocians, whether it be the Moon, or Pallas, or Bellona. This same goddess, to his thinking, stood by him, and put into his hand thunder and lightning, then naming his enemies one by one, bade him strike them, who, all of them, fell on the discharge and disappeared. Encouraged by this vision, and relating it to his colleague, next day he led on towards Rome. About Picinæ [6] being met by a deputation, beseeching him not to attack at once, in the heat of a march,

---

[6] An unknown place, perhaps a false reading. Picinæ should perhaps be Pictæ, a place mentioned by Strabo.

for that the senate had decreed to do him all the right imaginable, he consented to halt on the spot, and sent his officers to measure out the ground, as is usual, for a camp; so that the deputation, believing it, returned. They were no sooner gone, but he sent a party on under the command of Lucius Basillus and Caius Mummius, to secure the city gate, and the walls on the side of the Esquiline hill, and then close at their heels followed himself with all speed. Basillus made his way successfully into the city, but the unarmed multitude, pelting him with stones and tiles from off the houses, stopped his further progress, and beat him back to the wall. Sylla by this time was come up, and seeing what was going on, called aloud to his men to set fire to the houses, and taking a flaming torch, he himself led the way, and commanded the archers to make use of their fire-darts, letting fly at the tops of houses; all which he did, not upon any plan, but simply in his fury, yielding the conduct of that day's work to passion, and as if all he saw were enemies, without respect or pity either to friends, relations, or acquaintance, made his entry by fire, which knows no distinction betwixt friend or foe.

In this conflict, Marius being driven into the temple of Mother-Earth, thence invited the slaves by proclamation of freedom, but the enemy coming on he was overpowered and fled the city.

Sylla having called a senate, had sentence of death passed on Marius, and some few others, amongst whom was Sulpicius, tribune of the people. Sulpicius was killed, being betrayed by his servant, whom Sylla first made free, and then threw him headlong down the Tarpeian rock. As for Marius, he set a price on his life, by proclamation, neither gratefully nor politicly, if we consider into whose house, not long before, he put himself at mercy, and was safely dismissed.

Had Marius at that time not let Sylla go, but suffered him to be slain by the hands of Sulpicius, he might have been lord of all, nevertheless he spared his life, and a few days after when in a similar position himself, received a different measure.

By these proceedings, Sylla excited the secret distaste of the senate; but the displeasure and free indignation of the commonalty showed itself plainly by their actions. For they ignominiously rejected Nonius, his nephew, and Servius, who stood for offices of state by his interest, and elected others as magistrates, by honoring whom they thought they should most annoy him. He made semblance of extreme satisfaction at all this, as if the people by his means had again enjoyed the liberty of doing what seemed best to them. And to pacify the public hostility, he created Lucius Cinna consul, one of the adverse party, having first bound him under oaths and imprecations to be favorable to his interest. For Cinna, ascending the capitol with a stone in his hands, swore solemnly, and prayed with direful curses, that he himself, if he were not true to his friendship with Sylla, might be cast out of the city, as that stone out of his hand; and thereupon cast the stone to the ground, in the presence of many people. Nevertheless Cinna had no sooner entered on his charge, but he took measures to disturb the present settlement, and having prepared an impeachment against Sylla, got Virginius, one of the tribunes of the people, to be his accuser; but Sylla, leaving him and the court of judicature to themselves, set forth against Mithridates.

About the time that Sylla was making ready to put off with his forces from Italy, besides many other omens which befel Mithridates, then staying at Pergamus, there goes a story that a figure of Victory,

with a crown in her hand, which the Pergamenians
by machinery from above let down on him, when it
had almost reached his head, fell to pieces, and the
crown tumbling down into the midst of the theatre,
there broke against the ground, occasioning a general
alarm among the populace, and considerably disquiet-
ing Mithridates himself, although his affairs at that
time were succeeding beyond expectation. For having wrested Asia [7] from the Romans, and Bithynia
and Cappadocia from their kings, he made Pergamus
his royal seat, distributing among his friends riches,
principalities and kingdoms. Of his sons, one residing in Pontus and Bosporus held his ancient realm
as far as the deserts beyond the lake Mæotis, without
molestation; while Ariarathes, another, was reducing
Thrace and Macedon, with a great army, to obedience. His generals, with forces under them, were
establishing his supremacy in other quarters. Archelaus, in particular, with his fleet, held absolute mastery of the sea, and was bringing into subjection the
Cyclades, and all the other islands as far as Malea,
and had taken Euboea itself. Making Athens his
headquarters, from thence as far as Thessaly he was
withdrawing the States of Greece from the Roman
allegiance, without the least ill success, except at
Chæronea. For here Bruttius Sura, lieutenant to
Sentius, governor of Macedon, a man of singular
valor and prudence, met him, and though he came
like a torrent pouring over Bœotia, made stout resistance, and thrice giving him battle near Chæronea,

---

[7] Asia here and elsewhere in the narrative that follows is the
Roman province bearing that name, the chief town of which was
Ephesus, consisting of the greatest part of the western coast of
Asia Minor. Bosporus is the name for the southern part of the
Crimea.

repulsed and forced him back to the sea. But being commanded by Lucius Lucullus to give place to his successor, Sylla, and resign the war to whom it was decreed, he presently left Bœotia, and retired back to Sentius, although his success had outgone all hopes, and Greece was well disposed to a new revolution, upon account of his gallant behavior. These were the glorious actions of Bruttius.

Sylla, on his arrival, received by their deputations the compliments of all the cities of Greece, except Athens, against which, as it was compelled by the tyrant Aristion to hold for the king, he advanced with all his forces, and investing the Piræus, laid formal siege to it, employing every variety of engines, and trying every manner of assault; whereas, had he forborn but a little while, he might without hazard have taken the Upper City by famine, it being already reduced to the last extremity, through want of necessaries. But eager to return to Rome, and fearing innovation there, at great risk, with continual fighting and vast expense, he pushed on the war. Besides other equipage, the very work about the engines of battery was supplied with no less than ten thousand yoke of mules, employed daily in that service. And when timber grew scarce, for many of the works failed, some crushed to pieces by their own weight, others taking fire by the continual play of the enemy, he had recourse to the sacred groves, and cut down the trees of the Academy, the shadiest of all the suburbs, and the Lyceum. And a vast sum of money being wanted to carry on the war, he broke into the sanctuaries of Greece, that of Epidaurus and that of Olympia, sending for the most beautiful and precious offerings deposited there. He wrote, likewise, to the Amphictyons, at Delphi, that it were better to remit the wealth of the god to him, for that he would keep it more securely, or in case he made use of it, restore as much. He sent Caphis, the Phocian, one of his friends, with this message, commanding him to receive each item by weight. Caphis came to Delphi, but was loth to touch the holy things and with many tears, in the presence of the Amphictyons, bewailed the necessity. And on some of them declaring they heard the sound of a harp from the inner shrine, he, whether he himself believed it, or was willing to try the effect of religious fear upon Sylla, sent back an express. To which Sylla replied in a scoffing way, that it was surprising to him that Caphis did not know that music was a sign of joy, not anger; he should, therefore, go on boldly, and accept what a gracious and bountiful god offered.

Other things were sent away without much notice on the part of the Greeks in general, but in the case of the silver tun, that only relic of the regal donations [8] which its weight and bulk made it impossible for any carriage to receive, the Amphictyons were forced to cut it into pieces, and called to mind in so doing, how Titus Flamininus, and Manius Acilius, and again Paulus Æmilius, one of whom drove Antiochus out of Greece, and the others subdued the Macedonian kings, had not only abstained from violating the Greek temples, but had even given them new gifts and honors, and increased the general veneration for them. They, indeed, the lawful commanders of temperate and obedient soldiers, and themselves great in soul, and simple in expenses, lived within the bounds of the ordinary established charges, accounting it a greater disgrace to seek popularity with their men, than to feel fear of their enemy.

[8] The donations of Crœsus.

SYLLA 171

Whereas the commanders of these times, attaining to superiority by force, not worth, and having need of arms one against another, rather than against the public enemy, were constrained to temporize in authority, and in order to pay for the gratifications with which they purchased the labor of their soldiers, were driven, before they knew it, to sell the commonwealth itself, and, to gain the mastery over men better than themselves, were content to become slaves to the vilest of wretches. These practices drove Marius into exile, and again brought him in against Sylla. These made Cinna the assassin of Octavius, and Fimbria of Flaccus. To which courses Sylla contributed not the least; for to corrupt and win over those who were under the command of others, he would be munificent and profuse towards those who were under his own; and so, while tempting the soldiers of other generals to treachery, and his own to dissolute living, he was naturally in want of a large treasury, and especially during that siege.

Sylla had a vehement and an implacable desire to conquer Athens, whether out of emulation, fighting as it were against the shadow of the once famous city, or out of anger, at the foul words and scurrilous jests with which the tyrant Aristion, showing himself daily, with unseemly gesticulations, upon the walls, had provoked him and Metella.

The tyrant Aristion had his very being compounded of wantonness and cruelty, having gathered into himself all the worst of Mithridates's diseased and vicious qualities, like some fatal malady which the city, after its deliverance from innumerable wars, many tyrannies and seditions, was in its last days destined to endure. At the time when a medimnus of wheat was sold in the city for one thousand drachmas, and men were forced to live on the feverfew growing round the citadel, and to boil down shoes and oil-bags for their food, he, carousing and feasting in the open face of day, then dancing in armor, and making jokes at the enemy, suffered the holy lamp of the goddess to expire for want of oil, and to the chief priestess, who demanded of him the twelfth part of a medimnus of wheat, he sent the like quantity of pepper. The senators and priests, who came as suppliants to beg of him to take compassion on the city, and treat for peace with Sylla, he drove away and dispersed with a flight of arrows. At last, with much ado, he sent forth two or three of his revelling companions to parley, to whom Sylla, perceiving that they made no serious overtures towards an accommodation, but went on haranguing in praise of Theseus, Eumolpus, and the Median trophies, replied, "My good friends, you may put up your speeches and be gone. I was sent by the Romans to Athens, not to take lessons, but to reduce rebels to obedience."

In the mean time news came to Sylla that some old men, talking in the Ceramicus, had been overheard to blame the tyrant for not securing the passages and approaches near the Heptachalcum, the one point where the enemy might easily get over. Sylla neglected not the report, but going in the night, and discovering the place to be assailable, set instantly to work. Sylla himself makes mention in his Memoirs, that Marcus Teius, the first man who scaled the wall, meeting with an adversary, and striking him on the headpiece a home stroke, broke his own sword, but, notwithstanding, did not give ground, but stood and held him fast. The city was certainly taken from that quarter, according to the tradition of the oldest of the Athenians.

When they had thrown down the wall, and made

all level betwixt the Piraic and Sacred Gate, about midnight Sylla entered the breach, with all the terrors of trumpets and cornets sounding, with the triumphant shout and cry of an army let loose to spoil and slaughter, and scouring through the streets with swords drawn. There was no numbering the slain; the amount is to this day conjectured only from the space of ground overflowed with blood. For without mentioning the execution done in other quarters of the city, the blood that was shed about the market-place spread over the whole Ceramicus within the Double-gate, and, according to most writers, passed through the gate and overflowed the suburb. Nor did the multitudes which fell thus exceed the number of those, who, out of pity and love for their country, which they believed was now finally to perish, slew themselves; the best of them, through despair of their country's surviving, dreading themselves to survive, expecting neither humanity nor moderation in Sylla. At length, partly at the instance of Midias and Calliphon, two exiled men, beseeching and casting themselves at his feet, partly by the intercession of those senators who followed the camp, having had his fill of revenge, and making some honorable mention of the ancient Athenians, "I forgive," said he, "the many for the sake of the few, the living for the dead." He took Athens, according to his own Memoirs on the calends of March, coinciding pretty nearly with the new moon of Anthesterion, on which day it is the Athenian usage to perform various acts in commemoration of the ruins and devastations occasioned by the deluge, that being supposed to be the time of its occurrence.

At the taking of the town, the tyrant fled into the citadel, and was there besieged by Curio, who had that charge given him. He held out a considerable time, but at last yielded himself up for want of water, and divine power immediately intimated its agency in the matter. For on the same day and hour that Curio conducted him down, the clouds gathered in a clear sky, and there came down a great quantity of rain and filled the citadel with water.

Not long after, Sylla won the Piræus, and burnt most of it; amongst the rest, Philo's arsenal, a work very greatly admired.

In the mean time Taxiles, Mithridates's general, coming down from Thrace and Macedon, with an army of one hundred thousand foot, ten thousand horse, and ninety chariots, armed with scythes at the wheels, would have joined Archelaus, who lay with a navy on the coast near Munychia, reluctant to quit the sea, and yet unwilling to engage the Romans in battle, but desiring to protract the war and cut off the enemy's supplies. Which Sylla perceiving much better than himself, passed with his forces into Bœotia, quitting a barren district which was inadequate to maintain an army even in time of peace. He was thought by some to have taken false measures in thus leaving Attica, a rugged country, and ill suited for cavalry to move in, and entering the plain and open fields of Bœotia, knowing as he did the barbarian strength to consist most in horses and chariots. But as was said before, to avoid famine and scarcity, he was forced to run the risk of a battle. Moreover he was in anxiety for Hortensius, a bold and active officer, whom on his way to Sylla with forces from Thessaly, the barbarians awaited in the straits.[9] For these reasons Sylla drew off into Bœotia. Hortensius, meantime, was conducted by Caphis,[9] our coun-

---

[9] The straits, or pass of Thermopylæ. Caphis, a citizen of Chæronea, Plutarch's own home.

tryman, another way unknown to the barbarians, by Parnassus, just under Tithora, which was then not so large a town as it is now, but a mere fort, surrounded by steep precipices, whither the Phocians also, in old time, when flying from the invasion of Xerxes, carried themselves and their goods and were saved. Hortensius, encamping here, kept off the enemy by day, and at night descending by difficult passages to Patronis, joined the forces of Sylla, who came to meet him. Thus united they posted themselves on a fertile hill in the middle of the plain of Elatea, shaded with trees and watered at the foot. It is called Philobœotus, and its situation and natural advantages are spoken of with great admiration by Sylla.

As they lay thus encamped, they seemed to the enemy a contemptible number, for they were not above fifteen hundred horse, and less than fifteen thousand foot. Therefore the rest of the commanders, overpersuading Archelaus, and drawing up the army, covered the plain with horses, chariots, bucklers, targets. The clamor and cries of so many nations forming for battle rent the air, nor was the pomp and ostentation of their costly array altogether idle and unserviceable for terror; for the brightness of their armor, embellished magnificently with gold and silver, and the rich colors of their Median and Scythian coats, intermixed with brass and shining steel, presented a flaming and terrible sight as they swayed about and moved in their ranks, so much so that the Romans shrunk within their trenches, and Sylla, unable by any arguments to remove their fear, and unwilling to force them to fight against their wills, was fain to sit down in quiet, ill-brooking to become the subject of barbarian insolence and laughter. This, however, above all advantaged him, for the enemy, from contemning of him fell into disorder amongst themselves, being already less thoroughly under command, on account of the number of their leaders. Some few of them remained within the encampment, but others, the major part, lured out with hopes of prey and rapine, strayed about the country many days' journey from the camp, and are related to have destroyed the city of Panope,[10] to have plundered Lebadea, and robbed the oracle without any orders from their commanders.

Sylla, all this while, chafing and fretting to see the cities all around destroyed, suffered not the soldiery to remain idle, but leading them out, compelled them to divert the Cephisus from its ancient channel by casting up ditches, and giving respite to none, showed himself rigorous in punishing the remiss, that growing weary of labor, they might be induced by hardship to embrace danger. Which fell out accordingly, for on the third day, being hard at work as Sylla passed by, they begged and clamored to be led

[10] *Panope* is more correctly Panopeus; *the oracle* near Lebadea is that of Trophonius. The details in these pages taken, it would seem, from Sylla's own memoirs, and enlivened by Plutarch's knowledge of and interest in the localities, are examined at length by Col. Leake, who goes through the whole narrative (*Northern Greece, Vol. II., Chap. XIII., pages* 192 *to* 201). An antique chair of marble in the church is called Plutarch's chair. But a memorial more probably connected with him and his family existed in an inscription, read by Col. Leake on a stone near a fountain below the theatre, in remembrance of Demetrius Autobulus, a Platonic philosopher. And there is a record of another being extant in the time of Meletius the geographer, distinctly "in memory of Sextus Claudius Autobulus, *the sixth from Plutarch*, remarkable for every excellence in conduct and in words, erected by his grandmother Calliclea, his parents, and his sisters." Autobulus is a family name in Plutarch's minor works. Plutarch's own son Autobulus is there spoken of as married, and having a son of his own. See Vol. I., Life of Plutarch.

against the enemy. Sylla replied, that this demand of war proceeded rather from a backwardness to labor than any forwardness to fight, but if they were in good earnest martially inclined, he bade them take their arms and get up thither, pointing to the ancient citadel of the Parapotamians, of which at present, the city being laid waste, there remained only the rocky hill itself, steep and craggy on all sides, and severed from Mount Hedylium by the breadth of the river Assus, which running between, and at the bottom of the same hill falling into the Cephisus with an impetuous confluence, makes this eminence a strong positions for soldiers to occupy. Observing that the enemy's division, called the Brazen Shields, were making their way up thither, Sylla was willing to take first possession, and by the vigorous efforts of the soldiers succeeded. Archelaus, driven from hence, bent his forces upon Chæronea. The Chæroneans who bore arms in the Roman camp beseeching Sylla not to abandon the city, he despatched Gabinius, a tribune, with one legion, and sent out also the Chæroneans, who endeavored, but were not able to get in before Gabinius; so active was he, and more zealous to bring relief than those who had entreated it. Juba writes that Ericius was the man sent, not Gabinius. Thus narrowly did our native city escape.

From Lebadea and the cave of Trophonius there came favorable rumors and prophecies of victory to the Romans, of which the inhabitants of those places give a fuller account, but as Sylla himself affirms in the tenth book of his Memoirs, Quintus Titius, a man of some repute among the Romans who were engaged in mercantile business in Greece, came to him after the battle won at Chæronea, and declared that Trophonius had foretold another fight and victory on the same place, within a short time. After

him a soldier, by name Salvenius, brought an account
from the god of the future issue of affairs in Italy.
As to the vision, they both agreed in this, that they
had seen one who in stature and in majesty was similar to Jupiter Olympius.

Sylla, when he had passed over the Assus, marching under the Mount Hedylium, encamped close to
Archelaus, who had intrenched himself strongly between the mountains Acontium and Hedylium, close
to what are called the Assia. The place of his intrenchment is to this day named from him, Archelaus.
Sylla, after one day's respite, having left Murena
behind him with one legion and two cohorts to amuse
the enemy with continual alarms, himself went and
sacrificed on the banks of Cephisus, and the holy
rites ended, held on towards Chæronea to receive the
forces there and view Mount Thurium, where a party
of the enemy had posted themselves. This is a craggy
height running up in a conical form to a point, called
by us Orthopagus; at the foot of it is the river Morius
and the temple of Apollo Thurius. The god had his
surname from Thuro, mother of Chæron, whom
ancient record makes founder of Chæronea. Others
assert that the cow which Apollo gave to Cadmus for
a guide appeared there, and that the place took its
name from the beast, Thor being the Phœnician word
for a cow.

At Sylla's approach to Chæronea, the tribune who
had been appointed to guard the city led out his men
in arms, and met him with a garland of laurel in his
hand; which Sylla accepting, and at the same time
saluting the soldiers and animating them to the encounter, two men of Chæronea, Homoloichus and
Anaxidamus, presented themselves before him, and
offered, with a small party, to dislodge those who
were posted on Thurium. For there lay a path out

of sight of the barbarians, from what is called Petrochus along by the Museum,[11] leading right down from above upon Thurium. By this way it was easy to fall upon them and either stone them from above, or force them down into the plain. Sylla, assured of their faith and courage by Gabinius, bade them proceed with the enterprise, and meantime drew up the army, and disposing the cavalry on both wings, himself took command of the right; the left being committed to the direction of Murena. In the rear of all, Galba and Hortensius, his lieutenants, planted themselves on the upper grounds with the cohorts of reserve, to watch the motions of the enemy, who with numbers of horse and swift-footed, light-armed infantry, were noticed to have so formed their wing as to allow it readily to change about and alter its position, and thus gave reason for suspecting that they intended to carry it far out and so to inclose the Romans.

In the mean while, the Chæroneans, who had Ericius for commander by appointment of Sylla, covertly making their way around Thurium, and then discovering themselves, occasioned a great confusion and rout amongst the barbarians, and slaughter, for the most part, by their own hands. For they kept not their place, but making down the steep descent, ran themselves on their own spears, and violently sent each other over the cliffs, the enemy from above pressing on and wounding them where they exposed their bodies; insomuch that there fell three thousand about Thurium. Some of those who escaped, being met by Murena as he stood in array, were cut off and destroyed. Others breaking through to their friends and falling pell-mell into the ranks, filled most part

[11] That is, the temple or chapel, the building or piece of ground, consecrated to the Muses.

of the army with fear and tumult, and caused a hesitation and delay among the generals, which was no small disadvantage. For immediately upon the discomposure, Sylla coming full speed to the charge, and quickly crossing the interval between the armies, lost them the service of their armed chariots, which require a considerable space of ground to gather strength and impetuosity in their career, a short course being weak and ineffectual, like that of missiles without a full swing. Thus it fared with the barbarians at present, whose first chariots came feebly on and made but a faint impression; the Romans repulsing them with shouts and laughter, called out as they do at the races in the circus, for more to come. By this time the mass of both armies met; the barbarians on one side fixed their long pikes, and with their shields locked close together, strove so far as in them lay to preserve their line of battle entire. The Romans, on the other side, having discharged their javelins, rushed on with their drawn swords, and struggled to put by the pikes to get at them the sooner, in the fury that possessed them at seeing in the front of the enemy fifteen thousand slaves, whom the royal commanders had set free by proclamation, and ranged amongst the men of arms. And a Roman centurion is reported to have said at this sight, that he never knew servants allowed to play the masters, unless at the Saturnalia. These men by their deep and solid array, as well as by their daring courage, yielded but slowly to the legions, till at last by slinging engines, and darts, which the Romans poured in upon them behind, they were forced to give way and scatter.

As Archelaus was extending the right wing to encompass the enemy, Hortensius with his cohorts came down in force, with intention to charge him in the flank. But Archelaus wheeling about suddenly with two thousand horse, Hortensius, outnumbered and hard pressed, fell back towards the higher grounds, and found himself gradually getting separated from the main body and likely to be surrounded by the enemy. When Sylla heard this, he came rapidly up to his succor from the right wing, which as yet had not engaged. But Archelaus, guessing the matter by the dust of his troops, turned to the right wing, from whence Sylla came, in hopes to surprise it without a commander. At the same instant, likewise, Taxiles, with his Brazen Shields, assailed Murena, so that a cry coming from both places, and the hills repeating it around, Sylla stood in suspense which way to move. Deciding to resume his own station, he sent in aid to Murena four cohorts under Hortensius, and commanding the fifth to follow him, returned hastily to the right wing, which of itself held its ground on equal terms against Archelaus; and, at his appearance, with one bold effort forced them back, and, obtaining the mastery, followed them, flying in disorder to the river and Mount Acontium. Sylla, however, did not forget the danger Murena was in; but hasting thither and finding him victorious also, then joined in the pursuit. Many barbarians were slain in the field, many more were cut in pieces as they were making into the camp. Of all the vast multitude, ten thousand only got safe into Chalcis. Sylla writes that there were but fourteen of his soldiers missing, and that two of these returned towards evening; he, therefore, inscribed on the trophies the names of Mars, Victory, and Venus, as having won the day no less by good fortune than by management and force of arms. This trophy of the battle in the plain stands on the place where Archelaus first gave way, near the stream of the Molus; another is erected high on the top of Thurium, where the barbarians were environed, with an inscription in Greek, recording that the glory of the day belonged to Homoloichus and Anaxidamus. Sylla celebrated his victory at Thebes with spectacles, for which he erected a stage, near Œdipus's well. The judges of the performances were Greeks chosen out of other cities; his hostility to the Thebans being implacable, half of whose territory he took away and consecrated to Apollo and Jupiter, ordering that out of the revenue compensation should be made to the gods for the riches himself had taken from them.

After this, hearing that Flaccus, a man of the contrary faction, had been chosen consul, and was crossing the Ionian Sea with an army, professedly to act against Mithridates, but in reality against himself, he hastened towards Thessaly, designing to meet him, but in his march, when near Melitea, received advices from all parts that the countries behind him were overrun and ravaged by no less a royal army than the former. For Dorylaus, arriving at Chalcis with a large fleet, on board of which he brought over with him eighty thousand of the best appointed and best disciplined soldiers of Mithridates's army, at once invaded Bœotia, and occupied the country in hopes to bring Sylla to a battle, making no account of the dissuasions of Archelaus, but giving it out as to the last fight, that without treachery so many thousand men could never have perished. Sylla, however, facing about expeditiously, made it clear to him that Archelaus was a wise man, and had good skill in the Roman valor; insomuch that he himself, after some small skirmishes with Sylla near Tilphossium, was the first of those who thought it not advisable to put things to the decision of the sword, but rather to wear out the war by expense of time and treasure. The ground, however, near Orchomenus, where they then lay encamped, gave some encouragement to Archelaus, being a battle field admirably suited for an army superior in cavalry. Of all the plains in Bœotia that are renowned for their beauty and extent, this alone, which commences from the city of Orchomenus, spreads out unbroken and clear of trees to the edge of the fens in which the Melas, rising close under Orchomenus, loses itself, the only Greek river which is a deep and navigable water from the very head, increasing also about the summer solstice like the Nile, and producing plants similar to those that grow there, only small and without fruit. It does not run far before the main stream disappears among the blind and woody marsh-grounds; a small branch, however, joins the Cephisus, about the place where the lake is thought to produce the best flute-reeds.

Now that both armies were posted near each other, Archelaus lay still, but Sylla employed himself in cutting ditches from either side; that if possible, by driving the enemies from the firm and open champain, he might force them into the fens. They, on the other hand, not enduring this, as soon as their leaders allowed them the word of command, issued out furiously in large bodies; when not only the men at work were dispersed, but most part of those who stood in arms to protect the work fled in disorder. Upon this, Sylla leaped from his horse, and snatching hold of an ensign, rushed through the midst of the rout upon the enemy, crying out aloud, "To me, O Romans, it will be glorious to fall here. As for you, when they ask you where you betrayed your general, remember and say, at Orchomenus." His men rallying again at these words, and two cohorts coming to his succor from the right wing, he led them to the charge and turned the day. Then retiring some short distance and refreshing his men, he proceeded again with his works to block up the enemy's camp. They again sallied out in better order than before. Here Diogenes, step-son to Archelaus, fighting on the right wing with much gallantry, made an honorable end. And the archers, being hard pressed by the Romans, and wanting space for a retreat, took their arrows by handfuls, and striking with these as with swords, beat them back. In the end, however, they were all driven into the intrenchment and had a sorrowful night of it with their slain and wounded. The next day again, Sylla, leading forth his men up to their quarters, went on finishing the lines of intrenchment, and when they issued out again with larger numbers to give him battle, fell on them and put them to the rout, and in the consternation ensuing, none daring to abide, he took the camp by storm. The marshes were filled with blood, and the lake with dead bodies, insomuch that to this day many bows, helmets, fragments of iron, breastplates, and swords of barbarian make, continue to be found buried deep in mud, two hundred years after the fight. Thus much of the actions of Chæronea and Orchomenus.

At Rome, Cinna and Carbo were now using injustice and violence towards persons of the greatest eminence, and many of them to avoid this tyranny repaired, as to a safe harbor, to Sylla's camp, where, in a short space, he had about him the aspect of a senate. Metella, likewise, having with difficulty conveyed herself and children away by stealth, brought him word that his houses, both in town and country, had been burnt by his enemies, and entreated his help at home. Whilst he was in doubt what to do, being impatient to hear of his country being thus outraged, and yet not knowing how to leave so great a work as the Mithridatic war unfinished, there comes to him

Archelaus, a merchant of Delos, with hopes of an accommodation, and private instructions from Archelaus, the king's general. Sylla liked the business so well as to desire a speedy conference with Archelaus in person, and a meeting took place on the sea-coast near Delium, where the temple of Apollo stands. When Archelaus opened the conversation, and began to urge Sylla to abandon his pretensions to Asia and Pontus, and to set sail for the war in Rome, receiving money and shipping, and such forces as he should think fitting from the king, Sylla, interposing, bade Archelaus take no further care for Mithridates, but assume the crown to himself, and become a confederate of Rome, delivering up the navy. Archelaus professing his abhorrence of such treason, Sylla proceeded: "So you, Archelaus, a Cappadocian, and slave, or if it so please you, friend, to a barbarian king, would not, upon such vast considerations, be guilty of what is dishonorable, and yet dare to talk to me, Roman general and Sylla, of treason? as if you were not the selfsame Archelaus who ran away at Chæronea, with few remaining out of one hundred and twenty thousand men; who lay for two days in the fens of Orchomenus, and left Bœotia impassable for heaps of dead carcasses." Archelaus, changing his tone at this, humbly besought him to lay aside the thoughts of war, and make peace with Mithridates. Sylla consenting to this request, articles of agreement were concluded on. That Mithridates should quit Asia and Paphlagonia, restore Bithynia to Nicomedes, Cappadocia to Ariobarzanes, and pay the Romans two thousand talents, and give him seventy ships of war with all their furniture. On the other hand, that Sylla should confirm to him his other dominions, and declare him a Roman confederate. On these terms he proceeded by the way of Thessaly and

Macedon towards the Hellespont, having Archelaus with him, and treating him with great attention. For Archelaus being taken dangerously ill at Larissa, he stopped the march of the army, and took care of him, as if he had been one of his own captains, or his colleague in command. This gave suspicion of foul play in the battle of Chæronea; as it was also observed that Sylla had released all the friends of Mithridates taken prisoners in war, except only Aristion the tyrant, who was at enmity with Archelaus, and was put to death by poison; and, above all, ten thousand acres of land in Eubœa had been given to the Cappadocian, and he had received from Sylla the style of friend and ally of the Romans. On all which points Sylla defends himself in his Memoirs.

The ambassadors of Mithridates arriving and declaring that they accepted of the conditions, only Paphlagonia they could not part with; and as for the ships, professing not to know of any such capitulation, Sylla in a rage exclaimed, "What say you? Does Mithridates then withhold Paphlagonia? and as to the ships, deny that article? I thought to have seen him prostrate at my feet to thank me for leaving him so much as that right hand of his, which has cut off so many Romans. He will shortly, at my coming over into Asia, speak another language; in the mean time, let him at his ease in Pergamus sit managing a war which he never saw." The ambassadors in terror stood silent by, but Archelaus endeavored with humble supplications to assuage his wrath, laying hold on his right hand and weeping. In conclusion he obtained permission to go himself in person to Mithridates; for that he would either mediate a peace to the satisfaction of Sylla, or if not, slay himself. Sylla having thus despatched him away, made an inroad into Mædica, and after wide depopulations returned back again into Macedon, where he received Archelaus about Philippi, bringing word that all was well, and that Mithridates earnestly requested an interview. The chief cause of this meeting was Fimbria; for he having assassinated Flaccus, the consul of the contrary faction, and worsted the Mithridatic commanders, was advancing against Mithridates himself, who, fearing this, chose rather to seek the friendship of Sylla.

And so met at Dardanus in the Troad, on one side Mithridates, attended with two hundred ships, and land forces consisting of twenty thousand men at arms, six thousand horse, and a large train of scythed chariots; on the other, Sylla with only four cohorts, and two hundred horse. As Mithridates drew near and put out his hand Sylla demanded whether he was willing or no to end the war on the terms Archelaus had agreed to, but seeing the king made no answer, "How is this?" he continued, "ought not the petitioner to speak first, and the conqueror to listen in silence?" And when Mithridates, entering upon his plea, began to shift off the war, partly on the gods, and partly to blame the Romans themselves, he took him up, saying that he had heard, indeed, long since from others, and now he knew it himself for truth, that Mithridates was a powerful speaker, who in defence of the most foul and unjust proceedings, had not wanted for specious pretences. Then charging him with and inveighing bitterly against the outrages he had committed, he asked again whether he was willing or no to ratify the treaty of Archelaus? Mithridates answering in the affirmative, Sylla came forward, embraced and kissed him. Not long after he introduced Ariobarzanes and Nicomedes, the two kings, and made them friends. Mithridates, when he had handed over to Sylla seventy ships and five hundred archers, set sail for Pontus.

Sylla, perceiving the soldiers to be dissatisfied with the peace, (as it seemed indeed a monstrous thing that they should see the king who was their bitterest enemy, and who had caused one hundred and fifty thousand Romans to be massacred in one day in Asia, now sailing off with the riches and spoils of Asia, which he had pillaged, and put under contribution for the space of four years,) in his defence to them alleged, that he could not have made head against Fimbria and Mithridates, had they both withstood him in conjunction. Thence he set out and went in search of Fimbria, who lay with the army about Thyatira, and pitching his camp not far off, proceeded to fortify it with a trench. The soldiers of Fimbria came out in their single coats, and, saluting his men, lent ready assistance to the work; which change Fimbria beholding, and apprehending Sylla as irreconcilable, laid violent hands on himself in the camp.

Sylla imposed on Asia in general a tax of twenty thousand talents, and despoiled individually each family by the licentious behavior and long residence of the soldiery in private quarters. For he ordained that every host should allow his guest four tetradrachms [12] each day, and moreover entertain him, and as many friends as he should invite, with a supper; that a centurion should receive fifty drachmas a day, together with one suit of clothes to wear within doors, and another when he went abroad.

Having set out from Ephesus with the whole

---

[12] The tetradrachmon was a coin worth four drachmas, the ordinary large silver piece of the Greek currency, being in fact a sort of small dollar, a *four* franc piece.

navy, he came the third day to anchor in the Piræus. Here he was initiated in the mysteries, and seized for his use the library of Apellicon the Teian, in which were most of the works of Theophrastus and Aristotle, then not in general circulation. When the whole was afterwards conveyed to Rome, there, it is said, the greater part of the collection passed through the hands of Tyrannion the grammarian, and that Andronicus the Rhodian, having through his means the command of numerous copies, made the treatises public, and drew up the catalogues that are now current. The elder Peripatetics appear themselves, indeed, to have been accomplished and learned men, but of the writings of Aristotle and Theophrastus they had no large or exact knowledge, because Theophrastus bequeathing his books to the heir of Neleus of Scepsis,[18] they came into carless and illiterate hands.

During Sylla's stay about Athens, his feet were attacked by a heavy benumbing pain, which Strabo calls the first inarticulate sounds of the gout. Taking, therefore, a voyage to Ædepsus, he made use of the hot waters there, allowing himself at the same

[18] *The text of the passage about Neleus of Scepsis is uncertain. But the account is probably taken for the most part from Strabo (XIII. 1, 54), who, in speaking of Scepsis near Troy, tells us that Neleus, a native of the town, a scholar of Aristotle and Theophrastus, succeeded to the possession of Theophrastus's library, which included that of Aristotle, who left his to Theophrastus; Aristotle being the first man, to Strabo's knowledge, who collected a library, setting the example to the Egyptian kings. Neleus took the books to Scepsis, where those who afterwards came into his property kept them shut up without much care for their preservation; and when the kings of the house of Attalus were searching everywhere for books for the library at Pergamus, they buried them underground; and in the damaged condition they thus were in, the works of Theophrastus and Aristotle were bought at last by Apellicon the Teian, who was more, however, of*

time to forget all anxieties, and passing away his time with actors. As he was walking along the sea-shore, certain fishermen brought him some magnificent fish. Being much delighted with the gift, and understanding, on inquiry, that they were men of Halææ, "What," said he, "are there any men of Halææ surviving?" For after his victory at Orchomenus, in the heat of a pursuit, he had destroyed three cities of Bœotia, Anthedon, Larymna, and Halææ. The men not knowing what to say for fear, Sylla with a smile bade them cheer up and return in peace, as they had brought with them no insignificant intercessors. The Halæans say that this first gave them courage to reunite and return to their city.

Sylla, having marched through Thessaly and Macedon to the sea-coast, prepared, with twelve hundred vessels, to cross over from Dyrrhachium to Brundisium. Not far from hence is Apollonia, and near it the Nymphæum, a spot of ground where, from among green trees and meadows, there are found at various points springs of fire continually streaming out. Here, they say, a satyr, such as statuaries and painters represent, was caught asleep, and brought before Sylla, where he was asked by several interpreters who he was, and, after much trouble at last

a book-collector than a philosopher, and had copies made with the gaps filled in at a venture. Thus the earlier Peripatetics were left without the works of their master, and the later had faulty copies. And after Sylla, on taking Athens, carried Apellicon's library to Rome, Tyrannion the grammarian made a recension of them, and bad copies were made for booksellers, as is commonly the case, he says, with books written for sale both here (in Rome) *and in Alexandria. Strabo was Tyrannion's scholar, and probably gives the story from his account; the statement, however, that the early Peripatetics had no copies of Aristotle's writings, is said to be open to a good deal of exception.*

uttered nothing intelligible, but a harsh noise, something between the neighing of a horse and crying of a goat. Sylla, in dismay, and deprecating such an omen, bade it be removed.

At the point of transportation, Sylla being in alarm, lest at their first setting foot upon Italy, the soldiers should disband and disperse one by one among the cities, they of their own accord first took an oath to stand firm by him, and not of their goodwill to injure Italy; then seeing him in distress for money, they made, so to say, a freewill offering, and contributed each man according to his ability. However, Sylla would not accept of their offering, but praising their good-will, and arousing up their courage, put over (as he himself writes) against fifteen hostile generals in command of four hundred and fifty cohorts; but not without the most unmistakable divine intimations of his approaching happy successes. For when he was sacrificing at his first landing near Tarentum, the victim's liver showed the figure of a crown of laurel with two fillets hanging from it. And a little while before his arrival in Campania, near the mountain Hephæus,[14] two stately goats were seen in the daytime, fighting together, and performing all the motions of men in battle. It proved to be an apparition, and rising up gradually from the ground, dispersed in the air, like fancied representations in the clouds, and so vanished out of sight. Not long after, in the selfsame place, when Marius the younger, and Norbanus the consul, attacked him with two great armies, without prescribing the order of battle, or arranging his men according to their divisions, by

---

[14] *The mountain of Hephæus in Campania* seems to be quite unknown. It has been thought that Tifata (*Tiphata* in Greek) may have been the name originally written.

the sway only of one common alacrity and transport of courage, he overthrew the enemy, and shut up Norbanus into the city of Capua, with the loss of seven thousand of his men. And this was the reason, he says, that the soldiers did not leave him and disperse into the different towns, but held fast to him, and despised the enemy, though infinitely more in number.

At Silvium, (as he himself relates it,) there met him a servant of Pontius, in a state of divine possession, saying that he brought him the power of the sword and victory from Bellona, the goddess of war, and if he did not make haste, that the capitol would be burnt, which fell out on the same day the man foretold it, namely, on the sixth day of the month Quintilis, which we now call July.

At Fidentia, also, Marcus Lucullus, one of Sylla's commanders, reposed such confidence in the forwardness of the soldiers, as to dare to face fifty cohorts of the enemy, with only sixteen of his own; but because many of them were unarmed, delayed the onset. As he stood thus waiting, and considering with himself, a gentle gale of wind, bearing along with it from the neighboring meadows a quantity of flowers, scattered them down upon the army, on whose shields and helmets they settled, and arranged themselves spontaneously, so as to give the soldiers, in the eyes of the enemy, the appearance of being crowned with chaplets. Upon this, being yet further animated, they joined battle, and victoriously slaying eight thousand men, took the camp. This Lucullus was brother to that Lucullus who in after-times conquered Mithridates and Tigranes.

Sylla, seeing himself still surrounded by so many armies, and such mighty hostile powers, had recourse to art, inviting Scipio, the other consul, to a treaty of peace. The motion was willingly embraced, and several meetings and consultations ensued, in all which Sylla, still interposing matter of delay and new pretences, in the meanwhile debauched Scipio's men by means of his own, who were as well practised as the general himself, in all the artifices of inveigling. For entering into the enemy's quarters and joining in conversations, they gained some by present money, some by promises, others by fair words and persuasions; so that in the end, when Sylla with twenty cohorts drew near, on his men saluting Scipio's soldiers, they returned the greeting and came over, leaving Scipio behind them in his tent, where he was found all alone and dismissed. And having used his twenty cohorts as decoys to ensnare the forty of the enemy, he led them all back into the camp. On this occasion, Carbo was heard to say, that he had both a fox and a lion in the breast of Sylla to deal with, and was most troubled with the fox.

Some time after, at Signia, Marius the younger, with eighty-five cohorts, offered battle to Sylla, who was extremely desirous to have it decided on that very day; for the night before he had seen a vision in his sleep, of Marius the elder, who had been some time dead, advising his son to beware of the following day, as of fatal consequence to him. For this reason, Sylla, longing to come to a battle, sent off for Dolabella, who lay encamped at some distance. But because the enemy had beset and blocked up the passes, his soldiers got tired with skirmishing and marching at once. To these difficulties was added, moreover, tempestuous rainy weather, which distressed them most of all. The principal officers therefore came to Sylla, and besought him to defer the battle that day, showing him how the soldiers lay stretched on the ground, where they had thrown themselves down in their weariness, resting their heads upon their shields to gain some repose. When, with much reluctance, he had yielded, and given order for pitching the camp, they had no sooner begun to cast up the rampart and draw the ditch, but Marius came riding up furiously at the head of his troops, in hopes to scatter them in that disorder and confusion. Here the gods fulfilled Sylla's dream. For the soldiers, stirred up with anger, left off their work, and sticking their javelins into the bank, with drawn swords and a courageous shout, came to blows with the enemy, who made but small resistance, and lost great numbers in the flight. Marius fled to Præneste, but finding the gates shut, tied himself round by a rope that was thrown down to him, and was taken up on the walls. Some there are (as Fenestella for one) who affirm that Marius knew nothing of the fight, but, overwatched and spent with hard duty, had reposed himself, when the signal was given, beneath some shade, and was hardly to be awakened at the flight of his men. Sylla, according to his own account, lost only twenty-three men in this fight, having killed of the enemy twenty thousand, and taken alive eight thousand.

The like success attended his lieutenants, Pompey, Crassus, Metellus, Servilius, who with little or no loss cut off vast numbers of the enemy, insomuch that Carbo, the prime supporter of the cause, fled by night from his charge of the army, and sailed over into Libya.

In the last struggle, however, the Samnite Telesinus, like some champion, whose lot it is to enter last of all into the lists and take up the wearied conqueror, came nigh to have foiled and overthrown Sylla before the gates of Rome. For Telesinus with his second, Lamponius the Lucanian, having collected a large force, had been hastening towards Præneste, to, relieve Marius from the siege; but perceiving Sylla ahead of him, and Pompey behind, both hurrying up against him, straitened thus before and behind, as a valiant and experienced soldier, he arose by night, and marching directly with his whole army, was within a little of making his way unexpectedly into Rome itself. He lay that night before the city, at ten furlongs distance from the Colline gate, elated and full of hope, at having thus outgeneralled so many eminent commanders. At break of day, being charged by the noble youth of the city, among many others he overthrew Appius Claudius, renowned for high birth and character. The city, as is easy to imagine, was all in an uproar, the women shrieking and running about, as if it had already been entered forcibly by assault, till at last Balbus, sent forward by Sylla, was seen riding up with seven hundred horse at full speed. Halting only long enough to wipe the sweat from the horses, and then hastily bridling again, he at once attacked the enemy. Presently Sylla himself appeared, and commanding those who were foremost to take immediate refreshment, proceeded to form in order for battle. Dolabella and Torquatus were extremely earnest with him to desist awhile, and not with spent forces to hazard the last hope, having before them in the field, not Carbo or Marius, but two warlike nations bearing immortal hatred to Rome, the Samnites and Lucanians, to grapple with. But he put them by, and commanded the trumpets to sound a charge, when it was now about four o'clock in the afternoon. In the conflict which followed, as sharp a one as ever was, the right wing where Crassus was posted had clearly the advantage; the left suffered and was in distress, when Sylla came to its succor, mounted on a white courser, full of mettle and exceedingly swift, which two of the enemy knowing him by, had their lances ready to throw at him; he himself observed nothing, but his attendant behind him giving the horse a touch, he was, unknown to himself, just so far carried forward, that the points, falling beside the horse's tail, stuck in the ground. There is a story that he had a small golden image of Apollo from Delphi, which he was always wont in battle to carry about him in his bosom, and that he then kissed it with these words, "O Apollo Pythius, who in so many battles hast raised to honor and greatness the Fortunate Cornelius Sylla, wilt thou now cast him down, bringing him before the gate of his country, to perish shamefully with his fellow-citizens?" Thus, they say, addressing himself to the god, he entreated some of his men, threatened some, and seized others with his hand, till at length the left wing being wholly shattered, he was forced, in the general rout, to betake himself to the camp, having lost many of his friends and acquaintance. Many, likewise, of the city spectators who had come out, were killed or trodden underfoot. So that it was generally believed in the city that all was lost, and the siege of Præneste was all but raised; many fugitives from the battle making their way thither, and urging Lucretius Ofella, who was appointed to keep on the siege, to rise in all haste, for that Sylla had perished, and Rome fallen into the hands of the enemy.

About midnight there came into Sylla's camp messengers from Crassus, to fetch provision for him and his soldiers; for having vanquished the enemy, they had pursued him to the walls of Antemna, and had sat down there. Sylla, hearing this, and that most of the enemy were destroyed, came to Antemna by break of day, where three thousand of the besieged having sent forth a herald, he promised to receive them to mercy, on condition they did the enemy some mischief in their coming over. Trusting to his word, they fell foul on the rest of their companions, and made a great slaughter one of another. Nevertheless, Sylla gathered together in the circus, as well these as other survivors of the party, to the number of six thousand, and just as he commenced speaking to the senate, in the temple of Bellona, proceeded to cut them down, by men appointed for that service. The cry of so vast a multitude put to the sword, in so narrow a space, was naturally heard some distance, and startled the senators. He, however, continuing his speech with a calm and unconcerned countenance, bade them listen to what he had to say, and not busy themselves with what was doing out of doors; he had given directions for the chastisement of some offenders. This gave the most stupid of the Romans to understand, that they had merely exchanged, not escaped, tyranny. And Marius, being of a naturally harsh temper, had not altered, but merely continued what he had been, in authority; whereas Sylla, using his fortune moderately and unambitiously at first, and giving good hopes of a true patriot, firm to the interests both of the nobility and commonalty, being, moreover, of a gay and cheerful temper from his youth, and so easily moved to pity as to shed tears readily, has, perhaps deservedly, cast a blemish upon offices of great authority, as if they deranged men's former habits and character, and gave rise to violence, pride, and inhumanity. Whether this be a real change and revolution in the mind, caused by fortune, or rather a lurking viciousness of nature, discovering itself in authority, it were matter of another sort of disquisition to decide.

Sylla being thus wholly bent upon slaughter, and filling the city with executions without number or limit, many wholly uninterested persons falling a sacrifice to private enmity, through his permission and indulgence to his friends, Caius Metellus, one of the younger men, made bold in the senate to ask him what end there was of these evils, and at what point he might be expected to stop? "We do not ask you," said he, "to pardon any whom you have resolved to destroy, but to free from doubt those whom you are pleased to save." Sylla answering, that he knew not as yet whom to spare. "Why then," said he, "tell us whom you will punish." This Sylla said he would do. These last words, some authors say, were spoken not by Metellus, but by Afidius,[15] one of Sylla's fawning companions. Immediately upon this, without communicating with any of the magistrates, Sylla proscribed eighty persons, and notwithstanding the general indignation, after one day's respite, he posted two hundred and twenty more, and on the third again, as many. In an address to the people on this occasion, he told them he had put up as many names as he could think of; those which had escaped his memory, he would publish at a future time. He issued an edict likewise, making death the punishment of humanity, proscribing any who should dare to receive and cherish a proscribed person, without exception to brother, son, or parents. And to him who should slay any one proscribed person, he ordained two talents reward, even were it a slave who had killed his master, or a son his father. And what was thought most unjust of all, he caused the attainder to pass upon their sons, and son's sons, and made open sale of all their property. Nor did the proscription prevail only at Rome, but throughout all the cities of Italy the effusion of blood was such, that neither

---

[15] *Afidius* is probably a mistake (of Plutarch or of a transcriber) for Fufidius.

SYLLA

sanctuary of the gods, nor hearth of hospitality, nor ancestral home escaped. Men were butchered in the embraces of their wives, children in the arms of their mothers. Those who perished through public animosity, or private enmity, were nothing in comparison of the numbers of those who suffered for their riches. Even the murderers began to say, that "his fine house killed this man, a garden that, a third, his hot baths." Quintus Aurelius, a quiet, peaceable man, and one who thought all his part in the common calamity consisted in condoling with the misfortunes of others, coming into the forum to read the list, and finding himself among the proscribed, cried out, "Woe is me, my Alban farm has informed against me." He had not gone far, before he was dispatched by a ruffian, sent on that errand.

In the mean time, Marius, on the point of being taken, killed himself; and Sylla, coming to Præneste, at first proceeded judicially against each particular person, till at last, finding it a work of too much time, he cooped them up together in one place, to the number of twelve thousand men, and gave order for the execution of them all, his own host [16] alone excepted. But he, brave man, telling him he could not accept the obligation of life from the hands of one who had been the ruin of his country, went in among the rest, and submitted willingly to the stroke. What Lucius Catilina did was thought to exceed all other acts. For having, before matters came to an issue, made away with his brother, he besought Sylla to place him in the list of proscription, as though he had been alive, which was done; and Catiline, to return the kind of-

---

[16] The friend, that is, with whom he always stayed when he happened to be at Præneste, his *xenos:* a relationship much regarded in the Greek and Roman world.

fice, assassinated a certain Marcus Marius, one of the adverse party, and brought the head to Sylla, as he was sitting in the forum, and then going to the holy water of Apollo, which was nigh, washed his hands.

There were other things, besides this bloodshed, which gave offence. For Sylla had declared himself dictator, an office which had then been laid aside for the space of one hundred and twenty years. There was, likewise, an act of grace passed on his behalf, granting indemnity for what was passed, and for the future intrusting him with the power of life and death, confiscation, division of lands, erecting and demolishing of cities, taking away of kingdoms, and bestowing them at pleasure. He conducted the sale of confiscated property after such an arbitrary, imperious way, from the tribunal, that his gifts excited greater odium even than his usurpations; women, mimes, and musicians, and the lowest of the freed slaves had presents made them of the territories of nations, and the revenues of cities; and women of rank were married against their will to some of them. Wishing to insure the fidelity of Pompey the Great, by a nearer tie of blood, he bade him divorce his present wife, and forcing Æmilia, the daughter of Scaurus and Metella, his own wife, to leave her husband, Manius Glabrio, he bestowed her, though then with child, on Pompey, and she died in childbirth at his house.

When Lucretius Ofella, the same who reduced Marius by siege, offered himself for the consulship, he first forbade him; then, seeing he could not restrain him, on his coming down into the forum with a numerous train of followers, he sent one of the centurions who were immediately about him, and slew him, himself sitting on the tribunal in the temple of Castor, and beholding the murder from above. The citizens apprehending the centurion, and dragging him to the tribunal, he bade them cease their clamoring and let the centurion go, for he had commanded it.

His triumph was, in itself, exceedingly splendid, and distinguished by the rarity and magnificence of the royal spoils; but its yet greatest glory was the noble spectacle of the exiles. For in the rear followed the most eminent and most potent of the citizens, crowned with garlands, and calling Sylla savior and father, by whose means they were restored to their own country, and again enjoyed their wives and children. When the solemnity was over, and the time come to render an account of his actions, addressing the public assembly, he was as profuse in enumerating the lucky chances of war, as any of his own military merits. And, finally, from this felicity, he requested to receive the surname of Felix. In writing and transacting business with the Greeks, he styled himself Epaphroditus,[17] and on his trophies which are still extant with us, the name is given Lucius Cornelius Sylla Epaphroditus. Moreover, when his wife had brought him forth twins, he named the male Faustus, and the female Fausta, the Roman words for what is auspicious and of happy omen. The confidence which he reposed in his good genius, rather than in any abilities of his own, emboldened him, though deeply involved in bloodshed, and though he had been the author of such great changes and revolutions of State, to lay down his authority, and place

---

[17] The favored of Aphrodite or Venus, the preternatural power and divine principle, in Greek and Roman ideas, of all that is felicitous and beautiful,—of every happy stroke of genius alike and fortune; to whom would be referred any unaccountably successful acts, such as those things in the life of Sylla which it occurred to him, he knew not why, he says, to do, and led him, he knew not how, to the most successful results.

the right of consular elections once more in the hands of the people. And when they were held, he not only declined to seek that office, but in the forum exposed his person publicly to the people, walking up and down as a private man. And contrary to his will, a certain bold man and his enemy, Marcus Lepidus, was expected to become consul, not so much by his own interest, as by the power and solicitation of Pompey, whom the people were willing to oblige. When the business was over, seeing Pompey going home overjoyed with the success, he called him to him and said, "What a politic act, young man, to pass by Catulus, the best of men, and choose Lepidus, the worst! It will be well for you to be vigilant, now that you have strengthened your opponent against yourself." Sylla spoke this, it may seem, by a prophetic instinct, for, not long after, Lepidus grew insolent, and broke into open hostility to Pompey and his friends.

Sylla, consecrating the tenth of his whole substance to Hercules, entertained the people with sumptuous feastings. The provision was so much above what was necessary, that they were forced daily to throw great quantities of meat into the river, and they drank wine forty years old and upwards. In the midst of the banqueting, which lasted many days, Metella died of a disease. And because that the priest forbade him to visit the sick, or suffer his house to be polluted with mourning, he drew up an act of divorce, and caused her to be removed into another house whilst alive. Thus far, out of religious apprehension, he observed the strict rule to the very letter, but in the funeral expenses he transgressed the law he himself had made, limiting the amount, and spared no cost. He transgressed, likewise, his own sumptuary laws respecting expenditure in banquets, thinking to allay his grief by luxurious drinking parties and revellings with common buffoons.

Some few months after, at a show of gladiators, when men and women sat promiscuously in the theatre, no distinct places being as yet appointed, there sat down by Sylla a beautiful woman of high birth, by name Valeria, daughter of Messala, and sister to Hortensius the orator. Now it happened that she had been lately divorced from her husband. Passing along behind Sylla, she leaned on him with her hand, and plucking a bit of wool from his garment, so proceeded to her seat. And on Sylla looking up and wondering what it meant, "What harm, mighty Sir," said she, "if I also was desirous to partake a little in your felicity?" It appeared at once that Sylla was not displeased, but even tickled in his fancy, for he sent out to inquire her name, her birth, and past life. From this time there passed between them many side glances, each continually turning round to look at the other, and frequently interchanging smiles. In the end, overtures were made, and a marriage concluded on. All which was innocent, perhaps, on the lady's side, but, though she had been never so modest and virtuous, it was scarcely a temperate and worthy occasion of marriage on the part of Sylla, to take fire, as a boy might, at a face and a bold look, incentives not seldom to the most disorderly and shameless passions.

Notwithstanding this marriage, he kept company with actresses, musicians, and dancers, drinking with them on couches night and day. His chief favorites were Roscius the comedian, Sorex the arch mime, and Metrobius the player, for whom, though past his prime, he still professed a passionate fondness. By these courses he encouraged a disease which had begun from some unimportant cause; and for a long time he failed to observe that his bowels were ulcerated, till at length the corrupted flesh broke out into lice. Many were employed day and night in destroying them, but the work so multiplied under their hands, that not only his clothes, baths, basins, but his very meat was polluted with that flux and contagion, they came swarming out in such numbers. He went frequently by day into the bath to scour and cleanse his body, but all in vain; the evil generated too rapidly and too abundantly for any ablutions to overcome it. There died of this disease, amongst those of the most ancient times, Acastus, the son of Pelias; of later date, Alcman the poet, Pherecydes the theologian, Callisthenes the Olynthian, in the time of his imprisonment, as also Mucius the lawyer; and if we may mention ignoble, but notorious names, Eunus the fugitive, who stirred up the slaves of Sicily to rebel against their masters, after he was brought captive to Rome, died of this creeping sickness.

Sylla not only foresaw his end, but may be also said to have written of it. For in the two and twentieth book of his Memoirs, which he finished two days before his death, he writes that the Chaldeans foretold him, that after he had led a life of honor, he should conclude it in fulness of prosperity. He declares, moreover, that in a vision he had seen his son, who had died not long before Metella, stand by in mourning attire, and beseech his father to cast off further care, and come along with him to his mother Metella, there to live at ease and quietness with her. However, he could not refrain from intermeddling in public affairs. For, ten days before his decease, he composed the differences of the people of Dicæarchia,[18] and prescribed laws for their better govern-

---

[18] The Greek name of Puteoli, the modern Pozzuoli, which was originally, indeed, a Greek town, a colony like Naples itself,

ment. And the very day before his end, it being told him that the magistrate Granius deferred the payment of a public debt, in expectation of his death, he sent for him to his house, and placing his attendants about him, caused him to be strangled; but through the straining of his voice and body, the imposthume breaking, he lost a great quantity of blood. Upon this, his strength failing him, after spending a troublesome night, he died, leaving behind him two young children by Metella. Valeria was afterwards delivered of a daughter, named Posthuma; for so the Romans call those who are born after the father's death.

Many ran tumultuously together, and joined with Lepidus, to deprive the corpse of the accustomed solemnities; but Pompey, though offended at Sylla, (for he alone of all his friends, was not mentioned in his will,) having kept off some by his interest and entreaty, others by menaces, conveyed the body to Rome, and gave it a secure and honorable burial. It is said that the Roman ladies contributed such vast heaps of spices, that besides what was carried on two hundred and ten litters, there was sufficient to form a large figure of Sylla himself, and another, representing a lictor, out of the costly frankincense and cinnamon. The day being cloudy in the morning, they deferred carrying forth the corpse till about three in the afternoon, expecting it would rain. But a strong wind blowing full upon the funeral pile, and setting it all in a bright flame, the body was consumed so exactly in good time, that the pyre had begun to smoulder, and the fire was upon the point of expiring, when a violent rain came down, which con-

from the neighboring and ancient Greek settlement, Cumæ. Sylla was residing here.

tinued till night. So that his good fortune was firm even to the last, and did as it were officiate at his funeral. His monument stands in the Campus Martius, with an epitaph of his own writing; the substance of it being, that he had not been outdone by any of his friends in doing good turns, nor by any of his foes in doing bad.

COMPARISON OF LYSANDER WITH SYLLA.

HAVING completed this Life also, come we now to the comparison. That which was common to them both, was that they were founders of their own greatness, with this difference, that Lysander had the consent of his fellow-citizens, in times of sober judgment, for the honors he received; nor did he force any thing from them against their good-will, nor hold any power contrary to the laws.

> In civil strife e'en villians rise to fame.

And so then at Rome, when the people were distempered, and the government out of order, one or other was still raised to despotic power; no wonder, then, if Sylla reigned, when the Glauciæ and Saturnini drove out the Metelli, when sons of consuls were slain in the assemblies, when silver and gold purchased men and arms, and fire and sword enacted new laws, and put down lawful opposition. Nor do I blame any one, in such circumstances, for working himself into supreme power, only I would not have it thought a sign of great goodness, to be head of a State so wretchedly discomposed. Lysander, being employed in the greatest commands and affairs of State, by a sober and well-governed city, may be said to have had repute as the best and most virtuous man, in the best and most virtuous commonwealth. And thus, often returning the government into the hands of the citizens, he received it again as often, the superiority of his merit still awarding him them first place. Sylla, on the other hand, when he had once made himself general of an army, kept his command for ten years together, creating himself sometimes consul, sometimes proconsul, and sometimes dictator, but always remaining a tyrant.

It is true Lysander, as was said, designed to introduce a new form of government; by milder methods, however, and more agreeably to law than Sylla, not by force of arms, but persuasion, nor by subverting the whole State at once, but simply by amending the succession of the kings; in a way, moreover, which seemed the naturally just one, that the most deserving should rule, especially in a city which itself exercised command in Greece, upon account of virtue, not nobility. For as the hunter considers the whelp itself, not the bitch, and the horse-dealer the foal, not the mare, (for what if the foal should prove a mule?) so likewise were that politician extremely out, who, in the choice of a chief magistrate, should inquire, not what the man is, but how descended. The very Spartans themselves have deposed several of their kings for want of kingly virtues, as degenerated and good for nothing. As a vicious nature, though of an ancient stock, is dishonorable, it must be virtue itself, and not birth, that makes virtue honorable. Furthermore, the one committed his acts of injustice for the sake of his friends; the other extended his to his friends themselves. It is confessed on all hands, that Lysander offended most commonly for the sake of his companions, committing several slaughters to uphold their power and dominion; but as for Sylla, he, out of envy, reduced Pompey's command by land, and Dolabella's by sea, although he himself had given them those places; and ordered Lucretius Ofella, who sued for the consulship as the reward of many great services, to be slain before his eyes, exciting horror and alarm in the minds of all men, by his cruelty to his dearest friends.

As regards the pursuit of riches and pleasures, we yet further discover in one a princely, in the other a tyrannical disposition. Lysander did nothing that was intemperate or licentious, in that full command of means and opportunity, but kept clear, as much as ever man did, of that trite saying,

> Lions at home, but foxes out of doors;[1]

and ever maintained a sober, truly Spartan, and well-disciplined course of conduct. Whereas Sylla could never moderate his unruly affections, either by poverty when young, or by years when grown old, but would be still prescribing laws to the citizens concerning chastity and sobriety, himself living all that time, as Sallust affirms, in lewdness and adultery. By these ways he so impoverished and drained the city of her treasures, as to be forced to sell privileges and immunities to allied and friendly cities for money, although he daily gave up the wealthiest and greatest families to public sale and confiscation. There was no end of his favors vainly spent and thrown away on flatterers; for what hope could there be, or what likelihood of forethought or economy, in his more private moments over wine, when, in the open face of the people, upon the auction of a large estate, which he would have passed over to one of his friends at a small price, because another bid higher, and the officer announced the advance, he broke out into a passion,

---

[1] The proverb *Lions at home* occurs in verse, but not in the same form, in Aristophanes's play of the Peace (1189). The scholiast, in his note on the passage, says it was originally said of the Spartans after some mishap in Ionia, "Lions at home, but in Ephesus—mere Laconians." *Sallust's affirmation* about Sylla was probably made in one of his lost Histories.

saying, "What a strange and unjust thing is this, O citizens, that I cannot dispose of my own booty as I please!" But Lysander, on the contrary, with the rest of the spoil, sent home for public use even the presents which were made him. Nor do I commend him for it, for he, perhaps, by excessive liberality, did Sparta more harm, than ever the other did Rome by rapine; I only use it as an argument of his indifference to riches. They exercised a strange influence on their respective cities. Sylla, a profuse debauchee, endeavored to restore sober living amongst the citizens; Lysander, temperate himself, filled Sparta with the luxury he disregarded. So that both were blameworthy, the one for raising himself above his own laws, the other for causing his fellow-citizens to fall beneath his own example. He taught Sparta to want the very things which he himself had learned to do without. And thus much of their civil administration.

As for feats of arms, wise conduct in war, innumerable victories, perilous adventures, Sylla was beyond compare. Lysander, indeed, came off twice victorious in two battles by sea; I shall add to that the siege of Athens, a work of greater fame, than difficulty. What occurred in Bœotia, and at Haliartus, was the result, perhaps, of ill fortune; yet it certainly looks like ill counsel, not to wait for the king's forces, which had all but arrived from Platæa, but out of ambition and eagerness to fight, to approach the walls at disadvantage, and so to be cut off by a sally of inconsiderable men. He received his death-wound, not as Cleombrotus at Leuctra, resisting manfully the assault of an enemy in the field; not as Cyrus or Epaminondas, sustaining the declining battle, or making sure the victory; all these died the death of kings and generals; but he, as it had been some common skirmisher or scout, cast away his life ingloriously, giving testimony to the wisdom of the ancient Spartan maxim, to avoid attacks on walled cities, in which the stoutest warrior may chance to fall by the hand, not only of a man utterly his inferior, but by that of a boy or woman, as Achilles, they say, was slain by Paris in the gates. As for Sylla, it were hard to reckon up how many set battles he won, or how many thousands he slew; he took Rome itself twice, as also the Athenian Piræus, not by famine, as Lysander did, but by a series of great battles, driving Archelaus into the sea. And what is most important, there was a vast difference between the commanders they had to deal with. For I look upon it as an easy task, or rather sport, to beat Antiochus, Alcibiades's pilot, or to circumvent Philocles, the Athenian demagogue,

> Sharp only at the inglorious point of tongue,[2]

whom Mithridates would have scorned to compare with his groom, or Marius with his lictor. But of the potentates, consuls, commanders, and demagogues, to pass by all the rest who opposed themselves to Sylla, who amongst the Romans so formidable as Marius? what king more powerful than Mithridates? who of the Italians more warlike than Lamponius and Telesinus? yet of these, one he drove into banishment, one he quelled, and the others he slew.

And what is more important, in my judgment, than any thing yet adduced, is that Lysander had the assistance of the State in all his achievements; whereas Sylla, besides that he was a banished person, and overpowered by a faction, at a time when his wife was driven from home, his houses demolished, and adherents slain, himself then in Bœotia, stood embattled against countless numbers of the public enemy,

[2] A verse of which nothing is known.

and endangering himself for the sake of his country, raised a trophy of victory; and not even when Mithridates came with proposals of alliance and aid against his enemies, would he show any sort of compliance, or even clemency; did not so much as address him, or vouchsafe him his hand, until he had it from the king's own mouth, that he was willing to quit Asia, surrender the navy, and restore Bithynia and Cappadocia to the two kings. Than which action, Sylla never performed a braver, or with a nobler spirit, when, preferring the public good to the private, and like good hounds, where he had once fixed, never letting go his hold, till the enemy yielded, then, and not until then, he set himself to revenge his own private quarrels. We may perhaps let ourselves be influenced, moreover, in our comparison of their characters, by considering their treatment of Athens. Sylla, when he had made himself master of the city, which then upheld the dominion and power of Mithridates in opposition to him, restored her to liberty and the free exercise of her own laws; Lysander, on the contrary, when she had fallen from a vast height of dignity and rule, showed her no compassion, but abolishing her democratic government, imposed on her the most cruel and lawless tyrants. We are now qualified to consider, whether we should go far from the truth or no, in pronouncing that Sylla performed the more glorious deeds, but Lysander committed the fewer faults, as, likewise, by giving to one the preëminence for moderation and self-control, to the other, for conduct and valor.

CIMON[1]

TRANSLATED BY MAT. MORGAN, A. M., OF
ST. JOHN'S COLLEGE, OXFORD.

PERIPOLTAS, the prophet having brought the king Opheltas, and those under his command, from Thessaly into Bœotia, left there a family, which flourished a long time after; the greatest part of them inhabiting Chæronea, the first city out of which they expelled the barbarians. The descendants of this race, being men of bold attempts and warlike habits, exposed themselves to so many dangers, in the invasions of the Mede, and in battles against the Gauls, that at last they were almost wholly consumed.

There was left one orphan of this house, called Damon, surnamed Peripoltas, in beauty and greatness of spirit surpassing all of his age, but rude and undisciplined in temper. A Roman captain of a company that wintered in Chæronea became passionately fond of this youth, who was now pretty nearly grown a man. And finding all his approaches, his gifts, and his entreaties alike repulsed, he showed violent inclinations to assault Damon. Our native Chæronea was then in a distressed condition, too small and too poor to meet with any thing but neglect. Damon, being sensible of this, and looking upon himself as injured

---

[1] Born 504 B. C. His most brilliant success was in 466, when he defeated the Persian fleet. The death of Aristides and the banishment of Themistocles left Cimon without a rival at Athens for some years but his influence gradually declined as that of Pericles increased. He died in 449.—Dr. William Smith.

already, resolved to inflict punishment. Accordingly, he and sixteen of his companions conspired against the captain; but that the design might be managed without any danger of being discovered, they all daubed their faces at night with soot. Thus disguised and inflamed with wine, they set upon him by break of day, as he was sacrificing in the market-place; and having killed him, and several others that were with him, they fled out of the city, which was extremely alarmed and troubled at the murder. The council assembled immediately, and pronounced sentence of death against Damon and his accomplices. This they did to justify the city to the Romans. But that evening, as the magistrates were at supper together, according to the custom, Damon and his confederates breaking into the hall, killed them, and then again fled out of the town. About this time, Lucius Lucullus chanced to be passing that way with a body of troops, upon some expedition, and this disaster having but recently happened, he stayed to examine the matter. Upon inquiry, he found the city was in nowise faulty, but rather that they themselves had suffered; therefore he drew out the soldiers, and carried them away with him. Yet Damon continuing to ravage the country all about, the citizens, by messages and decrees, in appearance favorable, enticed him into the city, and upon his return, made him Gymnasiarch;[2] but afterwards as he was anointing himself in the vapor baths, they set upon him and killed him. For a long while after apparitions continuing to be seen, and groans to be heard in that place, so our fathers have told us, they ordered the gates of the baths to be built up; and

[2] Superintendent of the public gymnasia and palæstræ, gymnastic schools and exercising grounds; undoubtedly a public office, and regarded, most likely, as a considerable honor.

even to this day those who live in the neighborhood believe that they sometimes see spectres, and hear alarming sounds. The posterity of Damon, of whom some still remain, mostly in Phocis, near the town of Stiris, are called Asbolomeni, that is, in the Æolian idiom, men daubed with soot; because Damon was thus besmeared when he committed this murder.

But there being a quarrel between the people of Chæronea and the Orchomenians, their neighbors, these latter hired an informer, a Roman, to accuse the community of Chæronea, as if it had been a single person, of the murder of the Romans, of which only Damon and his companions were guilty; accordingly, the process was commenced, and the cause pleaded before the Prætor of Macedon, since the Romans as yet had not sent governors into Greece.

The advocates who defended the inhabitants appealed to the testimony of Lucullus, who, in answer to a letter the Prætor wrote to him, returned a true account of the matter-of-fact. By this means the town obtained its acquittal, and escaped a most serious danger. The citizens thus preserved erected a statue to Lucullus in the market-place, near that of the god Bacchus.

We also have the same impressions of gratitude; and though removed from the events by the distance of several generations, we yet feel the obligation to extend to ourselves; and as we think an image of the character and habits, to be a greater honor than one merely representing the face and the person, we will put Lucullus's life amongst our parallels of illustrious men, and without swerving from the truth, will record his actions. The commemoration will be itself a sufficient proof of our grateful feeling, and he himself would not thank us, if in recompense for a service, which consisted in speaking the truth, we should abuse his memory with a false and counterfeit narration. For as we would wish that a painter who is to draw a beautiful face, in which there is yet some imperfection, should neither wholly leave out, nor yet too pointedly express what is defective, because this would deform it, and that spoil the resemblance; so, since it is hard, or indeed perhaps impossible, to show the life of a man wholly free from blemish, in all that is excellent we must follow truth exactly, and give it fully; any lapses or faults that occur, through human passions or political necessities, we may regard rather as the short-comings of some particular virtue, than as the natural effects of vice; and may be content without introducing them, curiously and officiously, into our narrative, if it be but out of tenderness to the weakness of nature, which has never succeeded in producing any human character so perfect in virtue, as to be pure from all admixture, and open to no criticism. On considering with myself to whom I should compare Lucullus, I find none so exactly his parallel as Cimon.

They were both valiant in war, and successful against the barbarians; both gentle in political life, and more than any others gave their countrymen a respite from civil troubles at home, while abroad, each of them raised trophies and gained famous victories. No Greek before Cimon, nor Roman before Lucullus, ever carried the scene of war so far from their own country; putting out of the question the acts of Bacchus and Hercules, and any exploit of Perseus against the Ethiopians, Medes, and Armenians, or again of Jason, of which any record that deserves credit can be said to have come down to our days. Moreover in this they were alike, that they did not finish the enterprises they undertook. They brought their enemies near their ruin, but never entirely conquered them. There was yet a greater conformity in the free good-will and lavish abundance of their entertainments and general hospitalities, and in the youthful laxity of their habits. Other points of resemblance, which we have failed to notice, may be easily collected from our narrative itself.

Cimon was the son of Miltiades and Hegesipyle, who was by birth a Thracian, and daughter to the king. Olorus, as appears from the poems of Melanthius and Archelaus, written in praise of Cimon. By this means the historian Thucydides was his kinsman by the mother's side; for his father's name also, in remembrance of this common ancestor, was Olorous, and he was the owner of gold mines in Thrace, and met his death, it is said, by violence, in Scapte Hyle, a district of Thrace; and his remains having afterwards been brought into Attica, a monument is shown as his among those of the family of Cimon, near the tomb of Elpinice, Cimon's sister. But Thucydides was of the township of Halimus, and Miltiades and his family were Laciadæ.[3] Miltiades, being condemned in a fine of fifty talents to the State, and unable to pay it, was cast into prison, and there died. Thus Cimon was left an orphan very young, with his sister Elpinice, who was also young and unmarried. And at first he had but an indifferent reputation, being looked upon as disorderly in his habits, fond of drinking, and resembling his grandfather, also called Cimon, in character, whose simplicity got him the sur-

---

[3] *Miltiades and his family were Laciadæ,* or Laciads, this being the name of the members of the township or *demus* of Lacia, which itself was more commonly thus called, the township Laciadæ or the Laciads. For the quotation *Rude and unrefined,* see a note on the life of Marcellus at the end of Vol. II.

name of Coalemus.[4] Stesimbrotus of Thasos, who lived near about the same time with Cimon, reports of him that he had little acquaintance either with music, or any of the other liberal studies and accomplishments, then common among the Greeks; that he had nothing whatever of the quickness and the ready speech of his countrymen in Attica; that he had great nobleness and candor in his disposition, and in his character in general, resembled rather a native of Peloponnesus, than of Athens; as Euripides describes Hercules,

——— Rude
And unrefined, for great things well-endued;

for this may fairly be added to the character which Stesimbrotus has given of him.

They accused him, in his younger years, of cohabiting with his own sister Elpinice, who, indeed, otherwise had no very clear reputation, but was reported to have been over intimate with Polygnotus, the painter; and hence, when he painted the Trojan women in the porch, then called the Plesianactium, and now the Pœcile, he made Laodice [5] a portrait of her. Polygnotus was not an ordinary mechanic, nor was he paid for this work, but out of a desire to please the Athenians, painted the portico for nothing. So it is stated by the historians, and in the following verses by the poet Melanthius:—

Wrought by his hand the deeds of heroes grace
At his own charge our temples and our Place.[6]

[4] The simpleton.

[5] *Laodice, of the daughters of Priam the best in appearance,* occurs in the third Iliad (124). Iris took her form when she went to summon Helen to the walls, in the interval before the combat between Paris and Menelaus.

[6] The agŏra, the public meeting or market-place; the place

CIMON

Some affirm that Elpinice lived with her brother, not secretly, but as his married wife, her poverty excluding her from any suitable match. But afterward, when Callias, one of the richest men of Athens, fell in love with her, and proffered to pay the fine the father was condemned in, if he could obtain the daughter in marriage, with Elpinice's own consent, Cimon betrothed her to Callias. There is no doubt but that Cimon was, in general, of an amorous temper. For Melanthius, in his elegies, rallies him on his attachment for Asteria of Salamis, and again for a certain Mnestra. And there can be no doubt of his unusually passionate affection for his lawful wife Isodice, the daughter of Euryptolemus, the son of Megacles; nor of his regret, even to impatience, at her death, if any conclusion may be drawn from those elegies of condolence, addressed to him upon his loss of her. The philosopher Panætius is of opinion, that Archelaus, the writer on physics, was the author of them, and indeed the time seems to favor that conjecture. All the other points of Cimon's character were noble and good. He was as daring as Miltiades, and not inferior to Themistocles in judgment, and was incomparably more just and honest than either of them. Fully their equal in all military virtues, in the ordinary duties of a citizen at home he was immeasurably their superior. And this, too, when he was very young, his years not yet strengthened by any experience. For

---

found in every Greek town, where, as the Persian noble scoffingly said, "they met together to cheat each other"; the scene, however, not of business only, but of politics, law, and amusement. The *Place* of the cities of southern Europe, that of St. Mark, for example, at Venice, still gives the image of it. In northern towns, shelter from the weather confines within doors much that in Greece was done under the open sky, or under colonnades; yet the Exchange, in some cases, shows a resemblance.

when Themistocles, upon the Median invasion, advised the Athenians to forsake their city and their country, and to carry all their arms on shipboard, and fight the enemy by sea, in the straits of Salamis; when all the people stood amazed at the confidence and rashness of this advice, Cimon was seen, the first of all men, passing with a cheerful countenance through the Ceramicus, on his way with his companions to the citadel, carrying a bridle in his hand to offer to the goddess, intimating that there was no more need of horsemen now, but of mariners. There, after he had paid his devotions to the goddess, and offered up the bridle, he took down one of the bucklers that hung upon the walls of the temple, and went down to the port; by this example giving confidence to many of the citizens. He was also of a fairly handsome person, according to the poet Ion, tall and large, and let his thick and curly hair grow long. After he had acquitted himself gallantly in this battle of Salamis, he obtained great repute among the Athenians, and was regarded with affection, as well as admiration. He had many who followed after him, and bade him aspire to actions not less famous than his father's battle of Marathon. And when he came forward in political life, the people welcomed him gladly, being now weary of Themistocles; in opposition to whom, and because of the frankness and easiness of his temper, which was agreeable to every one, they advanced Cimon to the highest employments in the government. The man that contributed most to his promotion was Aristides, who early discerned in his character his natural capacity, and purposly raised him, that he might be a counterpoise to the craft and boldness of Themistocles.

After the Medes had been driven out of Greece, Cimon was sent out as admiral, when the Athenians had not yet attained their dominion by sea, but still followed Pausanias and the Lacedæmonians; and his fellow-citizens under his command were highly distinguished, both for the excellence of their discipline, and for their extraordinary zeal and readiness. And further, perceiving that Pausanias was carrying on secret communications with the barbarians, and writing letters to the king of Persia to betray Greece, and, puffed up with authority and success, was treating the allies haughtily, and committing many wanton injustices, Cimon, taking this advantage, by acts of kindness to those who were suffering wrong, and by his general humane bearing, robbed him of the command of the Greeks, before he was aware, not by arms, but by his mere language and character. The greatest part of the allies, no longer able to endure the harshness and pride of Pausanias, revolted from him to Cimon and Aristides, who accepted the duty, and wrote to the Ephors of Sparta, desiring them to recall a man who was causing dishonor to Sparta, and trouble to Greece. They tell of Pausanias, that when he was in Byzantium, he solicited a young lady of a noble family in the city, whose name was Cleonice, to debauch her. Her parents, dreading his cruelty, were forced to consent, and so abandoned their daughter to his wishes. The daughter asked the servants outside the chamber to put out all the lights; so that approaching silently and in the dark toward his bed, she stumbled upon the lamp, which she overturned. Pausanias, who was fallen asleep, awakened and startled with the noise, thought an assassin had taken that dead time of night to murder him, so that hastily snatching up his poniard that lay by him, he struck the girl, who fell with the blow, and died. After this, he never had rest, but was continually haunted by her, and saw an apparition visiting him in his sleep, and addressing him with these angry words:—

> Go on thy way, unto the evil end,
> That doth on lust and violence attend.

This was one of the chief occasions of indignation against him among the confederates, who now joining their resentments and forces with Cimon's, besieged him in Byzantium. He escaped out of their hands, and, continuing, as it is said, to be disturbed by the apparition, fled to the oracle of the dead at Heraclea, raised the ghost of Cleonice, and entreated her to be reconciled. Accordingly she appeared to him, and answered, that as soon as he came to Sparta, he should speedily be freed from all evils; obscurely foretelling, it would seem, his imminent death. This story is related by many authors.

Cimon, strengthened with the accession of the allies, went as general into Thrace. For he was told that some great men among the Persians, of the king's kindred, being in possession of Eion, a city situated upon the river Strymon, infested the neighboring Greeks. First he defeated these Persians in battle, and shut them up within the walls of their town. Then he fell upon the Thracians of the country beyond the Strymon, because they supplied Eion with victuals, and driving them entirely out of the country, took possession of it as conqueror, by which means he reduced the besieged to such straits, that Butes, who commanded there for the king, in desperation set fire to the town, and burned himself, his goods, and all his relations, in one common flame. By this means, Cimon got the town, but no great booty; as the barbarians had not only consumed themselves in the fire, but the richest of their effects. However, he put the country about into the hands of the Athenians, a most advantageous and desirable situation for a settlement. For this action, the people permitted him to erect the stone Mercuries, upon the first of which was this inscription:—

> Of bold and patient spirit, too, were those,
> Who, where the Strymon under Eion flows,
> With famine and the sword, to utmost need
> Reduced at last the children of the Mede.

Upon the second stood this:—

> The Athenians to their leaders this reward
> For great and useful service did accord;
> Others hereafter, shall, from their applause,
> Learn to be valiant in their country's cause.

and upon the third, the following:—

> With Atreus' sons, this city sent of yore
> Divine Menestheus to the Trojan shore;
> Of all the Greeks, so Homer's verses say,
> The ablest man an army to array:
> So old the title of her sons the name
> Of chiefs and champions in the field to claim.[7]

Though the name of Cimon is not mentioned in these inscriptions, yet his contemporaries considered them to be the very highest honors to him; as neither Miltiades nor Themistocles ever received the like. When Miltiades claimed a garland, Sochares of Decelea, stood up in the midst of the assembly and opposed it, using words which, though ungracious, were received with applause by the people. "When you have gained a victory by yourself, Miltiades, then you may

---

[7] These inscriptions are quoted by Æschines (*In Ctesiphont.*, p. 573), in his speech on the Crown; the simple honors of old times contrasting favorably for his purpose with those now offered to Demosthenes. *Butes* is Boges in Herodotus, and *Sochares* (p. 208) in Sophanes.

ask to triumph so too." What then induced them so particularly to honor Cimon? Was it that under other commanders they stood upon the defensive? but by his conduct, they not only attacked their enemies, but invaded them in their own country, and acquired new territory, becoming masters of Eion and Amphipolis, where they planted colonies, as also they did in the isle of Scyros, which Cimon had taken on the following occasion. The Dolopians were the inhabitants of this isle, a people who neglected all husbandry, and had, for many generations, been devoted to piracy; this they practised to that degree, that at last they began to plunder foreigners that brought merchandise into their ports. Some merchants of Thessaly, who had come to shore near Ctesium, were not only spoiled of their goods, but themselves put into confinement. These men afterwards escaping from their prison, went and obtained sentence against the Scyrians in a court of Amphictyons, and when the Scyrian people declined to make public restitution, and called upon the individuals who had got the plunder to give it up, these persons, in alarm, wrote to Cimon to succor them with his fleet, and declared themselves ready to deliver the town into his hands. Cimon, by these means, got the town, expelled the Dolopian pirates, and so opened the traffic of the Ægean sea. And, understanding that the ancient Theseus, the son of Ægeus, when he fled from Athens and took refuge in this isle, was here treacherously slain by king Lycomedes, who feared him, Cimon endeavored to find out where he was buried. For an oracle had commanded the Athenians to bring home his ashes, and pay him all due honors as a hero; but hitherto they had not been able to learn where he was interred, as the people of Scyros dissembled the knowledge of it, and were not willing to allow a search. But now, great inquiry being made, with some difficulty he found out the tomb, and carried the relics into his own galley, and with great pomp and show brought them to Athens, four hundred years, or thereabouts, after his expulsion. This act got Cimon great favor with the people, one mark of which was the judgment, afterwards so famous, upon the tragic poets. Sophocles, still a young man, had just brought forward his first plays; opinions were much divided, and the spectators had taken sides with some heat. So, to determine the case, Apsephion, who was at that time archon, would not cast lots who should be judges; but when Cimon, and his brother commanders with him, came into the theatre, after they had performed the usual rites to the god of the festival, he would not allow them to retire, but came forward and made them swear, (being ten in all, one from each tribe,) the usual oath; and so being sworn judges, he made them sit down to give sentence. The eagerness for victory grew all the warmer, from the ambition to get the suffrages of such honorable judges. And the victory was at last adjudged to Sophocles, which Æschylus is said to have taken so ill, that he left Athens shortly after, and went in anger to Sicily, where he died, and was buried near the city of Gela.

Ion relates that when he was a young man, and recently come from Chios to Athens, he chanced to sup with Cimon, at Laomedon's house. After supper, when they had, according to custom, poured out wine to the honor of the gods, Cimon was desired by the company to give them a song, which he did with sufficient success, and received the commendations of the company, who remarked on his superiority to Themistocles, who, on a like occasion, had declared he had never learnt to sing, nor to play, and only knew how to make a city rich and powerful. After talking of things incident to such entertainments, they entered upon the particulars of the several actions for which Cimon had been famous. And when they were mentioning the most signal, he told them they had omitted one, upon which he valued himself most for address and good contrivance. He gave this account of it. When the allies had taken a great number of the barbarians prisoners in Sestos and Byzantium, they gave him the preference to divide the booty; he accordingly put the prisoners in one lot, and the spoils of their rich attire and jewels in the other. This the allies complained of as an unequal division; but he gave them their choice to take which lot they would, for that the Athenians should be content with that which they refused. Herophytus of Samos advised them to take the ornaments for their share, and leave the slaves to the Athenians; and Cimon went away, and was much laughed at for his ridiculous division. For the allies carried away the golden bracelets, and armlets, and collars, and purple robes, and the Athenians had only the naked bodies of the captives, which they could make no advantage of, being unused to labor. But a little while after, the friends and kinsmen of the prisoners coming from Lydia and Phrygia, redeemed every one his relations at a high ransom; so that by this means Cimon got so much treasure that he maintained his whole fleet of galleys with the money for four months; and yet there was some left to lay up in the treasury at Athens.

Cimon now grew rich, and what he gained from the barbarians with honor, he spent yet more honorably upon the citizens. For he pulled down all the enclosures of his gardens and grounds, that strangers, and the needy of his follow-citizens, might gather of his fruits freely. At home, he kept a table, plain, but sufficient for a considerable number; to which any poor

CIMON

townsman had free access, and so might support himself without labor, with his whole time left free for public duties. Aristotle states, however, that this reception did not extend to all the Athenians, but only to his own fellow townsmen, the Laciadæ.[8] Besides this, he always went attended by two or three young companions, very well clad; and if he met with an elderly citizen in a poor habit, one of these would change clothes with the decayed citizen, which was looked upon as very nobly done. He enjoined them, likewise, to carry a considerable quantity of coin about them, which they were to convey silently into the hands of the better class of poor men, as they stood by them in the market-place. This, Cratinus the poet speaks of in one of his comedies, the Archilochi:—

> For I, Metrobius too, the scrivener poor,
> Of ease and comfort in my age secure,
> By Greece's noblest son in life's decline,
> Cimon, the generous-hearted, the divine,
> Well-fed and feasted hoped till death to be,
> Death which, alas! has taken him ere me.

Gorgias the Leontine gives him this character, that he got riches that he might use them, and used them that he might get honor by them. And Critias, one of

---

[8] Every Athenian citizen belonged, as such, to a particular town or township, one of the demi, of which there were above a hundred in Attica, in the latest times one hundred and seventy-four, all distinct localities; but, as a man, wherever he lived, continued to belong to his father's township, the relation was not strictly a local, but rather a personal one. The town-meetings were all held in Athens. Politically, the demi were, perhaps, hardly more than wards for registration, but socially, by connecting every man with a particular district, the institution seems to have exercised a good deal of practical influence. Cimon's town, Lacia, or the Laciadæ, was just out of Athens, on the road to Eleusis.

the thirty tyrants, makes it, in his elegies, his wish to have

> The Scopads' wealth, and Cimon's nobleness,
> And king Agesilaus's success.[9]

Lichas, we know, became famous in Greece, only because on the days of the sports, when the young boys run naked, he used to entertain the strangers that came to see these diversions. But Cimon's generosity outdid all the old Athenian hospitality and good-nature. For though it is the city's just boast that their forefathers taught the rest of Greece to sow corn, and how to use springs of water,[10] and to kindle fire, yet Cimon, by keeping [11] open house for his fellow-citizens, and giving travellers liberty to eat the fruits which the several seasons produced in his land, seemed to restore to the world that community of goods, which mythology says existed in the reign of Saturn. Those who object to him that he did this to be popular, and gain the applause of the vulgar, are confuted by the constant tenor of the rest of his actions, which all tended to uphold the interests of the nobility and the Spartan policy, of which he gave instances, when together with

---

[9] *King Agesilaus* is a doubtful reading; *Agesilas* or *Arcesilas* is more probable.

[10] "Ont aussi monstré *l'usage* des fonteines, and comment il faloit allumer et entretenir le feu," is Amyot's version. The word immediately preceding *"springs of water,"* has apparently been lost in the present Greek text, and it is hard to say what it was. The mere *use* of springs seems too obvious a thing to have been intended.

[11] Literally, "making his house a sort of private prytaneum, for his fellow-citizens." The prytaneum, or state-house, being frequently used for entertaining distinguished citizens, as well as strangers. Compare in the Life of Lucullus, the passage where his house is called a prytaneum for Greek visitors at Rome.

Aristides, he opposed Themistocles, who was advancing the authority of the people beyond its just limits, and resisted Ephialtes, who to please the multitude, was for abolishing the jurisdiction of the court of Areopagus. And when all of his time, except Aristides and Ephialtes, enriched themselves out of the public money, he still kept his hands clean and untainted, and to his last day never acted or spoke for his own private gain or emolument. They tell us that Rhœsaces, a Persian, who had traitorously revolted from the king his master, fled to Athens, and there, being harassed by sycophants, who were still accusing him to the people, he applied himself to Cimon for redress, and to gain his favor, laid down in his doorway two cups, the one full of gold, and the other of silver Darics. Cimon smiled and asked him whether he wished to have Cimon's hired service or his friendship. He replied, his friendship. "If so," said he, "take away these pieces, for being your friend, when I shall have occasion for them, I will send and ask for them."

The allies of the Athenians began now to be weary of war and military service, willing to have repose, and to look after their husbandry and traffic. For they saw their enemies driven out of the country, and did not fear any new vexations from them. They still paid the tax they were assessed at, but did not send men and galleys, as they had done before. This the other Athenian generals wished to constrain them to, and by judicial proceedings against defaulters, and penalties which they inflicted on them, made the government uneasy, and even odious. But Cimon practised a contrary method; he forced no man to go that was not willing, but of those that desired to be excused from service he took money and vessels unmanned, and let them yield to the temptation of staying at home, to attend to their private business. Thus they lost their military habits, and luxury, and their own folly quickly changed them into unwarlike husbandmen and traders, while Cimon, continually embarking large numbers of Athenians on board his galleys, thoroughly disciplined them in his expeditions, and ere long made them the lords of their own paymasters. The allies, whose indolence maintained them, while they thus went sailing about everywhere, and incessantly bearing arms and acquiring skill, began to fear and flatter them, and found themselves after a while allies no longer, but unwittingly become tributaries and slaves.

Nor did any man ever do more than Cimon did to humble the pride of the Persian king. He was not content with getting rid of him out of Greece; but following close at his heels, before the barbarians could take breath and recover themselves, he was already at work, and what with his devastations, and his forcible reduction of some places, and the revolts and voluntary accession of others, in the end, from Ionia to Pamphylia, all Asia was clear of Persian soldiers. Word being brought him that the royal commanders were lying in wait upon the coast of Pamphylia, with a numerous land army, and a large fleet, he determined to make the whole sea on this side the Chelidonian islands so formidable to them that they should never dare to show themselves in it; and setting off from Cnidos and the Triopian headland, with two hundred galleys, which had been originally built with particular care by Themistocles, for speed and rapid evolutions, and to which he now gave greater width and roomier decks along the sides to move to and fro upon, so as to allow a great number of full-armed soldiers to take part in the engagements and fight from them, he shaped his course first of all against the town of Phaselis, which, though inhabited by Greeks, yet would not quit the interests of Persia, but denied his galleys entrance into their port. Upon this he wasted the country, and drew up his army to their very walls; but the soldiers of Chios, who were then serving under him, being ancient friends to the Phaselites, endeavoring to propitiate the general in their behalf, at the same time shot arrows into the town, to which were fastened letters conveying intelligence. At length he concluded peace with them, upon the conditions that they should pay down ten talents and follow him against the barbarians. Ephorus says the admiral of the Persian fleet was Tithraustes, and the general of the land army Pherendates; but Callisthenes is positive that Ariomandes, the son of Gobryas, had the supreme command of all the forces. He lay waiting with the whole fleet at the mouth of the river Eurymedon, with no design to fight, but expecting a reinforcement of eighty Phœnician ships on their way from Cyprus. Cimon, aware of this, put out to sea, resolved, if they would not fight a battle willingly, to force them to it. The barbarians, seeing this, retired within the mouth of the river to avoid being attacked; but when they saw the Athenians come upon them, notwithstanding their retreat, they met them with six hundred ships, as Phanodemus relates, but according to Ephorus, only with three hundred and fifty. However, they did nothing worthy such mighty forces, but immediately turned the prows of their galleys toward the shore, where those that came first threw themselves upon the land, and fled to their army drawn up thereabout, while the rest perished with their vessels, or were taken. By this, one may guess at their number, for though a great many escaped out of the fight, and a great many others were sunk, yet two hundred galleys were taken by the Athenians.

When their land army drew toward the seaside,

Cimon was in suspense whether he should venture to try and force his way on shore; as he should thus expose his Greeks, wearied with slaughter in the first engagement, to the swords of the barbarians, who were all fresh men, and many times their number. But seeing his men resolute, and flushed with victory, he bade them land, though they were not yet cool from their first battle. As soon as they touched ground, they set up a shout and ran upon the enemy, who stood firm and sustained the first shock with great courage, so that the fight was a hard one, and some principal men of the Athenians in rank and courage were slain. At length, though with much ado, they routed the barbarians, and killing some, took others prisoners, and plundered all their tents and pavilions, which were full of rich spoil. Cimon, like a skilled athlete at the games, having in one day carried off two victories, wherein he surpassed that of Salamis by sea, and that of Platæa by land, was encouraged to try for yet another success. News being brought that the Phœnician succors, in number eighty sail, had come in sight of Hydrum, he set off with all speed to find them, while they as yet had not received any certain account of the larger fleet, and were in doubt what to think; so that thus surprised, they lost all their vessels, and most of their men with them. This success of Cimon so daunted the king of Persia, that he presently made that celebrated peace, by which he engaged that his armies should come no nearer the Grecian sea than the length of a horse's course; and that none of his galleys or vessels of war should appear between the Cyanean and Chelidonian isles. Callisthenes, however, says that he did not agree to any such articles, but that upon the fear this victory gave him, he did in reality thus act, and kept off so far from Greece, that when Pericles with fifty, and Ephialtes with thirty galleys, cruised beyond the Chelidonian isles, they did not discover one Persian vessel. But in the collection which Craterus made of the public acts of the people, there is a draft of this treaty given. And it is told, also, that at Athens they erected the altar of Peace upon this occasion, and decreed particular honors to Callias, who was employed as ambassador to procure the treaty.

The people of Athens raised so much money from the spoils of this war, which were publicly sold, that, besides other expenses, and raising the south wall of the citadel, they laid the foundation of the long walls, not, indeed, finished till at a later time, which were called the Legs. And the place where they built them being soft and marshy ground, they were forced to sink great weights of stone and rubble to secure the foundation, and did all this out of the money Cimon supplied them with. It was he, likewise, who first embellished the upper city with those fine and ornamental places of exercise and resort, which they afterward so much frequented and delighted in. He set the market-place with plane trees; and the Academy, which was before a bare, dry, and dirty spot, he converted into a well-watered grove, with shady alleys to walk in, and open courses for races.

When the Persians who had made themselves masters of the Chersonese, so far from quitting it, called in the people of the interior of Thrace to help them again Cimon, whom they despised for the smallness of his forces, he set upon them with only four galleys, and took thirteen of theirs; and having driven out the Persians, and subdued the Thracians, he made the whole Chersonese the property of Athens. Next, he attacked the people of Thasos, who had revolted from the Athenians; and, having defeated them in a fight at sea, where he took thirty-three of their vessels, he took their town by siege, and acquired for the Athenians all the mines of gold on the opposite coast, and the territory dependent on Thasos. This opened him a fair passage into Macedon, so that he might, it was thought, have acquired a good portion of that country; and because he neglected the opportunity, he was suspected of corruption, and of having been bribed off by king Alexander. So, by the combination of his adversaries, he was accused of being false to his country. In his defence he told the judges, that he had always shown himself in his public life the friend, not, like other men, of rich Ionians and Thessalians, to be courted, and to receive presents, but of the Lacedæmonians; for as he admired, so he wished to imitate the plainness of their habits, their temperance, and simplicity of living, which he preferred to any sort of riches; but that he always had been, and still was proud to enrich his country with the spoils of her enemies. Stesimbrotus, making mention of this trial, states that Elpinice, in behalf of her brother, addressed herself to Pericles, the most vehement of his accusers, to whom Pericles answered, with a smile, "You are old, Elpinice, to meddle with affairs of this nature." However, he proved the mildest of his prosecutors, and rose up but once all the while, almost as a matter of form, to plead against him. Cimon was acquitted.

In his public life after this, he continued, whilst at home, to control and restrain the common people, who would have trampled upon the nobility, and drawn all the power and sovereignty to themselves. But when he afterwards was sent out to war, the multitude broke loose, as it were, and overthrew all the ancient laws and customs they had hitherto observed, and, chiefly at the instigation of Ephialtes, withdrew the cognizance of almost all causes from the Areopagus; so that all jurisdiction now being transferred to them, the government was reduced to a perfect democracy, and this by the help of Pericles, who was already powerful, and had pronounced in favor of the common people. Cimon, when he returned, seeing the authority of this great council so upset, was exceedingly troubled, and endeavored to remedy these disorders by bringing the courts of law to their former state, and restoring the old aristocracy of the time of Clisthenes. This the others declaimed against with all the vehemence possible, and began to revive those stories concerning him and his sister, and cried out against him as the partisan of the Lacedæmonians. To these calumnies the famous verses of Eupolis, the poet, upon Cimon refer:—

> He was as good as others that one sees,
> But he was fond of drinking and of ease;
> And would at nights to Sparta often roam,
> Leaving his sister desolate at home.

But if, though slothful and a drunkard, he could capture so many towns, and gain so many victories, certainly if he had been sober and minded his business, there had been no Grecian commander, either before or after him, that could have surpassed him for exploits of war.

He was, indeed, a favorer of the Lacedæmonians even from his youth, and he gave the names of Lacedæmonius and Eleus to two sons, twins, whom he had, as Stesimbrotus says, by a woman of Clitorium, whence Pericles often upbraided them with their mother's blood. But Diodorus, the geographer, asserts that both these, and another son of Cimon's, whose name was Thessalus, were born of Isodice, the daughter of Euryptolemus, the son of Megacles.

However, this is certain, that Cimon was countenanced by the Lacedæmonians in opposition to Themistocles, whom they disliked; and while he was yet very young, they endeavored to raise and increase his credit in Athens. This the Athenians perceived at first with pleasure, and the favor the Lacedæmonians showed him was in various ways advantageous to them and their affairs; as at that time they were just rising to power, and were occupied in winning the allies to their side. So they seemed not at all offended with the honor and kindness shown to Cimon, who then had the chief management of all the affairs of Greece, and was acceptable to the Lacedæmonians, and courteous to the allies. But afterwards the Athenians, grown more powerful, when they saw Cimon so entirely devoted to the Lacedæmonians, began to be angry, for he would always in his speeches prefer them to the Athenians, and upon every occasion, when he would reprimand them for a fault, or incite them to emulation, he would exclaim, "The Lacedæmonians would not do thus." This raised the discontent, and got him in some degree the hatred of the citizens; but that which ministered chiefly to the accusation against him fell out upon the following occasion.

In the fourth year of the reign of Archidamus, the son of Zeuxidamus, king of Sparta, there happened in the country of Lacedæmon, the greatest earthquake that was known in the memory of man; the earth opened into chasms, and the mountain Taygetus was so shaken, that some of the rocky points of it fell down, and except five houses, all the town of Sparta was shattered to pieces. They say, that a little before any motion was perceived, as the young men and the boys just grown up were exercising themselves together in the middle of the portico, a hare, of a sudden, started out just by them, which the young men, though all naked and daubed with oil, ran after for sport. No sooner were they gone from the place, than the gymnasium fell down upon the boys who had stayed behind, and killed them all. Their tomb is to this day called Sismatias.[12] Archidamus, by the present danger made apprehensive of what might follow, and seeing the citizens intent upon removing the most valuable of their goods out of their houses, commanded an alarm to be sounded, as if an enemy were coming upon them, in order that they should collect about him in a body, with arms. It was this alone that saved Sparta at that time, for the Helots were got together from the country about, with design to surprise the Spartans, and overpower those whom the earthquake had spared. But finding them armed and well prepared, they retired into the towns and openly made war with them, gaining over a number of the Laconians of the country districts; while at the same time the Messenians, also, made an attack upon the Spartans, who therefore despatched Periclidas to Athens to solicit succors, of whom Aristophanes says in mockery that he came and

> In a red jacket, at the altars seated,
> With a white face, for men and arms entreated.[13]

This Ephialtes opposed, protesting that they ought not to raise up or assist a city that was a rival to Athens; but that being down, it were best to keep her so, and let the pride and arrogance of Sparta be trodden under. But Cimon, as Critias says, preferring the safety of Lacedæmon to the aggrandizement of his own country, so persuaded the people,

[12] From Seismos, or as it is written in Latin, Sismus, an earthquake.

[13] From the Lysistrata (1138).

that he soon marched out with a large army to their
relief. Ion records, also, the most successful expression which he used to move the Athenians. "They
ought not to suffer Greece to be lamed, nor their
own city to be deprived of her yoke-fellow."

In his return from aiding the Lacedæmonians, he
passed with his army through the territory of Corinth;
whereupon Lachartus reproached him for bringing
his army into the country, without first asking leave
of the people. For he that knocks at another man's
door ought not to enter the house till the master gives
him leave. "But you, Corinthians, O Lachartus,"
said Cimon, "did not knock at the gates of the Cle-
onæans and Megarians, but broke them down, and
entered by force, thinking that all places should be
open to the stronger." And having thus rallied the
Corinthian, he passed on with his army. Some time
after this, the Lacedæmonians sent a second time to
desire succors of the Athenians against the Messenians and Helots, who had seized upon Ithome. But
when they came, fearing their boldness and gallantry,
of all that came to their assistance, they sent them
only back, alleging they were designing innovations.
The Athenians returned home, enraged at this usage,
and vented their anger upon all those who were favor-
ers of the Lacedæmonians; and seizing some slight
occasion, they banished Cimon for ten years, which
is the time prescribed to those that are banished by the
ostracism. In the meantime, the Lacedæmonians, on
their return after freeing Delhi from the Phocians,
encamped their army at Tanagra, whither the Athenians presently marched with design to fight them.

Cimon, also, came thither armed, and ranged him-
self among those of his own tribe, which was the
Œneis, desirous of fighting with the rest against the
Spartans; but the council of five hundred being in-

formed of this, and frighted at it, his adversaries crying out he would disorder the army, and bring the Lacedæmonians to Athens, commanded the officers not to receive him. Wherefore Cimon left the army, conjuring Euthippus, the Anaphlystian, and the rest of his companions, who were most suspected as favoring the Lacedæmonians, to behave themselves bravely against their enemies, and by their actions make their innocence evident to their countrymen. These, being in all a hundred, took the arms of Cimon, and followed his advice; and making a body by themselves, fought so desperately with the enemy, that they were all cut off, leaving the Athenians deep regret for the loss of such brave men, and repentance for having so unjustly suspected them. Accordingly, they did not long retain their severity toward Cimon, partly upon remembrance of his former services, and partly, perhaps, induced by the juncture of the times. For being defeated at Tanagra in a great battle, and fearing the Peloponnesians would come upon them at the opening of the spring, they recalled Cimon by a decree, of which Pericles himself was author. So reasonable were men's resentments in those times, and so moderate their anger, that it always gave way to the public good. Even ambition, the least governable of all human passions, could then yield to the necessities of the State.

Cimon, as soon as he returned, put an end to the war, and reconciled the two cities. Peace thus established, seeing the Athenians impatient of being idle, and eager after the honor and aggrandizement of war, lest they should set upon the Greeks themselves, or with so many ships cruising about the isles and Peloponnesus, they should give occasions to intestine wars, or complaints of their allies against them, he equipped two hundred galleys, with design to make

an attempt upon Egypt and Cyprus; purposing, by
this means, to accustom the Athenians to fight
against the barbarians, and enrich themselves honestly by spoiling those who were the natural enemies
to Greece. But when all things were prepared, and
the army ready to embark, Cimon had this dream. It
seemed to him that there was a furious bitch barking
at him, and, mixed with the barking, a kind of human
voice uttered these words:—

> Come on, for thou shalt shortly be,
> A pleasure to my whelps and me.

This dream was hard to interpret, yet Astyphilus of
Posidonia,[14] a man skilled in divinations, and intimate
with Cimon, told him that his death was presaged by
this vision, which he thus explained. A dog is enemy
to him he barks at; and one is always most a pleasure
to one's enemies, when one is dead; the mixture of
human voice with barking signifies the Medes, for
the army of the Medes is mixed up of Greeks and barbarians. After this dream, as he was sacrificing to
Bacchus, and the priest cutting up the victim, a
number of ants, taking up the congealed particles of
the blood, laid them about Cimon's great toe. This
was not observed for a good while, but at the very
time when Cimon spied it, the priest came and showed
him the liver of the sacrifice imperfect, wanting that
part of it called the head. But he could not then
recede from the enterprise, so he set sail. Sixty of
his ships he sent toward Egypt; with the rest he
went and fought the king of Persia's fleet, composed
of Phœnician and Cilician galleys, recovered all the
cities thereabout, and threatened Egypt; designing

---

[14] Posidonia is Pæstum; this is one of the first things mentioned of it.

no less than the entire ruin of the Persian empire. And the rather, for that he was informed Themistocles was in great repute among the barbarians, having promised the king to lead his army, whenever he should make war upon Greece. But Themistocles, it is said, abandoning all hopes of compassing his designs, very much out of the despair of overcoming the valor and good-fortune of Cimon, died a voluntary death. Cimon, intent on great designs, which he was now to enter upon, keeping his navy about the isle of Cyprus, sent messengers to consult the oracle of Jupiter Ammon upon some secret matter. For it is not known about what they were sent, and the god would give them no answer, but commanded them to return again, for that Cimon was already with him. Hearing this, they returned to sea, and as soon as they came to the Grecian army, which was then about Egypt, they understood that Cimon was dead; and computing the time of the oracle, they found that his death had been signified, he being then already with the gods.

He died, some say, of sickness, while besieging Citium in Cyprus; according to others, of a wound he received in a skirmish with the barbarians. When he perceived he should die, he commanded those under his charge to return, and by no means to let the news of his death be known by the way; this they did with such secrecy that they all came home safe, and neither their enemies nor the allies knew what had happened. Thus, as Phanodemus relates, the Grecian army was, as it were, conducted by Cimon, thirty days after he was dead. But after his death there was not one commander among the Greeks that did any thing considerable against the barbarians, and instead of uniting against their common enemies, the popular leaders and partisans of war animated them against one another to that degree, that none could interpose their good offices to reconcile them. And while, by their mutual discord, they ruined the power of Greece, they gave the Persians time to recover breath, and repair all their losses. It is true, indeed, Agesilaus carried the arms of Greece into Asia, but it was a long time after; there were, indeed, some brief appearances of a war against the king's lieutenants in the maritime provinces, but they all quickly vanished; before he could perform any thing of moment, he was recalled by fresh civil dissensions and disturbances at home. So that he was forced to leave the Persian king's officers to impose what tribute they pleased on the Greek cities in Asia, the confederates and allies of the Lacedæmonians. Whereas, in the time of Cimon, not so much as a letter-carrier, or a single horseman, was ever seen to come within four hundred furlongs of the sea.

The monuments, called Cimonian to this day, in Athens, show that his remains were conveyed home, yet the inhabitants of the city Citium pay particular honor to a certain tomb which they call the tomb of Cimon, according to Nausicrates the rhetorician, who states that in a time of famine, when the crops of their land all failed, they sent to the oracle, which commanded them not to forget Cimon, but give him the honors of a superior being. Such was the Greek commander.[15]

---

[15] *Such was the Greek commander* is a translation that has come from Amyot, "telle donc a esté la vie du capitaine Grec." The text, as we have it (*agon*, not *hegĕmon*), means *Such is the Greek game,* i. e., thus much is to be said for the Greek competitor in the present pair of lives.

LUCULLUS[1]

TRANSLATED BY GILES THORNBURGH, A. M.

LUCULLUS's grandfather had been consul; his uncle by the mother's sister was Metellus, surnamed Numidicus. As for his parents, his father was convicted of extortion, and his mother Cæcilia's reputation was bad. The first thing that Lucullus did before ever he stood for any office, or meddled with the affairs of state, being then but a youth, was, to accuse the accuser of his father, Servilius the augur, having caught him in an offence against the state. This thing was much taken notice of among the Romans, who commended it as an act of high merit. Even without the provocation, the accusation was esteemed no unbecoming action, for they delighted to see young men as eagerly attacking injustice, as good dogs do wild beasts. But when great animosities ensued, insomuch that some were wounded and killed in the fray, Servilius escaped. Lucullus followed his studies, and became a competent speaker, in both Greek and Latin, insomuch that Sylla, when composing the commentaries of his own life and actions, dedicated them to him, as one who could have performed the task better himself. His speech was not only elegant and ready for purposes of mere business,

[1] He was born probably, about 110 B. C. Celebrated as the conqueror of Mithridates. He amassed vast treasures in Asia, supplying himself the means, after his return to Rome, for gratifying his taste for luxury and magnificence. He died in 57 or 56 B. C.— Dr. William Smith.

like the ordinary oratory which will in the public market-place,

> Lash as a wounded tunny does the sea,[2]

but on every other occasion shows itself

> Dried up and perished with the want of wit;

but even in his younger days he addicted himself to the study, simply for its own sake, of the liberal arts; and when advanced in years, after a life of conflicts, he gave his mind, as it were its liberty, to enjoy in full leisure the refreshment of philosophy; and summoning up his contemplative faculties, administered a timely check, after his difference with Pompey, to his feelings of emulation and ambition. Besides what has been said of his love of learning already, one instance more was, that in his youth, upon a suggestion of writing the Marsian war in Greek and Latin verse and prose, arising out of some pleasantry that passed into a serious proposal, he agreed with Hortensius the lawyer, and Sisenna the historian, that he would take his lot; and it seems that the lot directed him to the Greek tongue, for a Greek history of that war is still extant.

Among the many signs of the great love which he bore to his brother Marcus, one in particular is commemorated by the Romans. Though he was elder brother, he would not step into authority without him, but deferred his own advance until his brother was qualified to bear a share with him, and so won upon

---

[2] *Lash as a wounded tunny does the sea* is quoted again in Plutarch's Essay on the Tardiness of the Gods in inflicting Punishment (*de Sera Numinis Vindicta*), where Wyttenbach, in his note, conjectures merely that it comes from a lost play of Æschylus or Sophocles, and the fragment following from a Comic writer. But nothing further is known.

the people, as when absent to be chosen Ædile with him.

He gave many and early proofs of his valor and conduct, in the Marsian war, and was admired by Sylla for his constancy and mildness, and always employed in affairs of importance, especially in the mint; most of the money for carrying on the Mithridatic war being coined by him in Peloponnesus, which, by the soldiers' wants, was brought into rapid circulation, and long continued current under the name of Lucullean coin. After this, when Sylla conquered Athens, and was victorious by land, but found the supplies for his army cut off, the enemy being master at sea, Lucullus was the man whom he sent in Libya and Egypt, to procure him shipping. It was the depth of winter when he ventured with but three small Greek vessels, and as many Rhodian galleys, not only into the main sea, but also among multitudes of vessels belonging to the enemies, who were cruising about as absolute masters. Arriving at Crete, he gained it; and finding the Cyrenians harassed by long tyrannies and wars, he composed their troubles, and settled their government; putting the city in mind of that saying which Plato once had oracularly uttered of them, who, being requested to prescribe laws to them, and mould them into some sound form of government, made answer, that it was a hard thing to give laws to the Cyrenians, abounding, as they did, in wealth and plenty. For nothing is more intractable than man when in felicity, nor any thing more docile, when he has been reduced and humbled by fortune. This made the Cyrenians so willingly submit to the laws which Lucullus imposed upon them. From thence sailing into Egypt, and, pressed by pirates, he lost most of his vessels; but he himself narrowly escaping, made a magnificent entry into Alexandria. The whole fleet, a compliment due only to royalty, met him in full array, and the young Ptolemy showed wonderful kindness to him, appointing him lodging and diet in the palace, where no foreign commander before him had been received. Besides, he gave him gratuities and presents, not such as were usually given to men of his condition, but four times as much; of which, however, he took nothing more than served his necessity, and accepted of no gift, though what was worth eighty talents was offered him. It is reported he neither went to see Memphis, nor any of the celebrated wonders of Egypt. It was for a man of no business and much curiosity to see such things, not for him who had left his commander in the field, lodging under the ramparts of his enemies.

Ptolemy, fearing the issue of that war, deserted the confederacy, but nevertheless sent a convoy with him as far as Cyprus, and at parting, with much ceremony, wishing him a good voyage, gave him a very precious emerald set in gold. Lucullus at first refused it, but when the king showed him his own likeness cut upon it, he thought he could not persist in a denial, for had he parted with such open offence, it might have endangered his passage. Drawing a considerable squadron together, which he summoned, as he sailed by, out of all the maritime towns, except those suspected of piracy, he sailed for Cyprus; and there understanding that the enemy lay in wait under the promontories for him, he laid up his fleet, and sent to the cities to send in provisions for his wintering among them. But when time served, he launched his ships suddenly, and went off, and hoisting all his sails in the night, while he kept them down in the day, thus came safe to Rhodes. Being furnished with ships at Rhodes, he also prevailed upon the inhabi-

LUCULLUS 247

tants of Cos and Cnidus, to leave the king's side, and join in an expedition against the Samians. Out of Chios he himself drove the king's party, and set the Colophonians at liberty, having seized Epigonus the tyrant, who oppressed them.

About this time Mithridates left Pergamus, and retired to Pitane, where being closely besieged by Fimbria on the land, and not daring to engage with so bold and victorious a commander, he was concerting means for escape by sea, and sent for all his fleets from every quarter to attend him. Which when Fimbria perceived, having no ships of his own, he sent to Lucullus, entreating him to assist him with his, in subduing the most odious and warlike of kings, lest the opportunity of humbling Mithridates, the prize which the Romans had pursued with so much blood and trouble, should now at last be lost, when he was within the net, and easily to be taken. And were he caught, no one would be more highly commended than Lucullus, who stopped his passage and seized him in his flight. Being driven from the land by the one, and met in the sea by the other, he would give matter of renown and glory to them both, and the much applauded actions of Sylla at Orchomenus and about Chæronea, would no longer be thought of by the Romans. The proposal was no unreasonable thing; it being obvious to all men, that if Lucullus had harkened to Fimbria, and with his navy, which was then near at hand, had blocked up the haven, the war soon had been brought to an end, and infinite numbers of mischiefs prevented thereby. But he, whether from the sacredness of friendship between himself and Sylla, reckoning all other considerations of public or of private advantage inferior to it, or out of detestation of the wickedness of Fimbria, whom he abhorred for advancing himself by the late death of his friend and the general of the army, or by a divine fortune sparing Mithridates then, that he might have him for an adversary for a time to come, for whatever reason, refused to comply, and suffered Mithridates to escape and laugh at the attempts of Fimbria. He himself alone first, near Lectum in Troas, in a sea-fight, overcame the king's ships; and afterwards, discovering Neoptolemus lying in wait for him near Tenedos, with a greater fleet, he went aboard a Rhodian quinquereme galley, commanded by Damagoras, a man of great experience at sea, and friendly to the Romans, and sailed before the rest. Neoptolemus made up furiously at him, and commanded the master, with all imaginable might, to charge; but Damagoras, fearing the bulk and massy stem of the admiral, thought it dangerous to meet him prow to prow, and, rapidly wheeling round, bid his men back water, and so received him astern; in which place, though violently borne upon, he received no manner of harm, the blow being defeated by falling on those parts of the ship which lay under water. By which time, the rest of the fleet coming up to him, Lucullus gave order to turn again, and vigorously falling upon the enemy, put them to flight, and pursued Neoptolemus. After this he came to Sylla, in Chersonesus, as he was preparing to pass the strait, and brought timely assistance for the safe transportation of the army.

Peace being presently made, Mithridates sailed off to the Euxine sea, but Sylla taxed the inhabitants of Asia twenty thousand talents, and ordered Lucullus to gather and coin the money. And it was no small comfort to the cities under Sylla's severity, that a man of not only incorrupt and just behavior, but also of moderation, should be employed in so heavy and odious an office. The Mitylenæans, who absolutely revolted, he was willing should return to

LUCULLUS

their duty, and submit to a moderate penalty for the offence they had given in the case of Marius.[3] But, finding them bent upon their own destruction, he came up to them, defeated them at sea, blocked them up in their city and besieged them; then sailing off from them openly in the day to Elæa, he returned privately, and posting an ambush near the city, lay quiet himself. And on the Mitylenæans coming out eagerly and in disorder to plunder the deserted camp, he fell upon them, took many of them, and slew five hundred, who stood upon their defence. He gained six thousand slaves, and a very rich booty.

He was no way engaged in the great and general troubles of Italy which Sylla and Marius created, a happy providence at that time detaining him in Asia upon business. He was as much in Sylla's favor, however, as any of his other friends; Sylla, as was said before, dedicated his Memoirs to him as a token of kindness, and at his death, passing by Pompey, made him guardian to his son; which seems, indeed, to have been the rise of the quarrel and jealousy between them two, being both young men, and passionate for honor.

A little after Sylla's death, he was made consul with Marcus Cotta, about the one hundred and seventy-sixth Olympiad. The Mithridatic war being then under debate, Marcus declared that it was not finished, but only respited for a time, and therefore, upon choice of provinces, the lot falling to Lucullus to have Gaul within the Alps, a province where no

---

[3] *Marius* should in correctness be Manius, as appears from Velleius Paterculus (*II.*, 18), who relates how on the occupation of the coast and islands of Asia Minor by Mithridates, Manius Aquillius and other Romans were handed over to him by the Mitylenæans.

great action was to be done, he was ill-pleased. But chiefly, the success of Pompey in Spain fretted him, as, with the renown he got there, if the Spanish war were finished in time, he was likely to be chosen general before any one else against Mithridates. So that when Pompey sent for money, and signified by letter that, unless it were sent him, he would leave the country and Sertorius, and bring his forces home to Italy, Lucullus most zealously supported his request, to prevent any pretence of his returning home during his own consulship; for all things would have been at his disposal, at the head of so great an army. For Cethegus, the most influential popular leader at that time, owing to his always both acting and speaking to please the people, had, as it happened, a hatred to Lucullus, who had not concealed his disgust at his debauched, insolent, and lawless life. Lucullus, therefore, was at open warfare with him. And Lucius Quintius, also, another demagogue, who was taking steps against Sylla's constitution, and endeavoring to put things out of order, by private exhortations and public admonitions he checked in his designs, and repressed his ambition, wisely and safely remedying a great evil at the very outset.

At this time news came that Octavius, the governor of Cilicia, was dead, and many were eager for the place, courting Cethegus, as the man best able to serve them. Lucullus set little value upon Cilicia itself, no otherwise than as he thought, by his acceptance of it, no other man besides himself might be employed in the war against Mithridates, by reason of its nearness to Cappadocia. This made him strain every effort that that province might be allotted to himself, and to none other; which led him at last into an expedient not so honest or commendable, as it was serviceable for compassing his design, sub-

LUCULLUS 251

mitting to necessity against his own inclination. There was one Præcia, a celebrated wit and beauty, but in other respects nothing better than an ordinary harlot; who, however, to the charms of her person adding the reputation of one that loved and served her friends, by making use of those who visited her to assist their designs and promote their interests, had thus gained great power. She had seduced Cethegus, the first man at that time in reputation and authority of all the city, and enticed him to her love, and so had made all authority follow her. For nothing of moment was done in which Cethegus was not concerned, and nothing by Cethegus without Præcia. This woman Lucullus gained to his side by gifts and flattery, (and a great price it was in itself to so stately and magnificent a dame, to be seen engaged in the same cause with Lucullus,) and thus he presently found Cethegus his friend, using his utmost interest to procure Cilicia for him; which when once obtained, there was no more need of applying himself either to Præcia, or Cethegus; for all unanimously voted him to the Mithridatic war, by no hands likely to be so successfully managed as his. Pompey was still contending with Sertorius, and Metellus by age unfit for service; which two alone were the competitors who could prefer any claim with Lucullus for that command. Cotta, his colleague, after much ado in the senate, was sent away with a fleet to guard the Propontis, and defend Bithynia.

Lucullus carried with him a legion under his own orders, and crossed over into Asia and took the command of the forces there, composed of men who were all thoroughly disabled by dissoluteness and rapine, and the Fimbrians, as they were called, utterly unmanageable by long want of any sort of discipline. For these were they who under Fimbria had slain

Flaccus, the consul and general, and afterwards betrayed Fimbria to Sylla; a wilful and lawless set of men, but warlike, expert, and hardy in the field. Lucullus in a short time took down the courage of these, and disciplined the others, who then first, in all probability, knew what a true commander and governor was; whereas in former times they had been courted to service, and took up arms at nobody's command, but their own wills.

The enemy's provisions for war stood thus; Mithridates, like the Sophists,[4] boastful and haughty at first, set upon the Romans, with a very inefficient army, such, indeed, as made a good show, but was nothing for use; but being shamefully routed, and taught a lesson for a second engagement, he reduced his forces to a proper, serviceable shape. Dispensing with the mixed multitudes, and the noisy menaces of barbarous tribes of various languages, and with the ornaments of gold and precious stones, a greater temptation to the victors than security to the bearers, he gave his men broad swords like the Romans', and massy shields; chose horses better for service than show, drew up an hundred and twenty thousand foot in the figure of the Roman phalanx, and had sixteen thousand horse, besides chariots armed with scythes, no less than a hundred. Besides which, he set out a fleet not at all cumbered with gilded cabins, luxurious baths, and women's furniture, but stored with weapons and darts, and other necessaries, and thus made a descent upon Bithynia. Not only did these parts willingly receive him again, but almost all Asia re-

---

[4] The *Sophists* in Plato's dialogues always begin boldly with any showy, blustering piece of logic that occurs to them; and it is only when Socrates has quietly exposed the futility of this, that they bring forward something less pretentious and more to the point.

garded him as their salvation from the intolerable miseries which they were suffering from the Roman money-lenders, and revenue farmers. These afterwards, who like harpies stole away their very nourishment, Lucullus drove away, and at this time by reproving them, did what he could to make them more moderate, and to prevent a general secession, then breaking out in all parts. While Lucullus was detained in rectifying these matters, Cotta, finding affairs ripe for action, prepared for battle with Mithridates; and news coming from all hands that Lucullus had already entered Phrygia, on his march against the enemy, he, thinking he had a triumph all but actually in his hands, lest his colleague should share in the glory of it, hasted to battle without him. But being routed, both by sea and land, he lost sixty ships with their men, and four thousand foot, and himself was forced into and besieged in Chalcedon, there waiting for relief from Lucullus. There were those about Lucullus who would have had him leave Cotta and go forward, in hope of surprising the defenceless kingdom of Mithridates. And this was the feeling of the soldiers in general, who were indignant that Cotta should by his ill-counsel not only lose his own army, but hinder them also from conquest, which at that time, without the hazard of a battle, they might have obtained. But Lucullus, in a public address, declared to them that he would rather save one citizen from the enemy, than be master of all that they had.

Archelaus, the former commander in Bœotia under Mithridates, who afterwards deserted him and accompanied the Romans, protested to Lucullus that, upon his bare coming, he would possess himself of all Pontus. But he answered, that it did not become him to be more cowardly than huntsmen, to leave the wild beasts abroad, and seek after sport in their deserted dens. Having so said, he made towards Mithridates with thirty thousand foot, and two thousand five hundred horse. But on being come in sight of his enemies, he was astonished at their numbers, and thought to forbear fighting, and wear out time. But Marius, whom Sertorius had sent out of Spain to Mithridates with forces under him, stepping out and challenging him, he prepared for battle. In the very instant before joining battle, without any perceptible alteration preceding, on a sudden the sky opened, and a large luminous body fell down in the midst between the armies, in shape like a hogshead, but in color like melted silver, insomuch that both armies in alarm withdrew. This wonderful prodigy happened in Phrygia, near Otryæ. Lucullus after this began to think with himself that no human power and wealth could suffice to sustain such great numbers as Mithridates had, for any long time in the face of an enemy, and commanded one of the captives to be brought before him, and first of all asked him, how many companions had been quartered with him, and how much provision he had left behind him, and when he had answered him, commanded him to stand aside; then asked a second and a third the same question; after which, comparing the quantity of provision with the men, he found that in three or four days' time, his enemies would be brought to want. This all the more determined him to trust to time, and he took measures to store his camp with all sorts of provision, and thus living in plenty, trusted to watch the necessities of his hungry enemy.

This made Mithridates set out against the Cyzicenians, miserably shattered in the fight at Chalcedon, where they lost no less than three thousand citizens and ten ships. And that he might the safer steal away unobserved by Lucullus, immediately after supper, by the help of a dark and wet night, he went off, and by the morning gained the neighborhood of the city, and sat down with his forces upon the Adrastean mount. Lucullus, on finding him gone, pursued, but was well pleased not to overtake him with his own forces in disorder; and he sat down near what is called the Thracian village, an admirable position for commanding all the roads and the places whence, and through which the provisions for Mithridates's camp must of necessity come. And judging now of the event, he no longer kept his mind from his soldiers, but when the camp was fortified and their work finished, called them together, and with great assurance told them that in a few days, without the expense of blood, he would give them victory.

Mithridates besieged the Cyzicenians with ten camps by land, and with his ships occupied the strait that was betwixt their city and the main land, and so blocked them up on all sides; they, however, were fully prepared stoutly to receive him, and resolved to endure the utmost extremity, rather than forsake the Romans. That which troubled them most was, that they knew not where Lucullus was, and heard nothing of him, though at that time his army was visible before them. But they were imposed upon by the Mithridatians, who, showing them the Romans encamped on the hills, said, "Do ye see those? Those are the auxiliary Armenians and Medes, whom Tigranes has sent to Mithridates." They were thus overwhelmed with thinking of the vast numbers round them, and could not believe any way of relief was left them, even if Lucullus should come up to their assistance. Demonax, a messenger sent in by Archelaus, was the first who told them of Lucullus's arrival; but they disbelieved his report, and thought he came with a story invented merely to encourage them. At which time it happened that a boy, a prisoner who had run away from the enemy, was brought before them; who, being asked where Lucullus was, laughed at their jesting, as he thought, but, finding them in earnest, with his finger pointed to the Roman camp; upon which they took courage. The lake Dascylitis was navigated with vessels of some little size; one, the biggest of them, Lucullus drew ashore, and carrying her across in a wagon to the sea, filled her with soldiers, who sailing along unseen in the dead of the night, came safe into the city.

The gods themselves, too, in admiration of the constancy of the Cyzicenians, seem to have animated them with manifest signs, more especially now in the festival of Proserpine, where a black heifer being wanting for sacrifice, they supplied it by a figure made of dough, which they set before the altar. But the holy heifer set apart for the goddess, and at that time grazing with the other herds of the Cyzicenians on the other side of the strait, left the herd and swam over to the city alone, and offered herself for sacrifice. By night, also, the goddess appearing to Aristagoras, the town clerk, "I am come," said she, "and have brought the Libyan piper against the Pontic trumpeter; bid the citizens, therefore, be of good courage." While the Cyzicenians were wondering what the words could mean, a sudden wind sprung up and caused a considerable motion on the sea. The king's battering engines, the wonderful contrivance of Niconides of Thessaly, then under the walls, by their cracking and rattling, soon demonstrated what would follow; after which an extraordinarily tempestuous south wind succeeding shattered in a short space of time all the rest of the works, and by a violent concussion, threw down the wooden tower a hundred cubits high. It is said that in Ilium Minerva appeared to many that night in their sleep, with the sweat running down her person, and showed them her robe torn in one place, telling them that she had just arrived from relieving the Cyzicenians; and the inhabitants to this day show a monument with an inscription, including a public decree, referring to the fact.

Mithridates, through the knavery of his officers, not knowing for some time the want of provision in his camp, was troubled in mind that the Cyzicenians should hold out against him. But his ambition and anger fell, when he saw his soldiers in the extremity of want, and feeding on man's flesh; as, in truth, Lucullus was not carrying on the war as mere matter of show and stage-play, but according to the proverb, made the seat of war in the belly, and did everything to cut off their supplies of food. Mithridates, therefore, took advantage of the time, while Lucullus was storming a fort, and sent away almost all his horse to Bithynia, with the sumpter cattle, and as many of the foot as were unfit for service. On intelligence of which, Lucullus, while it was yet night, came to his camp, and in the morning, though it was stormy weather, took with him ten cohorts of foot, and the horse, and pursued them under falling snow and in cold so severe that many of his soldiers were unable to proceed; and with the rest coming upon the enemy, near the river Rhyndacus, he overthrew them with so great a slaughter, that the very women of Apollonia came out to seize on the booty and strip the slain. Great numbers, as we may suppose, were slain; six thousand horses were taken, with an infinite number of beasts of burden, and no less than fifteen thousand men. All which he led along by the enemy's camp. I cannot but wonder on this occasion at Sallust, who says that this was the first time camels were seen by the Romans, as if he thought those who, long before, under Scipio, defeated Antiochus, or those who lately

had fought against Archelaus near Orchomenus and
Chæronea, had not known what a camel was. Mithridates, himself fully determined upon flight, as mere
delays and diversions for Lucullus, sent his admiral
Aristonicus to the Greek sea; who, however, was betrayed in the very instant of going off, and Lucullus
became master of him, and ten thousand pieces of
gold which he was carrying with him to corrupt some
of the Roman army. After which, Mithridates himself made for the sea, leaving the foot officers to conduct the army, upon whom Lucullus fell, near the
river Granicus, where he took a vast number alive, and
slew twenty thousand. It is reported that the total
number killed, of fighting men and of others who
followed the camp, amounted to something not far
short of three hundred thousand.

Lucullus first went to Cyzicus, where he was received with all the joy and gratitude suiting the occasion, and then collected a navy, visiting the shores of
the Hellespont. And arriving at Troas, he lodged
in the temple of Venus, where, in the night, he thought
he saw the goddess coming to him, and saying,

> Sleep'st thou, great lion, when the fawns are nigh?

Rising up hereupon, he called his friends to him, it
being yet night, and told them his vision; at which
instant some Ilians came up and acquainted him that
thirteen of the king's quinqueremes were seen off the
Achæan harbor, sailing for Lemnos. He at once put
to sea, took these, and slew their admiral Isidorus.
And then he made after another squadron, who were
just come into port, and were hauling their vessels
ashore, but fought from the decks, and sorely galled
Lucullus's men; there being neither room to sail
round them, nor to bear upon them for any damage,
his ships being afloat, while theirs stood secure and

fixed on the sand. After much ado, at the only landing-place of the island, he disembarked the choicest of his men, who, falling upon the enemy behind, killed some, and forced others to cut their cables, and thus making from the shore, they fell foul upon one another, or came within the reach of Lucullus's fleet. Many were killed in the action. Among the captives was Marius, the commander sent by Sertorius, who had but one eye. And it was Lucullus's strict command to his men before the engagement, that they should kill no man who had but one eye, that he might rather die under disgrace and reproach.

This being over, he hastened his pursuit after Mithridates, whom he hoped to find still in Bithynia, intercepted by Voconius, whom he sent out before to Nicomedia with part of the fleet, to stop his flight. But Voconius, loitering in Samothrace to get initiated and celebrate a feast, let slip his opportunity, Mithridates being passed by with all his fleet. He, hastening into Pontus before Lucullus should come up to him, was caught in a storm, which dispersed his fleet and sunk several ships. The wreck floated on all the neighboring shore for many days after. The merchant ship, in which he himself was, could not well in that heavy swell be brought ashore by the masters for its bigness, and it being heavy with water and ready to sink, he left it and went aboard a pirate vessel, delivering himself into the hands of pirates, and thus unexpectedly and wonderfully came safe to Heraclea, in Pontus.

Thus the proud language Lucullus had used to the senate, ended without any mischance. For they having decreed him three thousand talents to furnish out a navy, he himself was against it and sent them word that without any such great and costly supplies, by the confederate shipping alone, he did not in the least doubt but to rout Mithridates from the sea. And so he did, by divine assistance, for it is said that the wrath of Diana of Priapus brought the great tempest upon the men of Pontus, because they had robbed her temple, and removed her image.

Many were persuading Lucullus to defer the war, but he rejected their counsel, and marched through Bithynia and Galatia into the king's country, in such great scarcity of provision at first, that thirty thousand Galatians followed, every man carrying a bushel of wheat at his back. But subduing all in his progress before him, he at last found himself in such great plenty, that an ox was sold in the camp for a single drachma, and a slave for four. The other booty they made no account of, but left it behind or destroyed it; there being no disposing of it, where all had such abundance. But when they had made frequent incursions with their cavalry, and had advanced as far as Themiscyra, and the plains of the Thermodon, merely laying waste the country before them, they began to find fault with Lucullus, asking "why he took so many towns by surrender, and never one by storm, which might enrich them with the plunder? and now, forsooth, leaving Amisus behind, a rich and wealthy city, of easy conquest, if closely besieged, he will carry us into the Tibarenian and Chaldean wilderness, to fight with Mithridates." Lucullus, little thinking this would be of such dangerous consequence as it afterwards proved, took no notice and slighted it; and was rather anxious to excuse himself to those who blamed his tardiness, in losing time about small pitiful places not worth the while, and allowing Mithridates opportunity to recruit. "That is what I design," said he, "and sit here contriving by my delay, that he may grow great again, and gather a considerable army, which may induce him to stand, and not fly away before us. For do you not see the wide and unknown wilderness behind? Caucasus is not far off, and a multitude of vast mountains, enough to conceal ten thousand kings that wished to avoid a battle. Besides this, a journey but of few days leads from Cabira to Armenia, where Tigranes reigns, king of kings, and holds in his hands a power that has enabled him to keep the Parthians in narrow bounds, to remove Greek cities bodily into Media, to conquer Syria and Palestine, to put to death the kings of the royal line of Seleucus, and carry away their wives and daughters by violence. This same is relation and son-in-law to Mithridates, and cannot but receive him upon entreaty, and enter into war with us to defend him; so that, while we endeavor to depose Mithridates, we shall endanger the bringing in of Tigranes against us, who already has sought occasion to fall out with us, but can never find one so justifiable as the succor of a friend and prince in his necessity. Why, therefore, should we put Mithridates upon this resource, who as yet does not see how he may best fight with us, and disdains to stoop to Tigranes; and not rather allow him time to gather a new army and grow confident again, that we may thus fight with Colchians, and Tibarenians, whom we have often defeated already, and not with Medes and Armenians."

Upon these motives, Lucullus sat down before Amisus, and slowly carried on the siege. But the winter being well spent, he left Murena in charge of it, and went himself against Mithridates, then rendezvousing at Cabira, and resolving to await the Romans, with forty thousand foot about him, and fourteen thousand horse, on whom he chiefly confided. Passing the river Lycus, he challenged the Romans into the plains, where the cavalry engaged, and the Romans were beaten. Pomponius, a man of some note, was

taken wounded; and sore, and in pain as he was, was
carried before Mithridates, and asked by the king, if
he would become his friend, if he saved his life. He
answered, "yes, if you become reconciled to the Romans; if not, your enemy." Mithridates wondered at
him, and did him no hurt. The enemy being with
their cavalry master of the plains, Lucullus was something afraid, and hesitated to enter the mountains, being very large, woody, and almost inaccessible, when,
by good luck, some Greeks who had fled into a cave
were taken, the eldest of whom, Artemidorus by
name, promised to bring Lucullus, and seat him in a
place of safety for his army, where there was a fort
that overlooked Cabira. Lucullus, believing him,
lighted his fires, and marched in the night; and safely
passing the defile, gained the place, and in the morning
was seen above the enemy, pitching his camp in a place
advantageous to descend upon them if he desired to
fight, and secure from being forced, if he preferred to
lie still. Neither side was willing to engage at present.
But it is related that some of the king's party were
hunting a stag, and some Romans wanting to cut them
off, came out and met them. Whereupon they skirmished, more still drawing together to each side, and
at last the king's party prevailed, on which the Romans, from their camp seeing their companions fly,
were enraged, and ran to Lucullus with entreaties to
lead them out, demanding that the sign might be given
for battle. But he, that they might know of what
consequence the presence and appearance of a wise
commander is in time of conflict and danger, ordered
them to stand still. But he went down himself into
the plains, and meeting with the foremost that fled,
commanded them to stand and turn back with him.
These obeying, the rest also turned and formed again
in a body, and thus, with no great difficulty, drove

back the enemies, and pursued them to their camp. After his return, Lucullus inflicted the customary punishment upon the fugitives, and made them dig a trench of twelve foot, working in their frocks unfastened, while the rest stood by and looked on.

There was in Mithridates's camp, one Olthacus a chief of the Dandarians, a barbarous people living near the lake Mæotis, a man remarkable for strength and courage in fight, wise in council, and pleasant and ingratiating in conversation. He, out of emulation, and a constant eagerness which possessed him to outdo one of the other chiefs of his country, promised a great piece of service to Mithridates, no less than the death of Lucullus. The king commended his resolution, and, according to agreement, counterfeited anger, and put some disgrace upon him; whereupon he took horse, and fled to Lucullus, who kindly received him, being a man of great name in the army. After some short trial of his sagacity and perseverance, he found way to Lucullus's board and council. The Dandarian, thinking he had a fair opportunity, commanded his servants to lead his horse out of the camp, while he himself, as the soldiers were refreshing and resting themselves, it being then high noon, went to the general's tent, not at all expecting that entrance would be denied to one who was so familiar with him, and came under pretence of extraordinary business with him. He had certainly been admitted, had not sleep, which has destroyed many captains, saved Lucullus. For so it was, and Menedemus, one of the bedchamber, was standing at the door, who told Olthacus that it was altogether unseasonable to see the general, since, after long watching and hard labor, he was but just before laid down to repose himself. Olthacus would not go away upon this denial, but still persisted, saying that he must go in to speak of some necessary affairs, whereupon Menedemus grew angry, and replied that nothing was more necessary than the safety of Lucullus, and forced him away with both hands. Upon which, out of fear, he straightway left the camp, took horse, and without effect returned to Mithridates. Thus in action as in physic, it is the critical moment that gives both the fortunate and the fatal effect.

After this, Sornatius being sent out with ten companies for forage, and pursued by Menander, one of Mithridates's captains, stood his ground, and after a sharp engagement, routed and slew a considerable number of the enemy. Adrianus being sent afterward, with some forces, to procure food enough and to spare for the camp, Mithridates did not let the opportunity slip, but despatched Menemachus and Myro, with a great force, both horse and foot, against him, all which except two men, it is stated, were cut off by the Romans. Mithridates concealed the loss, giving it out that it was a small defeat, nothing near so great as reported, and occasioned by the unskilfulness of the leaders. Bnt Adrianus in great pomp passed by his camp, having many wagons full of corn and other booty, filling Mithridates with distress, and the army with confusion and consternation. It was resolved, therefore, to stay no longer. But when the king's servants sent away their own goods quietly, and hindered others from doing so too, the soldiers in great fury thronged and crowded to the gates, seized on the king's servants and killed them, and plundered the baggage. Dorylaus, the general, in his confusion, having nothing else besides his purple cloak, lost his life for that, and Hermæus, the priest, was trod underfoot in the gate.

Mithridates, having not one of his guards, nor even a groom remaining with him, got out of the camp in the throng, but had none of his horses with him; until

Ptolemy, the eunuch, some little time after, seeing him in the press making his way among the others, dismounted and gave his horse to the king. The Romans were already close upon him in their pursuit, nor was it through want of speed that they failed to catch him, but they were as near as possible doing so. But greediness and a petty military avarice hindered them from acquiring that booty, which in so many fights and hazards they had sought after, and lost Lucullus the prize of his victory. For the horse which carried the king was within reach, but one of the mules that carried the treasure either by accident stepping in, or by order of the king so appointed to go between him and the pursuers, they seized and pilfered the gold, and falling out among themselves about the prey, let slip the great prize. Neither was their greediness prejudicial to Lucullus in this only, but also they slew Callistratus, the king's confidential attendant, under suspicion of having five hundred piece of gold in his girdle; whereas Lucullus had specially ordered that he should be conveyed safe into the camp. Notwithstanding all which, he gave them leave to plunder the camp.

After this, in Cabira, and other strongholds which he took, he found great treasures, and private prisons in which many Greeks and many of the king's relations had been confined, who, having long since counted themselves no other than dead men, by the favor of Lucullus, met not with relief so truly as with a new life and second birth. Nyssa, also, sister of Mithridates, enjoyed the like fortunate captivity; while those who seemed to be most out of danger, his wives and sisters at Phernacia, placed in safety, as they thought, miserably perished, Mithridates in his flight sending Bacchides the eunuch to them. Among others there were two sisters of the king, Roxana and Statira, unmarried women forty years old, and two Ionian wives, Berenice of Chios, and Monime of Miletus. This latter was the most celebrated among the Greeks, because she so long withstood the king in his courtship to her, though he presented her with fifteen thousand pieces of gold, until a covenant of marriage was made, and a crown was sent her, and she was saluted queen. She had been a sorrowful woman before, and often bewailed her beauty, that had procured her a keeper, instead of a husband, and a watch of barbarians, instead of the home and attendance of a wife; and, removed far from Greece, she enjoyed the pleasure which she proposed to herself, only in a dream, being in the meantime robbed of that which is real. And when Bacchides came and bade them prepare for death, as every one thought most easy and painless, she took the diadem from her head, and fastening the string to her neck, suspended herself with it; which soon breaking, "O wretched headband!" said she, "not able to help me even in this small thing!" And throwing it away she spat on it, and offered her throat to Bacchides. Berenice had prepared a potion for herself, but at her mother's entreaty, who stood by, she gave her part of it. Both drank of the potion, which prevailed over the weaker body. But Berenice, having drunk too little, was not released by it, but lingering on unable to die, was strangled by Bacchides for haste. It is said that one of the unmarried sisters drank the poison, with bitter execrations and curses; but Statira uttered nothing ungentle or reproachful, but, on the contrary, commended her brother, who in his own danger neglected not theirs, but carefully provided that they might go out of the world without shame or disgrace.

Lucullus, being a good and humane man, was concerned at these things. However, going on he came to Talaura, from whence four days before his arrival

Mithridates had fled, and was got to Tigranes in Armenia. He turned off, therefore, and subdued the Chaldeans and Tibarenians, with the lesser Armenia, and having reduced all their forts and cities, he sent Appius to Tigranes to demand Mithridates. He himself went to Amisus, which still held out under the command of Callimachus, who, by his great engineering skill, and his dexterity at all the shifts and subtleties of a siege, had greatly incommoded the Romans. For which afterward he paid dear enough, and was now out-manœuvred by Lucullus, who, unexpectedly coming upon him at the time of the day when the soldiers used to withdraw and rest themselves, gained part of the wall, and forced him to leave the city, in doing which he fired it, either envying the Romans the booty, or to secure his own escape the better. No man looked after those who went off in the ships, but as soon as the fire had seized on most part of the wall, the soldiers prepared themselves for plunder; while Lucullus, pitying the ruin of the city, brought assistance from without, and encouraged his men to extinguish the flames. But all, being intent upon the prey, and giving no heed to him, with loud outcries, beat and clashed their arms together, until he was compelled to let them plunder, that by that means he might at least save the city from fire. But they did quite the contrary, for in searching the houses with lights and torches everywhere, they were themselves the cause of the destruction of most of the buildings, insomuch that when Lucullus the next day went in, he shed tears, and said to his friends, that he had often before blessed the fortune of Sylla, but never so much admired it as then, because when he was willing, he was also able to save Athens, "but my infelicity is such, that while I endeavor to imitate him, I become like Mummius." Nevertheless, he endeavored to save as much of the city as he could, and at the same time, also, by a happy providence, a fall of rain concurred to extinguish the fire. He himself while present repaired the ruins as much as he could, receiving back the inhabitants who had fled, and settling as many other Greeks as were willing to live there, adding a hundred and twenty furlongs of ground to the place.

This city was a colony of Athens, built at that time when she flourished and was powerful at sea, upon which account many who fled from Aristion's tyranny settled here, and were admitted as citizens, but had the ill-luck to fly from evils at home, into greater abroad. As many of these as survived, Lucullus furnished every one with clothes, and two hundred drachmas, and sent them away into their own country. On this occasion, Tyrannion the grammarian was taken. Murena begged him of Lucullus, and took him and made him a freedman; but in this he abused Lucullus's favor, who, by no means liked that a man of high repute for learning should be first made a slave, and then freed; for freedom thus speciously granted again, was a real deprivation of what he had before. But not in this case alone Murena showed himself far inferior in generosity to the general.

Lucullus was now busy in looking after the cities of Asia, and having no war to divert his time, spent it in the administration of law and justice, the want of which had for a long time left the province a prey to unspeakable and incredible miseries; so plundered and enslaved by tax-farmers and usurers, that private people were compelled to sell their sons in the flower of their youth, and their daughters in their virginity, and the States publicly to sell their consecrated gifts, pictures, and statues. In the end their lot was to yield themselves up slaves to their creditors, but before this, worse troubles befell them, tortures, inflicted with ropes and by horses, standing abroad to be scorched when the sun was hot, and being driven into ice and clay in the cold; insomuch that slavery was no less than a redemption and joy to them. Lucullus in a short time freed the cities from all these evils and oppressions; for, first of all, he ordered there should be no more taken than one per cent.[5] Secondly, where the interest exceeded the principal, he struck it off. The third, and most considerable order was, that the creditor should receive the fourth part of the debtor's income; but if any lender had added the interest to the principal, it was utterly disallowed. Insomuch, that in the space of four years all debts were paid, and lands returned to their right owners. The public debt was contracted when Asia was fined twenty thousand talents by Sylla, but twice as much was paid to the collectors, who by their usury had by this time advanced it to a hundred and twenty thousand talents. And accordingly they inveighed against Lucullus at Rome, as grossly injured by him, and by their money's help (as, indeed, they were very powerful, and had many of the statesmen in their debt), they stirred up several leading men against him. But Lucullus was not only beloved by the cities which he obliged, but was also wished for by other provinces, who blessed the good-luck of those who had such a governor over them.

Appius Clodius, who was sent to Tigranes (the same Clodius was brother to Lucullus's wife), being led by the king's guides, a roundabout way, unnecessarily long and tedious, through the upper country, being informed by his freedman, a Syrian by nation, of the direct road, left that lengthy and fallacious

[5] One per cent. per *month,* twelve per cent.; centesimæ usuræ, a very general rate.

one; and bidding the barbarians, his guides, adieu, in a few days passed over Euphrates, and came to Antioch upon Daphne. There being commanded to wait for Tigranes, who at that time was reducing some towns in Phœnicia, he won over many chiefs to his side, who unwillingly submitted to the king of Armenia, among whom was Zarbienus, king of the Gordyenians; also many of the conquered cities corresponded privately with him, whom he assured of relief from Lucullus, but ordered them to lie still at present. The Armenian government was an oppressive one, and intolerable to the Greeks, especially that of the present king, who, growing insolent and overbearing with his success, imagined all things valuable and esteemed among men not only were his in fact, but had been purposely created for him alone. From a small and inconsiderable beginning, he had gone on to be the conqueror of many nations, had humbled the Parthian power more than any before him, and filled Mesopotamia with Greeks, whom he carried in numbers out of Cilicia and Cappadocia. He transplanted also the Arabs, who lived in tents, from their country and home, and settled them near him, that by their means he might carry on the trade.

He had many kings waiting on him, but four he always carried with him as servants and guards, who, when he rode, ran by his horse's side in ordinary under-frocks, and attended him, when sitting on his throne, and publishing his decrees to the people, with their hands folded together, which posture of all others was that which most expressed slavery, it being that of men who had bidden adieu to liberty, and had prepared their bodies more for chastisement, than the service of their masters. Appius, nothing dismayed or surprised at this theatrical desplay, as soon as audience was granted him, said he came to demand

LUCULLUS 271

Mithridates for Lucullus's triumph, otherwise to denounce war against Tigranes, insomuch that though Tigranes endeavored to receive him with a smooth countenance and a forced smile, he could not dissemble his discomposure to those who stood about him, at the bold language of the young man; for it was the first time, perhaps, in twenty-five years, the length of his reign, or, more truly, of his tyranny, that any free speech had been uttered to him. However, he made answer to Appius, that he would not desert Mithridates, and would defend himself, if the Romans attacked him. He was angry, also, with Lucullus for calling him only king in his letter, and not king of kings, and, in his answer, would not give him his title of imperator. Great gifts were sent to Appius, which he refused; but on their being sent again and augmented, that he might not seem to refuse in anger, he took one goblet and sent the rest back, and without delay went off to the general.

Tigranes before this neither vouchsafed to see nor speak with Mithridates, though a near kinsman, and forced out of so considerable a kingdom, but proudly and scornfully kept him at a distance, as a sort of prisoner, in a marshy and unhealthy district; but now, with much profession of respect and kindness, he sent for him, and at a private conference between them in the palace, they healed up all private jealousies between them, punishing their favorites, who bore all the blame; among whom Metrodorus of Scepsis was one, an eloquent and learned man, and so close an intimate as commonly to be called the king's father. This man, as it happened, being employed in an embassy by Mithridates to solicit help against the Romans, Tigranes asked him, "what would you, Metrodorus, advise me to in this affair?" In return to which, either out of good-will to Tigranes, or a want of solicitude for Mithridates, he made answer, that as ambassador he counselled him to it, but as a friend dissuaded him from it. This Tigranes reported, and affirmed to Mithridates, thinking that no irreparable harm would come of it to Metrodorus. But upon this he was presently taken off, and Tigranes was sorry for what he had done, though he had not, indeed, been absolutely the cause of his death; yet he had given the fatal turn to the anger of Mithridates, who had privately hated him before, as appeared from his cabinet papers when taken, among which there was an order that Metrodorus should die. Tigranes buried him splendidly, sparing no cost to his dead body, whom he betrayed when alive. In Tigranes's court died, also, Amphicrates the orator (if, for the sake of Athens, we may also mention him), of whom it is told that he left his country and fled to Seleucia, upon the river Tigris, and, being desired to teach logic among them, arrogantly replied, that the dish was too little to hold a dolphin. He, therefore, came to Cleopatra, daughter of Mithridates, and queen to Tigranes, but being accused of misdemeanors, and prohibited all commerce with his countrymen, ended his days by starving himself. He, in like manner, received from Cleopatra an honorable burial, near Sapha, a place so called in that country.

Lucullus, when he had reëstablished law and a lasting peace in Asia, did not altogether forget pleasure and mirth, but, during his residence at Ephesus, gratified the cities with sports, festival triumphs, wrestling games, and single combats of gladiators. And they, in requital, instituted others, called Lucullean games, in honor to him, thus manifesting their love to him, which was of more value to him than all the honor. But when Appius came to him, and told him he must prepare for war with Tigranes, he went again into

Pontus, and, gathering together his army, besieged Sinope, or rather the Cilicians of the king's side who held it; who thereupon killed a number of the Sinopians, and set the city on fire, and by night endeavored to escape. Which when Lucullus perceived, he entered the city, and killed eight thousand of them who were still left behind; but restored to the inhabitants what was their own, and took special care for the welfare of the city. To which he was chiefly prompted by this vision. One seemed to come to him in his sleep, and say, "Go on a little further, Lucullus, for Autolycus is coming to see thee." When he arose, he could not imagine what the vision meant. The same day he took the city, and as he was pursuing the Cilicians, who were flying by sea, he saw a statue lying on the shore, which the Cilicians carried so far, but had not time to carry aboard. It was one of the masterpieces of Sthenis. And one told him, that it was the statue of Autolycus, the founder of the city. This Autolycus is reported to have been son to Deimachus, and one of those who, under Hercules, went on the expedition out of Thessaly against the Amazons; from whence in his return with Demoleon and Phlogius, he lost his vessel on a point of the Chersonesus,[6] called Pedalium. He himself, with his companions and their weapons, being saved, came to Sinope, and dispossessed the Syrians there. The Syrians held it, descended from Syrus, as is the story, the son of Apollo, and Sinope the daughter of Asopus. Which as soon as Lucullus heard, he remembered the admonition of Sylla, whose advice it is in his Memoirs, to treat nothing as so certain and so worthy of reliance as an intimation given in dreams.

[6] The chersonesus, that is, or the peninsula, upon a part of which the modern as well as the ancient Sinope stands.

When it was now told him that Mithridates and Tigranes were just ready to transport their forces into Lycaonia and Cilicia, with the object of entering Asia before him, he wondered much why the Armenian, supposing him to entertain any real intention to fight with the Romans, did not assist Mithridates in his flourishing condition, and join forces when he was fit for service, instead of suffering him to be vanquished and broken in pieces, and now at last beginning the war, when its hopes were grown cold, and throwing himself down headlong with them, who were irrecoverably fallen already. But when Machares, the son of Mithridates, and governor of Bosporus, sent him a crown valued at a thousand pieces of gold, and desired to be enrolled as a friend and confederate of the Romans, he fairly reputed that war at an end, and left Sornatius, his deputy, with six thousand soldiers, to take care of Pontus. He himself with twelve thousand foot, and a little less than three thousand horse, went forth to the second war, advancing, it seemed very plain, with too great and ill-advised speed, into the midst of warlike nations, and many thousands upon thousands of horse, into an unknown extent of country, every way inclosed with deep rivers and mountains, never free from snow; which made the soldiers, already far from orderly, follow him with great unwillingness and opposition. For the same reason, also, the popular leaders at home publicly inveighed and declaimed against him, as one that raised up war after war, not so much for the interest of the republic, as that he himself, being still in commission, might not lay down arms, but go on enriching himself by the public dangers. These men, in the end, effected their purpose. But Lucullus by long journeys came to the Euphrates, where, finding the waters high and rough from the winter, he was much troubled for fear of delay and difficulty while he should procure boats and make a bridge of them. But in the evening the flood beginning to retire, and decreasing all through the night, the next day they saw the river far down within his banks, so much so that the inhabitants, discovering the little islands in the river, and the water stagnating among them, a thing which had rarely happened before, made obeisance to Lucullus, before whom the very river was humble and submissive, and yielded an easy and swift passage. Making use of the opportunity, he carried over his army, and met with a lucky sign at landing. Holy heifers are pastured on purpose for Diana Persia, whom, of all the gods, the barbarians beyond Euphrates chiefly adore. They use these heifers only for her sacrifices. At other times they wander up and down undisturbed, with the mark of the goddess, a torch, branded on them; and it is no such light or easy thing, when occasion requires, to seize one of them. But one of these, when the army had passed the Euphrates, coming to a rock consecrated to the goddess, stood upon it, and then laying down her neck, like others that are forced down with a rope, offered herself to Lucullus for sacrifice. Besides which, he offered also a bull to Euphrates, for his safe passage. That day he tarried there, but on the next, and those that followed, he travelled through Sophene, using no manner of violence to the people who came to him and willing received his army. And when the soldiers were desirous to plunder a castle that seemed to be well stored within, "That is the castle," said he, "that we must storm," showing them Taurus, at a distance; "the rest is reserved for those who conquer there." Wherefore hastening his march, and passing the Tigris, he came over into Armenia.

The first messenger that gave notice of Lucullus's

coming was so far from pleasing Tigranes, that he had his head cut off for his pains; and no man daring to bring further information, without any intelligence at all, Tigranes sat while war was already blazing around him, giving ear only to those who flattered him, by saying that Lucullus would show himself a great commander, if he ventured to wait for Tigranes at Ephesus, and did not at once fly out of Asia, at the mere sight of the many thousands that were come against him. He is a man of a strong body that can carry off a great quantity of wine, and of a powerful constitution of mind that can sustain felicity. Mithrobarzanes, one of his chief favorites, first dared to tell him the truth, but had no more thanks for his freedom of speech, than to be immediately sent out against Lucullus with three thousand horse, and a great number of foot, with peremptory commands to bring him alive, and trample down his army. Some of Lucullus's men were then pitching their camp, and the rest were coming up to them, when the scouts gave notice that the enemy was approaching, whereupon he was in fear lest they should fall upon him, while his men were divided and unarranged; which made him stay to pitch the camp himself, and send out Sextilius, the legate, with sixteen hundred horse, and about as many heavy and light arms, with orders to advance towards the enemy, and wait until intelligence came to him that the camp was finished. Sextilius designed to have kept this order; but Mithrobarzanes coming furiously upon him, he was forced to fight. In the engagement Mithrobarzanes himself was slain, fighting, and all his men, except a few who ran away, were destroyed. After this Tigranes left Tigranocerta, a great city built by himself, and retired to Taurus, and called all his forces about him.

But Lucullus, giving him no time to rendezvous,

sent out Murena to harass and cut off those who
marched to Tigranes, and Sextilius, also, to disperse a
great company of Arabians, then on the way to the
king. Sextilius fell upon the Arabians in their camp,
and destroyed most of them, and also Murena, in his
pursuit after Tigranes through a craggy and narrow
pass, opportunely fell upon him. Upon which Tigranes, abandoning all his baggage, fled; many of the
Armenians were killed, and more taken. After this
success, Lucullus went to Tigranocerta, and sitting
down before the city, besieged it. In it were many
Greeks carried away out of Cilicia, and many barbarians in like circumstances with the Greeks, Adiabenians, Assyrians, Gordyenians, and Cappadocians,
whose native cities he had destroyed, and forced away
the inhabitants to settle here. It was a rich and beautiful city; every common man, and every man of rank,
in imitation of the king, studied to enlarge and adorn
it. This made Lucullus more vigorously press the
siege, in the belief that Tigranes would not patiently
endure it, but even against his own judgment would
come down in anger to force him away; in which he
was not mistaken. Mithridates earnestly dissuaded
him from it, sending messengers and letters to him not
to engage, but rather with his horse to try and cut off
the supplies. Taxiles, also, who came from Mithridates, and who stayed with his army, very much entreated the king to forbear, and to avoid the Roman
arms, things it was not safe to meddle with. To this
he hearkened at first, but when the Armenians and
Gordyenians in a full body, and the whole forces of
Medes and Adiabenians, under their respective kings,
joined him; when many Arabians came up from the
sea beyond Babylon, and from the Caspian sea, the
Albanians and the Iberians their neighbors, and not
a few of the free people, without kings, living about

the Araxes, by entreaty and hire also came together
to him; and all the king's feasts and councils rang of
nothing but expectations, boastings, and barbaric
threatenings, Taxiles went in danger of his life, for
giving counsel against fighting, and it was imputed to
envy in Mithridates thus to discourage him from so
glorious an enterprise. Therefore Tigranes would by
no means tarry for him, for fear he should share in
the glory, but marched on with all his army, lamenting
to his friends, as it is said, that he should fight with
Lucullus alone, and not with all the Roman generals
together. Neither was his boldness to be accounted
wholly frantic or unreasonable, when he had so many
nations and kings attending him, and so many tens of
thousands of well-armed foot and horse about him.
He had twenty thousand archers and slingers, fifty-
five thousand horse, of which seventeen thousand were
in complete armor, as Lucullus wrote to the senate, a
hundred and fifty thousand heavy-armed men, drawn
up partly into cohorts, partly into phalanxes, besides
various divisions of men appointed to make roads and
lay bridges, to drain off waters and cut wood, and to
perform other necessary services, to the number of
thirty-five thousand, who, being quartered behind the
army, added to its strength, and made it the more
formidable to behold.

As soon as he had passed Taurus, and appeared
with his forces, and saw the Romans beleaguering Tigranocerta, the barbarous people within with shout-
ings and acclamations received the sight, and threatening the Romans from the wall, pointed to the Armenians. In a council of war, some advised Lucullus
to leave the siege, and march up to Tigranes, others
that it would not be safe to leave the siege, and so
many enemies behind. He answered that neither side
by itself was right, but together both gave sound ad-

vice; and accordingly he divided his army, and left Murena with six thousand foot in charge of the siege, and himself went out with twenty-four cohorts, in which were no more than ten thousand men at arms, and with all the horse, and about a thousand slingers and archers; and sitting down by the river in a large plain, he appeared, indeed, very inconsiderable to Tigranes, and a fit subject for the flattering wits about him. Some of whom jeered, others cast lots for the spoil, and every one of the kings and commanders came and desired to undertake the engagement alone, and that he would be pleased to sit still and behold. Tigranes himself, wishing to be witty and pleasant upon the occasion, made use of the well-known saying, that they were too many for ambassadors, and too few for soldiers. Thus they continued sneering and scoffing. As soon as day came, Lucullus brought out his forces under arms. The barbarian army stood on the eastern side of the river, and there being a bend of the river westward in that part of it, where it was easiest forded, Lucullus, while he led his army on in haste, seemed to Tigranes to be flying; who thereupon called Taxiles, and in derision said, "Do you not see these invincible Romans flying?" But Taxiles replied, "Would, indeed, O king, that some such unlikely piece of fortune might be destined you; but the Romans do not, when going on a march, put on their best clothes, nor use bright shields, and naked headpieces, as now you see them, with the leathern coverings all taken off, but this is a preparation for war of men just ready to engage with their enemies." While Taxiles was thus speaking, as Lucullus wheeled about, the first eagle appeared, and the cohorts, according to their divisions and companies, formed in order to pass over, when with much ado, and like a man that is just recovering from a drunken fit, Tigranes cried out twice or thrice, "What, are they upon us?" In great confusion, therefore, the army got in array, the king keeping the main body to himself, while the left wing was given in charge to the Adiabenian, and the right to the Mede, in the front of which latter were posted most of the heavy-armed cavalry. Some officers advised Lucullus, just as he was going to cross the river, to lie still, that day being one of the unfortunate ones which they call black days, for on it the army under Cæpio, engaging with the Cimbrians, was destroyed. But he returned the famous answer, "I will make it a happy day to the Romans." It was the day before the nones of October.

Having so said, he bade them take courage, passed over the river, and himself first of all led them against the enemy, clad in a coat of mail, with shining steel scales and a fringed mantle; and his sword might already be seen out of the scabbard, as if to signify that they must without delay come to a hand-to-hand combat with an enemy whose skill was in distant fighting, and by the speed of their advance curtail the space that exposed them to the archery. But when he saw the heavy-armed horse, the flower of the army, drawn up under a hill, on the top of which was a broad and open plain about four furlongs distant, and of no very difficult or troublesome access, he commanded his Thracian and Galatian horse to fall upon their flank, and beat down their lances with their swords. The only defence of these horsemen-at-arms are their lances; they have nothing else that they can use to protect themselves, or annoy their enemy, on account of the weight and stiffness of their armor, with which they are, as it were, built up. He himself, with two cohorts, made to the mountains, the soldiers briskly following, when they saw him in arms afoot first toiling and climbing up. Being on the top and standing in an open place, with a loud voice he cried out, "We have overcome, we have overcome, fellow-soldiers!" And having so said, he marched against the armed horsemen, commanding his men not to throw their javelins, but coming up hand to hand with the enemy, to hack their shins and thighs, which parts alone were unguarded in these heavy-armed horsemen. But there was no need of this way of fighting, for they stood not to receive the Romans, but with great clamor and worse flight they and their heavy horses threw themselves upon the ranks of the foot, before ever these could so much as begin the fight, insomuch that without a wound or bloodshed, so many thousands were overthrown. The greatest slaughter was made in the flight, or rather in the endeavoring to fly away, which they could not well do by reason of the depth and closeness of their own ranks, which hindered them. Tigranes at first fled with a few, but seeing his son in the same misfortune, he took the diadem from his head, and with tears gave it him, bidding him save himself by some other road if he could. But the young man, not daring to put it on, gave it to one of his trustiest servants to keep for him. This man, as it happened, being taken, was brought to Lucullus, and so, among the captives, the crown, also, of Tigranes was taken. It is stated that above a hundred thousand foot were lost, and that of the horse but very few escaped at all. Of the Romans, a hundred were wounded, and five killed. Antiochus the philosopher, making mention of this fight in his book about the gods, says that the sun never saw the like. Strabo, a second philosopher, in his historical collection says, that the Romans could not but blush and deride themselves for putting on armor against such pitiful slaves. Livy also says, that the Romans never fought an enemy with such unequal forces, for the conquerors were not so much as one twentieth part of the number of the conquered. The most sagacious and experienced Roman commanders made it a chief commendation of Lucullus, that he had conquered two great and potent kings by two most opposite ways, haste and delay. For he wore out the flourishing power of Mithridates by delay and time, and crushed that of Tigranes by haste; being one of the rare examples of generals who made use of delay for active achievement, and speed for security.

On this account it was that Mithridates had made no haste to come up to fight, imagining Lucullus would, as he had done before, use caution and delay, which made him march at his leisure to join Tigranes. And first, as he began to meet some straggling Armenians in the way, making off in great fear and consternation, he suspected the worst, and when greater numbers of stripped and wounded men met him and assured him of the defeat, he set out to seek for Tigranes. And finding him destitute and humiliated, he by no means requited him with insolence, but alighting from his horse, and condoling with him on their common loss, he gave him his own royal guard to attend him, and animated him for the future. And they together gathered fresh forces about them. In the city Tigranocerta, the Greeks meantime, dividing from the barbarians, sought to deliver it up to Lucullus, and he attacked and took it. He seized on the treasure himself, but gave the city to be plundred by the soldiers, in which were found, amongst other property, eight thousand talents of coined money. Besides this, also, he distributed eight hundred drachmas to each man, out of the spoils. When he understood that many players were taken in the city, whom Tigranes had invited from all parts for opening the theatre which he had built, he made use of them for celebrating his triumphal games and spectacles. The Greeks he sent home, allowing them money for their journey, and the barbarians also, as many as had been forced away from their own dwellings. So that by this one city being dissolved, many, by the restitution of their former inhabitants, were restored. By all of which Lucullus was beloved as a benefactor and founder. Other successes, also, attended him, such as he well deserved, desirous as he was far more of praise for acts of justice and clemency, than for feats in war, these being due partly to the soldiers, and very greatly to fortune, while those are the sure proofs of a gentle and liberal soul; and by such aids Lucullus, at that time, even without the help of arms, succeeded in reducing the barbarians. For the kings of the Arabians came to him, tendering what they had, and with them the Sophenians also submitted. And he so dealt with the Gordyenians, that they were willing to leave their own habitations, and to follow him with their wives and children. Which was for this cause. Zarbienus, king of the Gordyenians, as has been told, being impatient under the tyranny of Tigranes, had by Appius secretly made overtures of confederacy with Lucullus, but, being discovered, was executed, and his wife and children with him, before the Romans entered Armenia. Lucullus forgot not this, but coming to the Gordyenians made a solemn interment in honor of Zarbienus, and adorning the funeral pile with royal robes, and gold, and the spoils of Tigranes, he himself in person kindled the fire, and poured in perfumes with the friends and relations of the deceased, calling him his companion and the confederate of the Romans. He ordered, also, a costly monument to be built for him. There was a large treasure of gold and silver found in Zarbienus's palace, and no less than three million measures of corn, so that the soldiers were provided for, and Lucullus had the high commendation of maintaining the war at its own charge, without receiving one drachma from the public treasury.

After this came an embassy from the king of Parthia to him, desiring amity and confederacy; which being readily embraced by Lucullus, another was sent by him in return to the Parthian, the members of which discovered him to be a double-minded man, and to be dealing privately at the same time with Tigranes, offering to take part with him, upon condition Mesopotamia were delivered up to him. Which as soon as Lucullus understood, he resolved to pass by Tigranes and Mithridates as antagonists already overcome, and to try the power of Parthia, by leading his army against them, thinking it would be a glorious result, thus in one current of war, like an athlete in the games, to throw down three kings one after another, and successively to deal as a conqueror with three of the greatest powers under heaven. He sent, therefore, into Pontus to Sornatius and his colleagues, bidding them bring the army thence, and join with him in his expedition out of Gordyene. The soldiers there, however, who had been restive and unruly before, now openly displayed their mutinous temper. No manner of entreaty or force availed with them, but they protested and cried out that they would stay no longer even there, but would go away and desert Pontus. The news of which, when reported to Lucullus, did no small harm to the soldiers about him, who were already corrupted with wealth and plenty, and desirous of ease. And on hearing the boldness of the others, they called them men, and declared they themselves ought to follow their example, for the actions which they had done did now well deserve release from service, and repose.

Upon these and worse words, Lucullus gave up the thoughts of invading Parthia, and in the height of summer-time, went against Tigranes. Passing over Taurus, he was filled with apprehension at the greenness of the fields before him, so long is the season deferred in this region by the coldness of the air. But, nevertheless, he went down, and twice or thrice putting to flight the Armenians who dared to come out against him, he plundered and burnt their villages, and seizing on the provision designed for Tigranes, reduced his enemies to the necessity which he had feared for himself. But when, after doing all he could to provoke the enemy to fight, by drawing entrenchments round their camp and by burning the country before them, he could by no means bring them to venture out, after their frequent defeats before, he rose up and marched to Artaxata, the royal city of Tigranes, where his wives and young children were kept, judging that Tigranes would never suffer that to go without the hazard of a battle. It is related that Hannibal, the Carthaginian, after the defeat of Antiochus by the Romans, coming to Artaxas, king of Armenia, pointed out to him many other matters to his advantage, and observing the great natural capacities and the pleasantness of the site, then lying unoccupied and neglected, drew a model of a city for it, and bringing Artaxas thither, showed it to him and encouraged him to build. At which the king being pleased, and desiring him to oversee the work, erected a large and stately city, which was called after his own name, and made metropolis of Armenia.

And in fact, when Lucullus proceeded against it, Tigranes no longer suffered it, but came with his army, and on the fourth day sat down by the Romans, the river Arsanias lying between them, which of necessity Lucullus must pass in his march to Artaxata. Lucullus, after sacrifice to the gods, as if victory were already obtained, carried over his army, having twelve cohorts in the first division in front, the rest being disposed in the rear to prevent the enemy's inclosing them. For there were many choice horse drawn up against them; in the front stood the Mardian horse-archers, and Iberians with long spears, in whom, being the most warlike, Tigranes more confided than in any other of his foreign troops. But nothing of moment was done by them, for though they skirmished with the Roman horse at a distance, they were not able to stand when the foot came up to them; but being broken, and flying on both sides, drew the horse in pursuit after them. Though these were routed, yet Lucullus was not without alarm when he saw the cavalry about Tigranes with great bravery and in large numbers coming upon him; he recalled his horse from pursuing, and he himself, first of all, with the best of his men, engaged the Satrapenians [7] who were opposite him, and before ever they came to close fight, routed them with the mere terror. Of three kings in battle against him, Mithridates of Pontus fled away the most shamefully, being not so much as able to endure the shout of the Romans. The pursuit reached a long way, and all through the night the Romans slew and took prisoners, and carried off spoils and treasure, till they were weary. Livy says there were more taken and destroyed in the first battle, but in the second, men of greater distinction.

Lucullus, flushed and animated by this victory, determined to march on into the interior and there complete his conquests over the barbarians; but winter weather came on, contrary to expectation, as early as the autumnal equinox, with storms and frequent

---

[7] Probably a corrupt name; the editors correct it into Atropatenians or Sacapenians.

snows and, even in the most clear days, hoar frost and ice, which made the waters scarcely drinkable for the horses by their exceeding coldness, and scarcely passable through the ice breaking and cutting the horses' sinews. The country for the most part being quite uncleared, with difficult passes, and much wood, kept them continually wet, the snow falling thickly on them as they marched in the day, and the ground that they lay upon at night being damp and watery. After the battle they followed not Lucullus many days before they began to be refractory, first of all entreating and sending the tribunes to him, but presently they tumultuously gathered together, and made a shouting all night long in their tents, a plain sign of a mutinous army. But Lucullus as earnestly entreated them, desiring them to have patience but till they took the Armenian Carthage, and overturned the work of their great enemy, meaning Hannibal. But when he could not prevail, he led them back, and crossing Taurus by another road, came into the fruitful and sunny country of Mygdonia, where was a great and populous city, by the barbarians called Nisibis, by the Greeks Antioch of Mygdonia. This was defended by Guras, brother of Tigranes, with the dignity of governor, and by the engineering skill and dexterity of Callimachus, the same who so much annoyed the Romans at Amisus. Lucullus, however, brought his army up to it, and laying close siege, in a short time took it by storm. He used Guras, who surrendered himself, kindly, but gave no attention to Callimachus, though he offered to make discovery of hidden treasures, commanding him to be kept in chains, to be punished for firing the city of Amisus, which had disappointed his ambition of showing favor and kindness to the Greeks.

Hitherto, one would imagine fortune had attended

and fought with Lucullus, but afterward, as if the
wind had failed of a sudden, he did all things by force,
and, as it were, against the grain; and showed certainly the conduct and patience of a wise captain, but
in the results met with no fresh honor or reputation;
and, indeed, by bad success and vain embarrassments
with his soldiers, he came within a little of losing even
what he had before. He himself was not the least
cause of all this, being far from inclined to seek
popularity with the mass of the soldiers, and more
ready to think any indulgence shown to them an invasion of his own authority. But what was worst
of all, he was naturally unsociable to his great officers
in commission with him, despising others and thinking
them worthy of nothing in comparison with himself.
These faults, we are told, he had with all his many
excellences; he was of a large and noble person, an
eloquent speaker and a wise counsellor, both in the
forum and the camp. Sallust says, the soldiers were
ill affected to him from the beginning of the war,
because they were forced to keep the field two winters
at Cyzicus, and afterwards at Amisus. Their other
winters, also, vexed them, for they either spent them
in an enemy's country, or else were confined to their
tents in the open field among their confederates; for
Lucullus not so much as once went into a Greek confederate town with his army. To this ill affection
abroad, the tribunes yet more contributed at home,
invidiously accusing Lucullus, as one who for empire
and riches prolonged the war, holding, it might almost
be said, under his sole power Cilicia, Asia, Bithynia,
Paphlagonia, Pontus, Armenia, all as far as the river
Phasis; and now of late had plundered the royal city
of Tigranes, as if he had been commissioned not so
much to subdue, as to strip kings. This is what we
are told was said by Lucius Quintius, one of the

prætors, at whose instance, in particular, the people determined to send one who should succeed Lucullus in his province, and voted, also, to relieve many of the soldiers under him from further service.

Besides these evils, that which most of all prejudiced Lucullus, was Publius Clodius, an insolent man, very vicious and bold, brother to Lucullus's wife, a woman of bad conduct, with whom Clodius was himself suspected of criminal intercourse. Being then in the army under Lucullus, but not in as great authority as he expected, (for he would fain have been the chief of all, but on account of his character was postponed to many,) he ingratiated himself secretly with the Fimbrian troops, and stirred them up against Lucullus, using fair speeches to them, who of old had been used to be flattered in such a manner. These were those whom Fimbria before had persuaded to kill the consul Flaccus, and choose him their leader. And so they listened not unwillingly to Clodius, and called him the soldiers' friend, for the concern he professed for them, and the indignation he expressed at the prospect that "there must be no end of wars and toils, but in fighting with all nations, and wandering throughout all the world they must wear out their lives, receiving no other reward for their service than to guard the carriages and camels of Lucullus, laden with gold and precious goblets; while as for Pompey's soldiers, they were all citizens, living safe at home with their wives and children, on fertile lands, or in towns, and that, not after driving Mithridates and Tigranes into wild deserts, and overturning the royal cities of Asia, but after having merely reduced exiles in Spain, or fugitive slaves in Italy. Nay, if indeed we must never have an end of fighting, should we not rather reserve the remainder of our bodies and souls for a general who will reckon his chiefest glory to be the wealth of his soldiers."

By such practices the army of Lucullus being corrupted, neither followed him against Tigranes, nor against Mithridates, when he now at once returned into Pontus out of Armenia, and was recovering his kingdom, but under pretence of the winter, sat idle in Gordyene, every minute expecting either Pompey, or some other general, to succeed Lucullus. But when news came that Mithridates had defeated Fabius, and was marching against Sornatius and Triarius, out of shame they followed Lucullus. Triarius, ambitiously aiming at victory, before ever Lucullus came to him, though he was then very near, was defeated in a great battle, in which it is said that above seven thousand Romans fell, among whom were a hundred and fifty centurions, and four and twenty tribunes, and that the camp itself was taken. Lucullus, coming up a few days after, concealed Triarius from the search of the angry soldiers. But when Mithridates declined battle, and waited for the coming of Tigranes, who was then on his march with great forces, he resolved before they joined their forces to turn once more and engage with Tigranes. But in the way the mutinous Fimbrians deserted their ranks, professing themselves released from service by a decree, and that Lucullus, the provinces being allotted to others, had no longer any right to command them. There was nothing beneath the dignity of Lucullus which he did not now submit to bear, entreating them one by one, from tent to tent, going up and down humbly and in tears, and even taking some, like a suppliant, by the hand. But they turned away from his salutes, and threw down their empty purses, bidding him engage alone with the enemy, as he alone made advantage of it. At length, by the entreaty of the other soldiers, the Fimbrians, being prevailed upon, consented to tarry that summer under him, but if during that time no enemy came to fight them, to be free. Lucullus of necessity was forced to comply with this, or else to abandon the country to the barbarians. He kept them, indeed, with him, but without urging his authority upon them; nor did he lead them out to battle, being contented if they would but stay with him, though he then saw Cappadocia wasted by Tigranes, and Mithridates again triumphing, whom not long before he reported to the senate to be wholly subdued; and commissioners were now arrived to settle the affairs of Pontus, as if all had been quietly in his possession. But when they came, they found him not so much as master of himself, but contemned and derided by the common soldiers, who arrived at that height of insolence against their general, that at the end of summer they put on their armor and drew their swords, and defied their enemies then absent and gone off a long while before, and with great outcries and waving their swords in the air, they quitted the camp, proclaiming that the time was expired which they promised to stay with Lucullus The rest were. summoned by letters from Pompey to come and join him; he, by the favor of the people and by flattery of their leaders, having been chosen general of the army against Mithridates and Tigranes, though the senate and the nobility all thought that Lucullus was injured, having those put over his head who succeeded rather to his triumph, than to his commission, and that he was not so truly deprived of his command, as of the glory he had deserved in his command, which he was forced to yield to another.

It was yet more of just matter of pity and indignation to those who were present; for Lucullus remained no longer master of rewards or punishments for any actions done in the war; neither would Pompey suffer any man to go to him, or pay any respect to the orders and arrangements he made with advice of his ten commissioners, but expressly issued edicts to the contrary, and could not but be obeyed by reason of his greater power. Friends, however, on both sides, thought it desirable to bring them together, and they met in a village of Galatia, and saluted each other in a friendly manner, with congratulations on each other's successes. Lucullus was the elder, but Pompey the more distinguished by his more numerous commands and his two triumphs. Both had rods dressed with laurel carried before them for their victories. And as Pompey's laurels were withered with passing through hot and droughty countries, Lucullus's lictors courteously gave Pompey's some of the fresh and green ones which they had, which Pompey's friends counted a good omen, as indeed of a truth, Lucullus's actions furnished the honors of Pompey's command. The interview, however, did not bring them to any amicable agreement; they parted even less friends than they met. Pompey repealed all the acts of Lucullus, drew off his soldiers, and left him no more than sixteen hundred for his triumph, and even those unwilling to go with him. So wanting was Lucullus, either through natural constitution or adverse circumstances, in that one first and most important requisite of a general, which had he but added to his other many and remarkable virtues, his fortitude, vigilance, wisdom, justice, the Roman empire had not had Euphrates for its boundary, but the utmost ends of Asia and the Hyrcanian sea; as other nations were then disabled by the late conquests of Tigranes, and the power of Parthia had not in Lucullus's time shown itself so formidable as

Crassus afterwards found it, nor had as yet gained that consistency, being crippled by wars at home, and on its frontiers, and unable even to make head against the encroachments of the Armenians. And Lucullus, as it was, seems to me through others' agency to have done Rome greater harm, than he did her advantage by his own. For the trophies in Armenia, near the Parthian frontier, and Tigranocerta, and Nisibis, and the great wealth brought from thence to Rome, with the captive crown of Tigranes carried in triumph, all helped to puff up Crassus, as if the barbarians had been nothing else but spoil and booty, and he, falling among the Parthian archers, soon demonstrated that Lucullus's triumphs were not beholden to the inadvertency and effeminacy of his enemies, but to his own courage and conduct. But of this afterwards.

Lucullus, upon his return to Rome, found his brother Marcus accused by Caius Memmius, for his acts as quæstor, done by Sylla's orders; and on his acquittal, Memmius changed the scene, and animated the people against Lucullus himself, urging them to deny him a triumph for appropriating the spoils and prolonging the war. In this great struggle, the nobility and chief men went down and mingling in person among the tribes, with much entreaty and labor, scarce at length prevailed upon them to consent to his triumph. The pomp of which proved not so wonderful or so wearisome with the length of the procession and the number of things carried in it, but consisted chiefly in vast quantities of arms and machines of the king's, with which he adorned the Flaminian circus, a spectacle by no means despicable. In his progress there passed by a few horsemen in heavy armor, ten chariots armed with scythes, sixty friends and officers of the king's, and a hundred and ten brazen-beaked ships of war, which were conveyed along with them, a golden image of Mithridates six feet high, a shield set with precious stones, twenty loads of silver vessels, and thirty-two of golden cups, armor, and money, all carried by men. Besides which, eight mules were laden with golden couches, fifty-six with bullion, and a hundred and seven with coined silver, little less than two millions seven hundred thousand pieces. There were tablets, also, with inscriptions, stating what moneys he gave Pompey for prosecuting the piratic war, what he delivered into the treasury, and what he gave to every soldier, which was nine hundred and fifty drachmas each. After all which he nobly feasted the city and adjoining villages, or *vici*.[8]

Being divorced from Clodia, a dissolute and wicked woman, he married Servilia, sister to Cato. This also proved an unfortunate match, for she only wanted one of all Clodia's vices, the criminality she was accused of with her brothers. Out of reverence to Cato, he for a while connived at her impurity and immodesty, but at length dismissed her. When the senate expected great things from him, hoping to find in him a check to the usurpations of Pompey, and that with the greatness of his station and credit he would come forward as the champion of the nobility, he retired from business and abandoned public life; either because he saw the State to be in a difficult and diseased condition, or, as others say, because he was as great as he could well be, and inclined to a quiet and easy life, after those many labors and toils which had ended with him so far from fortunately. There are

---

[8] *The city and adjoining villages* or vici; such is Plutarch's expression; but the *vici* are properly the subdivisions of the *regions*, or wards, of the city, each under its proper officers or *vici-magistri*. Augustus made them four hundred and twenty-four in number. Many of these might in Lucullus's time have been called *vici*, but not included in the city.

those who highly commend his change of life, saying that he thus avoided that rock on which Marius split. For he, after the great and glorious deeds of his Cimbrian victories, was not contented to retire upon his honors, but out of an insatiable desire of glory and power, even in his old age, headed a political party against young men, and let himself fall into miserable actions, and yet more miserable sufferings. Better, in like manner, they say, had it been for Cicero, after Catiline's conspiracy, to have retired and grown old, and for Scipio, after his Numantine and Carthaginian conquests, to have sat down contented. For the administration of public affairs has, like other things, its proper term, and statesmen as well as wrestlers will break down, when strength and youth fail. But Crassus and Pompey, on the other hand, laughed to see Lucullus abandoning himself to pleasure and expense, as if luxurious living were not a thing that as little became his years, as government of affairs at home, or of an army abroad.

And, indeed, Lucullus's life, like the Old Comedy, presents us at the commencement with acts of policy and of war, at the end offering nothing but good eating and drinking, feastings and revellings, and mere play. For I give no higher name to his sumptuous buildings, porticos and baths, still less to his paintings and sculptures, and all his industry about these curiosities, which he collected with vast expense, lavishly bestowing all the wealth and treasure which he got in the war upon them, insomuch that even now, with all the advance of luxury, the Lucullean gardens [9] are counted the noblest the emperor has. Tubero

---

[9] The *Lucullean gardens* were those of the Garden Hill (the Collis Hortulorum), the Pincian of the present time. *Horace,* in the last line, is in the original *Flaccus.*

the stoic, when he saw his buildings at Naples, where he suspended the hills upon vast tunnels, brought in the sea for moats and fish-ponds round his house, and built pleasure-houses in the waters, called him Xerxes in a gown. He had also fine seats in Tusculum, belvederes, and large open balconies for men's apartments, and porticos to walk in, where Pompey coming to see him, blamed him for making a house which would be pleasant in summer, but uninhabitable in winter; whom he answered with a smile, "You think me, then, less provident than cranes and storks, not to change my home with the season." When a prætor, with great expense and pains, was preparing a spectacle for the people, and asked him to lend him some purple robes for the performers in a chorus, he told him he would go home and see, and if he had got any, would let him have them; and the next day asking how many he wanted, and being told that a hundred would suffice, bade him to take twice as many: on which the poet Horace observes, that a house is but a poor one, where the valuables unseen and unthought of do not exceed all those that meet the eye.[10]

Lucullus's daily entertainments were ostentatiously extravagant, not only with purple coverlets, and plate adorned with precious stones, and dancings, and interludes, but with the greatest diversity of

---

[10] In the Epistles, I. 6, 40, where the story is told a little differently:—

> Chlamydes Lucullus, ut aiunt,
> Si posset centum cœnæ præbere rogatus,
> Quî possum tot? ait; tamen et quæram et quot habebo
> Mittam; postpaulo scribit sibi millia quinque
> Esse domi chlamydum; partem vel tolleret omnes.
> Exilis domus est ubi non et multa supersunt,
> Et dominum fallunt et prosunt furibus.

dishes and the most elaborate cookery, for the vulgar to admire and envy. It was a happy thought of Pompey in his sickness, when his physician prescribed a thrush for his dinner, and his servants told him that in summer time thrushes were not to be found anywhere but in Lucullus's fattening coops, that he would not suffer them to fetch one thence, but observing to his physician, "So if Lucullus had not been an epicure, Pompey had not lived," ordered something else that could easily be got to be prepared for him. Cato was his friend and connection, but, nevertheless, so hated his life and habits, that when a young man in the senate made a long and tedious speech in praise of frugality and temperance, Cato got up and said, "How long do you mean to go on making money like Crassus, living like Lucullus, and talking like Cato?" There are some, however, who say the words were said, but not by Cato.

It is plain from the anecdotes on record of him, that Lucullus was not only pleased with, but even gloried in his way of living. For he is said to have feasted several Greeks upon their coming to Rome day after day, who, out of a true Grecian principle, being ashamed, and declining the invitation, where so great an expense was every day incurred for them, he with a smile told them, "Some of this, indeed, my Grecian friends, is for your sakes, but more for that of Lucullus." Once when he supped alone, there being only once course, and that but moderately furnished, he called his steward and reproved him, who, professing to have supposed that there would be no need of any great entertainment, when nobody was invited, was answered, "What, did not you know, then, that to-day Lucullus dines with Lucullus?" Which being much spoken of about the city, Cicero and Pompey one day met him loitering in the forum, the former his intimate friend and familiar, and, though there had been some ill-will between Pompey and him about the command in the war, still they used to see each other and converse on easy terms together. Cicero accordingly saluted him, and asked him whether to-day were a good time for asking a favor of him, and on his answering, "Very much so," and begging to hear what it was, "Then," said Cicero, "we should like to dine with you to-day, just on the dinner that is prepared for yourself." Lucullus being surprised, and requesting a day's time, they refused to grant it, neither suffered him to talk with his servants, for fear he should give order for more than was appointed before. But thus much they consented to, that before their faces he might tell his servant, that to-day he would sup in the Apollo, (for so one of his best dining-rooms was called,) and by this evasion he outwitted his guests. For every room, as it seems, had its own assessment of expenditure, dinner at such a price, and all else in accordance; so that the servants, on knowing where he would dine, knew also how much was to be expended, and in what style and form dinner was to be served. The expense for the Apollo was fifty thousand drachmas,[11] and thus much being that day laid out, the greatness of the cost did not so much amaze Pompey and Cicero, as the rapidity of the outlay. One might believe Lucullus thought his money really captive and barbarian, so wantonly and contumeliously did he treat it.

His furnishing a library, however, deserves praise and record, for he collected very many choice manuscripts; and the use they were put to was even more magnificent than the purchase, the library being always open, and the walks and reading-rooms about it

[11] About $10,000.

free to all Greeks, whose delight it was to leave their other occupations and hasten thither as to the habitation of the Muses, there walking about, and diverting one another. He himself often passed his hours there, disputing with the learned in the walks, and giving his advice to statesmen who required it, insomuch that his house was altogether a home, and in a manner a Greek prytaneum for those that visited Rome. He was fond of all sorts of philosophy, and was well-read and expert in them all. But he always from the first specially favored and valued the Academy; not the New one, which at that time under Philo flourished with the precepts of Carneades, but the Old one, then sustained and represented by Antiochus of Ascalon, a learned and eloquent man. Lucullus with great labor made him his friend and companion, and set him up against Philo's auditors, among whom Cicero was one, who wrote an admirable treatise in defence of his sect, in which he puts the argument in favor of *comprehension*[12] in the mouth of Lucullus, and the opposite argument in his own. The book is called Lucullus. For as has been said, they were great friends, and took the same side in politics. For Lucullus did not wholly retire from the republic, but only from ambition, and from the dangerous and often lawless struggle for political preeminence, which he left to Crassus and Cato, whom the senators, jealous of Pompey's greatness, put for-

---

[12] *Comprehensio* is Cicero's literal Latin version of the Greek philosophical term *catalepsis,* equivalent in the doctrine of Antiochus and of the Stoics to what we might rather call apprehension, as opposed to mere sensation, or impression. The argument, placed in the mouth of Lucullus, in the book which bears his name, the second of the Prior Academics, is in favor of the possibility of certain and real knowledge, in opposition to the sceptical views of human capacities.

ward as their champions, when Lucullus refused to head them. For his friends' sake he came into the forum and into the senate, when occasion offered to humble the ambition and pride of Pompey, whose settlement, after his conquests over the kings, he got cancelled, and by the assistance of Cato, hindered a division of lands to his soldiers, which he proposed. So Pompey went over to Crassus and Cæsar's alliance, or rather conspiracy, and filling the city with armed men, procured the ratification of his decrees by force, and drove Cato and Lucullus out of the forum. Which being resented by the nobility, Pompey's party produced one Vettius, pretending they apprehended him in a design against Pompey's life. Who in the senate-house accused others, but before the people named Lucullus, as if he had been suborned by him to kill Pompey. Nobody gave heed to what he said, and it soon appeared that they had put him forward to make false charges and accusations. And after a few days the whole intrigue became yet more obvious, when the dead body of Vettius was thrown out of the prison, he being reported, indeed, to have died a natural death, but carrying marks of a halter and blows about him, and seeming rather to have been taken off by those who suborned him. These things kept Lucullus at a greater distance from the republic.

But when Cicero was banished the city, and Cato sent to Cyprus, he quitted public affairs altogether. It is said, too, that before his death, his intellects failed him by degrees. But Cornelius Nepos denies that either age or sickness impaired his mind, which was rather affected by a potion, given him by Callisthenes his freedman. The potion was meant by Callisthenes to strengthen his affection for him, and was supposed to have that tendency but it acted quite otherwise, and so disabled and unsettled his mind, that while he was yet alive, his brother took charge of his affairs. At his death, as though it had been the death of one taken off in the very height of military and civil glory, the people were much concerned, and flocked together, and would have forcibly taken his corpse, as it was carried into the market-place by young men of the highest rank, and have buried it in the field of Mars, where they buried Sylla. Which being altogether unexpected, and necessaries not easily to be procured on a sudden, his brother, after much entreaty and solicitation, prevailed upon them to suffer him to be buried on his Tusculan estate as had been appointed. He himself survived him but a short time, coming not far behind in death, as he did in age and renown, in all respects, a most loving brother.

COMPARISON OF LUCULLUS WITH CIMON

ONE might bless the end of Lucullus, which was so timed as to let him die before the great revolution, which fate by intestine wars, was already effecting against the established government, and to close his life in a free, though troubled commonwealth. And in this, above all other things, Cimon and he are alike. For he died also when Greece was as yet undisordered, in its highest felicity; though in the field at the head of his army, not recalled, nor out of his mind, nor sullying the glory of his wars, engagements, and conquests, by making feastings and debauches seem the apparent end and aim of them all; as Plato says scornfully of Orpheus,[1] that he makes an eternal debauch hereafter, the reward of those who lived well here. Indeed, ease and quiet, and the study of pleasant and speculative learning, to an old man retiring from command and office, is a most suitable and becoming solace; but to misguide virtuous actions to pleasure as their utmost end, and, as the conclusion of campaigns and commands, to keep the feast of Venus, did not become the noble Academy, and the follower of Xenocrates, but rather one that inclined to Epicurus. And this is one surprising point of contrast between them; Cimon's[2] youth was ill-reputed and

---

[1] *Plato says* it *scornfully* not of Orpheus, but Musæus, in the Republic (*II.*, p. 363). *The feast of Venus,* the Aphrodisia, is often spoken of as kept formally by sailors on their return to port, and, in a general way, the phrase is used of all indulgence and feasting after business, labor, or danger.

[2] Plato's words about Cimon's ostracism are in the Gorgias (*p.* 516).

intemperate, Lucullus's well disciplined and sober. Undoubtedly we must give the preference to the change for good, for it argues the better nature, where vice declines and virtue grows. Both had great wealth, but employed it in different ways; and there is no comparison between the south wall of the acropolis built by Cimon, and the chambers and galleries, with their sea-views, built at Naples by Lucullus, out of the spoils of the barbarians. Neither can we compare Cimon's popular and liberal table with the sumptuous oriental one of Lucullus, the former receiving a great many guests every day at small cost, the latter expensively spread for a few men of pleasure, unless you will say that different times made the alteration. For who can tell but that Cimon, if he had retired in his old age from business and war to quiet and solitude, might have lived a more luxurious and self-indulgent life, as he was fond of wine and company, and accused, as has been said, of laxity with women? The better pleasures gained in successful action and effort leave the baser appetites no time or place, and make active and heroic men forget them. Had but Lucullus ended his days in the field, and in command, envy and detraction itself could never have accused him. So much for their manner of life.

In war, it is plain they were both soldiers of excellent conduct, both at land and sea. But as in the games they honor those champions who on the same day gain the garland, both in wrestling and in the pancratium, with the name of "Victors and more," [3] so Cimon, honoring Greece with a sea and land victory on the same day, may claim a certain pre-

---

[3] The text is uncertain; "paradoxonicas," i. e. "victors contrary to all probability," seems the most reasonable conjecture.

eminence among commanders. Lucullus received command from his country, whereas Cimon brought it to his. He annexed the territories of enemies to her, who ruled over confederates before, but Cimon made his country, which when he began was a mere follower of others, both rule over confederates, and conquer enemies too, forcing the Persians to relinquish the sea, and inducing the Lacedæmonians to surrender their command. If it be the chiefest thing in a general to obtain the obedience of his soldiers by good-will, Lucullus was despised by his own army, but Cimon highly prized even by others. His soldiers deserted the one, the confederates came over to the other. Lucullus came home without the forces which he led out; Cimon, sent out at first to serve as one confederate among others, returned home with authority even over these also, having successfully effected for his city three most difficult services, establishing peace with the enemy, dominion over confederates, and concord with Lacedæmon. Both aiming to destroy great kingdoms, and subdue all Asia, failed in their enterprise, Cimon by a simple piece of illfortune, for he died when general, in the height of success; but Lucullus no man can wholly acquit of being in fault with his soldiers, whether it were he did not know, or would not comply with the distastes and complaints of his army, which brought him at last into such extreme unpopularity among them. But did not Cimon also suffer like him in this? For the citizens arraigned him, and did not leave off till they had banished him, that, as Plato says, they might not hear him for the space of ten years. For high and noble minds seldom please the vulgar, or are acceptable to them; for the force they use to straighten their distorted actions gives the same pain as surgeons' bandages do in bringing dislocated bones to their natural position. Both of them, perhaps, come off pretty much with an equal acquittal on this count.

Lucullus very much outwent him in war, being the first Roman who carried an army over Taurus, passed the Tigris, took and burnt the royal palaces of Asia in the sight of the kings, Tigranocerta, Cabira, Sinope, and Nisibis, seizing and overwhelming the northern parts as far as the Phasis, the east as far as Media, and making the South and Red Sea his own through the kings of the Arabians. He shattered the power of the kings, and narrowly missed their persons, while like wild beasts they fled away into deserts and thick and impassable woods. In demonstration of this superiority, we see that the Persians, as if no great harm had befallen them under Cimon, soon after appeared in arms against the Greeks, and overcame and destroyed their numerous forces in Egypt. But after Lucullus, Tigranes and Mithridates were able to do nothing; the latter, being disabled and broken in the former wars, never dared to show his army to Pompey outside the camp, but fled away to Bosporus, and there died. Tigranes threw himself, naked and unarmed, down before Pompey, and taking his crown from his head, laid it at his feet, complimenting Pompey with what was not his own, but, in real truth, the conquest already effected by Lucullus. And when he received the ensigns of majesty again, he was well pleased, evidently because he had forfeited them before. And the commander, as the wrestler, is to be accounted to have done most who leaves an adversary almost conquered for his successor. Cimon, moreover, when he took the command, found the power of the king broken, and the spirits of the Persians humbled by their great defeats and incessant routs under Themistocles, Pausanias, and Leotychides, and thus easily overcame the bodies of men whose souls were quelled and defeated beforehand. But Tigranes had never yet in many combats been beaten, and was flushed with success when he engaged with Lucullus. There is no comparison between the numbers, which came against Lucullus, and those subdued by Cimon. All which things being rightly considered, it is a hard matter to give judgment. For supernatural favor also appears to have attended both of them, directing the one what to do, the other what to avoid, and thus they have, both of them, so to say, the vote of the gods, to declare them noble and divine characters.

NICIAS[1]

TRANSLATED BY THOMAS RYMER, ESQ., (THE CRITIC AND ANTIQUARY).

CRASSUS, in my opinion, may most properly be set against Nicias, and the Parthian disaster compared with that in Sicily. But here it will be well for me to entreat the reader, in all courtesy, not to think that I contend with Thucydides in matters so pathetically, vividly, and eloquently, beyond all imitation, and even beyond himself, expressed by him; nor to believe me guilty of the like folly with Timæus, who, hoping in his history to surpass Thucydides in art, and to make Philistus appear a trifler and a novice, pushes on in his descriptions, through all the battles, sea-fights, and public speeches, in recording which they have been most successful, without meriting so much as to be compared in Pindar's phrase to

> One that on his feet
> Would with the Lydian cars compete.[2]

He simply shows himself all along a half-lettered, childish writer; in the words of Diphilus,

> ——— of wit obese,
> O'erlarded with Sicilian grease.

[1] A celebrated Athenian general during the Peloponnesian war, several times associated with Pericles, noted for his great prudence and high character. With Demosthenes he was put to death by the Syracusans (413 B. C.).—Dr. William Smith.

[2] The fragment from Pindar is No. 119, in the Uncertain Fragments of Boeckh's edition. Diphilus is a Comic poet.

Often he sinks to the very level of Xenarchus, telling us that he thinks it ominous to the Athenians, that their general, who had victory [3] in his name, was unwilling to take command in the expedition; and that the defacing of the Hermæ was a divine intimation that they should suffer much in the war by Hermocrates, the son of Hermon; and, moreover, how it was likely that Hercules should aid the Syracusans for the sake of Proserpine, by which means he took Cerberus, and should be angry with the Athenians for protecting the Egesteans, descended from Trojan ancestors, whose city he, for an injury of their king Laomedon, had overthrown. However, all these may be merely other instances of the same happy taste that makes him correct the diction of Philistus, and abuse Plato and Aristotle. This sort of contention and rivalry with others in matter of style, to my mind, in any case, seems petty and pedantic, but when its objects are works of inimitable excellence, it is absolutely senseless. Such actions in Nicias's life as Thucydides and Philistus have related, since they cannot be passed by, illustrating as they do most especially his character and temper, under his many and great troubles, that I may not seem altogether negligent, I shall briefly run over. And such things as are not commonly known, and lie scattered here and there in other men's writings, or are found amongst the old monuments and archives, I shall endeavor to bring together; not collecting mere useless pieces of learning, but adducing what may make his disposition and habit of mind understood.

First of all, I would mention what Aristotle has said of Nicias, that there had been three good citizens, eminent above the rest for their hereditary affection

---

[3] Nikë, or nicë, victory, in the name Nikias, or Nicias.

and love to the people, Nicias, the son of Niceratus, Thucydides the son of Melesias, and Theramenes the son of Hagnon, but the last less than the others; for he had his dubious extraction cast in his teeth, as a foreigner from Ceos, and his inconstancy, which made him side sometimes with one party, sometimes with another in public life, and which obtained him the nickname of the Buskin.[4]

Thucydides came earlier, and, on the behalf of the nobility, was a great opponent of the measures by which Pericles courted the favor of the people.

Nicias was a younger man, yet was in some reputation even whilst Pericles lived; so much so as to have been his colleague in the office of general, and to have held command by himself more than once. But on the death of Pericles, he presently rose to the highest place, chiefly by the favor of the rich and eminent citizens, who set him up for their bulwark against the presumption and insolence of Cleon; nevertheless, he did not forfeit the good-will of the commonalty, who, likewise, contributed to his advancement. For though Cleon got great influence by his exertions

——— to please
The old men, who trusted him to find them fees.[5]

Yet even those, for whose interest, and to gain whose favor he acted, nevertheless observing the avarice, the arrogance, and the presumption of the man, many of them supported Nicias. For his was not that sort of gravity which is harsh and offensive, but he tempered it with a certain caution and deference, winning upon the people, by seeming afraid of them. And being

[4] Which would fit indifferently on either foot.

[5] The quotation is loosely taken from the Knights of Aristophanes (Equites, 1096).

naturally diffident and unhopeful in war, his good fortune supplied his want of courage, and kept it from being detected, as in all his commands he was constantly successful. And his timorousness in civil life, and his extreme dread of accusers, was thought very suitable in a citizen of a free State; and from the people's good-will towards him, got him no small power over them, they being fearful of all that despised them, but willing to promote one who seemed to be afraid of them; the greatest compliment their betters could pay them being not to contemn them.

Pericles, who by solid virtue and the pure force of argument ruled the commonwealth, had stood in need of no disguises nor persuasions with the people. Nicias, inferior in these respects, used his riches, of which he had abundance, to gain popularity. Neither had he the nimble wit of Cleon, to win the Athenians to his purposes by amusing them with bold jests; unprovided with such qualities, he courted them with dramatic exhibitions, gymnastic games, and other public shows, more sumptuous and more splendid than had been ever known in his, or in former ages. Amongst his religious offerings, there was extant, even in our days, the small figure of Minerva in the citadel, having lost the gold that covered it; and a shrine in the temple of Bacchus, under the tripods, that were presented by those who won the prize in the shows of plays. For at these he had often carried off the prize, and never once failed. We are told that on one of these occasions, a slave of his appeared in the character of Bacchus, of a beautiful person and noble stature, and with as yet no beard upon his chin; and on the Athenians being pleased with the sight, and applauding a long time, Nicias stood up, and said he could not in piety keep as a slave one whose person had been consecrated to represent a god. And forthwith he set the young man free. His performances at Delos are, also, on record, as noble and magnificent works of devotion. For whereas the choruses which the cities sent to sing hymns to the god were wont to arrive in no order, as it might happen, and, being there met by a crowd of people crying out to them to sing, in their hurry to begin, used to disembark confusedly, putting on their garlands, and changing their dresses as they left the ships, he, when he had to convoy the sacred company, disembarked the chorus at Rhenea, together with the sacrifice, and other holy appurtenances. And having brought along with him from Athens a bridge fitted by measurement for the purpose, and magnificently adorned with gilding and coloring, and with garlands and tapestries; this he laid in the night over the channel betwixt Rhenea and Delos, being no great distance. And at break of day he marched forth with all the procession to the god, and led the chorus, sumptuously ornamented, and singing their hymns, along over the bridge. The sacrifices, the games, and the feast being over, he set up a palm-tree of brass for a present to the god, and bought a parcel of land with ten thousand drachmas, which he consecrated; with the revenue the inhabitants of Delos were to sacrifice and to feast, and to pray the gods for many good things to Nicias. This he engraved on a pillar, which he left in Delos to be a record of his bequest. This same palm-tree, afterwards broken down by the wind, fell on the great statue which the men of Naxos presented, and struck it to the ground.

It is plain that much of this might be vainglory, and the mere desire of popularity and applause; yet from other qualities and carriage of the man, one might believe all this cost and public display to be the effect of devotion. For he was one of those who dreaded the divine powers extremely, and, as Thucydides tells us, was much given to arts of divination. In one of Pasiphon's dialogues, it is stated that he daily sacrificed to the gods, and keeping a diviner at his house, professed to be consulting always about the commonwealth, but for the most part, inquired about his own private affairs, more especially concerning his silver mines; for he owned many works at Laurium, of great value, but somewhat hazardous to carry on. He maintained there a multitude of slaves, and his wealth consisted chiefly in silver. Hence he hand many hangers-on about him, begging and obtaining. For he gave to those who could do him mischief, no less than to those who deserved well. In short, his timidity was a revenue to rogues, and his humanity to honest men. We find testimony in the comic writers, as when Teleclides, speaking of one of the professed informers, says:—

> Charicles [6] gave the man a pound, the matter not to name,
> That from inside a money-bag into the world he came;
> And Nicias, also, paid him four; I know the reason well,
> But Nicias is a worthy man, and so I will not tell.

So, also, the informer whom Eupolis introduces in his Maricas, attacking a good, simple, poor man:—

> How long ago did you and Nicias meet?
>
> I did but see him just now in the street.
>
> The man has seen him and denies it not,
> 'T is evident that they are in a plot.

---

[6] The allusion of Teleclides in the case of Charicles is to the habit, apparently very frequent with rich and childless women in Greece, of introducing supposititious children into a family. For the words of *Cleon* (or, more correctly, of Agoracritus, Cleon's opponent), *in Aristophanes*, see the Knights, 358.

NICIAS

> See you, O citizen! 't is fact,
> Nicias is taken in the act.
>
> Taken, Fools! take so good a man
> In aught that's wrong none will or can.[7]

Cleon, in Aristophanes, makes it one of his threats:—

> I'll outscream all the speakers, and make Nicias stand aghast!

Phrynichus also implies his want of spirit, and his easiness to be intimidated in the verses,

> A noble man he was, I well can say,
> Nor walked like Nicias, cowering on his way.

So cautious was he of informers, and so reserved, that he never would dine out with any citizen, nor allowed himself to indulge in talk and conversation with his friends, nor gave himself any leisure for such amusements; but when he was general he used to stay at the office [8] till night, and was the first that came to the council-house, and the last that left it. And if no public business engaged him, it was very hard to have access, or to speak with him, he being retired at home and locked up. And when any came to the door, some friend of his gave them good words, and begged them to excuse him, Nicias was very busy; as if affairs of State and public duties still kept his occupied. He who principally acted this part for him, and contributed most to this state and show, was Hiero, a man educated in Nicias's family, and instructed by him in letters and music. He professed to be the son of Dionysius, surnamed Chalcus, whose poems are yet

---

[7] One half of the citizens take the part of the informer, the other that of the accused.

[8] The office of the Board of Generals, ten in number, by whom all the military business was transacted.

extant, and had led out the colony to Italy, and
founded Thurii. This Hiero transacted all his secrets for Nicias with the diviners; and gave out to the
people, what a toilsome and miserable life he led, for
the sake of the commonwealth. "He," said Hiero,
"can never be either at the bath, or at his meat, but
some public business interferes. Careless of his own,
and zealous for the public good, he scarcely ever goes
to bed till after others have had their first sleep. So
that his health is impaired, and his body out of order,
nor is he cheerful or affable with his friends, but loses
them as well as his money in the service of the State,
while other men gain friends by public speaking, enrich themselves, fare delicately, and make government
their amusement." And in fact this was Nicias's manner of life, so that he well might apply to himself the
words of Agamemnon:—

> Vain pomp's the ruler of the life we live,
> And a slave's service to the crowd we give.[9]

He observed that the people, in the case of men of
eloquence, or of eminent parts, made use of their
talents upon occasion, but were always jealous of their
abilities, and held a watchful eye upon them, taking
all opportunities to humble their pride and abate their
reputation; as was manifest in their condemnation of
Pericles, their banishment of Damon, their distrust
of Antiphon the Rhamnusian, but especially in the
case of Paches who took Lesbos, who, having to give
an account of his conduct, in the very court of justice
unsheathed his sword and slew himself. Upon such
considerations, Nicias declined all difficult and lengthy
enterprises; if he took a command, he was for doing
what was safe; and if, as thus was likely, he had for

---

[9] *The words of Agamemnon* are from the Iphigenia in Aulis
of Euripides (449).

the most part success, he did not attribute it to any wisdom, conduct, or courage of his own, but, to avoid envy, he thanked fortune for all, and gave the glory to the divine powers. And the actions themselves bore testimony in his favor; the city met at that time with several considerable reverses, but he had not a hand in any of them. The Athenians were routed in Thrace by the Chalcidians, Calliades and Xenophon commanding in chief. Demosthenes was the general when they were unfortunate in Ætolia. At Delium, they lost a thousand citizens under the conduct of Hippocrates; the plague was principally laid to the charge of Pericles, he, to carry on the war, having shut up close together in the town the crowd of people from the country, who, by the change of place, and of their usual course of living, bred the pestilence. Nicias stood clear of all this; under his conduct was taken Cythera, an island most commodious against Laconia, and occupied by the Lacedæmonian settlers; many places, likewise, in Thrace, which had revolted, were taken or won over by him; he, shutting up the Megarians within their town, seized upon the isle of Minoa; and soon after, advancing from thence to Nisæa, made himself master there, and then making a descent upon the Corinthian territory, fought a successful battle, and slew a great number of the Corinthians with their captain Lycophron. There it happened that two of his men were left by an oversight, when they carried off the dead, which when he understood, he stopped the fleet, and sent a herald to the enemy for leave to carry off the dead; though by law and custom, he that by a truce craved leave to carry off the dead, was hereby supposed to give up all claim to the victory. Nor was it lawful for him that did this to erect a trophy, for his is the victory who is master of the field, and he is not master who asks leave, as wanting power to take. But he chose rather to renounce his victory and his glory, than to let two citizens lie unburied. He scoured the coast of Laconia all along, and beat the Lacedæmonians that made head against him. He took Thyrea, occupied by the Æginetans, and carried the prisoners to Athens.

When Demosthenes had fortified Pylos, and the Peloponnesians brought together both their sea and land forces before it, after the fight, about the number of four hundred native Spartans were left ashore in the isle Sphacteria. The Athenians thought it a great prize, as indeed it was, to take these men prisoners. But the siege, in places that wanted water, being very difficult and untoward, and to convey necessaries about by sea in summer tedious and expensive, in winter doubtful, or plainly impossible, they began to be annoyed, and to repent their having rejected the embassy of the Lacedæmonians, that had been sent to propose a treaty of peace, which had been done at the importunity of Cleon, who opposed it chiefly out of a pique to Nicias; for, being his enemy, and observing him to be extremely solicitous to support the offers of the Lacedæmonians, he persuaded the people to refuse them.

Now, therefore, that the siege was protracted, and they heard of the difficulties that pressed their army, they grew enraged against Cleon. But he turned all the blame upon Nicias, charging it on his softness and cowardice, that the besieged were not yet taken. "Were I general," said he, "they should not hold out so long." The Athenians not unnaturally asked the question, "Why then, as it is, do you not go with a squadron against them?" And Nicias, standing up resigned his command at Pylos to him, and bade him take what forces he pleased along with him, and not

NICIAS

be bold in words, out of harm's way, but go forth and perform some real service for the commonwealth. Cleon, at the first, tried to draw back, disconcerted at the proposal, which he had never expected; but the Athenians insisting, and Nicias loudly upbraiding him, he thus provoked, and fired with ambition, took upon him the charge, and said further, that within twenty days after he embarked, he would either kill the enemy upon the place, or bring them alive to Athens. This the Athenians were readier to laugh at than to believe, as on other occasions, also, his bold assertions and extravagances used to make them sport, and were pleasant enough. As, for instance, it is reported that once when the people were assembled, and had waited his coming a long time, at last he appeared with a garland on his head, and prayed them to adjourn to the next day. "For," said he, "I am not at leisure to-day; I have sacrificed to the gods, and am to entertain some strangers. Whereupon the Athenians laughing rose up, and dissolved the assembly. However, at this time he had good fortune, and in conjunction with Demosthenes, conducted the enterprise so well, that within the time he had limited, he carried captive to Athens all the Spartans that had not fallen in battle.

This brought great disgrace on Nicias; for this was not to throw away his shield, but something yet more shameful and ignominious, to quit his charge voluntarily out of cowardice, and voting himself, as it were, out of his command of his own accord, to put into his enemy's hand the opportunity of achieving so brave an action. Aristophanes has a jest against him on this occasion in the Birds [10]:—

[10] For the first quotation, see the Birds (643); the second is from a lost play.

> Indeed, not now the word that must be said
> Is, do like Nicias, or retire to bed.

And, again, in his Husbandmen:—

> I wish to stay at home and farm.
>   What then?
> Who should prevent you?
>   You, my countrymen;
> Whom I would pay a thousand drachmas down,
> To let me give up office and leave town.
>
> Enough; content; the sum two thousand is,
> With those that Nicias paid to give up his.

Besides all this, he did great mischief to the city by suffering the accession of so much reputation and power to Cleon, who now assumed such lofty airs, and allowed himself in such intolerable audacity, as led to many unfortunate results, a sufficient part of which fell to his own share. Amongst other things, he destroyed all the decorum of public speaking; he was the first who ever broke out into exclamations, flung open his dress, smote his thigh, and ran up and down whilst he was speaking, things which soon after introduced amongst those who managed the affairs of State, such license and contempt of decency, as brought all into confusion.

Already, too, Alcibiades was beginning to show his strength at Athens, a popular leader, not, indeed, as utterly violent as Cleon, but as the land of Egypt, through the richness of its soil, is said,

> ——— great plenty to produce,
> Both wholesome herbs, and drugs of deadly juice,[11]

so the nature of Alcibiades was strong and luxuriant in both kinds, and made way for many serious innovations. Thus it fell out that after Nicias had got

---

[11] Thus described in the fourth Odyssey (230).

his hands clear of Cleon, he had not opportunity to settle the city perfectly into quietness. For having brought matters to a pretty hopeful condition, he found every thing carried away and plunged again into confusion by Alcibiades, through the wildness and vehemence of his ambition, and all embroiled again in war worse than ever. Which fell out thus. The persons who had principally hindered the peace were Cleon and Brasidas. War setting off the virtue of the one, and hiding the villany of the other, gave to the one occasions of achieving brave actions, to the other opportunity of committing equal dishonesties. Now when these two were in one battle both slain near Amphipolis, Nicias was aware that the Spartans had long been desirous of a peace, and that the Athenians had no longer the same cofidence in the war. Both being alike tired, and, as it were by consent, letting fall their hands, he, therefore, in this nick of time, employed his efforts to make a friendship betwixt the two cities, and to deliver the other States of Greece from the evils and calamities they labored under, and so establish his own good name for success as a statesman for all future time. He found the men of substance, the elder men, and the land-owners and farmers pretty generally, all inclined to peace. And when, in addition to these, by conversing and reasoning, he had cooled the wishes of a good many others for war, he now encouraged the hopes of the Lacedæmonians, and counselled them to seek peace. They confided in him, as on account of his general character for moderation and equity, so, also, because of the kindness and care he had shown to the prisoners taken at Pylos and kept in confinement, making their misfortune the more easy for them.

The Athenians and the Spartans had before this concluded a truce for a year, and during this, by associating with one another, they had tasted again the sweets of peace and security, and unimpeded intercourse with friends and connections, and thus longed for an end of that fighting and bloodshed, and heard with delight the chorus sing such verses as

————my lance I'll leave
Laid by, for spiders to o'erweave,[12]

and remembered with joy the saying, In peace, they who sleep are awaked by the cock-crow, not by the trumpet. So shutting their ears, with loud reproaches, to the forebodings of those who said that the Fates decreed this to be a war of thrice nine years, the whole question having been debated, they made a peace. And most people thought, now, indeed, they had got an end of all their evils. And Nicias was in every man's mouth, as one especially beloved of the gods, who, for his piety and devotion, had been appointed to give a name to the fairest and greatest of all blessings. For in fact they considered the peace Nicias's work, as the war the work of Pericles; because he, on light occasions, seemed to have plunged the Greeks into great calamities, while Nicias had induced them to forget all the evils they had done each other and to be friends again; and so to this day it is called the Peace of Nicias.

The articles being, that the garrisons and towns taken on either side, and the prisoners should be restored, and they to restore the first to whom it should fall by lot, Nicias, as Theophrastus tells us, by a sum of money procured that the lot should fall for the Lacedæmonians to deliver the first. Afterwards,

[12] *My lance I'll leave* is a fragment of the lost Erechtheus of Euripides. It is found at greater length in Stobæus. See Matthiæ's fragments of the play, No. xiii.

when the Corinthians and the Bœotians showed their
dislike of what was done, and by their complaints and
accusations were wellnigh bringing the war back
again, Nicias persuaded the Athenians and the Lacedæmonians,
besides the peace, to make a treaty of
alliance, offensive and defensive, as a tie and confirmation
of the peace, which would make them more
terrible to those that held out, and the firmer to each
other. Whilst these matters were on foot, Alcibiades,
who was no lover of tranquillity, and who was offended
with the Lacedæmonians because of their applications
and attentions to Nicias, while they overlooked and
despised himself, from first to last, indeed, had opposed
the peace, though all in vain, but now finding
that the Lacedæmonians did not altogether continue
to please the Athenians, but were thought to have
acted unfairly in having made a league with the
Bœotians, and had not given up Panactum, as they
should have done, with its fortifications unrazed, nor
yet Amphipolis, he laid hold on these occasions for his
purpose, and availed himself of every one of them to
irritate the people. And, at length, sending for ambassadors
from the Argives, he exerted himself to effect
a confederacy between the Athenians and them.
And now, when Lacedæmonian ambassadors were
come with full powers, and at their preliminary audience
by the council seemed to come in all points with
just proposals, he, fearing that the general assembly,
also, would be won over to their offers, overreached
them with false professions and oaths of assistance, on
the condition that they would not avow that they
came with full powers, this, he said, being the only
way for them to attain their desires. They being overpersuaded
and decoyed from Nicias to follow him, he
introduced them to the assembly, and asked them presently
whether or no they came in all points with full

powers, which when they denied, he, contrary to their
expectation, changing his countenance, called the
council to witness their words, and now bade the
people beware how they trust, or transact any thing
with such manifest liars, who say at one time one
thing, and at another the very opposite upon the
same subject. These plenipotentiaries were, as well
they might be, confounded at this, and Nicias, also,
being at a loss what to say, and struck with amazement
and wonder, the assembly resolved to send immediately
for the Argives, to enter into a league with them.
An earthquake, which interrupted the assembly, made
for Nicias's advantage; and the next day the people
being again assembled, after much speaking and soliciting,
with great ado he brought it about, that the
treaty with the Argives should be deferred, and he be
sent to the Lacedæmonians, in full expectation that so
all would go well.

When he arrived at Sparta, they received him
there as a good man, and one well inclined towards
them; yet he effected nothing, but, baffled by the party
that favored the Bœotians, he returned home, not only
dishonored and hardly spoken of, but likewise in fear
of the Athenians, who were vexed and enraged that
through his persuasions they had released so many
and such considerable persons, their prisoners, for the
men who had been brought from Pylos were of the
chiefest families of Sparta, and had those who were
highest there in place and power for their friends and
kindred. Yet did they not in their heat proceed
against him, otherwise than that they chose Alcibiades
general, and took the Mantineans and Eleans, who
had thrown up their alliance with the Lacedæmonians,
into the league, together with the Argives, and sent
to Pylos freebooters to infest Laconia, whereby the
war began to break out afresh.

But the enmity betwixt Nicias and Alcibiades running higher and higher, and the time being at hand for decreeing the ostracism or banishment, for ten years, which the people, putting the name on a sherd, were wont to inflict at certain times on some person suspected or regarded with jealousy for his popularity or wealth, both were now in alarm and apprehension, one of them, in all likelihood, being to undergo this ostracism; as the people abominated the life of Alcibiades, and stood in fear of his boldness and resolution, as is shown particularly in the history of him; while as for Nicias, his riches made him envied, and his habits of living, in particular, his unsociable and exclusive ways, not like those of a fellow-citizen, or even a fellow-man, went against him, and having many times opposed their inclinations, forcing them against their feelings to do what was their interest, he had got himself disliked.

To speak plainly, it was a contest of the young men who were eager for war, against the men of years and lovers of peace, they turning the ostracism upon the one, these upon the other. But

> In civil strife e'en villains rise to fame.

And so now it happened that the city, distracted into two factions, allowed free course to the most impudent and profligate persons, among them was Hyperbolus of the Perithœdæ, one who could not, indeed, be said to be presuming upon any power, but rather by his presumption rose into power, and by the honor he found in the city, became the scandal of it. He, at this time, thought himself far enough from the ostracism, as more properly deserving the slave's gallows, and made account, that one of these men being dispatched out of the way, he might be able to play a part against the other that should be left, and openly showed his pleasure at the dissension, and his desire to inflame the people against both of them. Nicias and Alcibiades, perceiving his malice, secretly combined together, and setting both their interests jointly at work, succeeded in fixing the ostracism not on either of them, but even on Hyperbolus. This, indeed, at the first, made sport, and raised laughter among the people; but afterwards it was felt as an affront, that the thing should be dishonored by being employed upon so unworthy a subject; punishment, also, having its proper dignity, and ostracism being one that was appropriate rather for Thucydides, Aristides, and such like persons; whereas for Hyperbolus it was a glory, and a fair ground for boasting on his part, when for his villany he suffered the same with the best men. As Plato, the comic poet, said of him,

> The man deserved the fate, deny who can;
> Yes, but the fate did not deserve the man;
> Not for the like of him and his slave-brands,
> Did Athens put the sherd into our hands.

And, in fact, none ever afterwards suffered this sort of punishment, but Hyperbolus was the last, as Hipparchus [13] the Cholargian, who was kin to the tyrant, was the first.

There is no judgment to be made of fortune; nor can any reasoning bring us to a certainty about it. If Nicias had run the risk with Alcibiades, whether of the two should undergo the ostracism, he had either prevailed, and, his rival being expelled the city, he had remained secure; or, being overcome, he had avoided the utmost disasters, and preserved the reputation of a most excellent commander. Meantime I am not ignorant that Theophrastus says, that when Hyper-

---

[13] Hipparchus was kin to the tyrant Pisistratus.

NICIAS

bolus was banished, Phæax, not Nicias, contested it with Alcibiades; but most authors differ from him.

It was Alcibiades, at any rate, whom when the Ægestean and Leontine ambassadors arrived and urged the Athenians to make an expedition against Sicily, Nicias opposed, and by whose persuasions and ambition he found himself overborne, who even before the people could be assembled, had preoccupied and corrupted their judgment with hopes and with speeches; insomuch that the young men at their sports, and the old men in their workshops, and sitting together on the benches,[14] would be drawing maps of Sicily, and making charts showing the seas, the harbors, and general character of the coast of the island opposite Africa. For they made not Sicily the end of the war, but rather its starting point and head-quarters from whence they might carry it to the Carthaginians, and possess themselves of Africa, and of the seas as far as the pillars of Hercules. The bulk of the people, therefore, pressing this way, Nicias, who opposed them, found but few supporters, nor those of much influence; for the men of substance, fearing lest they should seem to shun the public charges and ship-money, were quiet against their inclination; nevertheless he did not tire nor give it up, but even after the Athenians decreed a war and chose him in the first place general, together with Alcibiades and Lamachus, when they were again assembled, he stood up, dissuaded them, and protested against the decision, and laid the blame on Alcibiades, charging him with going about to involve the city in foreign dangers and

[14] *The benches*, literally *the semicircles*, are probably the seats of this form, which were set in public places, in porches and gardens and exercise grounds, rather perhaps than the regular seats of theatres.

difficulties, merely with a view to his own private lucre and ambition. Yet it came to nothing. Nicias, because of his experience, was looked upon as the fitter for the employment, and his wariness with the bravery of Alcibiades, and the easy temper of Lamachus, all compounded together, promised such security, that he did but confirm the resolution. Demostratus, who, of the popular leaders, was the one who chiefly pressed the Athenians to the expedition, stood up and said he would stop the mouth of Nicias from urging any more excuses, and moved that the generals should have absolute power both at home and abroad, to order and to act as they thought best; and this vote the people passed.

The priests, however, are said to have very earnestly opposed the enterprise. But Alcibiades had his diviners of another sort, who from some old prophesies announced that "there shall be great fame of the Athenians in Sicily," and messengers came back to him from Jupiter Ammon, with oracles importing that "the Athenians shall take all the Syracusans." Those, meanwhile, who knew any thing that boded ill, concealed it, lest they might seem to forespeak ill-luck. For even prodigies that were obvious and plain would not deter them; not the defacing of the Hermæ, all maimed in one night except one, called the Hermes of Andocides, erected by the tribe of Ægeus, placed directly before the house then occupied by Andocides; nor what was perpetrated on the altar of the twelve gods, upon which a certain man leaped suddenly up, and then turning round, mutilated himself with a stone. Likewise at Delphi, there stood a golden image of Minerva, set on a palm-tree of brass, erected by the city of Athens from the spoils they won from the Medes; this was pecked at several days together by crows flying upon it, who, also, plucked off and knocked down the fruit, made of gold, upon the palm-tree. But the Athenians said these were all but inventions of the Delphians, corrupted by the men of Syracuse. A certain oracle bade them bring from Clazomenæ the priestess of Minerva there; they sent for the woman and found her named *Hesychia, Quietness,* this being, it would seem, what the divine powers advised the city at this time, to be quiet. Whether, therefore, the astrologer Meton feared these presages, or that from human reason he doubted its success, (for he was appointed to a command in it,) feigning himself mad, he set his house on fire. Others say he did not counterfeit madness, but set his house on fire in the night, and the next morning came before the assembly in great distress, and besought the people, in consideration of the sad disaster, to release his son from the service, who was about to go captain of a galley for Sicily. The genius, also, of the philosopher Socrates, on this occasion, too, gave him intimation by the usual tokens, that the expedition would prove the ruin of the commonwealth; this he imparted to his friends and familiars, and by them it was mentioned to a number of people. Not a few were troubled because the days on which the fleet set sail happened to be the time when the women celebrated the death of Adonis; there being everywhere then exposed to view images of dead men, carried about with mourning and lamentation, and women beating their breasts. So that such as laid any stress on these matters were extremely troubled, and feared lest that all this warlike preparation, so splendid and so glorious, should suddenly, in a little time, be blasted in its very prime of magnificence, and come to nothing.

Nicias, in opposing the voting of this expedition, and neither being puffed up with hopes, nor transported with the honor of his high command so as to

modify his judgment, showed himself a man of virtue
and constancy. But when his endeavors could not
divert the people from the war, nor get leave for
himself to be discharged of the command, but the
people, as it were, violently took him up and carried
him, and against his will put him in the office of general, this was no longer now a time for his excessive
caution and his delays, nor was it for him, like a child,
to look back from the ship, often repeating and reconsidering over and over again how that his advice had
not been overruled by fair arguments, thus blunting
the courage of his fellow commanders and spoiling the
season of action. Whereas, he ought speedily to have
closed with the enemy and brought the matter to an
issue, and put fortune immediately to the test in battle. But, on the contrary, when Lamachus counselled
to sail directly to Syracuse, and fight the enemy under
their city walls, and Alcibiades advised to secure the
friendship of the other towns, and then to march
against them, Nicias dissented from them both, and
insisted that they should cruise quietly around the
island and display their armament, and, having landed
a small supply of men for the Egesteans, return to
Athens, weakening at once the resolution and casting
down the spirits of the men. And when, a little while
after, the Athenians called home Alcibiades in order
to his trial, he being, though joined nominally with
another in commission, in effect the only general, made
now no end of loitering, of cruising, and considering,
till their hopes were grown stale, and all the disorder
and consternation which the first approach and view
of their forces had cast amongst the enemy was worn
off, and had left them.

Whilst yet Alcibiades was with the fleet, they went
before Syracuse with a squadron of sixty galleys, fifty
of them lying in array without the harbor, while the

other ten rowed in to reconnoitre, and by a herald called upon the citizens of Leontini to return to their own country. These scouts took a galley of the enemy's, in which they found certain tablets, on which was set down a list of all the Syracusans, according to their tribes. These were wont to be laid up at a distance from the city, in the temple of Jupiter Olympius, but were now brought forth for examination to furnish a muster-roll of young men for the war. These being so taken by the Athenians, and carried to the officers, and the multitude of names appearing the diviners thought it unpropitious, and were in apprehension lest this should be the only destined fulfilment of the prophecy, that "the Athenians shall take all the Syracusans." Yet, indeed, this was said to be accomplished by the Athenians at another time, when Callippus the Athenian, having slain Dion, became master of Syracuse. But when Alcibiades shortly after sailed away from Sicily, the command fell wholly to Nicias. Lamachus was, indeed, a brave and honest man, and ready to fight fearlessly with his own hand in battle, but so poor and ill off, that whenever he was appointed general, he used always, in accounting for his outlay of public money, to bring some little reckoning or other of money for his very clothes and shoes. On the contrary, Nicias, as on other accounts, so, also, because of his wealth and station, was very much thought of. The story is told that once upon a time the commission of generals being in consultation together in their public office, he bade Sophocles the poet give his opinion first, as the senior of the board. "I," replied Sophocles, "am the older, but you are the senior." And so now, also, Lamachus, who better understood military affairs, being quite his subordinate, he himself, evermore delaying and avoiding risk, and faintly employing his forces, first by his sailing about Sicily at the greatest distance aloof from the enemy, gave them confidence, then by afterwards attacking Hybla, a petty fortress, and drawing off before he could take it, made himself utterly despised. At the last he retreated to Catana without having achieved any thing, save that he demolished Hyccara, a humble town of the barbarians, out of which the story goes that Lais the courtesan, yet a mere girl, was sold amongst the other prisoners, and carried thence away to Peloponnesus.

But when the summer was spent, after reports began to reach him that the Syracusans were grown so confident that they would come first to attack him, and troopers skirmishing to the very camp twitted his soldiers, asking whether they came to settle with the Catanians, or to put the Leontines in possession of their city, at last, with much ado, Nicias resolved to sail against Syracuse. And wishing to form his camp safely and without molestation, he procured a man to carry from Catana intelligence to the Syracusans that they might seize the camp of the Athenians unprotected, and all their arms, if on such a day they should march with all their forces to Catana; and that, the Athenians living mostly in the town, the friends of the Syracusans had concerted, as soon as they should perceive them coming, to possess themselves of one of the gates, and to fire the arsenal; that many now were in the conspiracy and awaited their arrival. This was the ablest thing Nicias did in the whole of his conduct of the expedition. For having drawn out all the strength of the enemy, and made the city destitute of men, he set out from Catana, entered the harbor, and chose a fit place for his camp, where the enemy could least incommode him with the means in which they were superior to him, while with the means in which he was superior to them, he might expect to carry on the war without impediment.

When the Syracusans returned from Catana, and stood in battle array before the city gates, he rapidly led up the Athenians and fell on them and defeated them, but did not kill many, their horse hindering the pursuit. And his cutting and breaking down the bridges that lay over the river gave Hermocrates, when cheering up the Syracusans, occasion to say, that Nicias was ridiculous, whose great aim seemed to be to avoid fighting, as if fighting were not the thing he came for. However, he put the Syracusans into a very great alarm and consternation, so that instead of fifteen generals then in service, they chose three others, to whom the people engaged by oath to allow absolute authority.

There stood near them the temple of Jupiter Olympius, which the Athenians (there being in it many consecrated things of gold and silver) were eager to take, but were purposely withheld from it by Nicias, who let the opportunity slip, and allowed a garrison of the Syracusans to enter it, judging that if the soldiers should make booty of that wealth, it would be no advantage to the public, and he should bear the guilt of the impiety. Not improving in the least this success, which was everywhere famous, after a few days' stay, away he goes to Naxos, and there winters, spending largely for the maintenance of so great an army, and not doing any thing except some matters of little consequence with some native Sicilians that revolted to him. Insomuch that the Syracusans took heart again, made excursions to Catana, wasted the country, and fired the camp of the Athenians. For which everybody blamed Nicias, who, with his long reflection, his deliberateness, and his caution, had let slip the time for action. None ever found fault with the man when once at work, for in the brunt he showed vigor and activity enough, but was slow and wanted assurance to engage.

When, therefore, he brought again the army to Syracuse, such was his conduct, and with such celerity, and at the same time security, he came upon them, that nobody knew of his approach, when already he had come to shore with his galleys at Thapsus, and had landed his men; and before any could help it, he had surprised Epipolæ, had defeated the body of picked men that came to its succor, took three hundred prisoners, and routed the cavalry of the enemy, which had been thought invincible. But what chiefly astonished the Syracusans, and seemed incredible to the Greeks, was, in so short a space of time the walling about of Syracuse, a town not less than Athens, and far more difficult, by the unevenness of the ground, and the nearness of the sea and the marshes adjacent, to have such a wall drawn in a circle round it; yet this, all within a very little, finished by a man that had not even his health for such weighty cares, but lay ill of the stone, which may justly bear the blame for what was left undone. I admire the industry of the general, and the bravery of the soldiers for what they succeeded in. Euripides, after their ruin and disaster, writing their funeral elegy, said that

> Eight victories over Syracuse they gained,
> While equal yet to both the gods remained.

And in truth one shall not find eight, but many more victories, won by these men against the Syracusans, till the gods, in real truth, or fortune intervened to check the Athenians in this advance to the height of power and greatness.

Nicias, therefore, doing violence to his body, was present in most actions. But once, when his disease was the sharpest upon him, he lay in the camp with some few servants to attend him. And Lamachus having the command fought the Syracusians, who were bringing a cross-wall from the city along to that of the Athenians, to hinder them from carrying it round; and in the victory, the Athenians hurrying in some disorder to the pursuit, Lamachus getting separated from his men, had to resist the Syracusan horse that came upon him. Before the rest advanced Callicrates, a man of good courage and skill in war. Lamachus, upon a challenge, engaged with him in single combat, and receiving the first wound, returned it so home to Callicrates, that they both fell and died together. The Syracusans took away his body and arms, and at full speed advanced to the wall of the Athenians, where Nicias lay without any troops to oppose to them, yet roused by this necessity, and seeing the danger, he bade those about him to go and set on fire all the wood and materials that lay provided before the wall for the engines, and the engines themselves; this put a stop to the Syracusans, saved Nicias, saved the walls, and all the money of the Athenians. For when the Syracusans saw such a fire blazing up between them and the wall, they retired.

Nicias now remained sole general, and with great prospects; for cities began to come over to alliance with him, and ships laden with corn from every coast came to the camp, every one favoring when matters went well. And some proposals from among the Syracusans despairing to defend the city, about a capitulation, were already conveyed to him. And in fact Gylippus, who was on his way with a squadron to their aid from Lacedæmon, hearing, on his voyage, of the wall surrounding them, and of their distress, only continued his enterprise thenceforth, that, giving Sicily up for lost, he might, if even that should be possible,

secure the Italians their cities. For a strong report
was everywhere spread about that the Athenians carried all before them, and had a general alike for conduct and for fortune invincible.

And Nicias himself, too, now against his nature
grown bold in his present strength and success, especially from the intelligence he received under hand of
the Syracusans, believing they would almost immediately surrender the town upon terms, paid no manner
of regard to Gylippus coming to their assistance, nor
kept any watch of his approach, so that, neglected
altogether and despised, Gylippus went in a longboat
ashore[15] without the knowledge of Nicias, and, having
landed in the remotest parts from Syracuse, mustered
up a considerable force, the Syracusans not so much as
knowing of his arrival nor expecting him; so that an
assembly was summoned to consider the terms to be
arranged with Nicias, and some were actually on the
way, thinking it essential to have all despatched before
the town should be quite walled round, for now there
remained very little to be done, and the materials for
the building lay all ready along the line.

In this very nick of time and danger arrived Gongylus in one galley from Corinth, and every one, as may
be imagined, flocking about him, he told them that Gylippus would be with them speedily, and that other
ships were coming to relieve them. And, ere yet they
could perfectly believe Gongylus, an express was
brought from Gylippus, to bid them go forth to meet
him. So now taking good heart, they armed themselves; and Gylippus at once led on his men from their

---

[15] This is an uncertain reading; very likely the genuine text
(*dia tou porthmou,* instead of *dia porthemeiou,*) should mean
"passed through the straits" between Italy and Sicily, which is
the account given in Thucydides, who, indeed, uses these very
words.

march in battle array against the Athenians, as Nicias also embattled these. And Gylippus, piling his arms in view of the Athenians, sent a herald to tell them he would give them leave to depart from Sicily without molestation. To this Nicias would not vouchsafe any answer, but some of his soldiers laughing asked if with the sight of one coarse coat and Laconian staff the Syràcusan prospects had become so brilliant that they could despise the Athenians, who had released to the Lacedæmonians three hundred, whom they held in chains, bigger men than Gylippus, and longer-haired? Timæus, also, writes that even the Syracusans made no account of Gylippus, at the first sight mocking at his staff and long hair, as afterwards they found reason to blame his covetousness and meanness. The same author, however, adds that on Gylippus's first appearance, as it might have been at the sight of an owl abroad in the air, there was a general flocking together of men to serve in the war. And this is the truer saying of the two; for in the staff and the cloak they saw the badge and authority of Sparta, and crowded to him accordingly. And not only Thucydides affirms that the whole thing was done by him alone, but so, also, does Philistus, who was a Syracusan and an actual witness of what happened.

However, the Athenians had the better in the first encounter, and slew some few of the Syracusans, and amongst them Gongylus of Corinth. But on the next day Gylippus showed what it is to be a man of experience; for with the same arms, the same horses, and on the same spot of ground, only employing them otherwise he overcame the Athenians; and they fleeing to their camp, he set the Syracusans to work, and with the stone and materials that had been brought together for finishing the wall of the Athenians, he built a cross-wall to intercept theirs and break it off, so that even if they were successful in the field, they would not be able to do any thing. And after this the Syracusans taking courage manned their galleys, and with their horse and followers ranging about took a good many prisoners; and Gylippus going himself to the cities, called upon them to join with him, and was listened to and supported vigorously by them. So that Nicias fell back again to his old views, and, seeing the face of affairs change, desponded, and wrote to Athens, bidding them either send another army, or recall this out of Sicily, and that he might, in any case, be wholly relieved of the command, because of his disease.

Before this, the Athenians had been intending to send another army to Sicily, but envy of Nicias's early achievements and high fortune had occasioned, up to this time, many delays; but now they were all eager to send off succors. Eurymedon went before, in midwinter, with money, and to announce that Euthydemus and Menander were chosen out of those that served there under Nicias, to be joint commanders with him. Demosthenes was to go after in the spring with a great armament. In the mean time Nicias was briskly attacked, both by sea and land; in the beginning he had the disadvantage on the water, but in the end repulsed and sunk many of the galleys of the enemy. But by land he could not provide succor in time, so Gylippus surprised and captured Plemmyrium, in which the stores for the navy, and a great sum of money being there kept, all fell into his hands, and many were slain, and many taken prisoners. And what was of greatest importance, he now cut off Nicias's supplies, which had been safely and readily conveyed to him under Plemmyrium, while the Athenians still held it, but now that they were beaten out, he could only procure them with great difficulty, and with opposition from the enemy, who lay in wait with their ships under that fort. Moreover, it seemed manifest to the Syracusans that their navy had not been beaten by strength, but by their disorder in the pursuit. Now, therefore, all hands went to work to prepare for a new attempt, that should succeed better than the former. Nicias had no wish for a sea-fight, but said it was mere folly for them, when Demosthenes was coming in all haste with so great a fleet and fresh forces to their succor, to engage the enemy with a less number of ships and ill provided. But, on the other hand, Menander and Euthydemus, who were just commencing their new command, prompted by a feeling of rivalry and emulation of both the generals, were eager to gain some great success before Demosthenes came, and to prove themselves superior to Nicias. They urged the honor of the city, which, said they, would be blemished and utterly lost, if they should decline a challenge from the Syracusans. Thus they forced Nicias to a sea-fight; and by the stratagem of Ariston, the Corinthian pilot, (his trick, described by Thucydides, about the men's dinners,) they were worsted, and lost many of their men, causing the greatest dejection to Nicias, who had suffered so much from having the sole command, and now again miscarried through his colleagues.

But now, by this time, Demosthenes with his splendid fleet came in sight outside the harbor, a terror to the enemy. He brought along, in seventy-three galleys, five thousand men at arms; of darters, archers, and slingers, not less than three thousand; with the glittering of their armor, the flags waving from the galleys, the multitude of coxswains and flute-players giving time to the rowers, setting off the whole with all possible warlike pomp and ostentation to dismay the enemy. Now, one may believe the Syracusans were again in extreme alarm, seeing no end or prospect of release before them, toiling, as it seemed, in vain, and perishing to no purpose. Nicias, however, was not long overjoyed with the reinforcement, for the first time he conferred with Demosthenes, who advised forthwith to attack the Syracusans, and to put all to the speediest hazard, to win Syracuse, or else return home, afraid, and wondering at his promptness and audacity, he besought him to do nothing rashly and desperately, since delay would be the ruin of the enemy, whose money would not hold out, nor their confederates be long kept together; that when once they came to be pinched with want, they would presently come again to him for terms, as formerly. For, indeed, many in Syracuse held secret correspondence with him, and urged him to stay, declaring that even now the people were quite worn out with the war, and weary of Gylippus. And if their necessities should the least sharpen upon them they would give up all.

Nicias glancing darkly at these matters, and unwilling to speak out plainly, made his colleagues imagine that it was cowardice which made him talk in this manner. And saying that this was the old story over again, the well-known procrastinations and delays and refinements with which at first he let slip the opportunity in not immediately falling on the enemy, but suffering the armament to become a thing of yesterday, that nobody was alarmed with, they took the side of Demosthenes, and with much ado forced Nicias to comply. And so Demosthenes, taking the land-forces, by night made an assault upon Epipolæ; part of the enemy he slew ere they took the alarm, the rest defending themselves he put to flight. Nor was he content with this victory there, but pushed on further, till he met the Bœotians. For these were the first that made head against the Athenians, and charged them with a shout, spear against spear,, and killed many on the place. And now at once there ensued a panic and confusion throughout the whole army; the victorious portion got infected with the fears of the flying part, and those who were still disembarking and coming forward, falling foul of the retreaters, came into conflict with their own party, taking the fugitives for pursuers, and treating their friends as if they were the enemy.

Thus huddled together in disorder, distracted with fear and uncertainties, and unable to be sure of seeing any thing, the night not being absolutely dark, nor yielding any steady light, the moon then towards setting, shadowed with the many weapons and bodies that moved to and fro, and glimmering so as not to show an object plain, but to make friends through fear suspected for foes, the Athenians fell into utter perplexity and desperation. For, moreover, they had the moon at their backs, and consequently their own shadows fell upon them, and both hid the number and the glittering of their arms; while the reflection of the moon from the shields of the enemy made them show more numerous and better appointed than, indeed, they were. At last, being pressed on every side, when once they had given way, they took to rout, and in their flight were destroyed, some by the enemy, some by the hand of their friends, and some tumbling down the rocks, while those that were dispersed and straggled about were picked off in the morning by the horsemen and put to the sword. The slain were two thousand; and of the rest few came off safe with their arms.

Upon this disaster, which was to him not wholly an unexpected one, Nicias accused the rashness of Demosthenes; but he, making his excuses for the past, now advised to be gone in all haste, for neither were other forces to come, nor could the enemy be beaten with the present. And, indeed, even supposing they were yet too hard for the enemy in any case, they ought to remove and quit a situation which they understood to be always accounted a sickly one, and dangerous for an army, and was more particularly unwholesome now, as they could see themselves, because of the time of year. It was the beginning of autumn, and many now lay sick, and all were out of heart.

It grieved Nicias to hear of flight and departing home, not that he did not fear the Syracusans, but he was worse afraid of the Athenians, their impeachments and sentences; he professed that he apprehended no further harm there, or if it must be, he would rather die by the hand of an enemy, than by his fellow-citizens. He was not of the opinion which Leo of Byzantium declared to his fellow-citizens: "I had rather," said he, "perish by you, than with you." As to the matter of place and quarter whither to remove their camp, that, he said, might be debated at leisure. And Demosthenes, his former counsel having succeeded so ill, ceased to press him further; others thought Nicias had reasons for expectation, and relied on some assurance from people within the city, and that this made made him so strongly oppose their retreat, so they acquiesced. But fresh forces now coming to the Syracusans, and the sickness growing worse in his camp, he, also, now approved of their retreat, and commanded the soldiers to make ready to go aboard. And when all were in readiness, and none of the enemy had observed them, not expecting such a thing, the moon was eclipsed in the night, to the great fright of Nicias and others, who, for want of experience, or out of superstition, felt alarm at such appearances. That the sun might be darkened about the close of the month, this even ordinary people now understood

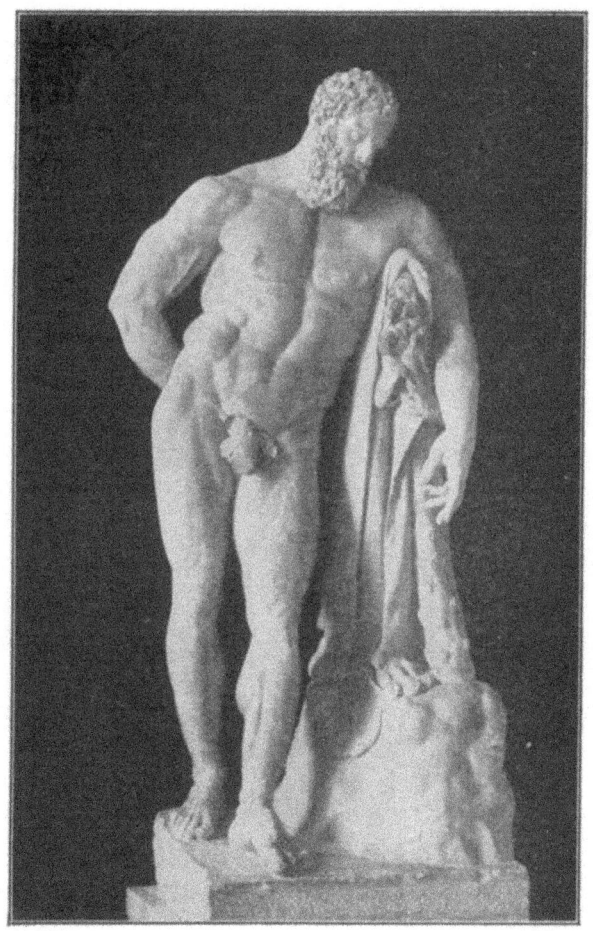

HERCULES

pretty well to be the effect of the moon; but the moon itself to be darkened, how that could come about, and how, on the sudden, a broad full moon should lose her light, and show such various colors, was not easy to be comprehended; they concluded it to be ominous, and a divine intimation of some heavy calamities. For he who the first, and the most plainly of any, and with the greatest assurance committed to writing how the moon is enlightened and overshadowed, was Anaxagoras; and he was as yet but recent, nor was his argument much known, but was rather kept secret, passing only amongst a few, under some kind of caution and confidence. People would not then tolerate natural philosophers, and theorists, as they then called them, about things above;[16] as lessening the divine power, by explaining away its agency into the operation of irrational causes and senseless forces acting by necessity, without any thing of Providence, or a free agent. Hence it was that Protagoras was banished, and Anaxagoras cast into prison, so that Pericles had much difficulty to procure his liberty; and Socrates, though he had no concern whatever with this sort of learning, yet was put to death for philosophy. It was only afterwards that the reputation of Plato, shining forth by his life, and because he subjected natural necessity to divine and more excellent principles, took away the obloquy and scandal that had attached to such contemplations, and obtained these studies currency among all people. So his friend Dion, when the moon, at the time he was to embark from Zacynthus to go against Dionysius, was eclipsed, was not in the least disturbed, but went on, and, arriving at Syr-

[16] *Meteōroleschæ*, talkers about *meteōra*, or things in the air, between the earth and the sky, one of the terms of reproach commonly applied, as, for example, by Aristophanes in the Clouds, to speculators about astronomical phenomena.

acuse, expelled the tyrant. But it so fell out with
Nicias, that he had not at this time a skilful diviner
with him; his former habitual adviser who used to
moderate much of his superstition, Stilbides, had died
a little before. For in fact, this prodigy, as Philochorus observes, was not unlucky for men wishing
to fly, but on the contrary very favorable; for things
done in fear require to be hidden, and the light is their
foe. Nor was it usual to observe signs in the sun or
moon more than three days, as Autoclides[17] states in
his Commentaries. But Nicias persuaded them to
wait another full course of the moon, as if he had not
seen it clear again as soon as ever it had passed the
region of shadow where the light was obstructed by
the earth.

In a manner abandoning all other cares, he betook
himself wholly to his sacrifices, till the enemy came
upon them with their infantry, besieging the forts and
camp, and placing their ships in a circle about the harbor. Nor did the men in the galleys only, but the
little boys everywhere got into the fishing-boats and
rowed up and challenged the Athenians, and insulted
over them. Amongst these a youth of noble parentage, Heraclides by name, having ventured out beyond
the rest, an Athenian ship pursued and wellnigh took
him. His uncle Pollichus, in fear for him, put out
with ten galleys which he commanded, and the rest, to
relieve Pollichus, in like manner drew forth; the result
of it being a very sharp engagement, in which the Syra-

[17] Instead of *Autoclides*, we have elsewhere *Anticlides*. His
Commentaries, or *Exegetics*, as the Greek term is, would be a
book of directions or prescriptions as to what to do in a particular case of good or bad omens; *exegesis* referring specially
to the oral instructions given by a priest, for example, to a
worshipper for the performance of a ceremony; it is applied, for
instance, to the dictation of the words of an oath.

cusans had the victory, and slew Eurymedon, with many others. After this the Athenian soldiers had no patience to stay longer, but raised an outcry against their officers, requiring them to depart by land; for the Syracusans, upon their victory, immediately shut and blocked up the entrance of the harbor; but Nicias would not consent to this, as it was a shameful thing to leave behind so many ships of burden, and galleys little less than two hundred. Putting, therefore, on board the best of the foot, and the most serviceable darters, they filled one hundred and ten galleys; the rest wanted oars. The remainder of his army Nicias posted along by the sea-side, abandoning the great camp and the fortifications adjoining the temple of Hercules; so the Syracusans, not having for a long time performed their usual sacrifice to Hercules, went up now, both priests and captains, to sacrifice.

And their galleys being manned, the diviners predicted from their sacrifices victory and glory to the Syracusans, provided they would not be the aggressors, but fight upon the defensive; for so Hercules overcame all, by only defending himself when set upon. In this confidence they set out; and this proved the hottest and fiercest of all their sea-fights, raising no less concern and passion in the beholders than in the actors; as they could oversee the whole action with all the various and unexpected turns of fortune which, in a short space, occurred in it; the Athenians suffering no less from their own preparations, than from the enemy; for they fought against light and nimble ships, that could attack from any quarter, with theirs laden and heavy. And they were thrown at with stones that fly indifferently any way, for which they could only return darts and arrows, the direct aim of which the motion of the water disturbed, preventing their coming true, point foremost to their mark. This the Syracusans had learned from Ariston the Corinthian pilot, who, fighting stoutly, fell himself in this very engagement, when the victory had already declared for the Syracusans.

The Athenians, their loss and slaughter being very great, their flight by sea cut off, their safety by land so difficult, did not attempt to hinder the enemy towing away their ships under their eyes, nor demanded their dead, as, indeed, their want of burial seemed a less calamity than the leaving behind the sick and wounded which they now had before them. Yet more miserable still than those did they reckon themselves, who were to work on yet, through more such sufferings after all to reach the same end.

They prepared to dislodge that night. And Gylippus and his friends seeing the Syracusans engaged in their sacrifices and at their cups, for their victories, and it being also a holiday, did not expect either by persuasion or by force to rouse them up and carry them against the Athenians as they decamped. But Hermocrates, of his own head, put a trick upon Nicias, and sent some of his companions to him, who pretended they came from those that were wont to hold secret intelligence with him, and advised him not to stir that night, the Syracusans having laid ambushes and beset the ways. Nicias, caught with this stratagem, remained, to encounter presently in reality, what he had feared when there was no occasion. For they the next morning, marching before seized the defiles, fortified the passes where the rivers were fordable, cut down the bridges, and ordered their horsemen to range the plains and ground that lay open, so as to leave no part of the country where the Athenians could move without fighting. They stayed both that day and another night, and then went along as if they were leaving their own, not an enemy's country, lamenting and bewailing for want of necessaries, and for their parting from friends and companions that were not able to help themselves; and, nevertheless, judging the present evils lighter than those they expected to come. But among the many miserable spectacles that appeared up and down in the camp, the saddest sight of all was Nicias himself, laboring under his malady, and unworthily reduced to the scantiest supply of all the accomodations necessary for human wants, of which he in his condition required more than ordinary, because of his sickness; yet bearing up under all this illness, and doing and undergoing more than many in perfect health. And it was plainly evident, that all this toil was not for himself, or from any regard to his own life, but that purely for the sake of those under his command he would not abandon hope. And, indeed, the rest were given over to weeping and lamentation through fear or sorrow, but he, whenever he yielded to any thing of the kind, did so, it was evident, from reflection upon the shame and dishonor of the enterprise, contrasted with the greatness and glory of the success he had anticipated, and not only the sight of his person, but, also, the recollection of the arguments and the dissuasions he used to prevent this expedition, enhanced their sense of the undeservedness of his sufferings, nor had they any heart to put their trust in the gods, considering that a man so religious, who had performed to the divine powers so many and so great acts of devotion, should have no more favorable treatment than the wickedest and meanest of the army.

Nicias, however, endeavored all the while by his voice, his countenance, and his carriage, to show himself undefeated by these misfortunes. And all along the way shot at, and receiving wounds eight days continually from the enemy, he yet preserved the forces

with him in a body entire, till that Demosthenes was
taken prisoner with the party that he led, whilst they
fought and made a resistance, and so got behind and
were surrounded near the country house of Polyzelus.
Demosthenes thereupon drew his sword, and wounded
but did not kill himself, the enemy speedily running
in and seizing upon him. So soon as the Syracusans
had gone and informed Nicias of this, and he had sent
some horsemen, and by them knew the certainty of the
defeat of that division, he then vouchsafed to sue to
Gylippus for a truce for the Athenians to depart out
of Sicily, leaving hostages for payment of the money
that the Syracusans had expended in the war.

But now they would not hear of these proposals, but
threatening and reviling them, angrily and insultingly
continued to ply their missiles at them, now destitute
of every necessary. Yet Nicias still made good his
retreat all that night, and the next day, through all
their darts, made his way to the river Asinarus. There,
however, the enemy encountering them, drove some
into the stream, while others ready to die for thirst
plunged in headlong, while they drank at the same
time, and were cut down by their enemies. And here
was the cruellest and the most immoderate slaughter.
Till at last Nicias falling down to Gylippus, "Let
pity, O Gylippus," said he, "move you in your victory; not for me, who was destined, it seems, to bring
the glory I once had to this end, but for the other
Athenians; as you well know that the chances of war
are common to all, and the Athenians used them moderately and mildly towards you in their prosperity."

At these words, and at the sight of Nicias, Gylippus
was somewhat troubled, for he was sensible that the
Lacedæmonians had received good offices from Nicias
in the late treaty; and he thought it would be a great
and glorius thing for him to carry off the chief com-

manders of the Athenians alive. He, therefore, raised
Nicias with respect, and bade him be of good cheer,
and commanded his men to spare the lives of the rest.
But the word of command being communicated
slowly, the slain were a far greater number than the
prisoners. Many, however, were privily conveyed away
by particular soldiers. Those taken openly were hurried together in a mass; their arms and spoils hung up
on the finest and largest trees along the river. The
conquerors, with garlands on their heads, with their
own horses splendidly adorned, and cropping short the
manes and tails of those of their enemies, entered the
city, having, in the most signal conflict ever waged by
Greeks against Greeks, and with the greatest strength
and the utmost effort of valor and manhood, won a
most entire victory.

And a great assembly of the people of Syracuse and
their confederates sitting, Eurycles, the popular leader, moved, first, that the day on which they took Nicias
should thenceforward be kept holiday by sacrificing
and forbearing all manner of work, and from the river
be called the Asinarian Feast. This was the twenty-sixth day of the month Carneus, the Athenian Metagitnion. And that the servants of the Athenians with
the other confederates be sold for slaves, and they
themselves and the Sicilian auxiliaries be kept and
employed in the quarries, except the generals, who
should be put to death. The Syracusans favored the
proposal, and when Hermocrates said, that to use well
a victory was better than to gain a victory, he was met
with a great clamor and outcry. When Gylippus, also,
demanded the Athenian generals to be delivered to
him, that he might carry them to the Lacedæmonians,
the Syracusans, now insolent with their good fortune,
gave him ill words. Indeed, before this, even in the
war, they had been impatient at his rough behavior

and Lacedæmonian haughtiness, and had, as Timæus tells us, discovered sordidness and avarice in his character, vices which may have descended to him from his father Cleandrides, who was convicted of bribery and banished. And the very man himself, of the one thousand talents which Lysander sent to Sparta, embezzled thirty, and hid them under the tiles of his house, and was detected and shamefully fled his country. But this is related more at large in the life of Lysander. Timæus says that Demosthenes and Nicias did not die, as Thucydides and Philistus have written, by the order of the Syracusans, but that upon a message sent them from Hermocrates, whilst yet the assembly were sitting, by the connivance of some of their guards, they were enabled to put an end to themselves. Their bodies, however, were thrown out before the gates and offered for a public spectacle. And I have heard that to this day in a temple at Syracuse is shown a shield, said to have been Nicias's, curiously wrought and embroidered with gold and purple intermixed. Most of the Athenians perished in the quarries by diseases and ill diet, being allowed only one pint of barley every day, and one half pint of water. Many of them, however, were carried off by stealth, or, from the first, were supposed to be servants, and were sold as slaves. These latter were branded on their foreheads with the figure of a horse. There were, however, Athenians,[18] who, in addition to slavery, had to endure even this. But their discreet and orderly conduct was

---

[18] The latest editor, Sintenis, conceives that the word "few" has dropped out here. As it stands, the passage must mean, that as many free Athenians were in the first instance passed off as domestic slaves, and thus saved from the quarries and sold, and as the prisoners who were sold were branded, there were Athenians who suffered the indignity of becoming branded slaves.

an advantage to them; they were either soon set free, or won the respect of their masters with whom they continued to live. Several were saved for the sake of Euripides, whose poetry, it appears, was in request among the Sicilians more than among any of the settlers out of Greece. And when any travellers arrived that could tell them some passage, or give them any specimen of his verses, they were delighted to be able to communicate them to one another. Many of the captives who got safe back to Athens are said, after they reached home, to have gone and made their acknowledgements to Euripides, relating how that some of them had been released from thir slavery by teaching what they could remember of his poems, and others, when straggling after the fight, been relieved with meat and drink for repeating some of his lyrics. Nor need this be any wonder, for it is told that a ship of Caunus fleeing into one of their harbors for protection, pursued by pirates, was not received, but forced back, till one asked if they knew any of Euripide's verses, and on their saying they did, they were admitted, and their ship brought into harbor.

It is said that the Athenians would not believe their loss, in a great degree because of the person who first brought them news of it. For a certain stranger, it seems, coming to Piræus, and there sitting in a barber's shop, began to talk of what had happened, as if the Athenians already knew all that had passed; which the barber hearing, before he acquainted anybody else, ran as fast as he could up into the city, addressed himself to the Archons, and presently spread it about in the public Place. On which, there being everywhere, as may be imagined, terror and consternation, the Archons summoned a general assembly, and there brought in the man and questioned him how he came to know. And he, giving no satisfactory account, was taken for a spreader of false intelligence and a disturber of the city, and was, therefore, fastened to the wheel and racked a long time, till other messengers arrived and related the whole disaster particularly. So hardly was Nicias believed to have suffered the calamity which he had often predicted.

CRASSUS[1]

TRANSLATED BY —AMHURST, ESQ.

MARCUS CRASSUS, whose father had borne the office of a censor, and received the honor of a triumph, was educated in a little house together with his two brothers, who both married in their parents' lifetime; they kept but one table amongst them; all which, perhaps, was not the least reason of his own temperance and moderation in diet. One of his brothers dying, he married his widow, by whom he had his children; neither was there in these respects any of the Romans who lived a more orderly life than he did, though later in life he was suspected to have been too familiar with one of the vestal virgins, named Licinia, who was, nevertheless, acquitted, upon an impeachment brought against her by one Plotinus. Licinia stood possessed of a beautiful property in the suburbs, which Crassus desiring to purchase at a low price, for this reason was frequent in his attentions to her, which gave occasion to the scandal, and his avarice, so to say, serving to clear him of the crime, he was acquitted. Nor did he leave the lady till he had got the estate.

People were wont to say that the many virtues of Crassus were darkened by the one vice of avarice, and indeed he seemed to have no other but that; for it being the most predominant, obscured others to which he

---

[1] Joined with Pompey and Cæsar, forming the so-called triumviate, 60 B. C. His ruling passion was money, and he devoted all his energies to its accumulation. Assassinated by order of Surenas, 53 B. C.—Dr. William Smith.

was inclined. The arguments in proof of his avarice were the vastness of his estate, and the manner of raising it; for whereas at first he was not worth above three hundred talents, yet, though in the course of his political life[2] he dedicated the tenth of all he had to Hercules, and feasted the people, and gave to every citizen corn enough to serve him three months, upon casting up his accounts, before he went upon his Parthian expedition, he found his possession to amount to seven thousand one hundred talents; most of which, if we may scandal him with a truth, he got by fire and rapine, making his advantages of the public calamities. For when Sylla seized the city, and exposed to sale the goods of those that he had caused to be slain, accounting them booty and spoils, and, indeed, calling them so too, and was desirous of making as many, and as eminent men as he could, partakers in the crime, Crassus never was the man that refused to accept or give money for them. Moreover observing how extremely subject the city was to fire, and falling down of houses, by reason of their height and their standing so near together, he bought slaves that were builders and architects, and when he had collected these to the number of more than five hundred, he made it his practice to buy houses that were on fire, and those in the neighborhood, which, in the immediate danger and uncertainty, the proprietors were willing to part with for little or nothing; so that the greatest part of Rome, at one time or other, came into his hands. Yet for all he had so many workmen, he never built any thing but his own house, and used to say that those that were addicted to building would

[2] These were the munificent acts of his consulship, as we presently read in the account of it; and accordingly some of the editors correct the passage, "in his hupateian," or consulship, instead of "in his politeian," or political life.

undo themselves soon enough without the help of other enemies. And though he had many silver mines, and much valuable land, and laborers to work in it, yet all this was nothing in comparison of his slaves, such a number and variety did he possess of excellent readers, amanuenses, silversmiths, stewards, and table-waiters, whose instruction he always attended to himself, superintending in person while they learned, and teaching them himself accounting it the main duty of a master to look over the servants, that are, indeed, the living tools of housekeeping; and in this, indeed, he was in the right in thinking, that is, as he used to say, that servants ought to look after all other things, and the master after them. For economy, which in things inanimate is but money-making, when exercised over men becomes policy.[3] But it was surely a mistaken judgment, when he said no man was to be accounted rich that could not maintain an army at his own cost and charges, for war, as Archidamus well observed, is not fed at a fixed allowance, so that there is no saying what wealth suffices for it, and certainly it was one very far removed from that of Marius; for when he had distributed fourteen acres of land a man, and understood that some desired more, "God forbid," said he, "that any Roman should think that too little which is enough to keep him alive and well."

Crassus, however was very eager to be hospitable to strangers; he kept open house, and to his friends he would lend money without interest, but called it in precisely at the time; so that his kindness was often

[3] *Œconomia*, or the art of keeping and managing a house, household and property,—*husbandry* in the old sense of the word. —so long as its subject is inanimate things, is merely an art of profit, or money-making—*chrematistic*, but as it extends its exercise to men, it rises into the political or social art, the art of government.

thought worse than the paying the interest would have been. His entertainments were, for the most part, plain and citizenlike, the company general and popular; good taste and kindness made them pleasanter than sumptuosity would have done. As for learning, he chiefly cared for rhetoric, and what would be serviceable with large numbers; he became one of the best speakers at Rome, and by his pains and industry outdid the best natural orators. For there was no trial how mean and contemptible soever that he came to unprepared; nay, several times he undertook and concluded a cause, when Pompey and Cæsar and Cicero refused to stand up, upon which account particularly he got the love of the people, who looked upon him as a diligent and careful man, ready to help and succor his fellow-citizens. Besides, the people were pleased with his courteous and unpretending salutations and greetings; for he never met any citizen however humble and low, but he returned him his salute by name. He was looked upon as a man well-read in history, and pretty well versed in Aristotle's philosophy, in which one Alexander instructed him, a man whose intercourse with Crassus gave a sufficient proof of his good-nature, and gentle disposition; for it is hard to say whether he was poorer when he entered into his service, or while he continued in it; for being his only friend that used to accompany him when travelling, he used to receive from him a cloak for the journey, and when he came home had it demanded from him again; poor patient sufferer, when even the philosophy he professed did not look upon poverty as a thing indifferent.[4] But of this hereafter.

[4] The point of difference between Aristotle and the Stoics; his theory not allowing happiness or well-being to be perfect in the absence of external goods. The concluding clause, however, is not quite certainly Plutarch's writing.

When Cinna and Marius got the power in their hands, it was soon perceived that they had not come back for any good they intended to their country, but to effect the ruin and utter destruction of the nobility. And as many as they could lay their hands on they slew, amongst whom were Crassus's father and brother; he himself, being very young, for the moment escaped the danger; but understanding that he was every way beset and hunted after by the tyrants, taking with him three friends and ten servants, with all possible speed he fled into Spain, having formerly been there and secured a great number of friends, while his father was prætor of that country. But finding all people in a consternation, and trembling at the cruelty of Marius, as if he was already standing over them in person, he durst not discover himself to anybody, but hid himself in a large cave, which was by the sea-shore, and belonged to Vibius Pacianus, to whom he sent one of his servants to sound him, his provisions, also, beginning to fail. Vibius was well pleased at his escape, and inquiring the place of his abode and the number of his companions, he went not to him himself, but commanded his steward to provide every day a good meal's meat, and carry it and leave it near such a rock, and so return without taking any further notice or being inquisitive, promising him his liberty if he did as he commanded, and that he would kill him if he intermeddled. The cave is not far from the sea; a small and insignificant looking opening in the cliffs conducts you in; when you are entered, a wonderfully high roof spreads above you, and large chambers open out one beyond another, nor does it lack either water or light, for a very pleasant and wholesome spring runs at the foot of the cliffs, and natural chinks, in the most advantageous place, let in the light all day long; and the thickness

of the rock makes the air within pure and clear, all
the wet and moisture being carried off into the spring.

While Crassus remained here, the steward brought
them what was necessary, but never saw them, nor
knew any thing of the matter, though they within saw,
and expected him at the customary times. Neither
was their entertainment such as just to keep them
alive, but given them in abundance and for their enjoyment; for Pacianus resolved to treat him with all
imaginable kindness, and considering he was a young
man, thought it well to gratify a little his youthful
inclinations; for to give just what is needful, seems
rather to come from necessity than from a hearty
friendship. Once taking with him two female servants, he showed them the place and bade them go in
boldly, whom when Crassus and his friends saw, they
were afraid of being betrayed, and demanded what
they were, and what they would have. They, according as they were instructed, answered, they came to
wait upon their master who was hid in that cave. And
so Crassus perceiving it was a piece of pleasantry and
of good-will on the part of Vibius, took them in and
kept them there with him as long as he stayed, and
employed them to give information to Vibius of what
they wanted, and how they were. Fenestella says he
saw one of them, then very old, and often heard her
speak of the time and repeat the story with pleasure.

After Crassus had lain concealed there eight
months, on hearing that Cinna was dead, he appeared
abroad, and a great number of people flocking to him,
out of whom he selected a body of two thousand five
hundred, he visited many cities, and, as some write,
sacked Malaca, which he himself, however, always denied, and contradicted all who said so. Afterwards,
getting together some ships, he passed into Africa, and
joined with Metellus Pius, an eminent person that

had raised a very considerable force; but upon some difference between him and Metellus, he stayed not long there, but went over to Sylla, by whom he was very much esteemed. When Sylla passed over into Italy, he was anxious to put all the young men that were with him in employment; and as he despatched some one way, and some another, Crassus, on its falling to his share to raise men among the Marsians, demanded a guard, being to pass through the enemy's country, upon which Sylla replied sharply, "I give you for guard your father, your brother, your friends and kindred, whose unjust and cruel murder I am now going to revenge;" and Crassus, being nettled, went his way, broke boldly through the enemy, collected a considerable force, and in all Sylla's wars acted with great zeal and courage. And in these times and occasions, they say, began the emulation and rivalry for glory between him and Pompey; for though Pompey was the younger man, and had the disadvantage to be descended of a father that was disesteemed by the citizens, and hated as much as ever man was, yet in these actions he shone out, and was proved so great, that Sylla always used, when he came in, to stand up and uncover his head, an honor which he seldom showed to older men and his own equals, and always saluted him *Imperator*. This fired and stung Crassus, though, indeed, he could not with any fairness claim to be preferred; for he both wanted experience, and his two innate vices, sordidness and avarice, tarnished all the lustre of his actions. For when he had taken Tudertia,[5] a town of the Umbrians, he converted, it was said, all the spoil to his own use, for which he was complained of to Sylla. But in the last and greatest battle before Rome itself, where Sylla

[5] Or Tuder.

was worsted, some of his battalions giving ground, and others being quite broken, Crassus got the victory on the right wing, which he commanded, and pursued the enemy till night, and then sent to Sylla to acquaint him with his success, and demand provision for his soldiers. In the time, however, of the proscriptions and sequestrations, he lost his repute again, by making great purchases for little or nothing, and asking for grants. Nay, they say he proscribed one of the Bruttians without Sylla's order, only for his own profit, and that, on discovering this, Sylla never after trusted him in any public affairs. As no man was more cunning than Crassus to ensnare others by flattery, so no man lay more open to it, or swallowed it more greedily than himself. And this particularly was observed of him, that though he was the most covetous man in the world, yet he habitually disliked and cried out against others who were so.

It troubled him to see Pompey so successful in all his undertakings; that he had had a triumph before he was capable to sit in the senate, and that the people had surnamed him Magnus, or the Great. When somebody was saying Pompey the Great was coming, he smiled, and asked him, "How big is he?" Despairing to equal him by feats of arms, he betook himself to civil life, where by doing kindnesses, pleading, lending money, by speaking and canvassing among the people for those who had objects to obtain from them, he gradually gained as great honor and power as Pompey had from his many famous expeditions. And it was a curious thing in their rivalry, that Pompey's name and interest in the city was greatest when he was absent, for his renown in war, but when present he was often less successful than Crassus, by reason of his superciliousness and haughty way of living, shunning crowds of people, and appearing rarely in the forum, and assisting only some few, and that not readily, that his interest might be the stronger when he came to use it for himself. Whereas, Crassus, being a friend always at hand, ready to be had and easy of access, and always with his hands full of other people's business, with his freedom and courtesy, got the better of Pompey's formality. In point of dignity of person, eloquence of language, and attractiveness of countenance, they were pretty equally excellent. But, however, this emulation never transported Crassus so far as to make him bear enmity, or any ill-will; for though he was vexed to see Pompey and Cæsar preferred to him, yet he never mingled any hostility or malice with his jealousy; though Cæsar when he was taken captive by the corsairs in Asia, cried out, "O Crassus, how glad you will be at the news of my captivity!" Afterwards they lived together on friendly terms, for when Cæsar was going prætor into Spain, and his creditors, he being then in want of money, came upon him and seized his equipage, Crassus then stood by him and relieved him, and was his security for eight hundred and thirty talents. And, in general, Rome being divided into three great interests, those of Pompey, Cæsar, and Crassus, (for as for Cato, his fame was greater than his power, and he was rather admired than followed,) the sober and quiet part were for Pompey, the restless and hotheaded followed Cæsar's ambition, but Crassus trimmed between them, making advantages of both, and changed sides continually, being neither a trusty friend nor an implacable enemy, and easily abandoned both his attachments and his animosities, as he found it for his advantage, so that in short spaces of time, the same men and the same measures had him both as their supporter and as their opponent. He was much liked, but was feared as much or even more. At any rate, when Sicinius, who was the greatest troubler of the magistrates and ministers of his time, was asked how it was he let Crassus alone, "Oh," said he, "he carries hay on his horns," alluding to the custom of tying hay to the horns of a bull that used to butt, that people might keep out of his way.

The insurrection of the gladiators and the devastation of Italy, commonly called the war of Spartacus, began upon this occasion. One Lentulus Batiates trained up a great many gladiators in Capua, most of them Gauls and Thracians, who, not for any fault by them committed, but simply through the cruelty of their masters, were kept in confinement for this object of fighting one with another. Two hundred of these formed a plan to escape, but their plot being discovered, those of them who became aware of it in time to anticipate their master, being seventy-eight, got out of a cook's shop chopping-knives and spits, and made their way through the city, and lighting by the way on several wagons that were carrying gladiator's arms to another city, they seized upon them and armed themselves. And seizing upon a defensible place, they chose three captains, of whom Spartacus was chief, a Thracian of one of the nomad tribes, and a man not only of high spirit and valiant, but in understanding, also, and in gentleness, superior to his condition, and more of a Grecian than the people of his country usually are. When he first came to be sold at Rome, they say a snake coiled itself upon his face as he lay asleep, and his wife, who at this latter time also accompanied him in his flight, his country-woman, a kind of prophetess, and one of those possessed with the bacchanal frenzy, declared that it was a sign portending great and formidable power to him with no happy event.

First, then, routing those that came out of Capua

against them, and thus procuring a quantity of proper soldiers' arms, they gladly threw away their own as barbarous and dishonorable. Afterwards Clodius, the prætor, took the command against them with a body of three thousand men from Rome, and besieged them within a mountain, accessible only by one narrow and difficult passage, which Clodius kept guarded, encompassed on all other sides with steep and slippery precipices. Upon the top, however, grew a great many wild vines, and cutting down as many of their boughs as they had need of, they twisted them into strong ladders long enough to reach from thence to the bottom, by which, without any danger, they got down all but one, who stayed there to throw them down their arms, and after this succeeded in saving himself. The Romans were ignorant of all this, and, therefore, coming upon them in the rear, they assaulted them unawares and took their camp. Several, also, of the shepherds and herdsmen that were there, stout and nimble fellows, revolted over to them, to some of whom they gave complete arms, and made use of others as scouts and light-armed soldiers. Publius Varinus, the prætor, was now sent against them, whose lieutenant, Furius, with two thousand men, they fought and routed. Then Cossinius was sent, with considerable forces, to give his assistance and advice, and him Spartacus missed but very little of capturing in person, as he was bathing at Salinæ;[6] for he with great difficulty made his escape, while Spartacus possessed himself of his baggage, and following the chase with a great slaughter, stormed his camp and took it, where Cossinius himself was slain. After many successful skirmishes with the prætor himself, in one of

[6] Salenæ or *Salinæ* (the latter is a conjecture), and *the Lucanian lake,* in page 343, are uncertain localities; *the mountains of Petelia,* page 344, are near Petelia in Bruttium.

which he took his lictors and his own horse, he began
to be great and terrible; but wisely considering that
he was not to expect to match the force of the empire,
he marched his army towards the Alps, intending,
when he had passed them, that every man should go
to his own home, some to Thrace, some to Gaul. But
they, grown confident in their numbers, and puffed
up with their success, would give no obedience to him,
but went about and ravaged Italy; so that now the
senate was not only moved at the indignity and baseness, both of the enemy and of the insurrection, but,
looking upon it as a matter of alarm and of dangerous consequence, sent out both the consuls to it, as to
a great and difficult enterprise. The consul Gellius,
falling suddenly upon a party of Germans, who
through contempt and confidence had straggled from
Spartacus, cut them all to pieces. But when Lentulus
with a large army besieged Spartacus, he sallied out
upon him, and, joining battle, defeated his chief officers, and captured all his baggage. As he made
towards the Alps, Cassius, who was prætor of that
part of Gaul that lies about the Po, met him with ten
thousand men, but being overcome in battle, he had
much ado to escape himself, with the loss of a great
many of his men.

When the senate understood this, they were displeased at the consuls, and ordering them to meddle
no further, they appointed Crassus general of the war,
and a great many of the nobility went volunteers with
him, partly out of friendship, and partly to get honor.
He stayed himself on the borders of Picenum, expecting Spartacus would come that way and sent his lieutenant, Mummius, with two legions, to wheel about
and observe the enemy's motions, but upon no account
to engage or skirmish. But he, upon the first opportunity, joined battle, and was routed, having a great

CRASSUS

many of his men slain, and a great many only saving their lives, with the loss of their arms. Crassus rebuked Mummius severely, and arming the soldiers again, he made them find sureties for their arms, that they would part with them no more, and five hundred that were the beginners of the flight, he divided into fifty tens, and one of each was to die by lot, thus reviving the ancient Roman punishment of decimation, where ignominy is added to the penalty of death, with a variety of appalling and terrible circumstances, presented before the eyes of the whole army, assembled as spectators. When he had thus reclaimed his men, he led them against the enemy; but Spartacus retreated through Lucania toward the sea, and in the straits meeting with some Cilician pirate ships, he had thoughts of attempting Sicily, where, by landing two thousand men, he hoped to new kindle the war of the slaves, which was but lately extinguished, and seemed to need but a little fuel to set it burning again. But after the pirates had struck a bargain with him, and received his earnest, they deceived him and sailed away. He thereupon retired again from the sea, and established his army in the peninsula of Rhegium; there Crassus came upon him, and considering the nature of the place, which of itself suggested the undertaking, he set to work to build a wall across the isthmus; thus keeping his soldiers at once from idleness, and his foes from forage. This great and difficult work he perfected in a space of time short beyond all expectation, making a ditch from one sea to the other, over the neck of land, three hundred furlongs long, fifteen feet broad, and as much in depth, and above it built a wonderfully high and strong wall. All which Spartacus at first slighted and despised, but when provisions began to fail, and on his proposing to pass further, he found he was walled in, and no more was to be had in the peninsula, taking the opportunity of a snowy, stormy night, he filled up part of the ditch with earth and boughs of trees, and so passed the third part of his army over.

Crassus was afraid lest he should march directly to Rome, but was soon eased of that fear when he saw many of his men break out in a mutiny and quit him, and encamp by themselves upon the Lucanian lake. This lake they say changes at intervals of time, and is sometimes sweet, and sometimes so salt that it cannot be drunk. Crassus falling upon these beat them from the lake, but he could not pursue the slaughter, because of Spartacus suddenly coming up, and checking the flight. Now he began to repent that he had previously written to the senate to call Lucullus out of Thrace, and Pompey out of Spain; so that he did all he could to finish the war before they came, knowing that the honor of the action would redound to him that came to his assistance. Resolving, therefore, first to set upon those that had mutinied and encamped apart, whom Caius Cannicius and Castus commanded, he sent six thousand men before to secure a little eminence, and to do it as privately as possible, which that they might do, they covered their helmets, but being discovered by two women that were sacrificing for the enemy, they had been in great hazard, had not Crassus immediately appeared, and engaged in a battle which proved a most bloody one. Of twelve thousand three hundred whom he killed, two only were found wounded in their backs, the rest all having died standing in their ranks, and fighting bravely. Spartacus, after this discomfiture, retired to the mountains of Petelia, but Quintius, one of Crassus's officers, and Scrofa, the quæstor, pursued and overtook him. But when Spartacus rallied and faced them, they were utterly routed and fled, and had much ado to carry off their quæstor, who was wounded. This success, however, ruined Spartacus, because it encouraged the slaves, who now disdained any longer to avoid fighting, or to obey their officers, but as they were upon their march, they came to them with their swords in their hand, and compelled them to lead them back again through Lucania, against the Romans, the very thing which Crassus was eager for. For news was already brought that Pompey was at hand; and people began to talk openly, that the honor of this war was reserved for him, who would come and at once oblige the enemy to fight and put an end to the war. Crassus, therefore, eager to fight a decisive battle, encamped very near the enemy, and began to make lines of circumvallation; but the slaves made a sally, and attacked the pioneers. As fresh supplies came in on either side, Spartacus, seeing there was no avoiding it, set all his army in array, and when his horse was brought him, he drew out his sword and killed him, saying, if he got the day, he should have a great many better horses of the enemies, and if he lost it, he should have no need of this. And so making directly towards Crassus himself, through the midst of arms and wounds, he missed him, but slew two centurions that fell upon him together. At last being deserted by those that were about him, he himself stood his ground, and, surrounded by the enemy, bravely defending himself, was cut in pieces. But though Crassus had good fortune, and not only did the part of a good general, but gallantly exposed his person, yet Pompey had much of the credit of the action. For he met with many of the fugitives, and slew them, and wrote to the senate that Crassus indeed had vanquished the slaves in a pitched battle, but that he had put an end to the war. Pompey was honored with a magnificent triumph for his conquest over Sertorius and Spain, while Crassus could not himself so much as desire a triumph in its full form, and indeed it was thought to look but meanly in him to accept of the lesser honor, called the ovation, for a servile war, and perform a procession on foot. The difference between this and the other, and the origin of the name, are explained in the life of Marcellus.

And Pompey being immediately invited to the consulship, Crassus, who had hoped to be joined with him, did not scruple to request his assistance. Pompey most readily seized the opportunity, as he desired by all means to lay some obligation upon Crassus, and zealously promoted his interest; and at last he declared in one of his speeches to the people, that he should be not less beholden to them for his colleague, than for the honor of his own appointment. But once entered upon the employment, this amity continued not long; but differing almost in every thing, disagreeing, quarrelling, and contending, they spent the time of their consulship, without effecting any measure of consequence, except that Crassus made a great sacrifice to Hercules, and feasted the people at ten thousand tables, and measured them out corn for three months. When their command was now ready to expire, and they were, as it happened, addressing the people, a Roman knight, one Onatius [7] Aurelius, an ordinary private person, living in the country, mounted the hustings, and declared a vision he had in his sleep: "Jupiter," said he, "appeared to me, and commanded me to tell you, that you should not suffer your consuls to law down their charge before they are made friends." When he had spoken, the people cried out that they should be reconciled. Pompey stood still

[7] The text is probably corrupt. The word Onatius is made up most likely of the name Caius and another word. He is called Caius Aurelius in the life of Pompey.

and said nothing, but Cassus, first offering him his hand, said, "I cannot think, my countrymen, that I do any thing humiliating or unworthy of myself, if I make the first offers of accommodation and friendship with Pompey, whom you yourselves styled the Great, before he was of man's estate, and decreed him a triumph before he was capable of sitting in the senate."

This is what was memorable in Crassus's consulship, but as for his censorship, that was altogether idle and inactive, for he neither made a scrutiny of the senate, nor took a review of the horsemen, nor a census of the people, though he had as mild a man as could be desired for his colleague, Lutatius Catulus. It is said, indeed, that when Crassus intended a violent and unjust measure, which was the reducing Egypt to be tributary to Rome, Catulus strongly opposed it, and falling out about it, they laid down their office by consent. In the great conspiracy of Catiline, which was very near subverting the government, Crassus was not without some suspicion of being concerned, and one man came forward and declared him to be in the plot; but nobody credited him. Yet Cicero, in one of his orations, clearly charges both Crassus and Cæsar with the guilt of it, though that speech was not published till they were both dead. But in his speech upon his consulship, he declares that Crassus came to him by night, and brought a letter concerning Catiline, stating the details of the conspiracy. Crassus hated him ever after, but was hindered by his son from doing him any open injury; for Publius was a great lover of learning and eloquence, and a constant follower of Cicero, insomuch that he put himself into mourning when he was accused, and induced the other young men to do the same. And at last he reconciled him to his father.

Cæsar now returning from his command, and

designing to get the consulship, and seeing that
Crassus and Pompey were again at variance, was
unwilling to disoblige one by making application to
the other, and despaired of success without the help
of one of them; he therefore made it his business to
reconcile them, making it appear that by weakening
each other's influence, they were promoting the interest of the Ciceros, the Catuli, and the Catos, who
would really be of no account if they would join
their interests and their factions, and act together in
public with one policy and one united power. And so
reconciling them by his persuasions, out of the three
parties he set up one irresistible power, which utterly
subverted the government both of senate and people.
Not that he made either Pompey or Crassus greater
than they were before, but by their means made himself greatest of all; for by the help of the adherents
of both, he was at once gloriously declared consul,
which office when he administered with credit, they
decreed him the command of an army, and allotted
him Gaul for his province, and so placed him as it
were in the citadel, not doubting but they should
divide the rest at their pleasure between themselves,
when they had confirmed him in his allotted command.
Pompey was actuated in all this by an immoderate
desire of ruling, but Crassus, adding to his old disease
of covetousness, a new passion after trophies and triumphs, emulous of Cæsar's exploits, not content to
be beneath him in these points, though above him in
all others, could not be at rest, till it ended in an
ignominious overthrow, and a public calamity. When
Cæsar came out of Gaul to Lucca, a great many went
thither from Rome to meet him. Pompey and
Crassus had various conferences with him in secret,
in which they came to the resolution to proceed to
still more decisive steps, and to get the whole manage-

THE CATILINIAN CONSPIRACY

ment of affairs into their hands, Cæsar to keep his army, and Pompey and Crassus to obtain new ones and new provinces. To effect all which there was but one way, the getting the consulate a second time, which they were to stand for, and Cæsar to assist them by writing to his friends, and sending many of his soldiers to vote.

But when they returned to Rome, their design was presently suspected, and a report was soon spread that this interview had been for no good. When Marcellinus and Domitius asked Pompey in the senate if he intended to stand for the consulship, he answered, perhaps he would, perhaps not; and being urged again, replied, he would ask it of the honest citizens, but not of the dishonest. Which answer appearing too haughty and arrogant, Crassus, said, more modestly, that he would desire it if it might be for the advantage of the public, otherwise he would decline it. Upon this some others took confidence and came forward as candidates, among them Domitius. But when Pompey and Crassus now openly appeared for it, the rest were afraid and drew back; only Cato encouraged Domitius, who was his friend and relation, to proceed, exciting him to persist, as though he was now defending the public liberty, as these men, he said, did not so much aim at the consulate, as at arbitrary government, and it was not a petition for office, but a seizure of provinces and armies. Thus spoke and thought Cato, and almost forcibly compelled Domitius to appear in the forum, where many sided with them. For there was, indeed, much wonder and question among the people, "Why should Pompey and Crassus want another consulship? and why they two together, and not with some third person? We have a great many men not unworthy to be fellow-consuls with either the one or the other." Pompey's party, being apprehensive of this, committed all manner of indecencies and violences, and amongst other things lay in wait for Domitius, as he was coming thither before daybreak with his friends; his torchbearer they killed, and wounded several others, of whom Cato was one. And these being beaten back and driven into a house, Pompey and Crassus were proclaimed consuls. Not long after, they surrounded the house[8] with armed men, thrust Cato out of the forum, killed some that made resistance, and decreed Cæsar his command for five years longer, and provinces for themselves, Syria, and both the Spains, which being divided by lots, Syria fell to Crassus, and the Spains to Pompey.

All were well pleased with the chance, for the people were desirous that Pompey should not go far from the city, and he, being extremely fond of his wife, was very glad to continue there; but Crassus was so transported with his fortune, that it was manifest he thought he had never had such good luck befall him as now, so that he had much to do to contain himself before company and strangers; but amongst his private friends he let fall many vain and childish words, which were unworthy of his age, and contrary to his usual character, for he had been very little given to boasting hitherto. But then being strangely puffed up, and his head heated, he would not limit his fortune to Parthia and Syria; but looking on the actions of Lucullus against Tigranes and the exploits of Pompey against Mithridates as but child's play, he proposed to himself in his hopes to pass as far as Bactria and India, and the utmost

---

[8] This, the commentators say, may mean the senate-house, if the reading is correct. It is more likely, however, that the Greek should be, not *oikema*, but *bema*, the hustings, "la tribune aux harangues" (Amyot's translation), the rostra.

ocean. Not that he was called upon by the decree which appointed him to his office to undertake any expedition against the Parthians, but it was well known that he was eager for it, and Cæsar wrote to him out of Gaul, commending his resolution, and inciting him to the war. And when Ateius, the tribune of the people, designed to stop his journey, and many others murmured that one man should undertake a war against a people that had done them no injury, and were at amity with them, he desired Pompey to stand by him and accompany him out of the town, as he had a great name amongst the common people. And when several were ready prepared to interfere and raise an outcry, Pompey appeared with a pleasing countenance, and so mollified the people, that they let Crassus pass quietly. Ateius, however, met him, and first by word of mouth warned and conjured him not to proceed, and then commanded his attendant officer to seize him and detain him; but the other tribunes not permitting it, the officer released Crassus. Ateius, therefore, running to the gate, when Crassus was come thither, set down a chafing-dish with lighted fire in it, and burning incense and pouring libations on it, cursed him with dreadful imprecations, calling upon and naming several strange and horrible deities. In the Roman belief there is so much virtue in these sacred and ancient rites, that no man can escape the effects of them, and that the utterer himself seldom prospers; so that they are not often made use of, and but upon a great occasion. And Ateius was blamed at the time for resorting to them, as the city itself, in whose cause he used them, would be the first to feel the ill effects of these curses and supernatural terrors.

Crassus arrived at Brundusium, and though the sea was very rough, he had not patience to wait, but went on board, and lost many of his ships. With the remnant of his army he marched rapidly through Galatia, where meeting with king Deiotarus, who, though he was very old, was about building a new city, Crassus scoffingly told him, "Your majesty begins to build at the twelfth hour." "Neither do you," said he, "O general, undertake your Parthian expedition very early." For Crassus was then sixty years old, and he seemed older than he was. At his first coming, things went as he would have them, for he made a bridge over Euphrates without much difficulty, and passed over his army in safety, and occupied many cities of Mesopotamia, which yielded voluntarily. But a hundred of his men were killed in one, in which Apollonius was tyrant; therefore, bringing his forces against it, he took it by storm, plundered the goods, and sold the inhabitants. The Greeks called this city Zenodotia, upon the taking of which, he permitted the army to salute him Imperator,[9] but this was very ill thought of, and it looked as if he despaired a nobler achievement, that he made so much of this little success. Putting garrisons of seven thousand foot and one thousand horse in the new conquests, he returned to take up his winter quarters in Syria, where his son was to meet him coming from Cæsar out of Gaul, decorated with rewards for his valor, and bringing with him one thousand select horse. Here Crassus seemed to commit his first error, and except, indeed, the whole expedition, his greatest; for, whereas he ought to have gone forward and

[9] Imperator, though the original of Emperor, was never the title of any office, but was merely a name of honor given by the soldiery after some success, and assumed by the general in command when he recognized that success as sufficient to deserve it. Thenceforward, however, he would use it as a title, and Crassus would now in his letters style himself Marcus Crassus Imperator.

CRASSUS

seized Babylon and Seleucia, cities that were ever at enmity with the Parthians, he gave the enemy time to provide against him. Besides, he spent his time in Syria more like an usurer than a general, not in taking an account of the arms, and in improving the skill and discipline of his soldiers, but in computing the revenue of the cities, wasting many days in weighing by scale and balance the treasure that was in the temple of Hierapolis,[10] issuing requisitions for levies of soldiers upon particular towns and kingdoms, and then again withdrawing them on payment of sums of money, by which he lost his credit and became despised. Here, too, he met with the first ill-omen from that goddess, whom some call Venus, others Juno, others Nature, or the Cause that produces out of moisture the first principles and seeds of all things, and gives mankind their earliest knowledge of all that is good for them. For as they were going out of the temple, young Crassus stumbled, and his father fell upon him.

When he drew his army out of winter quarters, ambassadors came to him from Arsaces,[11] with this

[10] *Hierapolis*, the "holy city," so called by the Greeks (Bambyce by the natives), was the seat of the worship of the Syrian Venus or Astarte, the personified divine prolific moisture of the universe, out of which all things are born and grow, and seek their proper good. In this sense, she would be Hera or Juno, perhaps, rather than Venus. See Lucian On the Syrian Goddess, a little narrative in imitation of the style of Herodotus, giving an account, apparently, of his own visit to the place. This holy city was on the way from Antioch to Zeugma, the Crossing, the ordinary passage of the Euphrates, and so to Seleucia, or Seleuceia, on the Tigris, at this time (Ctesiphon not as yet having outgrown it), the Greek capital of the Parthian kings.

[11] Arsaces is the title common to all the kings of the dynasty called the Arsacidæ; as Cæsar to the Roman emperors. Hyrodes, which occurs presently, more usually written Orodes, is the proper name.

short speech: If the army was sent by the people of Rome, he denounced mortal war, but if, as he understood was the case, against the consent of his country, Crassus for his own private profit had invaded his territory, then their king would be more merciful, and taking pity upon Crassus's dotage, would send those soldiers back, who had been left not so truly to keep guard on him as to be his prisoners. Crassus boastfully told them he would return his answer at Seleucia, upon which Vagises, the eldest of them, laughed and showed the palm of his hand, saying, "Hair will grow here before you will see Seleucia"; so they returned to their king, Hyrodes, telling him it was war. Several of the Romans that were in garrison in Mesopotamia with great hazard made their escape, and brought word that the danger was worth consideration, urging their own eye-witness of the numbers of the enemy, and the manner of their fighting, when they assaulted their towns; and, as men's manner is, made all seem greater than really it was. By flight it was impossible to escape them, and as impossible to overtake them when they fled, and they had a new and strange sort of darts, as swift as sight, for they pierced whatever they met with, before you could see who threw; their men-at-arms were so provided that their weapons would cut through any thing, and their armor give way to nothing. All which when the soldiers heard, their hearts failed them; for till now they thought there was no difference between the Parthians and the Armenians or Cappadocians, whom Lucullus grew weary with plundering, and had been persuaded that the main difficulty of the war consisted only in the tediousness of the march, and the trouble of chasing men that durst not come to blows, so that the danger of a battle was beyond their expectation; accordingly, some of the officers advised Crassus to proceed no further at present, but reconsider the whole enterprise, amongst whom in particular was Cassius, the quæstor. The soothsayers, also, told him privately the signs found in the sacrifices were continually adverse and unfavorable. But he paid no heed to them, or to anybody who gave any other advice than to proceed. Nor did Artabazes,[12] king of Armenia, confirm him a little, who came to his aid with six thousand horse; who, however, were said to be only the king's lifeguard and suite, for he promised ten thousand cuirassiers more, and thirty thousand foot, at his own charge. He urged Crassus to invade Parthia by the way of Armenia, for not only would he be able there to supply his army with abundant provision, which he would give him, but his passage would be more secure in the mountains and hills, with which the whole country was covered, making it almost impassable to horse, in which the main strength of the Parthians consisted. Crassus returned him but cold thanks for his readiness to serve him, and for the splendor of his assistance, and told him he was resolved to pass through Mesopotamia, where he had left a great many brave Roman soldiers; whereupon the Armenian went his way. As Crassus was taking the army over the river at Zeugma, he encountered preternaturally violent thunder, and the lightning flashed in the faces of the troops, and during the storm a hurricane broke upon the bridge, and carried part of it away; two thunderbolts fell upon the very place where the army was going to encamp; and one of the general's horses magnificently caparisoned, dragged away the groom into the river and was drowned. It is said, too, that when they went to take up the first standard,

---

[12] Or Artavasdes, as Plutarch presently writes it.

the eagle of itself turned its head backward; and after he had passed over his army, as they were distributing provisions, the first thing they gave was lentils and salt, which with the Romans are the food proper to funerals, and are offered to the dead. And as Crassus was haranguing his soldiers, he let fall a word which was thought very ominous in the army; for "I am going," he said, "to break down the bridges, that none of you may return;" and whereas he ought, when he had perceived his blunder, to have corrected himself, and explained his meaning, seeing the men alarmed at the expression, he would not do it out of mere stubbornness. And when at the last general sacrifice the priest gave him the entrails, they slipt out of his hand, and when he saw the standers-by concerned at it, he laughed and said, "See what it is to be an old man; but I shall hold my sword fast enough."

So he marched his army along the river with seven legions, little less than four thousand horse, and as many light-armed soldiers, and the scouts returning declared that not one man appeared, but that they saw the footing of a great many horses which seemed to be retiring in flight, whereupon Crassus conceived great hopes, and the Romans began to despise the Parthians, as men that would not come to combat, hand to hand. But Cassius spoke with him again, and advised him to refresh his army in some of the garrison towns, and remain there till they could get some certain intelligence of the enemy, or at least to make toward Seleucia, and keep by the river, that so they might have the convenience of having provision constantly supplied by the boats, which might always accompany the army, and the river would secure them from being environed, and, if they should fight, it might be upon equal terms.

While Crassus was still considering, and as yet undetermined, there came to the camp an Arab chief named Ariamnes, a cunning and wily fellow, who, of all the evil chances which combined to lead them on to destruction, was the chief and the most fatal. Some of Pompey's old soldiers knew him, and remembered him to have received some kindnesses of Pompey, and to have been looked upon as a friend to the Romans, but he was now suborned by the king's generals, and sent to Crassus to entice him if possible from the river and hills into the wide open plain, where he might be surrounded. For the Parthians desired any thing, rather than to be obliged to meet the Romans face to face. He, therefore, coming to Crassus, (and he had a persuasive tongue,) highly commended Pompey as his benefactor, and admired the forces that Crassus had with him, but seemed to wonder why he delayed and made preparations, as if he should not use his feet more than any arms, against men that, taking with them their best goods and chattels, had designed long ago to fly for refuge to the Scythians or Hyrcanians. "If you meant to fight, you should have made all possible haste, before the king should recover courage, and collect his forces together; at present you see Surena and Silaces opposed to you, to draw you off in pursuit of them, while the king himself keeps out of the way." But this was all a lie, for Hyrodes had divided his army in two parts, with one he in person wasted Armenia, revenging himself upon Artavasdes, and sent Surena against the Romans, not out of contempt, as some pretend, for there is no likelihood that he should despise Crassus, one of the chiefest men of Rome, to go and fight with Artavasdes, and invade Armenia; but much more probably he really apprehended the danger, and therefore waited to see the event, intending that

Surena should first run the hazard of a battle, and
draw the enemy on. Nor was this Surena an ordinary
person, but in wealth, family, and reputation, the
second man in the kingdom, and in courage and
prowess the first, and for bodily stature and beauty
no man like him. Whenever he travelled privately,
he had one thousand camels to carry his baggage, two
hundred chariots for his concubines, one thousand
completely armed men for his life-guards, and a great
many more light-armed; and he had at least ten
thousand horsemen altogether, of his servants and
retinue. The honor had long belonged to his family,
that at the king's coronation he put the crown upon
his head, and when this very king Hyrodes had been
exiled, he brought him in; it was he, also, that took
the great city of Seleucia, was the first man that
scaled the walls, and with his own hand beat off the
defenders. And though at this time he was not above
thirty years old, he had a great name for wisdom and
sagacity, and, indeed, by these qualities chiefly, he
overthrew Crassus, who first through his overweening
confidence, and afterwards because he was cowed by
his calamities, fell a ready victim to his subtlety.
When Ariamnes had thus worked upon him, he drew
him from the river into vast plains, by a way that at
first was pleasant and easy, but afterwards very
troublesome by reason of the depth of the sand; no
tree, nor any water, and no end of this to be seen;
so that they were not only spent with thirst, and the
difficulty of the passage, but were dismayed with the
uncomfortable prospect of not a bough, not a stream,
not a hillock, not a green herb, but in fact a sea of
sand, which encompassed the army with its waves.
They began to suspect some treachery, and at the
same time came messengers from Artavasdes, that he
was fiercely attacked by Hyrodes, who had invaded

his country, so that now it was impossible for him to send any succors, and that he therefore advised Crassus to turn back, and with joint forces to give Hyrodes battle, or at least that he should march and encamp where horses could not easily come, and keep to the mountains. Crassus, out of anger and perverseness, wrote him no answer, but told them, at present he was not at leisure to mind the Armenians, but he would call upon them another time, and revenge himself upon Artavasdes for his treachery. Cassius and his friends began again to complain, but when they perceived that it merely displeased Crassus, they gave over, but privately railed at the barbarian, "What evil genius, O thou worst of men, brought thee to our camp, and with what charms and potions hast thou bewitched Crassus, that he should march his army through a vast and deep desert, through ways which are rather fit for a captain of Arabian robbers, than for the general of a Roman army?" But the barbarian, being a wily fellow, very submissively exhorted them, and encouraged them to sustain it a little further, and ran about the camp, and, professing to cheer up the soldiers, asked them, jokingly, "What, do you think you march through Campania, expecting everywhere to find springs, and shady trees, and baths, and inns of entertainment? Consider you now travel through the confines of Arabia and Assyria." Thus he managed them like children, and before the cheat was discovered, he rode away; not but that Crassus was aware of his going, but he had persuaded him that he would go and contrive how to disorder the affairs of the enemy.

It is related that Crassus came abroad that day not in his scarlet robe, which Roman generals usually wear, but in a black one, which, as soon as he perceived, he changed. And the standard-bearers had

much ado to take up their eagles, which seemed to
be fixed to the place. Crassus laughed at it, and
hastened their march, and compelled his infantry to
keep pace with his cavalry, till some few of the scouts
returned and told them that their fellows were slain
and they hardly escaped, that the enemy was at hand
in full force, and resolved to give them battle. On
this all was in an uproar; Crassus was struck with
amazement, and for haste could scarcely put his army
in good order. First, as Cassius advised, he opened
their ranks and files that they might take up as much
space as could be, to prevent their being surrounded,
and distributed the horse upon the wings, but afterwards changing his mind, he drew up his army in a
square, and made a front every way, each of which
consisted of twelve cohorts, to every one of which
he allotted a troop of horse, that no part might be
destitute of the assistance that the horse might give,
and that they might be ready to assist everywhere,
as need should require. Cassius commanded one of
the wings, young Crassus the other, and he himself
was in the middle. Thus they marched on till they
came to a little river named Balissus, a very inconsiderable one in itself, but very grateful to the soldiers, who had suffered so much by drouth and heat
all along their march. Most of the commanders were
of the opinion that they ought to remain there that
night, and to inform themselves as much as possible
of the number of the enemies, and their order, and so
march against them at break of day; but Crassus was
so carried away by the eagerness of his son, and the
horsemen that were with him, who desired and urged
him to lead them on and engage, that he commanded
those that had a mind to it to eat and drink as they
stood in their ranks, and before they had all well
done, he led them on, not leisurely and with halts to

take breath, as if he was going to battle, but kept on his pace as if he had been in haste, till they saw the enemy, contrary to their expectation, neither so many nor so magnificently armed as the Romans expected. For Surena had hid his main force behind the first ranks, and ordered them to hide the glittering of their armor with coats and skins. But when they approached and the general gave the signal, immediately all the field rung with a hideous noise and terrible clamor. For the Parthians do not encourage themselves to war with cornets and trumpets, but with a kind of kettle-drum, which they strike all at once in various quarters. With these they make a dead hollow noise like the bellowing of beasts, mixed with sounds resembling thunder, having, it would seem, very correctly observed, that of all our senses hearing most confounds and disorders us, and that the feelings excited through it most quickly disturb, and most entirely overpower the understanding.

When they had sufficiently terrified the Romans with their noise, they threw off the covering of their armor, and shone like lightning in their breastplates and helmets of polished Margianian steel, and with their horses covered with brass and steel trappings. Surena was the tallest and finest looking man himself, but the delicacy of his looks and effeminacy of his dress did not promise so much manhood as he really was master of; for his face was painted, and his hair parted after the fashion of the Medes, whereas the other Parthians made a more terrible appearance, with their shaggy hair gathered in a mass upon their foreheads after the Scythian mode. Their first design was with their lances to beat down and force back the first ranks of the Romans, but when they perceived the depth of their battle, and that the soldiers firmly kept their ground, they made a retreat, and pretending to break their order and disperse, they encompassed the Roman square before they were aware of it. Crassus commanded his light-armed soldiers to charge, but they had not gone far before they were received with such a shower of arrows that they were glad to retire amongst the heavy-armed, with whom this was the first occasion of disorder and terror, when they perceived the strength and force of their darts, which pierced their arms, and passed through every kind of covering, hard and soft alike. The Parthians now placing themselves at distances began to shoot from all sides, not aiming at any particular mark, (for, indeed, the order of the Romans was so close, that they could not miss if they would,) but simply sent their arrows with great force out of strong bent bows, the strokes from which came with extreme violence. The position of the Romans was a very bad one from the first; for if they kept their ranks, they were wounded, and if they tried to charge, they hurt the enemy none the more, and themselves suffered none the less. For the Parthians threw their darts as they fled, an art in which none but the Scythians excel them, and it is, indeed, a cunning practice, for while they thus fight to make their escape, they avoid the dishonor of a flight.

However, the Romans had some comfort to think that when they had spent all their arrows, they would either give over or come to blows; but when they presently understood that there were numerous camels loaded with arrows, and that when the first ranks had discharged those they had, they wheeled off and took more, Crassus seeing no end of it, was out of all heart, and sent to his son that he should endeavor to fall in upon them before he was quite surrounded; for the enemy advanced most upon that quarter, and seemed to be trying to ride round and come upon the rear.

Therefore the young man, taking with him thirteen hundred horse, one thousand of which he had from Cæsar, five hundred archers, and eight cohorts of the full-armed soldiers that stood next him, led them up with design to charge the Parthians. Whether it was that they found themselves in a piece of marshy ground, as some think, or else designing to entice young Crassus as far as they could from his father, they turned and began to fly; whereupon he crying out that they durst not stand, pursued them, and with him Censorinus and Megabacchus, both famous, the latter for his courage and prowess, the other for being of a senator's family, and an excellent orator, both intimates of Crassus, and of about the same age. The horse thus pushing on, the infantry stayed little behind, being exalted with hopes and joy, for they supposed they had already conquered, and now were only pursuing; till when they were gone too far, they perceived the deceit, for they that seemed to fly, now turned again, and a great many fresh ones came on. Upon this they made an halt, for they doubted not but now the enemy would attack them, because they were so few. But they merely placed their cuirassiers to face the Romans, and with the rest of their horse rode about scouring the field, and thus stirring up the sand, they raised such a dust that the Romans could neither see nor speak to one another, and being driven in upon one another in one close body, they were thus hit and killed, dying, not by a quick and easy death, but with miserable pains and convulsions; for writhing upon the darts in their bodies, they broke them in their wounds, and when they would by force pluck out the barbed points, they caught the nerves and veins, so that they tore and tortured themselves. Many of them died thus, and those that survived were disabled for any service, and when Publius[13] exhorted them to charge the cuirassiers, they showed him their hands nailed to their shields, and their feet stuck to the ground, so that they could neither fly nor fight. He charged in himself boldly, however, with his horse, and came to close quarters with them, but was very unequal, whether as to the offensive or defensive part; for with his weak and little javelins, he struck against targets that were of tough raw hides and iron, whereas the lightly clad bodies of his Gaulish horsemen were exposed to the strong spears of the enemy. For upon these he mostly depended, and with them he wrought wonders; for they would catch hold of the great spears, and close upon the enemy, and so pull them off from their horses, where they could scarce stir by reason of the heaviness of their armor, and many of the Gauls quitting their own horses, would creep under those of the enemy, and stick them in the belly; which, growing unruly with the pain, trampled upon their riders and upon the enemies promiscuously. The Gauls were chiefly tormented by the heat and drouth, being not accustomed to either, and most of their horses were slain by being spurred on against the spears, so that they were forced to retire among the foot, bearing off Publius grievously wounded. Observing a sandy hillock not far off, they made to it, and tying their horses to one another, and placing them in the midst, and joining all their shields together before them, they thought they might make some defence against the barbarians. But it fell out quite contrary, for when they were drawn up in a plain, the front in some measure secured those that were behind; but when they were upon the hill, one being of necessity higher up than another, none were in shelter, but all

---

[13] That is, young Crassus.

alike stood equally exposed, bewailing their inglorious and useless fate. There were with Publius two Greeks that lived near there at Carrhæ, Hieronymus and Nicomachus; these men urged him to retire with them and fly to Ichnæ, a town not far from thence, and friendly to the Romans. "No," said he, "there is no death so terrible, for the fear of which Publius would leave his friends that die upon his account;" and bidding them to take care of themselves, he embraced them and sent them away, and, because he could not use his arm, for he was run through with a dart, he opened his side to his armor-bearer, and commanded him to run him through. It is said that Censorinus fell in the same manner. Megabacchus slew himself, as did also the rest of best note. The Parthians coming upon the rest with their lances, killed them fighting, nor were there above five hundred taken prisoners. Cutting off the head of Publius, they rode off directly towards Crassus.

His condition was thus. When he had commanded his son to fall upon the enemy, and word was brought him that they fled and that there was a distant pursuit, and perceiving also that the enemy did not press upon him so hard as formerly, for they were mostly gone to fall upon Publius, he began to take heart a little; and drawing his army towards some sloping ground, expected when his son would return from the pursuit. Of the messengers whom Publius sent to him (as soon as he saw his danger,) the first were intercepted by the enemy, and slain; the last hardly escaping, came and declared that Publius was lost, unless he had speedy succors. Crassus was terribly distracted, not knowing what counsel to take, and indeed no longer capable of taking any; overpowered now by fear for the whole army, now by desire to help his son. At last he resolved to move with his forces. Just upon this, up came the enemy with their shouts and noises more terrible than before, their drums sounding again in the ears of the Romans, who now feared a fresh engagement. And they who brought Publius's head upon the point of a spear, riding up near enough that it could be known, scoffingly inquired where were his parents, and what family he was of, for it was impossible that so brave and gallant a warrior should be the son of so pitiful a coward as Crassus. This sight above all the rest dismayed the Romans, for it did not incite them to anger as it might have done, but to horror and trembling, though they say Crassus outdid himself in this calamity, for he passed through the ranks and cried out to them, "This, O my countrymen, is my own peculiar loss, but the fortune and the glory of Rome is safe and untainted so long as you are safe. But if any one be concerned for my loss of the best of sons, let him show it in revenging him upon the enemy. Take away their joy, revenge their cruelty, nor be dismayed at what is past; for whoever tries for great objects must suffer something. Neither did Lucullus overthrow Tigranes without bloodshed, nor Scipio Antiochus; our ancestors lost one thousand ships about Sicily, and how many generals and captains in Italy? no one of which losses hindered them from overthrowing their conquerors; for the State of Rome did not arrive to this height by fortune, but by perseverance and virtue in confronting danger."

While Crassus thus spoke exhorting them, he saw but few that gave much heed to him, and when he ordered them to shout for the battle, he could no longer mistake the despondency of his army, which made but a faint and unsteady noise, while the shout of the enemy was clear and bold. And when they came to the business, the Parthian servants and dependents riding about shot their arrows, and the horsemen in the foremost ranks with their spears drove the Romans close together, except those who rushed upon them for fear of being killed by their arrows. Neither did these do much execution, being quickly despatched; for the strong thick spears made large and mortal wounds, and often run through two men at once. As they were thus fighting, the night coming on parted them, the Parthians boasting that they would indulge Crassus with one night to mourn his son, unless upon better consideration he would rather go to Arsaces, than be carried to him. These, therefore, took up their quarters near them, being flushed with their victory. But the Romans had a sad night of it; for neither taking care for the burial of their dead, nor the cure of the wounded, nor the groans of the expiring, every one bewailed his own fate. For there was no means of escaping, whether they should stay for the light, or venture to retreat into the vast desert in the dark. And now the wounded men gave them new trouble, since to take them with them would retard their flight, and if they should leave them, they might serve as guides to the enemy by their cries. However, they were all desirous to see and hear Crassus, though they were sensible that he was the cause of all their mischief. But he wrapped his cloak around him, and hid himself, where he lay as an example, to ordinary minds, of the caprice of fortune, but to the wise, of inconsiderateness and ambition; who, not content to be superior to so many millions of men, being inferior to two, esteemed himself as the lowest of all. Then came Octavius, his lieutenant, and Cassius, to comfort him, but he being altogether past helping, they themselves called together the centurions and tribunes, and agreeing that the best way was to fly, they ordered the army out, without sound of trumpet, and at first with silence. But before long, when the disabled men found they were left behind, strange confusion and disorder, with an outcry and lamentation, seized the camp, and a trembling and dread presently fell upon them, as if the enemy were at their heels. By which means, now and then turning out of their way, now and then standing to their ranks, sometimes taking up the wounded that followed, sometimes laying them down, they wasted the time, except three hundred horse, whom Egnatius brought safe to Carrhæ about midnight; where calling, in the Roman tongue, to the watch, as soon as they heard him, he bade them tell Coponius, the governor, that Crassus had fought a very great battle with the Parthians; and having said but this, and not so much as telling his name, he rode away at full speed to Zeugma. And by this means he saved himself and his men, but lost his reputation by deserting his general. However, his message to Coponius was for the advantage of Crassus; for he, suspecting by this hasty and confused delivery of the message that all was not well, immediately ordered the garrison to be in arms, and as soon as he understood that Crassus was upon the way towards him, he went out to meet him, and received him with his army into the town.

The Parthians, although they perceived their dislodgement in the night, yet did not pursue them, but as soon as it was day, they came upon those that were left in the camp, and put no less than four thousand to the sword, and with their light-horse picked up a great many stragglers. Varguntinus, the lieutenant, while it was yet dark, had broken off from the main body with four cohorts, which had strayed out of the way; and the Parthians encompassing these on a small hill, slew every man of them excepting twenty, who with their drawn swords forced their way through the thickest, and they admiring their courage, opened their ranks to the right and left, and let them pass without molestation to Carrhæ.

Soon after a false report was brought to Surena, that Crassus, with his principal offiers, had escaped, and that those who were got into Carrhæ were but a confused rout of insignificant people, not worth further pursuit. Supposing, therefore, that he had lost the very crown and glory of his victory, and yet being uncertain whether it were so or not, and anxious to ascertain the fact, that so he should either stay and besiege Carrhæ or follow Crassus, he sent one of his interpreters to the walls, commanding him in Latin to call for Crassus or Cassius, for that the general, Surena, desired a conference. As soon as Crassus heard this, he embraced the proposal, and soon after there came up a band of Arabians, who very well knew the faces of Crassus and Cassius, as having been frequently in the Roman camp before the battle. They having espied Cassius from the wall, told him that Surena desired a peace, and would give them safe convoy, if they would make a treaty with the king his master, and withdraw all their troops out of Mesopotamia; and this he thought most advisable for them both, before things came to the last extremity; Cassius, embracing the proposal, desired that a time and place might be appointed where Crassus and Surena might have an interview. The Arabians, having charged themselves with the message, went back to Surena, who was not a little rejoiced that Crassus was there to be besieged.

Next day, therefore, he came up with his army, insulting over the Romans, and haughtily demanding of them Crassus and Cassius bound, if they expected any mercy. The Romans, seeing themselves deluded and mocked, were much troubled at it, but advising Crassus to lay aside his distant and empty hopes of aid from the Armenians, resolved to fly for it; and this design ought to have been kept private, till they were upon their way, and not have been told to any of the people of Carrhæ. But Crassus let this also be known to Andromachus, the most faithless of men, nay he was so infatuated as to choose him for his guide. The Parthians then, to be sure, had punctual intelligence of all that passed; but it being contrary to their usage, and also difficult for them to fight by night, and Crassus having chosen that time to set out, Andromachus, lest he should get the start too far of his pursuers, led them hither and thither, and at last conveyed him into the midst of morasses and places full of ditches, so that the Romans had a troublesome and perplexing journey of it, and some there were who, supposing by these windings and turnings of Andromachus that no good was intended, resolved to follow him no further. And at last Cassius himself returned to Carrhæ, and his guides, the Arabians, advising him to tarry there till the moon was got out of Scorpio, he told them that he was most afraid of Sagittarius, and so with five hundred horse went off to Syria. Others there were, who having got honest guides, took their way by the mountains called Sinnaca, and got into places of security by daybreak; these were five thousand under the command of Octavius, a very gallant man. But Crassus fared worse; day overtook him still deceived by Andromachus, and entangled in the fens and the difficult country. There were with him four cohorts of legionary soldiers, a very few horsemen, and five lictors, with whom having with great difficulty got into the way, and not being a mile and a half from Octavius, instead of going to join him, although the enemy were already upon him, he retreated to another hill, neither so defensible nor impassable for the horse, but lying under the hills of Sinnaca, and continued so as to join them in a long ridge through the plain. Octavius could see in what danger the general was, and himself, at first but slenderly followed, hurried to the rescue. Soon after, the rest, upbraiding one another with baseness in forsaking their officers, marched down, and falling upon the Parthians, drove them from the hill, and compassing Crassus about, and fencing him with their shields, declared proudly, that no arrow in Parthia should ever touch their general, so long as there was a man of them left alive to protect him.

Surena, therefore, perceiving his soldiers less inclined to expose themselves, and knowing that if the Romans should prolong the battle till night, they might then gain the mountains and be out of his reach, betook himself to his usual craft. Some of the prisoners were set free, who had, as it was contrived, been in hearing, while some of the barbarians spoke of a set purpose in the camp to the effect that the king did not design the war to be pursued to extremity against the Romans, but rather desired, by his gentle treatment of Crassus, to make a step towards reconciliation. And the barbarians desisted from fighting, and Surena himself, with his chief officers, riding gently to the hill, unbent his bow and held out his hand, inviting Crassus to an agreement, and saying that it was beside the king's intentions, that they had thus had experience of the courage and the strength of his soldiers; that now he desired no other contention but that of kindness and friendship, by making a truce, and permitting them to go away in safety. These words of Surena the rest received joyfully, and were eager to accept the offer; but Crassus, who had had sufficient experience of their perfidiousness, and was unable to see any reason for the sudden change, would give no ear to them, and only took time to consider. But the soldiers cried out and advised him to treat, and then went on to upbraid and affront him, saying that it was very unreasonable that he should bring them to fight with such men armed, whom himself, without their arms, durst not look in the face. He tried first to prevail with them by entreaties, and told them that if they would have patience till evening, they might get into the mountains and passes, inaccessible for horse, and be out of danger, and withal he pointed out the way with his hand entreating them not to abandon their preservation, now close before them. But when they mutinied and clashed their targets in a threatening manner, he was overpowered and forced to go, and only turning about at parting, said, "You, Octavius and Petronius, and the rest of the officers who are present, see the necessity of going which I lie under, and cannot but be sensible of the indignities and violence offered to me. Tell all men when you have escaped, that Crassus perished rather by the subtility of his enemies, than by the disobedience of his countrymen."

Octavius, however, would not stay there, but with Petronius went down from the hill; as for the lictors, Crassus bade them be gone. The first that met him were two half-blood Greeks, who, leaping from their horses, made a profound reverence to Crassus, and desired him, in Greek, to send some before him, who might see that Surena himself was coming towards them, his retinue disarmed, and not having so much as their wearing swords along with them. But Crassus answered, that if he had the least concern for his life, he would never have intrusted himself in their hands, but sent two brothers of the name of Roscius, to inquire on what terms, and in what numbers they should meet. These Surena ordered immediately to be seized, and himself with his principal officers came up on horseback, and greeting him, said, "How is this, then? A Roman commander is on foot, while I and my train are mounted." But Crassus replied, that there was no error committed on either side, for they both met according to the custom of their own country. Surena told him that from that time there was a league between the king his master and the Romans, but that Crassus must go with him to the river to sign it, "for you Romans," said he, "have not good memories for conditions," and so saying, reached out his hand to him. Crassus, therefore, gave order that one of his horses should be brought; but Surena told him there was no need, "the king, my master, presents you with this;" and immediately a horse with a golden bit was brought up to him, and himself was forcibly put into the saddle by the grooms, who ran by the side and struck the horse to make the more haste. But Octavius running up, got hold of the bridle, and soon after one of the officers, Petronius, and the rest of the company came up, striving to stop the horse, and pulling back those who on both sides of him forced Crassus forward. Thus from pulling and thrusting one another, they came to a tumult, and soon after to blows. Octavius, drawing his sword, killed a groom of one of the barbarians, and one of them, getting behind Octavius, killed him. Petronius was not armed, but being struck on the breastplate, fell down from his horse, though without hurt. Crassus was killed by a Parthian, called Pomaxathres; others say, by a different man, and that Pomaxathres only cut off his head and right hand after he had fallen. But this is conjecture rather than certain knowledge, for those that were by had not leisure to observe particulars, and were either killed fighting about Crassus, or ran off at once to get to their comrades on the hill. But the Parthians coming up to them, and saying that Crassus had the punishment he justly deserved, and that Surena bade the rest come down from the hill without fear, some of them came down and surrendered themselves, others were scattered up and down in the night, a very few of whom got safe home, and others the Arabians, beating through the country, hunted down and put to death. It is generally said, that in all twenty thousand men were slain, and ten thousand taken prisoners.

Surena sent the head and hand of Crassus to Hyrodes, the king, into Armenia, but himself by his messengers scattering a report that he was bringing Crassus alive to Seleucia, made a ridiculous procession, which by way of scorn, he called a triumph. For one Caius Paccianus, who of all the prisoners was most like Crassus, being put in a woman's dress of the fashion of the barbarians, and instructed to answer to the title of Crassus and Imperator, was brought sitting upon his horse, while before him went a parcel of trumpeters and lictors upon camels. Purses were hung at the ends of the bundles of rods, and the heads of the slain fresh bleeding at the end of their axes. After them followed the Seleucian singing women, repeating scurrilous and abusive songs upon the effeminacy and cowardliness of Crassus. This show was seen by everybody; but Surena, calling together the senate of Seleucia, laid before them certain wanton books, of the writings of Aristides, his Milesiaca; neither, indeed, was this any forgery, for they had been found among the baggage of Rustius, and were a good subject to supply Surena with insulting remarks upon the Romans, who were not able even in the time of war to forget such writings and practices. But the people of Seleucia had reason to commend the wisdom of Æsop's fable of the wallet,[14] seeing their general Surena carrying a bag full of loose Milesian stories before him, but keeping behind him a whole Parthian Sybaris in his many wagons full of concubines; like the vipers and asps people talk of, all the foremost and more visible parts fierce and terrible with spears and arrows and horsemen, but the rear terminating in loose women and castanets, music of the lute, and midnight revellings. Rustius, indeed, is not to be excused, but the Parthians had forgot, when they mocked at the Milesian stories, that many of the royal line of their Arsacidæ had been born of Milesian and Ionian mistresses.

Whilst these things were doing, Hyrodes had struck up a peace with the king of Armenia, and made a match between his son Pacorus and the king of Armenia's sister. Their feastings and entertainments in consequence were very sumptuous, and various Grecian compositions, suitable to the occasion, were recited before them. For Hyrodes was not ignorant of the Greek language and literature, and Artavasdes was so expert in it, that he wrote tragedies and orations and histories, some of which are still extant. When the head of Crassus was brought to the door, the tables were just taken away, and one Jason, a tragic actor, of the town of Tralles, was singing the scene in the Bacchæ of Euripides concerning Agave. He was receiving much applause, when Sillaces coming to the room, and having made obeisance to the king, threw down the head of Crassus into the midst

[14] The two wallets, filled, the one with other men's faults, which we carry before us; the other with our own, which hangs out of our sight, upon our backs.

of the company. The Parthians receiving it with joy
and acclamations, Sillaces, by the king's command,
was made to sit down, while Jason[15] handed over the
costume of Pentheus to one of the dancers in the
chorus, and taking up the head of Crassus, and acting
the part of a bacchante in her frenzy, in a rapturous
impassioned manner, sang the lyric passages,

> We've hunted down a mighty chase to-day,
> And from the mountain bring the noble prey;

to the great delight of all the company; but when the
verses of the dialogue followed,

> What happy hand the glorious victim slew?
> I claim that honor to my courage due;

Pomaxathres, who happened to be there at the supper, started up and would have got the head into his
own hands, "for it is my due," said he, "and no man's
else." The king was greatly pleased, and gave presents, according to the custom of the Parthians, to
them, and to Jason, the actor, a talent. Such was the
burlesque that was played, they tell us, as the afterpiece to the tragedy of Crassus's expedition. But
divine justice failed not to punish both Hyrodes, for

---

[15] Jason, at the time of the interruption, was acting, it seems,
the part of Pentheus; he put off his dress and took that, apparently, of Agave. The lines that follow are from the scene
in the Bacchæ, (1170,) where Agave, returning from Cithæron,
presents herself with the head of her son Pentheus, whom in
her frenzy, she has killed, which she carries in her hand, thinking it a lion's. The lyric dialogue sung between Agave and the
chorus of her attendant bacchantes opens on her part with, "We
bring from the mountain a young one new killed to the house,
a fortunate prey," (this is Mr. Long's translation,) and presently,
to the question of the chorus, which Plutarch quotes from memory
a little inexactly, "Whose hand struck him first?" exclaims in
answer, "Mine is the honor."

his cruelty, and Surena for his perjury; for Surena not long after was put to death by Hyrodes, out of mere envy to his glory; and Hyrodes himself, having lost his son Pacorus, who was beaten in a battle with the Romans, falling into a disease which turned to a dropsy, had aconite given him by his second son, Phraates; but the poison working only upon the disease, and carrying away the dropsical matter with itself, the king began suddenly to recover, so that Phraates at length was forced to take the shortest course, and strangled him.

COMPARISON OF CRASSUS WITH NICIAS

IN the comparison of these two, first, if we compare the estate of Nicias with that of Crassus, we must acknowledge Nicias's to have been more honestly got. In itself, indeed, one cannot much approve of gaining riches by working mines, the greatest part of which is done by malefactors and barbarians, some of them, too, bound, and perishing in those close and unwholesome places. But if we compare this with the sequestrations of Sylla, and the contracts for houses ruined by fire, we shall then think Nicias came very honestly by his money. For Crassus publicly and avowedly made use of these arts, as other men do of husbandry, and putting out money to interest; while as for other matters which he used to deny, when taxed with them, as namely, selling his voice in the senate for gain's sake, and injuring allies, and courting women, and conniving at criminals, these are things which Nicias was never so much as falsely accused of; nay, he was rather laughed at for giving money to those who made a trade of impeachments, merely out of timorousness, a course, indeed, that would by no means become Pericles and Aristides, but necessary for him who by nature was wanting in assurance, even as Lycurgus, the orator, frankly acknowledged to the people; for when he was accused for buying off an evidence, he said that he was very much pleased that having administered their affairs for so long a time, he was at last accused, rather for giving, than receiving. Again, Nicias, in his expenses, was of a more public spirit than Crassus, priding himself much on the dedication of gifts in temples, on presiding at gymnastic games, and furnishing choruses for the plays, and adorning processions, while the expenses of Crassus, in feasting and afterwards providing food for so many myriads of people, were much greater than all that Nicias possessed as well as spent, put together. So that one might wonder at any one's failing to see that vice is a certain inconsistency and incongruity of habit, after such an example of money dishonorably obtained, and wastefully lavished away.

Let so much be said of their estates; as for their management of public affairs, I see not that any dishonesty, injustice, or arbitrary action can be objected to Nicias, who was rather the victim of Alcibiades's tricks, and was always careful and scrupulous in his dealings with the people. But Crassus is very generally blamed for his changeableness in his friendships and enmities, for his unfaithfulness, and his mean and underhand proceedings; since he himself could not deny that to compass the consulship, he hired men to lay violent hands upon Domitius and Cato. Then at the assembly held for assigning the provinces, many were wounded and four actually killed, and he himself, which I had omitted in the narrative of his life, struck with his fist one Lucius Analius, a senator, for contradicting him, so that he left the place bleeding. But as Crassus was to be blamed for his violent and arbitrary courses, so is Nicias no less to be blamed for his timorousness and meanness of spirit, which made him submit and give in to the basest people, whereas in this respect Crassus showed himself lofty-spirited and magnanimous, who having to do not with such as Cleon or Hyperbolus, but with the splendid acts of Cæsar and the three triumphs of Pompey, would not stoop, but bravely bore up against their joint interests, and in obtaining the office of censor, surpassed even Pompey himself. For a statesman ought not to regard how invidious[1] the thing is, but how noble, and by his greatness to overpower envy; but if he will be always aiming at security and quiet, and dread Alcibiades upon the hustings, and the Lacedæmonians at Pylos, and Perdiccas in Thrace, there is room and opportunity enough for retirement, and he may sit out of the noise of business, and weave himself, as one of the sophists says, his triumphal garland of inactivity. His desire of peace, indeed, and of finishing the war, was a divine and truly Grecian ambition, nor in this respect would Crassus deserve to be compared to him, though he had enlarged the Roman empire to the Caspian Sea or the Indian Ocean.

In a State where there is a sense of virtue, a powerful man ought not to give way to the ill-affected, or expose the government to those that are incapable of it, nor suffer high trusts to be committed to those who want common honesty. Yet Nicias, by his connivance, raised Cleon, a fellow remarkable for nothing but his loud voice and brazen face, to the command of an army. Indeed, I do not commend Crassus, who in the war with Spartacus was more forward to fight than became a discreet general, though he was urged into it by a point of

---

[1] *A statesman ought not to regard how invidious the thing is, but how noble* (or, more exactly, the part of the statesman is to strive upon the highest conditions to attain, not exemption from odium, but glory), is a sentiment taken from Thucydides, which Plutarch himself cites expressly unpopularity all must experience who seek dominion over others; he is wisest who takes the odium on the loftiest terms. The unpopularity does not last; the present splendor, and the glory that follows it, remain to an everlasting remembrance." (II., 64.)

honor, lest Pompey by his coming should rob him of the glory of the action, as Mummius did Metellus at the taking of Corinth, but Nicias's proceedings are inexcusable. For he did not yield up a mere opportunity of getting honor and advantage to his competitor, but believing that the expedition would be very hazardous, was thankful to take care of himself, and left the Commonwealth to shift for itself. And whereas Themistocles, lest a mean and incapable fellow should ruin the State by holding command in the Persian war, bought him off, and Cato, in a most dangerous and critical conjuncture, stood for the tribuneship for the sake of his country, Nicias, reserving himself for trifling expeditions against Minoa and Cythera, and the miserable Melians, if there be occasion to come to blows with the Lacedæmonians, slips off his general's cloak and hands over to the unskilfulness and rashness of Cleon, fleet, men, and arms, and the whole command, where the utmost possible skill was called for. Such conduct, I say, is not to be thought so much carelessness of his own fame, as of the interest and preservation of his country. By this means it came to pass he was compelled to the Sicilian war, men generally believing that he was not so much honestly convinced of the difficulty of the enterprise, as ready out of mere love of ease and cowardice to lose the city the conquest of Sicily. But yet it is a great sign of his integrity, that though he was always averse from war, and unwilling to command, yet they always continued to appoint him as the best experienced and ablest general they had. On the other hand Crassus, though always ambitious of command, never attained to it, except by mere necessity in the servile war, Pompey and Metellus and the two brothers Lucullus being absent, although at that time he was at his highest pitch of interest and reputation. Even those who thought most of him seem to have thought him, as the comic poet says:—

A brave man anywhere but in the field.[2]

There was no help, however, for the Romans, against his passion for command and for distinction. The Athenians sent out Nicias against his will to the war, and Crassus led out the Romans against theirs; Crassus brought misfortune on Rome, as Athens brought it on Nicias.

Still this is rather ground for praising Nicias, than for finding fault with Crassus. His experience and sound judgment as a general saved him from being carried away by the delusive hopes of his fellow-citizens, and made him refuse to entertain any prospect of conquering Sicily. Crassus, on the other hand, mistook, in entering on a Parthian war as an easy matter. He was eager, while Cæsar was subduing the west, Gaul, Germany, and Britain, to advance for his part to the east and the Indian Sea, by the conquest of Asia, to complete the incursions of Pompey and the attempts of Lucullus, men of prudent temper and of unimpeachable worth, who, nevertheless, entertained the same projects as Crassus, and acted under the same convictions. When Pompey was appointed to the like command, the senate was opposed to it; and after Cæsar had routed three hundred thousand Germans, Cato recommended that he should be surrendered to the defeated enemy, to expiate in his own person the guilt of breach of faith. The people, meantime, (their service to Cato!) kept holiday for fifteen days, and were overjoyed. What would have been their feelings, and how many holidays would

---

[2] *A brave man anywhere but in the field,* is, I believe, an unknown fragment.

they have celebrated, if Crassus had sent news from Babylon of victory, and thence marching onward had converted Media and Persia, the Hyrcanians, Susa, and Bactra, into Roman provinces?

If wrong we must do, as Euripides [3] says, and cannot be content with peace and present good things, let it not be for such results as destroying Mende or Scandea, or beating up the exiled Æginetans in the coverts to which like hunted birds they had fled, when expelled from their homes, but let it be for some really great remuneration; nor let us part with justice, like a cheap and common thing, for a small and trifling price. Those who praise Alexander's enterprise and blame that of Crassus, judge of the beginning unfairly by the results.

In actual service, Nicias did much that deserves high praise. He frequently defeated the enemy in battle, and was on the very point of capturing Syracuse; nor should he bear the whole blame of the disaster, which may fairly be ascribed in part to his want of health and to the jealousy entertained of him at home. Crassus, on the other hand, committed so many errors as not to leave fortune room to show him favor. It is no surprise to find such imbecility fall a victim to the power of Parthia; the only wonder is to see it prevailing over the wonted good-fortune of Rome. One scrupulously observed, the other entirely slighted the arts of divination; and as both equally

---

[3] *If wrong we must do,* says Euripides in the Phœnissæ, 521-525; it is the reply of Eteocles to the expostulations of his mother:—

      Come fire, come sword, yoke-to the steeds apace,
      Through all the plain let the war chariots race,
      I to my rival will not yield my place;
      If wrong we must do, let us, to 't is best,
      To become kings do wrong, and right in all the rest.

perished, it is difficult to see what inference we should draw. Yet the fault of over-caution, supported by old and general opinion, better deserves forgiveness than that of self-willed and lawless transgression.

In his death, however, Crassus has the advantage, as he did not surrender himself, nor submit to bondage, or let himself be taken in by trickery, but was the victim only of the entreaties of his friends and the perfidy of his enemies; whereas Nicias enhanced the shame of his death by yielding himself up in the hope of a disgraceful and inglorious escape.

SERTORIUS[1]

TRANSLATED BY EDWARD BROWNE, M. D.

IT is no great wonder if in long process of time, while fortune takes her course hither and thither, numerous coincidences should spontaneously occur. If the number and variety of subjects to be wrought upon be infinite, it is all the more easy for fortune, with such an abundance of material, to effect this similarity of results. Or if, on the other hand, events are limited to the combinations of some finite number, then of necessity the same must often recur, and in the same sequence. There are people who take a pleasure in making collections of all such fortuitous occurrences that they have heard or read of, as look like works of a rational power and design; they observe, for example, that two eminent persons, whose names were Attis, the one a Syrian, the other of Arcadia, were both slain by a wild boar; that of two whose names were Actæon, the one was torn in pieces by his dogs, the other by his lovers; that of two famous Scipios, the one overthrew the Carthaginians in war, the other totally ruined and destroyed them; the city of Troy was the first time taken by Hercules for the horses promised him by Laomedon, the second time by Agamemnon, by means of the celebrated great wooden horse, and the third time by Charidemus, by

[1] One of the most extraordinary men in the later times of the Roman republic. Waged war, generally with success, against the Sullan commanders and was at length assassinated in 72 B. C. —Dr. William Smith.

occasion of a horse falling down at the gate, which
hindered the Trojans, so that they could not shut
them soon enough; and of two cities which take their
names from the most agreeable odoriferous plants,
Ios and Smyrna, the one from a violet, the other from
myrrh, the poet Homer is reported to have been born
in the one, and to have died in the other. And so to
these instances let us further add, that the most warlike commanders, and most remarkable for exploits
of skilful stratagem, have had but one eye; as Philip,
Antigonus, Hannibal, and Sertorius, whose life and
actions we describe at present; of whom, indeed, we
might truly say, that he was more continent than
Philip, more faithful to his friend than Antigonus,
and more merciful to his enemies than Hannibal; and
that for prudence and judgment he gave place to
none of them, but in fortune was inferior to them all.
Yet though he had continually in her a far more difficult adversary to contend against than his open enemies, he nevertheless maintained his ground, with the
military skill of Metellus, the boldness of Pompey,
the success of Sylla, and the power of the Roman
people, all to be encountered by one who was a banished man and a stranger at the head of a body of
barbarians. Among Greek commanders, Eumenes
of Cardia may be best compared with him; they were
both of them men born for command, for warfare,
and for stratagem; both banished from their countries, and holding command over strangers; both had
fortune for their adversary, in their last days so
harshly so, that they were both betrayed and murdered by those who served them, and with whom they
had formerly overcome their enemies.

Quintus Sertorius was of a noble family, born in
the city of Nursia, in the country of the Sabines; his
father died when he was young, and he was carefully

and decently educated by his mother, whose name was Rhea, and whom he appears to have extremely loved and honored. He paid some attention to the study of oratory and pleading in his youth, and acquired some reputation and influence in Rome by his eloquence; but the splendor of his actions in arms, and his successful achievements in the wars, drew off his ambition in that direction.

At his first beginning, he served under Cæpio, when the Cimbri and Teutones invaded Gaul; where the Romans fighting unsuccessfully, and being put to flight, he was wounded in many parts of his body, and lost his horse, yet, nevertheless, swam across the river Rhone in his armor, with his breastplate and shield, bearing himself up against the violence of the current; so strong and so well inured to hardship was his body.

The second time that the Cimbri and Teutones came down with some hundreds of thousands, threatening death and destruction to all, when it was no small piece of service for a Roman soldier to keep his ranks and obey his commander, Sertorius undertook, while Marius led the army, to spy out the enemy's camp. Procuring a Celtic dress, and acquainting himself with the ordinary expressions of their language requisite for common intercourse, he threw himself in amongst the barbarians; where having carefully seen with his own eyes, or having been fully informed by persons upon the place of all their most important concerns, he returned to Marius, from whose hands he received the rewards of valor; and afterwards giving frequent proofs both of conduct and courage in all the following war, he was advanced to places of honor and trust under his general. After the wars with the Cimbri and Teutones, he was sent into Spain, having the command of a thousand men under Didius, the Roman general, and wintered in the country of the Celtiberians, in the city of Castulo, where the soldiers enjoying great plenty, and growing insolent, and continually drinking, the inhabitants despised them and sent for aid by night to the Gyriscenians, their near neighbors, who fell upon the Romans in their lodgings and slew a great number of them. Sertorius, with a few of his soldiers, made his way out, and rallying together the rest who escaped, he marched round about the walls, and finding the gate open, by which the Gyriscenians had made their secret entrance, he gave not them the same opportunity, but placing a guard at the gate, and seizing upon all quarters of the city, he slew all who were of age to bear arms, and then ordering his soldiers to lay aside their weapons and put off their own clothes, and put on the accoutrements of the barbarians, he commanded them to follow him to the city, from whence the men came who had made this night attack upon the Romans. And thus deceiving the Gyriscenians with the sight of their own armor, he found the gates of their city open, and took a great number prisoners, who came out thinking to meet their friends and fellow-citizens come home from a successful expedition. Most of them were thus slain by the Romans at their own gates, and the rest within yielded up themselves and were sold for slaves.

This action made Sertorius highly renowned throughout all Spain, and as soon as he returned to Rome he was appointed quæstor of Cisalpine Gaul, at a very seasonable moment for his country, the Marsian war being on the point of breaking out. Sertorius was ordered to raise soldiers and provide arms, which he performed with a diligence and alacrity, so contrasting with the feebleness and slothfulness of other officers of his age, that he got the repute of a man whose life would be one of action. Nor did he relinquish the part of a soldier, now that he had arrived at the dignity of a commander, but performed wonders with his own hands, and never sparing himself, but exposing his body freely in all conflicts, he lost one of his eyes. This he always esteemed an honor to him; observing that others do not continually carry about with them the marks and testimonies of their valor but must often lay aside their chains of gold, their spears and crowns; whereas his ensigns of honor, and the manifestations of his courage always remained with him, and those who beheld his misfortune, must at the same time recognize his merits. The people also paid him the respect he deserved, and when he came into the theatre, received him with plaudits and joyful acclamations, an honor rarely bestowed even on persons of advanced standing and established reputation. Yet, notwithstanding this popularity, when he stood to be tribune of the people, he was disappointed, and lost the place, being opposed by the party of Sylla, which seems to have been the principal cause of his subsequent enmity to Sylla.

After that Marius was overcome by Sylla and fled into Africa, and Sylla had left Italy to go to the wars against Mithridates, and of the two consuls Octavius and Cinna, Octavius remained steadfast to the policy of Sylla, but Cinna, desirous of a new revolution, attempted to recall the lost interest of Marius, Sertorius joined Cinna's party, more particularly as he saw that Octavius was not very capable, and was also suspicious of any one that was a friend to Marius. When a great battle was fought between the two consuls in the forum, Octavius overcame, and Cinna and Sertorius, having lost not less than ten thousand men, left the city, and gaining over most part of the troops who were dispersed about and remained still in many

parts of Italy, they in a short time mustered up a
force against Octavius sufficient to give him battle
again, and Marius, also, now coming by sea out of
Africa, proffered himself to serve under Cinna, as a
private soldier under his consul and commander.

Most were for the immediate reception of Marius,
but Sertorius openly declared against it, whether he
thought that Cinna would not now pay as much attention to himself, when a man of higher military repute was present, or feared that the violence of Marius would bring all things to confusion, by his bound-
less wrath and vengeance after victory. He insisted
upon it with Cinna that they were already victorious,
that there remained little to be done, and that, if they
admitted Marius, he would deprive them of the glory
and advantage of the war, as there was no man less
easy to deal with, or less to be trusted in, as a partner
in power. Cinna answered, that Sertorius rightly
judged the affair, but that he himself was at a loss,
and ashamed, and knew not how to reject him, after
he had sent for him to share in his fortunes. To which
Sertorius immediately replied, that he had thought
that Marius came into Italy of his own accord, and
therefore had deliberated as to what might be most
expedient, but that Cinna ought not so much as to
have questioned whether he should accept him whom
he had already invited, but should have honorably
received and employed him, for his word once past
left no room for debate. Thus Marius being sent for
by Cinna, and their forces being divided into three
parts, under Cinna, Marius, and Sertorius, the war
was brought to a successful conclusion; but those
about Cinna and Marius committing all manner of
insolence and cruelty, made the Romans think the
evils of war a golden time in comparison. On the
contrary, it is reported of Sertorius, that he never

slew any man in his anger, to satisfy his own private revenge, nor ever insulted over any one whom he had overcome, but was much offended with Marius, and often privately entreated Cinna to use his power more moderately. And in the end, when the slaves whom Marius had freed at his landing to increase his army, being made not only his fellow-soldiers in the war, but also now his guard in his usurpation, enriched and powerful by his favor, either by the command or permission of Marius, or by their own lawless violence, committed all sorts of crimes, killed their masters, ravished their masters' wives, and abused their children, their conduct appeared so intolerable to Sertorius that he slew the whole body of them, four thousand in number, commanding his soldiers to shoot them down with their javelins, as they lay encamped together.

Afterwards, when Marius died, and Cinna shortly after was slain, when the younger Marius made himself consul against Sertorius's wishes and contrary to law, when Carbo, Norbanus, and Scipio fought unsuccessfully against Sylla, now advancing to Rome, when much was lost by the cowardice and remissness of the commanders, but more by the treachery of their party, when with the want of prudence in the chief leaders, all went so ill that his pressence could do no good, in the end when Sylla had placed his camp near to Scipio, and by pretending friendship, and putting him in hopes of a peace, corrupted his army, and Scipio could not be made sensible of this, although often forewarned of it by Sertorius,—at last he utterly despaired of Rome, and hastened into Spain, that by taking possession there beforehand, he might secure a refuge to his friends, from their misfortunes at home. Having bad weather in his journey, and travelling through mountainous countries, and the in-

habitants stopping the way, and demanding a toll and
money for passage, those who were with him were
out of all patience at the indignity and shame it would
be for a proconsul of Rome to pay tribute to a crew
of wretched barbarians. But he little regarded their
censure, and slighting that which had only the appearance of an indecency, told them he must buy time, the
most precious of all things to those who go upon great
enterprises; and pacifying the barbarous people with
money, he hastened his journey, and took possession
of Spain, a country flourishing and populous, abounding with young men fit to bear arms; but on account
of the insolence and covetousness of the governors
from time to time sent thither from Rome, they had
generally an aversion to the Roman supemacy. He,
however, soon gained the affection of their nobles by
intercourse with them, and the good opinion of the
people by remitting their taxes. But that which won
him most popularity, was his exempting them from
finding lodgings for the soldiers, when he commanded
his army to take up their winter quarters outside the
cities, and to pitch their camp in the suburbs; and
when he himself, first of all, caused his own tent to be
raised without the walls. Yet not being willing to
rely totally upon the good inclination of the inhabitants, he armed all the Romans who lived in those
countries that were of military age, and undertook
the building of ships and the making of all sorts of
warlike engines, by which means he kept the cities in
due obedience, showing himself gentle in all peaceful
business, and at the same time formidable to his enemies by his great preparations for war.

As soon as he was informed that Sylla had made
himself master of Rome, and that the party which
sided with Marius and Carbo was going to destruction, he expected that some commander with a con-

siderable army would speedily come against him, and therefore sent away Julius Salinator immediately, with six thousand men fully armed, to fortify and defend the passes of the Pyrenees. And Caius Annius not long after being sent out by Sylla, finding Julius unassailable, sat down short at the foot of the mountains in perplexity. But a certain Calpurnius, surnamed Lanarius, having treacherously slain Julius, and his soldiers then forsaking the heights of the Pyrenees, Caius Annius advanced with large numbers and drove before him all who endeavored to hinder his march. Sertorius, also, not being strong enough to give him battle, retreated with three thousand men into New Carthage, where he took shipping, and crossed the seas into Africa. And coming near the coast of Mauritania, his men went on shore to water, and straggling about negligently, the natives fell upon them and slew a great number. This new misfortune forced him to sail back again into Spain, whence he was also repulsed, and, some Cilician pirate ships joining with him, they made for the island of Pityussa,[2] where they landed and overpowered the garrison placed there by Annius, who, however, came not long after with a great fleet of ships, and five thousand soldiers. And Sertorius made ready to fight him by sea, although his ships were not built for strength, but for lightness and swift sailing; but a violent west wind raised such a sea that many of them were run aground and shipwrecked, and he himself, with a few vessels, being kept from putting further out to sea by the fury of the weather, and from landing by the power of his enemies, was tossed about painfully for ten days together, amidst the boisterous and adverse waves.

[2] The modern Ivica.

He escaped with difficulty, and after the wind
ceased, ran for certain desert islands scattered in those
seas, affording no water, and after passing a night
there, making out to sea again, he went through the
straits of Cadiz,[3] and sailing outward, keeping the
Spanish shore on his right hand, he landed a little
above the mouth of the river Bætis, where it falls into
the Atlantic sea, and gives the name to that part of
Spain. Here he met with seamen recently arrived from
the Atlantic islands, two in number, and divided from
another only by a narrow channel, and distant from
the coast of Africa ten thousand furlongs. These are
called the Islands of the Blest; rains fall there seldom, and in moderate showers, but for the most part
they have gentle breezes, bringing along with them
soft dews, which render the soil not only rich for
ploughing and planting, but so abundantly fruitful
that it produces spontaneously an abundance of delicate fruits, sufficient to feed the inhabitants, who may
here enjoy all things without trouble or labor. The
seasons of the year are temperate, and the transitions
from one to another so moderate, that the air is almost
always serene and pleasant. The rough northerly and
easterly winds which blow from the coasts of Europe
and Africa, dissipated in the vast open space, utterly
lose their force before they reach the islands. The
soft western and southerly winds which breathe upon
them sometimes produce gentle sprinkling showers,
which they convey along with them from the sea, but
more usually bring days of moist bright weather,
cooling and gently fertilizing the soil, so that the firm
belief prevails even among the barbarians, that this is

[3] The Straits of Gibraltar.

the seat of the blessed, and that these are the Elysian Fields celebrated by Homer.[4]

When Sertorius heard this account, he was seized with a wonderful passion for these islands, and had an extreme desire to go and live there in peace and quietness, and safe from oppression and unending wars; but his inclinations being perceived by the Cilican pirates, who desired not peace nor quiet, but riches and spoils, they immediately forsook him, and sailed away into Africa to assist Ascalis, the son of Iphtha, and to help to restore him to his kingdom of Mauritania. Their sudden departure noways discouraged Sertorius; he presently resolved to assist the enemies of Ascalis, and by this new adventure trusted to keep his soldiers together, who from this might conceive new hopes, and a prospect of a new scene of action. His arrival in Mauritania being very acceptable to the Moors, he lost no time, but immediately giving battle to Ascalis, beat him out of the field and besieged him; and Paccianus being sent by Sylla, with a powerful supply, to raise the siege, Sertorius slew him in the field, gained over all his forces, and took the city of Tingis, into which Ascalis and his brothers were fled for refuge. The Africans tell that Antæus was buried in this city, and Sertorius had the grave opened, doubting the story because of the prodigious size, and finding there his body, in effect, it is said, full sixty cubits long, he was infinitely astonished, offered sacrifice, and heaped up the tomb again, gave his confirmation to the story, and added new honors

---

[4] Menelaus shall not die in Argos; the deities will convey him to the Elysian field, and the limits of the earth, where the yellow-haired Rhadamanthus lives. In that land man's life is easiest; there is no snow, no long bad weather, and no falls of rain; but Oceanus sends in to refresh them continually the whistling breezes of Zephyrus.—*Odyssey,* iv. 563.

to the memory of Antæus. The Africans tell that after the death of Antæus, his wife Tinga lived with Hercules, and had a son by him called Sophax, who was king of these countries, and gave his mother's name to this city, whose son, also, was Diodorus, a great conqueror, who brought the greatest part of the Libyan tribes under his subjection, with an army of Greeks, raised out of the colonies of the Olbians and Myceneans placed here by Hercules. Thus much I may mention for the sake of king Juba, of all monarchs the greatest student of history, whose ancestors are said to have sprung from Diodorus and Sophax.

When Sertorius had made himself absolute master of the whole country, he acted with great fairness to those who had confided in him, and who yielded to his mercy; he restored to them their property, cities, and government, accepting only of such acknowledgments as they themselves freely offered. And whilst he considered which way next to turn his arms, the Lusitanians sent ambassadors to desire him to be their general; for being terrified with the Roman power, and finding the necessity of having a commander of great authority and experience in war, being also sufficiently assured of his worth and valor by those who had formerly known him, they were desirous to commit themselves especially to his care. And in fact Sertorius is said to have been of a temper unassailable either by fear or pleasure, in adversity and dangers undaunted, and noways puffed up with prosperity. In straightforward fighting, no commander in his time was more bold and daring, and in whatever was to be performed in war by stratagem, secrecy, or surprise, if any strong place was to be secured, any pass to be gained speedily, for deceiving and overreaching an enemy, there was no man equal to him in subtlety and skill. In bestowing rewards and conferring honors upon those who had performed good service in the wars he was bountiful and magnificent, and was no less sparing and moderate in inflicting punishment. It is true that that piece of harshness and cruelty which he executed in the latter part of his days upon the Spanish hostages, seems to argue that his clemency was not natural to him, but only worn as a dress, and employed upon calculation, as his occasion or necessity required. As to my own opinion, I am persuaded that pure virtue, established by reason and judgment, can never be totally perverted or changed think it at the same time possible, that virtuous inclinations and natural good qualities may, when unations and natural good qualities may, when unworthily oppressed by calamities, show, with change of fortune, some change and alteration of their temper; and thus I conceive it happened to Sertorius, who when prosperity failed him, became exasperated by his disasters against those who had done him wrong.

The Lusitanians having sent for Sertorius, he left Africa, and being made general with absolute authority, he put all in order amongst them, and brought the neighboring parts of Spain under subjection. Most of the tribes voluntarily submitted themselves, won by the fame of his clemency and of his courage, and, to some extent, also, he availed himself of cunning artifices of his own devising to impose upon them and gain influence over them. Amongst which, certainly, that of the hind was not the least. Spanus, a countryman who lived in those parts, meeting by chance a hind that had recently calved, flying from the hunters, let the dam go, and pursuing the fawn, took it, being wonderfully pleased with the rarity of the color, which was all milk white. And as at that time Sertorius was living in the neighborhood, and accepted gladly any presents of fruit, fowl, or venison, that the country

afforded, and rewarded liberally those who presented
them, the countryman brought him his young hind,
which he took and was well pleased with at the first
sight, but when in time he had made it so tame and
gentle that it would come when he called, and follow
him wheresoever he went, and could endure the noise
and tumult of the camp, knowing well that uncivi-
lized people are naturally prone to superstition, by
little and little he raised it into something preternatural, saying that it was given him by the goddess
Diana, and that it revealed to him many secrets. He
added, also, further contrivances. If he had received
at any time private intelligence that the enemies had
made an incursion into any part of the districts under
his command, or had solicited any city to revolt, he
pretended that the hind had informed him of it in his
sleep, and charged him to keep his forces in readiness.
Or if again he had notice that any of the commanders
under him had got a victory, he would hide the messengers and bring forth the hind crowned with flowers,
for joy of the good news that was to come, and would
encourage them to rejoice and sacrifice to the gods for
the good account they should soon receive of their
prosperous success.

By such practices, he brought them to be more
tractable and obedient in all things; for now they
thought themselves no longer to be led by a stranger,
by rather conducted by a god, and the more so, as the
facts themselves seemed to bear witness to it, his
power, contrary to all expectation or probability; continually increasing. For with two thousand six hundred men, whom for honor's sake he called Romans,
combined with seven hundred Africans, who landed
with him when he first entered Lusitania, together
with four thousand targeteers, and seven hundred
horse of the Lusitanians themselves, he made war

against four Roman generals, who commanded a hundred and twenty thousand foot, six thousand horse, two thousand archers and slingers, and had cities innumerable in their power; whereas at the first he had not above twenty cities in all. And from this weak and slender beginning, he raised himself to the command of large nations of men, and the possession of numerous cities; and of the Roman commanders who were sent against him, he overthrew Cotta in a sea-fight, in the channel near the town of Mellaria; he routed Fufidius, the governor of Bætica, with the loss of two thousand Romans, near the banks of the river Bætis; Lucius Domitius,[5] proconsul of the other province of Spain, was overthrown by one of his lieutenants; Thoranius, another commander sent against him by Metellus with a great force, was slain, and Metellus, one of the greatest and most approved Roman generals then living, by a series of defeats, was reduced to such extremities, that Lucius Manlius came to his assistance out of Gallia Narbonensis, and Pompey the Great, was sent from Rome, itself, in all haste, with considerable forces. Nor did Metellus know which way to turn himself, in a war with such a bold and ready commander, who was continually molesting him, and yet could not be brought to a set battle, but

[5] *Lucius Domitius* is the old reading, followed by Amyot, but it may be Domitius Calvisius, or Domitius Calvinus. The Roman names in Plutarch must always be accepted under protest. Fufidius, just above, is a correction, and for Thoranius just below, and Lucius Manlius in the next page, there are other readings. Lucius Manilius appears to be the proper original of the latter, and "the true name of Thoranius," says Mr. Long, "is Thorius." Perpenna, in like manner, ought in correctness to be written Perperna, and Marcus Marius, the envoy to Mithridates, should most likely, both here and in the Life of Lucullus (p. 242), be Varius. And the same uncertainty attaches to the orthography of the names of the Spanish localities.

by the swiftness and dexterity of his Spanish soldiery, was enabled to shift and adapt himself to any change of circumstances. Metellus had had experience in battles fought by regular legions of soldiers, fully armed and drawn up in due order into a heavy standing phalanx, admirably trained for encountering and overpowering an enemy who came to close combat, hand to hand, but entirely unfit for climbing among the hills, and competing incessantly with the swift attacks and retreats of a set of fleet mountaineers, or to endure hunger and thirst, and live exposed like them to the wind and weather, without fire or covering.

Besides, being now in years, and having been formerly engaged in many fights and dangerous conflicts, he had grown inclined to a more remiss, easy, and luxurious life, and was the less able to contend with Sertorius, who was in the prime of his strength and vigor, and had a body wonderfully fitted for war, being strong, active and temperate, continually accustomed to endure hard labor, to take long tedious journeys, to pass many nights together without sleep, to eat little, and to be satisfied with very coarse fare, and who was never stained with the least excess in wine, even when he was most at leisure. What leisure time he allowed himself, he spent in hunting and riding about, and so made himself thoroughly acquainted with every passage for escape when he would fly, and for overtaking and intercepting in pursuit, and gained a perfect knowledge of where he could and where he could not go. Insomuch that Metellus suffered all the inconveniences of defeat, although he earnestly desired to fight, and Sertorius, though he refused the field, reaped all the advantages of a conqueror. For he hindered them from foraging, and cut them off from water; if they advanced, he was nowhere to be found; if they stayed in any place and encamped, he continually molested and alarmed them; if they besieged any town, he presently appeared and besieged them again, and put them to extremities for want of necessaries. And thus he so wearied out the Roman army, that when Sertorius challenged Metellus to fight singly with him, they commended it, and cried out, it was a fair offer, a Roman to fight against a Roman, and a general against a general; and when Metellus refused the challenge, they reproached him. Metellus derided and contemned this, and rightly so; for, as Theophrastus observes, a general should die like a general, and not like a skirmisher. But perceiving that the town of the Langobritæ, who gave great assistance to Sertorius, might easily be taken for want of water, as there was but one well within the walls, and the besieger would be master of the springs and fountains in the suburbs, he advanced against the place, expecting to carry it in two days' time, there being no more water, and gave command to his soldiers to take five days' provision only. Sertorius, however, resolving to send speedy relief, ordered two thousand skins to be filled with water, naming a considerable sum of money for the carriage of every skin; and many Spaniards and Moors undertaking the work, he chose out those who were the strongest and swiftest of foot, and sent them through the mountains, with order that when they had delivered the water, they should convey away privately all those who would be least serviceable in the siege, that there might be water sufficient for the defendants. As soon as Metellus understood this, he was disturbed, as he had already consumed most part of the necessary provisions for his army, but he sent out Aquinus with six thousand soldiers to fetch in fresh supplies. But Sertorius having notice of it, laid an ambush for him, and having sent out

beforehand three thousand men to take post in a
thickly wooded watercourse, with these he attacked
the rear of Aquinus in his return, while he himself
charging him in the front, destroyed part of his army,
and took the rest prisoners, Aquinus only escaping,
after the loss of both his horse and his armor. And
Metellus, being forced shamefully to raise the siege,
withdrew amidst the laughter and contempt of the
Spaniards; while Sertorius became yet more the object of their esteem and admiration.

He was also highly honored for his introducing
discipline and good order amongst them, for he altered their furious savage manner of fighting, and
brought them to make use of the Roman armor,
taught them to keep their ranks, and observe signals
and watchwords; and out of a confused number of
thieves and robbers, he constituted a regular, well-disciplined army. He bestowed silver and gold upon
them liberally to gild and adorn their helmets, he had
their shields worked with various figures and designs,
he brought them into the mode of wearing flowered
and embroidered cloaks and coats, and by supplying
money for these purposes, and joining with them in
all improvements, he won the hearts of all. That,
however, which delighted them most, was the care that
he took of their children. He sent for all the boys of
noblest parentage out of all their tribes, and placed
them in the great city of Osca, where he appointed
masters to instruct them in the Grecian and Roman
learning, that when they came to be men, they might,
as he professed, be fitted to share with him in authority, and in conducting the government, although
under this pretext he really made them hostages.
However, their fathers were wonderfully pleased to
see their children going daily to the schools in good
order, handsomely dressed in gowns edged with pur-

ple, and that Sertorius paid for their lessons, examined them often, distributed rewards to the most deserving, and gave them the golden bosses to hang about their necks, which the Romans called bullæ.

There being a custom in Spain, that when a commander was slain in battle, those who attended his person fought it out till they all died with him, which the inhabitants of those countries called an *offering,* or libation, there were few commanders that had any considerable guard or number of attendants; but Sertorius was followed by many thousands who offered themselves, and vowed to spend their blood with his. And it is told that when his army was defeated near a city in Spain, and the enemy pressed hard upon them, the Spaniards, with no care for themselves, but being totally solicitous to save Sertorius, took him up on their shoulders and passed him from one to another, till they carried him into the city, and only when they had thus placed their general in safety, provided afterwards each man for his own security.

Nor were the Spaniards alone ambitious to serve him, but the Roman soldiers, also, that came out of Italy, were impatient to be under his command; and when Perpenna Vento, who was of the same faction with Sertorius, came into Spain with a quantity of money and a large number of troops, and designed to make war against Metellus on his own account, his own soldiers opposed it, and talked continually of Sertorius, much to the mortification of Perpenna, who was puffed up with the grandeur of his family and his riches. And when they afterwards received tidings that Pompey was passing the Pyrenees, they took up their arms, laid hold on their ensigns, called upon Perpenna to lead them to Sertorius, and threatened him that if he refused they would go without him, and place themselves under a commander who was able to defend himself and those that served him. And so Perpenna was obliged to yield to their desires, and joining Sertorius, added to his army three and fifty cohorts.

And when now all the cities on this side of the river Ebro also united their forces together under his command, his army grew great, for they flocked together and flowed in upon him from all quarters. But when they continually cried out to attack the enemy, and were impatient of delay, their inexperienced, disorderly rashness caused Sertorius much trouble, who at first strove to restrain them with reason and good counsel, but when he perceived them refractory and unseasonably violent, he gave way to their impetuous desires, and permitted them to engage with the enemy, in such sort that they might, being repulsed, yet not totally routed, become more obedient to his commands for the future. Which happening as he had anticipated, he soon rescued them, and brought them safe into his camp. And after a few days, being willing to encourage them again, when he had called all his army together, he caused two horses to be brought into the field, one an old, feeble, lean animal, the other a lusty, strong horse, with a remarkably thick and long tail. Near the lean one he placed a tall strong man, and near the strong young horse a weak despicable-looking fellow; and at a sign given, the strong man took hold of the weak horse's tail with both his hands and drew it to him with his whole force, as if he would pull it off; the other, the weak man, in the mean time, set to work to pluck off hair by hair from the great horse's tail. And when the strong man had given trouble enough to himself in vain, and sufficient diversion to the company, and had abandoned his attempt, whilst the weak pitiful fellow in a short time and with little pains had left not a hair on the great horse's tail, Sertorius rose up and spoke to his army, "You see, fellow-soldiers, that perseverance is more prevailing than violence, and that many things which cannot be overcome when they are together, yield themselves up when taken little by little. Assiduity and persistence are irresistible, and in time overthrow and destroy the greatest powers whatever. Time being the favorable friend and assistant of those who use their judgment to await his occasions, and the destructive enemy of those who are unseasonably urging and pressing forward." With a frequent use of such words and such devices, he soothed the fierceness of the barbarous people, and taught them to attend and watch for their opportunities.

Of all his remarkable exploits, none raised greater admiration than that which he put in practice against the Characitanians. These are a people beyond the river Tagus, who inhabit neither cities nor towns, but live in a vast high hill, within the deep dens and caves of the rocks, the mouths of which open all towards the north. The country below is of a soil resembling a light clay, so loose as easily to break into powder, and is not firm enough to bear any one that treads upon it, and if you touch it in the least, it flies about like ashes or unslaked lime. In any danger of war, these people descend into their caves, and carrying in their booty and prey along with them, stay quietly within, secure from every attack. And when Sertorius, leaving Metellus some distance off, had placed his camp near this hill, they slighted and despised him, imagining that he retired into these parts, being overthrown by the Romans. And whether out of anger and resentment, or out of his unwillingness to be thought to fly from his enemies, early in the morning he rode up to view the situation of the place. But finding there was no way to come at it, as he rode about, threatening them in vain and disconcerted, he took notice that the wind raised the dust and carried it up towards the caves of the Characitanians, the mouths of which, as I said before, opened towards the north; and the northerly wind, which some call Cæcias, prevailing most in those parts, coming up out of moist plains or mountains covered with snow, at this particular time, in the heat of summer, being further supplied and increased by the melting of the ice in the northern regions, blew a delightful fresh gale, cooling and refreshing the Characitanians and their cattle all the day long. Sertorius, considering well all circumstances in which either the information of the inhabitants, or his own experience had instructed him, commanded his soldiers to shovel up a great quantity of this light, dusty earth, to heap it up together, and make a mount of it over against the hill in which these barbarous people resided, who, imagining that all this preparation was for raising a mound to get at them, only mocked and laughed at it. However, he continued the work till the evening, and brought his soldiers back into their camp. The next morning a gentle breeze at first arose, and moved the lightest parts of the earth, and dispersed it about as the chaff before the wind; but when the sun coming to be higher, the strong northerly wind had covered the hills with the dust, the soldiers came and turned this mound of earth over and over, and broke the hard clods in pieces, whilst others on horseback rode through it backward and forward, and raised a cloud of dust into the air: there with the wind the whole of it was carried away and blown into the dwellings of the Characitanians, all lying open to the north. And there being no other vent or breathing-place than that through which the Cæcias rushed in upon them, it quickly blinded their eyes, and filled their lungs, and all but choked them, while they strove to draw in the rough air mingled with dust and powdered earth. Nor were they able, with all they could do, to hold out above two days, but yielded up themselves on the third, adding, by their defeat, not so much to the power of Sertorius, as to his renown, in proving that he was able to conquer places by art, which were impregnable by the force of arms.

So long as he had to do with Metellus, he was thought to owe his successes to his opponent's age and slow temper, which were ill-suited for coping with the daring and activity of one who commanded a light army more like a band of robbers than regular soldiers. But when Pompey also passed over the Pyrenees, and Sertorius pitched his camp near him, and offered and himself accepted every occasion by which military skill could be put to the proof, and in this contest of dexterity was found to have the better, both in baffling his enemy's designs and in counter-scheming himself, the fame of him now spread even to Rome itself, as the most expert commander of his time. For the renown of Pompey was not small, who had already won much honor by his achievements in the wars of Sylla, from whom he received the title of Magnus, and was called Pompey the Great; and who had risen to the honor of a triumph before the beard had grown on his face. And many cities which were under Sertorius were on the very eve of revolting and going over to Pompey, when they were deterred from it by that great action, amongst others, which he performed near the city of Lauron, contrary to the expectation of all.

For Sertorius had laid siege to Lauron, and Pompey came with his whole army to relieve it; and there being a hill near this city very advantageously situated, they both made haste to take it. Sertorius was beforehand, and took possession of it first, and Pompey, having drawn down his forces, was not sorry that it had thus happened, imagining that he had hereby inclosed his enemy between his own army and the city, and sent in a messenger to the citizens of Lauron, to bid them be of good courage, and to come upon their walls, where they might see their besieger besieged. Sertorius, perceiving their intentions, smiled, and said, he would now teach Sylla's scholar, for so he called Pompey in derision, that it was the part of a general to look as well behind him as before him, and at the same time showed them six thousand soldiers, whom he had left in his former camp, from whence he marched out to take the hill, where if Pompey should assault him, they might fall upon his rear. Pompey discovered this too late, and not daring to give battle, for fear of being encompassed, and yet being ashamed to desert his friends and confederates in their extreme danger, was thus forced to sit still, and see them ruined before his face. For the besieged despaired of relief, and delivered up themselves to Sertorius, who spared their lives and granted them their liberty, but burnt their city, not out of anger or cruelty, for of all commanders that ever were, Sertorius seems least of all to have indulged these passions, but only for the greater shame and confusion of the admirers of Pompey, and that it might be reported amongst the Spaniards, that though he had been so close to the fire which burnt down the city of his confederates as actually to feel the heat of it, he still had not dared to make any opposition.

Sertorius, however, sustained many losses; but he always maintained himself and those immediately with him undefeated, and it was by other commanders under him that he suffered; and he was more admired for being able to repair his losses, and for recovering the victory, than the Roman generals against him for gaining these advantages; as at the battle of the Sucro against Pompey, and at the battle near Tuttia, against him and Metellus together. The battle near the Sucro was fought, it is said, through the impatience of Pompey, lest Metellus should share with him in the victory, Sertorius being also willing to engage Pompey before the arrival of Metellus. Sertorius delayed the time till the evening, considering that the darkness of the night would be a disadvantage to his enemies, whether flying or pursuing, being strangers, and having no knowledge of the country. When the fight began, it happened that Sertorius was not placed directly against Pompey, but against Afranius, who had command of the left wing of the Roman army, as he commanded the right wing of his own; but when he understood that his left wing began to give way, and yield to the assault of Pompey, he committed the care of his right wing to other commanders, and made haste to relieve those in distress; and rallying some that were flying, and encouraging others that still kept their ranks, he renewed the fight, and attacked the enemy in their pursuit so effectively as to cause a considerable rout, and brought Pompey into great danger of his life. For after being wounded and losing his horse, he escaped unexpectedly. For the Africans with Sertorius, who took Pompey's horse, set out with gold, and covered with rich trappings, fell out with one another; and upon the dividing of the spoil, gave over the pursuit. Afranius, in the mean time, as soon as Sertorius had left his right wing, to assist the other part of his army, overthrew all that opposed him; and pursuing them to their camp, fell in together with them, and plundered them till it was dark night; knowing nothing of Pompey's overthrow, nor being able to restrain his soldiers from pillaging; when Sertorius, returning with victory, fell upon him and upon his men, who were all in disorder, and slew many of them. And the next morning he came into the field again, well armed and offered battle, but perceiving that Mettellus was near, he drew off, and returned to his camp, saying, " If this old woman had not come up, I would have whipped that boy soundly and sent him to Rome."

He was much concerned that his white hind could nowhere be found; as he was thus destitute of an admirable contrivance to encourage the barbarous people, at a time when he most stood in need of it. Some men, however, wandering in the night, chanced to meet her, and knowing her by her color, took her; to whom Sertorius promised a good reward, if they would tell no one of it; and immediately shut her up. A few days after, he appeared in public with a very cheerful look, and declared to the chief men of the country, that the gods had foretold him in a dream that some great good fortune should shortly attend him; and, taking his seat, proceeded to answer the petitions of those who applied themselves to him. The keepers of the hind, who were not far off, now let her loose, and she no sooner espied Sertorius, but she came leaping with great joy to his feet, laid her head upon his knees and licked his hands as she formerly used to do. And Sertorius stroking her, and making much of her again, with that tenderness that the tears stood in his eyes, all that were present were immediately filled with wonder and astonishment, and accompanying him to his house with loud shouts for joy, looked upon him as a person above the rank of mortal men, and highly beloved by the gods; and were in great courage and hope for the future.

When he had reduced his enemies to the last extremity for want of provision, he was forced to give them battle, in the plains near Saguntum, to hinder them from foraging, and plundering the country. Both parties fought gloriously. Memmius, the best commander in Pompey's army, was slain in the heat of the battle. Sertorius overthrew all before him, and with great slaughter of his enemies pressed forward towards Metellus. This old commander, making a resistance beyond what could be expected from one of his years, was wounded with a lance; an occurrence which filled all who either saw it or heard of it, with shame, to be thought to have left their general in distress, but at the same time it provoked them to revenge and fury against their enemies; they covered Metellus with their shields, and brought him off in safety, and then valiantly repulsed the Spaniards; and so victory changed sides, and Sertorius, that he might afford a more secure retreat to his army, and that fresh forces might more easily be raised, retired into a strong city in the mountains. And though it was the least of his intention to sustain a long siege, yet he began to repair the walls, and to fortify the gates, thus deluding his enemies, who came and sat down before the town, hoping to take it without much resistance; and meantime gave over the pursuit of the Spaniards, and allowed opportunity for raising new forces for Sertorius, to which purpose he had sent commanders to all their cities, with orders, when they had sufficiently increased their numbers, to send him word of it. This news he no sooner received, but he sallied out and forced his way through his enemies, and easily joined them with the rest of his army. And having received this considerable reinforcement, he set upon the Romans again, and by rapidly assaulting them, by alarming them on all sides, by ensnaring, circumventing, and laying ambushes for them, he cut off all provisions by land, while with his piratical vessels, he kept all the coast in awe, and hindered their supplies by sea. He thus forced the Roman generals to dislodge, and to separate from one another: Metellus departed into Gaul, and Pompey wintered among the Vaccæans, in a wretched condition, where, being in extreme want of money, he wrote a letter to the senate, to let them know that if they did not speedily supply him, he must draw off his army for he had already spent his own money in the defence of Italy. To these extremities, the chiefest and the most powerful commanders of the age were reduced by the skill of Sertorius; and it was the common opinion in Rome, that he would be in Italy before Pompey.

How far Metellus was terrified, and at what rate he esteemed him, he plainly declared, when he offered by proclamation an hundred talents, and twenty thousand acres of land, to any Roman that should kill him, and leave, if he were banished, to return; attempting villanously to buy his life by treachery, when he despaired of ever being able to overcome him in open war. And when once he gained the advantage in a battle against Sertorius, he was so pleased and transported with his good fortune, that he caused himself to be publicly proclaimed imperator; and all the cities which he visited received him with altars and sacrifices; he allowed himself, it is said, to have garlands placed on his head, and accepted sumptuous entertainments, at which he sat drinking in triumphal robes, while images and figures of victory were introduced by the motion of machines, bringing in with them crowns and trophies of gold to present to him, and companies of young men and women danced before him, and sang to him songs of joy and triumph. By all which he rendered himself deservedly ridiculous, for being so excessively delighted and puffed up with the thoughts of having followed one who was retiring of his own accord, and for having once had the better of him whom he used to call Sylla's runaway slave, and his forces, the remnant of the defeated troops of Carbo.

Sertorius, meantime, showed the loftiness of his temper in calling together all the Roman senators who had fled from Rome, and had come and resided with him, and giving them the name of a senate; and out of these he chose prætors and quæstors, and adorned his government with all the Roman laws and institutions. And though he made use of the arms, riches, and cities of the Spaniards, yet he would never, even in word, remit to them the imperial authority, but set Roman officers and commanders over them, intimating his purpose to restore liberty to the Romans, not to raise up the Spaniard's power against them. For he was a sincere lover of his country, and had a great desire to return home; but in his adverse fortune he showed undaunted courage, and behaved himself towards his enemies in a manner free from all dejection and mean-spiritedness; and when he was in his prosperity, and in the height of his victories, he sent word to Metellus and Pompey, that he was ready to lay down his arms, and live a private life, if he were allowed to return home, declaring that he had rather live as the meanest citizen in Rome, than, exiled from it, be supreme commander of all other cities together. And it is thought that his great desire for his country was in no small measure promoted by the tenderness he had for his mother, under whom he was brought up after the death of his father, and upon whom he had placed his entire affection. And after that his friends had sent for him into Spain to be their general, as soon as he heard of his mother's death, he had almost cast away himself and died for grief; for he lay seven days together continually in his tent, without giving the word, or being seen by the nearest of his friends; and when the chief commanders of the army, and persons of the greatest note came about his tent, with great difficulty they prevailed with him at last to come abroad, and speak to his soldiers, and to take upon him the management of affairs, which were in a prosperous condition. And thus, to many men's judgment, he seemed to have been in himself of a mild and compassionate temper, and naturally given to ease and quietness, and to have accepted of the command of military forces contrary to his own inclination, and not being able to live in safety otherwise, to have been driven by his enemies to have recourse to arms, and to espouse the wars as a necessary guard for the defence of his person.

His negotiations with king Mithridates further argue the greatness of his mind. For when Mithridates, recovering himself from his overthrow by Sylla, like a strong wrestler that gets up to try another fall, was again endeavoring to reëstablish his power in Asia, at this time the great fame of Sertorius was celebrated in all places; and when the merchants who came out of the western parts of Europe, bringing these, as it were, among their other foreign wares, had filled the kingdom of Pontus with their stories of his exploits in war, Mithridates was extremely desirous to send an embassy to him, being also highly encouraged to it by the boastings of his flattering courtiers, who, comparing Mithridates to Pyrrhus, and Sertorius to Hannibal, professed that the Romans would never be able to make any considerable resistance against such great forces, and such admirable commanders, when they should be set upon on both sides at once, on one by the most warlike general, and on the other by the most powerful prince in existence.

Accordingly, Mithridates sends ambassadors into Spain to Sertorius with letters and instructions, and commission to promise ships and money towards the charge of the war; if Sertorius would confirm his pretentions upon Asia, and authorize him to possess all that he had surrendered to the Romans in his treaty with Sylla. Sertorius summoned a full council which he called a senate, where, when others joyfully approved of the conditions, and were desirous immediately to accept of his offer, seeing that he desired nothing of them but a name, and an empty title to places not in their power to dispose of, in recompense of which they should be supplied with what they then stood most in need of, Sertorius would by no means agree to it; declaring that he was willing that king Mithridates should exercise all royal power and authority over Bithynia and Cappadocia, countries accustomed to a monarchical government, and not belonging to Rome, but he could never consent that he should seize or detain a province, which, by the justest right and title, was possessed by the Romans, which Mithridates had formerly taken away from them, and had afterwards lost in open war to Fimbria, and quitted upon a treaty of peace with Sylla. For he looked upon it as his duty to enlarge the Roman possessions by his conquering arms, and not to increase his own power by the diminution of the Roman territories. Since a noble-minded man, though he willingly accepts of victory when it comes with honor, will never so much as endeavor to save his own life upon any dishonorable terms.

When this was related to Mithridates, he was struck with amazement, and said to his intimate friends, "What will Sertorius enjoin us to do when he comes to be seated in the Palatium in Rome, who at present, when he is driven out to the borders of the Atlantic sea, sets bounds to our kingdoms in the east, and threatens us with war, if we attempt the recovery of Asia?" However, they solemnly, upon oath, concluded a league between them, upon these terms: that Mithridates should enjoy the free possession of Cappadocia and Bithynia, and that Sertorius should send him soldiers, and a general for his army, in recompense of which the king was to supply him with three thousand talents and forty ships. Marcus Marius, a Roman senator who had quitted Rome to follow Sertorius, was sent general into Asia, in company with whom when Mithridates had reduced divers of the Asian cities, Marius made his entrance with rods and axes carried before him, and Mithridates followed in the second place, voluntarily waiting upon him. Some of these cities he set at liberty, and others he freed from taxes, signifying to them that these privileges were granted to them by the favor of Sertorius, and hereby Asia, which had been miserably tormented by the revenue-farmers, and oppressed by the insolent pride and covetousness of the soldiers, began to rise again to new hopes, and to look forward with joy to the expected change of government.

But in Spain, the senators about Sertorius, and others of the nobility, finding themselves strong enough for their enemies, no sooner laid aside fear, but their minds were possessed by envy and irrational jealousies of Sertorius's power. And chiefly Perpenna, elevated by the thoughts of his noble birth, and carried away with a fond ambition of commanding the army, threw out villanous discourses in private amongst his acquaintance. "What evil genius," he would say, "hurries us perpetually from worse to worse? We who disdained to obey the dictates of Sylla, the ruler of sea and land, and thus to live at home in peace and quiet, are come hither to our destruction, hoping to enjoy our liberty, and have made ourselves slaves of our own accord, and are become the contemptible guards and attendants of the banished Sertorius, who, that he may expose us the further, gives us a name that renders us ridiculous to all that hear it, and calls us the Senate, when at the same time he makes us undergo as much hard labor, and forces us to be as subject to his haughty commands and insolences, as any Spaniards and Lusitanians." With these mutinous discourses, he seduced them; and though the greater number could not be led into open rebellion against Sertorius, fearing his power, they were prevailed with to endeavor to destroy his interest secretly. For by abusing the Lusitanians and Spaniards, by inflicting severe punishments upon them, by raising exorbitant taxes, and by pretending that all this was done by the strict command of Sertorius, they caused great troubles, and made many cities to revolt; and those who were sent to mitigate and heal these differences, did rather exasperate them, and increase the number of his enemies, and left them at their return more obstinate and rebellious than they found them. And Sertorius, incensed with all this, now so far forgot his former clemency and goodness, as to lay hands on the sons of the Spaniards, educated in the city of Osca; and, contrary to all justice, he cruelly put some of them to death, and sold others.

In the mean time, Perpenna, having increased the number of his conspirators, drew in Manlius, a commander in the army, who, at that time being attached to a youth, to gain his affections the more, discovered the confederacy to him, bidding him neglect others, and be constant to him alone; who, in a few days, was to be a person of great power and authority. But the youth having a greater inclination for Aufidius, disclosed all to him, which much surprised and amazed him. For he was also one of the confederacy, but knew not that Manlius was anyways engaged in it; but when the youth began to name Perpenna, Gracinus, and others, whom he knew very well to be sworn conspirators, he was very much terrified and astonished; but made light of it to the youth, and bade him not regard what Manlius said, a vain boasting fellow. However, he went presently to Perpenna, and giving him notice of the danger they were in, and of the shortness of their time, desired him immediately to put their designs in execution. And when all the confederates had consented to it, they provided a messenger who brought feigned letters to Sertorius, in which he had notice of a victory obtained, it said, by one of his lieutenants, and of the great slaughter of his enemies; and as Sertorius, being extremely well pleased, was sacrificing and giving thanks to the gods for his prosperous success, Perpenna invited him, and those with him, who were also of the conspiracy, to an entertainment, and being very importunate, prevailed with him to come. At all suppers and entertainments where Sertorius was present, great order and decency was wont to be observed, for he would not endure to hear or see any thing that was rude or unhandsome, but made it the habit of all who kept his company, to entertain themselves with quiet and inoffensive amusements. But in the middle of this entertainment, those who sought occasion to quarrel, fell into dissolute discourse openly, and making as if they were very drunk, committed many insolences on purpose to provoke him. Sertorius, being offended with their ill behavior, or perceiving the

state of their minds by their way of speaking and
their unusually disrespectful manner, changed the
posture of his lying, and leaned backward, as one
that neither heard nor regarded them. Perpenna
now took a cup full of wine, and, as he was drinking,
let it fall out of his hand and make a noise, which was
the sign agreed upon amongst them; and Antonius,
who was next to Sertorius, immediately wounded
him with his sword. And whilst Sertorius, upon receiving the wound, turned himself, and strove to get
up, Antonius threw himself upon his breast, and held
both his hands, so that he died by a number of blows,
without being able even to defend himself.

Upon the first news of his death, most of the
Spaniards left the conspirators, and sent embassadors
to Pompey and Metellus, and yielded themselves up
to them. Perpenna attempted to do something with
those that remained, but he made only so much use of
Sertorius's arms and preparations for war, as to disgrace himself in them, and to let it be evident to all,
that he understood no more how to command, than
he knew how to obey; and when he came against
Pompey, he was soon overthrown, and taken prisoner.
Neither did he bear this last affliction with any bravery, but having Sertorius's papers and writings in his
hands, he offered to show Pompey letters from persons of consular dignity, and of the highest quality
in Rome, written with their own hands, expressly
to call Sertorius into Italy, and to let him know what
great numbers there were that earnestly desired to
alter the present state of affairs, and to introduce
another manner of government. Upon this occasion,
Pompey behaved not like a youth, or one of a light
inconsiderate mind, but as a man of a confirmed,
mature, and solid judgment; and so freed Rome from
great fears and dangers of change. For he put all

Sertorius's writings and letters together and read not one of them, nor suffered any one else to read them, but burnt them all, and caused Perpenna immediately to be put to death, lest by discovering their names, further troubles and revolutions might ensue.

Of the rest of the conspirators with Perpenna, some were taken and slain by the command of Pompey, others fled into Africa, and were set upon by the Moors, and run through with their darts; and in a short time, not one of them was left alive, except only Aufidius, the rival of Manlius, who, hiding himself, or not being much inquired after, died an old man, in an obscure village in Spain, in extreme poverty, and hated by all.

EUMENES[1]

TRANSLATED FOR DRYDEN'S EDITION BY
SOME ONE UNNAMED.

DURIS reports that Eumenes, the Cardian, was the son of a poor wagoner in the Thracian Chersonesus, yet liberally educated, both as a scholar and a soldier; and that while he was but young, Philip, passing through Cardia, diverted himself with a sight of the wrestling-matches and other exercises of the youth of that place, among whom Eumenes performing with success, and showing signs of intelligence and bravery, Philip was so pleased with him, as to take him into his service. But they seem to speak more probably, who tell us that Philip advanced Eumenes for the friendship he bore to his father, whose guest he had sometime been. After the death of Philip, he continued in the service of Alexander, with the title of his principal secretary, but in as great favor as the most intimate of his familiars, being esteemed as wise and faithful as any person about him, so that he went with troops under his immediate command as general in the expedition against India, and succeeded to the post of Perdiccas, when Perdiccas was advanced to that of Hephæstion, then newly deceased. And therefore, after the death of Alexander, when Neoptolemus, who had been captain of his lifeguard, said that he had followed Alexander

[1] He was forty-five years old at the time of his death, 316 B. C. Of his ability, both as a general and a statesman, no doubt can be entertained.—Dr. William Smith.

with shield and spear, but Eumenes only with pen and paper, the Macedonians laughed at him, as knowing very well that, besides other marks of favor, the king had done him the honor to make him a kind of kinsman to himself by marriage. For Alexander's first mistress in Asia, by whom he had his son Hercules, was Barsine, the daughter of Artabazus; and in the distribution of the Persian ladies amongst his captains, Alexander gave Apame, one of her sisters, to Ptolemy, and another, also called Barsine, to Eumenes.

Notwithstanding, he frequently incurred Alexander's displeasure, and put himself into some danger, through Hephæstion. The quarters that had been taken up for Eumenes, Hephæstion assigned to Euius, the flute-player. Upon which, in great anger, Eumenes and Mentor came to Alexander, and loudly complained, saying that the way to be regarded was to throw away their arms, and turn flute-players or tragedians; so much so that Alexander took their part and chid Hephæstion; but soon after changed his mind again, and was angry with Eumenes, and accounted the freedom he had taken to be rather an affront to the king, than a reflection upon Hephæstion. Afterwards, when Nearchus, with a fleet, was to be sent to the Southern Sea, Alexander borrowed money of his friends, his own treasury being exhausted, and would have had three hundred talents of Eumenes, but he sent a hundred only, pretending that it was not without great difficulty he had raised so much from his stewards. Alexander neither complained nor took the money, but gave private order to set Eumenes's tent on fire, designing to take him in a manifest lie, when his money was carried out. But before that could be done, the tent was consumed, and Alexander repented of his orders, all his papers

ALEXANDER THE GREAT

being burnt; the gold and silver, however, which was melted down in the fire, being afterwards collected, was found to be more than one thousand talents; yet Alexander took none of it, and only wrote to the several governors and generals to send new copies of the papers that were burnt, and ordered them to be delivered to Eumenes.

Another difference happened between him and Hephæstion concerning a gift, and a great deal of ill language passed between them, yet Eumenes still continued in favor. But Hephæstion dying soon after, the king, in his grief, presuming all those that differed with Hephæstion in his lifetime were now rejoicing at his death, showed much harshness and severity in his behavior with them, especially towards Eumenes, whom he often upbraided with his quarrels and ill language to Hephæstion. But he, being a wise and dexterous courtier, made advantage of what had done him prejudice, and struck in with the king's passion for glorifying his friend's memory, suggesting various plans to do him honor, and contributing largely and readily towards erecting his monument.

After Alexander's death, when the quarrel broke out between the troops of the phalanx and the officers, his companions, Eumenes, though in his judgment he inclined to the latter, yet in his professions stood neuter, as if he thought it unbecoming him, who was a stranger, to interpose in the private quarrels of the Macedonians. And when the rest of Alexander's friends left Babylon, he stayed behind, and did much to pacify the foot-soldiers, and to dispose them towards an accommodation. And when the officers had agreed among themselves, and, recovering from the first disorder, proceeded to share out the several commands and provinces, they made Eumenes governor of Cappadocia and Paphlagonia, and all the coast upon the Pontic Sea as far as Trebizond, which at that time was not subject to the Macedonians, for Ariarathes kept it as king, but Leonnatus and Antigonus, with a large army, were to put him in possession of it. Antigonus, already filled with hopes of his own, and despising all men, took no notice of Perdiccas's letters; but Leonnatus with his army came down into Phrygia to the service of Eumenes. But being visited by Hecatæus, the tyrant of the Cardians, and requested rather to relieve Antipater and the Macedonians that were besieged in Lamia, he resolved upon that expedition, inviting Eumenes to a share in it, and endeavoring to reconcile him to Hecatæus. For there was an hereditary feud between them, arising out of political differences, and Eumenes had more than once been known to denounce Hecatæus as a tyrant, and to exhort Alexander to restore the Cardians their liberty. Therefore at this time, also, he declined the expedition proposed, pretending that he feared lest Antipater, who already hated him, should for that reason and to gratify Hecatæus, kill him. Leonnatus so far believed, as to impart to Eumenes his whole design, which, as he had pretended and given out, was to aid Antipater, but in truth was to seize the kingdom of Macedon; and he showed him letters from Cleopatra,[2] in which, it appeared, she invited him to Pella, with promises to marry him. But Eumenes, whether fearing Antipater, or looking upon Leonnatus as a rash, headstrong, and unsafe man, stole away from him by night, taking with him all his men, namely, three hundred horse, and two hundred of his own servants armed, and all his gold, to the value of five thousand

[2] Alexander's own sister; at the celebration of whose marriage with Alexander of Epirus, Philip was killed.

talents of silver, and fled to Perdiccas, discovered to him Leonnatus's design, and thus gained great interest with him, and was made of the council. Soon after, Perdiccas, with a great army, which he led himself, conducted Eumenes into Cappadocia, and, having taken Ariarathes prisoner, and subdued the whole country, declared him governor of it. He accordingly proceeded to dispose of the chief cities among his own friends and made captains of garrisons, judges, receivers, and other officers, of such as he thought fit himself, Perdiccas not at all interposing. Eumenes, however, still continued to attend upon Perdiccas, both out of respect to him, and a desire not to be absent from the royal family.

But Perdiccas, believing he was able enough to attain his own further objects without assistance, and that the country he left behind him might stand in need of an active and faithful governor, when he came into Cilicia, dismissed Eumenes under color of sending him to his command, but in truth to secure Armenia, which was on its frontier, and was unsettled through the practices of Neoptolemus. Him a proud and vain man, Eumenes exerted himself to gain by personal attentions; but to balance the Macedonian foot, whom he found insolent and self-willed, he contrived to raise an army of horse, excusing from tax and contribution all those of the country that were able to serve on horseback, and buying up a number of horses, which he distributed among such of his own men as he most confided in, stimulating the courage of his new soldiers by gifts and honors, and inuring their bodies to service by frequent marching and exercising; so that the Macedonians were some of them astonished, others overjoyed, to see that in so short a time he had got together a body of no less than six thousand three hundred horsemen.

But when Craterus and Antipater, having subdued the Greeks, advanced into Asia, with intentions to quell the power of Perdiccas, and were reported to design an invasion of Cappadocia, Perdiccas, resolving himself to march against Ptolemy, made Eumenes commander-in-chief of all the forces of Armenia and Cappadocia, and to that purpose wrote letters, requiring Alcetas and Neoptolemus to be obedient to Eumenes, and giving full commission to Eumenes to dispose and order all things as he thought fit. Alcetas flatly refused to serve, because his Macedonians, he said, were ashamed to fight against Antipater, and loved Craterus so well, they were ready to receive him for their commander. Neoptolemus designed treachery against Eumenes, but was discovered; and being summoned, refused to obey, and put himself in a posture of defence. Here Eumenes first found the benefit of his own foresight and contrivance, for his foot being beaten, he routed Neoptolemus with his horse, and took all his baggage; and coming up with his whole force upon the phalanx while broken and disordered in its flight, obliged the men to lay down their arms, and take an oath to serve under him. Neoptolemus, with some few stragglers whom he rallied, fled to Craterus and Antipater. From them had come an embassy to Eumenes, inviting him over to their side, offering to secure him in his present government and to give him additional command, both of men and of territory, with the advantage of gaining his enemy Antipater to become his friend, and keeping Craterus his friend from turning to be his enemy. To which Eumenes replied, that he could not so suddenly be reconciled to his old enemy Antipater, especially at a time when he saw him use his friends like enemies, but was ready to reconcile Craterus to Perdiccas, upon any just and equitable terms;

but in case of any aggression, he would resist the injustice to his last breath, and would rather lose his life than betray his word.

Antipater, receiving this answer, took time to consider upon the whole matter; when Neoptolemus arrived from his defeat, and acquainted them with the ill success of his arms, and urged them to give him assistance, to come, both of them, if possible, but Craterus at any rate, for the Macedonians loved him so excessively, that if they saw but his hat,[3] or heard his voice, they would all pass over in a body with their arms. And in truth, Craterus had a mighty name among them, and the soldiers after Alexander's death were extremely fond of him, remembering how he had often for their sakes incurred Alexander's displeasure, doing his best to withhold him when he began to follow the Persian fashions, and always maintaining the customs of his country, when, through pride and luxuriousness, they began to be disregarded. Craterus, therefore, sent on Antipater into Cilicia, and himself and Neoptolemus marched with a large division of the army against Eumenes; expecting to come upon him unawares, and to find his army disordered with revelling after the late victory. Now that Eumenes should suspect his coming, and be prepared to receive him, is an argument of his vigilance, but not perhaps a proof of any extraordinary sagacity, but that he should contrive both to conceal from his enemies the disadvantages of his position, and from his own men whom they were to fight with, so that he led them on against Craterus himself, without their knowing that he commanded the enemy, this,

---

[3] *His hat* should be rather, perhaps, *his bonnet;* it is the Macedonian broad-flapping *causia,* which their kings, even in Egypt, retained as a mark of their nationality. See the account in the Life of Antony, Vol. V.

indeed, seems to show peculiar address and skill in the general. He gave out that Neoptolemus and Pigres were approaching with some Cappadocian and Paphlagonian horse. And at night, having resolved on marching, he fell asleep, and had an extraordinary dream. For he thought he saw two Alexanders ready to engage, each commanding his several phalanx, the one assisted by Minerva, the other by Ceres; and that after a hot dispute, he on whose side Minerva was, was beaten, and Ceres, gathering ears of corn, wove them into a crown for the victor. This vision Eumenes interpreted at once as boding success to himself, who was to fight for a fruitful country, and at that very time covered with the young ears, the whole being sowed with corn, and the fields so thick with it, that they made a beautiful show of a long peace. And he was further emboldened, when he understood that the enemy's pass-word was Minerva and Alexander. Accordingly he also gave out as his, Ceres and Alexander, and gave his men orders to make garlands for themselves, and to dress their arms with wreaths of corn. He found himself under many temptations to discover to his captains and officers whom they were to engage with, and not to conceal a secret of such moment in his own breast alone, yet he kept to his first resolutions, and ventured to run the hazard of his own judgment.

When he came to give battle, he would not trust any Macedonian to engage Craterus, but appointed two troops of foreign horse, commanded by Pharnabazus, son to Artabazus, and Phœnix of Tenedos, with order to charge as soon as ever they saw the enemy, without giving them leisure to speak or retire, or receiving any herald or trumpet from them. For he was exceedingly afraid about his Macedonians, lest, if they found out Craterus to be there, they should go over to his side. He himself, with three hundred of his best horse, led the right wing against Neoptolemus. When having passed a little hill they came in view, and were seen advancing with more than ordinary briskness, Craterus was amazed, and bitterly reproached Neoptolemus for deceiving him with hopes of the Macedonians' revolt, but he encouraged his men to do bravely, and forthwith charged. The first engagement was very fierce, and the spears being soon broken to pieces, they came to close fighting with their swords; and here Craterus did by no means dishonor Alexander, but slew many of his enemies, and repulsed many assaults, but at last received a wound in his side from a Thracian, and fell off his horse. Being down, many not knowing him went past him, but Gorgias, one of Eumenes's captains, knew him, and alighting from his horse, kept guard over him, as he lay badly wounded and slowly dying. In the mean time Neoptolemus and Eumenes were engaged; who, being inveterate and mortal enemies, sought for one another, but missed for the two first courses, but in the third discovering one another, they drew their swords, and with loud shouts immediately charged. And their horses striking against one another like two galleys, they quitted their reins, and taking mutual hold pulled at one another's helmets, and at the armor from their shoulders. While they were thus struggling, their horses went from under them, and they fell together to the ground, there again still keeping their hold and wrestling. Neoptolemus was getting up first, but Eumenes wounded him in the ham, and got upon his feet before him. Neoptolemus supporting himself upon one knee, the other leg being disabled, and himself undermost, fought courageously, though his blows were not mortal, but receiving a stroke in the neck he fell and

ceased to resist. Eumenes, transported with passion
and his inveterate hatred to him, fell to reviling and
stripping him, and perceived not that his sword was
still in his hand. And with this he wounded Eumenes
under the bottom of his corselet in the groin, but in
truth more frightened than hurt him; his blow being
faint for want of strength. Having stript the dead
body, ill as he was with the wounds he had received
in his legs and arms, he took horse again, and hurried
towards the left wing of his army, which he supposed
to be still engaged. Hearing of the death of Craterus,
he rode up to him, and finding there was yet
some life in him, alighted from his horse and wept,
and laying his right hand upon him, inveighed bitterly
against Neoptolemus, and lamented both Craterus's
misfortune and his own hard fate, that he
should be necessitated to engage against an old friend
and acquaintance, and either do or suffer so much
mischief.

This victory Eumenes obtained about ten days
after the former, and got great reputation alike for
his conduct and his valor in achieving it. But on the
other hand, it created him great envy among his own
troops, and his enemies, that he, a stranger and a
foreigner, should employ the forces and arms of
Macedon, to cut off the bravest and most approved
man among them. Had the news of this defeat come
timely enough to Perdiccas, he had doubtless been the
greatest of all the Macedonians; but now, he being
slain in a mutiny in Egypt, two days before the news
arrived, the Macedonians in a rage decreed Eumenes's
death, giving joint commission to Antigonus and
Antipater to prosecute the war against him. Passing
by Mount Ida, where there was a royal establishment
of horses, Eumenes took as many as he had
occasion for, and sent an account of his doing so to

the overseers, at which Antipater is said to have laughed, calling it truly laudable in Eumenes thus to hold himself prepared for giving in to them [4] (or would it be taking from them?) strict account of all matters of administration. Eumenes had designed to engage in the plains of Lydia, near Sardis, both because his chief strength lay in horse, and to let Cleopatra see how powerful he was. But at her particular request, for she was afraid to give any umbrage to Antipater, he marched into the upper Phrygia, and wintered in Celænæ; when Alcetas, Polemon, and Docimus disputing with him who should command in chief, " You know," said he, " the old saying, That destruction regards no punctilios." Having promised his soldiers pay within three days, he sold them all the farms and castles in the country, together with the men and beasts with which they were filled; every captain or officer that bought, received from Eumenes the use of his engines to storm the place, and divided the spoil among his company, proportionably to every man's arrears. By this Eumenes came again to be popular, so that when letters were found thrown about the camp by the enemy, promising one hundred talents, besides great honors, to any one that should kill Eumenes, the Macedonians were extremely offended, and made an order that from that time forward one thousand of their best men should continually guard his person, and keep strict watch about him by night in their several turns. This order was cheerfully obeyed, and they gladly received of

---

[4] That is, to Antipater and (under him) Antigonus, the former of whom, since Perdiccas's death, held the regency. Eumenes, who had been faithful to Perdiccas, as regent, and was now, therefore, treated as an enemy by his successors, was anxious to maintain his relations with the royal family, all that now was left for him.

Eumenes the same honors which the kings used to confer upon their favorites. He now had leave to bestow purple hats and cloaks, which among the Macedonians is one of the greatest honors the king can give.

Good fortune will elevate even petty minds, and gives them the appearance of a certain greatness and stateliness, as from their high place they look down upon the world; but the truly noble and resolved spirit raises itself, and becomes more conspicuous in times of disaster and ill fortune, as was now the case with Eumenes. For having by the treason of one of his own men lost the field to Antigonus at Orcynii, in Cappadocia, in his flight he gave the traitor no opportunity to escape to the enemy, but immediately seized and hanged him. Then in his flight, taking a contrary course to his pursuers, he stole by them unawares, returned to the place where the battle had been fought, and encamped. There he gathered up the dead bodies, and burnt them with the doors and windows of the neighboring villages, and raised heaps of earth upon their graves; insomuch that Antigonus, who came thither soon after, expressed his astonishment at his courage and firm resolution. Falling afterwards upon the baggage of Antigonus, he might easily have taken many captives, both bond and freemen, and much wealth collected from the spoils of so many wars; but he feared lest his men, overladen with so much booty, might become unfit for rapid retreat, and too fond of their ease to sustain the continual marches and endure the long waiting on which he depended for success, expecting to tire Antigonus into some other course. But then considering it would be extremely difficult to restrain the Macedonians from plunder, when it seemed to offer itself, he gave them order to refresh themselves, and bait their horses, and then attack the enemy. In the mean time he sent privately to Menander, who had care of all his baggage, professing a concern for him upon the score of old friendship and acquaintance; and therefore advising him to quit the plain and secure himself upon the sides of the neighboring hills, where the horse might not be able to hem him in. When Menander, sensible of his danger, had speedily packed up his goods and decamped, Eumenes openly sent his scouts to discover the enemy's posture, and commanded his men to arm, and bridle their horses, as designing immediately to give battle; but the scouts returning with news that Menander had secured so difficult a post it was impossible to take him, Eumenes, pretending to be grieved with the disappointment, drew off his men another way. It is said that when Menander reported this afterwards to Antigonus, and the Macedonians commended Eumenes, imputing it to his singular good-nature, that having it in his power to make slaves of their children, and outrage their wives, he forebore and spared them all, Antigonus replied, " Alas, good friends, he had no regard to us, but to himself, being loath to wear so many shackles when he designed to fly."

From this time Eumenes, daily flying and wandering about, persuaded many of his men to disband, whether out of kindness to them, or unwillingness to lead about such a body of men as were too few to engage, and too many to fly undiscovered. Taking refuge at Nora, a place on the confines of Lycaonia and Cappadocia, with five hundred horse, and two hundred heavy-armed foot, he again dismissed as many of his friends as desired it, through fear of the probable hardships to be encountered there, and embracing them with all demonstrations of kindness, gave them license to depart. Antigonus, when he came before this fort, desired to have an interview with Eumenes before the siege; but he returned answer, that Antigonus had many friends who might command in his room; but they whom Eumenes defended, had no body to substitute if he should miscarry; therefore, if Antigonus thought it worth while to treat with him, he should first send him hostages. And when Antigonus required that Eumenes should first address himself to him as his superior, he replied, " While I am able to wield a sword, I shall think no man greater than myself." At last, when according to Eumenes's demand, Antigonus sent his own nephew Ptolemy to the fort, Eumenes went out to him, and they mutually embraced with great tenderness and friendship, as having formerly been very intimate. After long conversation, Eumenes making no mention of his own pardon and security, but requiring that he should be confirmed in his several governments, and restitution be made him of the rewards of his service, all that were present were astonished at his courage and gallantry. And many of the Macedonians flocked to see what sort of person Eumenes was, for since the death of Craterus, no man had been so much talked of in the army. But Antigonus, being afraid lest he might suffer some violence, first commanded the soldiers to keep off, calling out and throwing stones at those who pressed forwards. At last, taking Eumenes in his arms, and keeping off the crowd with his guards, not without great difficulty, he returned him safe into the fort.

Then Antigonus, having built a wall round Nora, left a force sufficient to carry on the siege, and drew off the rest of his army; and Eumenes was beleaguered and kept garrison, having plenty of corn and water and salt, but no other thing, either for food, or delicacy; yet with such as he had, he kept a cheerful table for his friends, inviting them severally in their turns, and seasoning his entertainment with a gentle and affable behavior. For he had a pleasant countenance, and looked not like an old and practised soldier, but was smooth and florid, and his shape as delicate as if his limbs had been carved by art in the most accurate proportions. He was not a great orator, but winning and persuasive, as may be seen in his letters. The greatest distress of the besieged was the narrowness of the place they were in, their quarters being very confined, and the whole place but two furlongs in compass; so that both they and their horses fed without exercise. Accordingly, not only to prevent the listlessness of such inactive living, but to have them in condition to fly if occasion required, he assigned a room one and twenty feet long, the largest in all the fort, for the men to walk in, directing them to begin their walk gently, and so gradually mend their pace. And for the horses, he tied them to the roof with great halters, fastening which about their necks, with a pulley he gently raised them, till standing upon the ground with their hinder feet, they just touched it with the very ends of their fore feet. In this posture the grooms plied them with whips and shouts, provoking them to curvet and kick out with their hind legs, struggling and stamping at the same time to find support for their fore feet, and thus their whole body was exercised, till they were all in a foam and sweat; excellent exercise, whether for strength or speed; and then he gave them their corn already coarsely ground, that they might sooner despatch, and better digest it.

The siege continuing long, Antigonus received advice that Antipater was dead in Macedon, and that affairs were embroiled by the differences of Cassander and Polysperchon, upon which he conceived no mean hopes, purposing to make himself master of all, and, in order to his design, thought to bring over Eumenes, that he might have his advice and assistance. He, therefore, sent Hieronymus [5] to treat with him, proposing a certain oath, which Eumenes first corrected, and then referred himself to the Macedonians themselves that besieged him, to be judged by them, which of the two forms were the most equitable. Antigonus in the beginning of his had slightly mentioned the kings [6] as by way of ceremony, while all the sequel referred to himself alone; but Eumenes changed the form of it to Olympias and the kings, and proceeded to swear not to be true to Antigonus only, but to them, and to have the same friends and enemies, not with Antigonus, but with Olympias and the kings. This form the Macedonians thinking the more reasonable, swore Eumenes according to it, and raised the siege, sending also to Antigonus, that he should swear in the same form to Eumenes. Meantime, all the hostages of the Cappadocians whom Eumenes had in Nora he returned, obtaining from their friends war horses, beasts of carriage, and tents in exchange. And collecting again all the soldiers who had dispersed at the time of his flight, and were now wandering about the country, he got together a body of near a thousand horse, and with them fled from Antigonous whom he justly feared. For he had sent orders not only to have him blocked up and besieged again, but had given a very sharp answer to the Mace-

[5] Hieronymus of Cardia, his countryman, who afterwards wrote his life.

[6] Arrhidæus Philip, and Alexander Ægus, the former the son of Philip, the latter Alexander's posthumous child by Roxana, the regents for whom had been, first, Perdiccas, on his death Antipater, and now, by Antipater's will, Polysperchon.

donians, for admitting Eumenes's amendment of the oath.

While Eumenes was flying, he received letters from those in Macedonia, who were jealous of Antigonus's greatness, from Olympias, inviting him thither, to take the charge and protection of Alexander's infant son, whose person was in danger, and other letters from Polysperchon, and Philip the king, requiring him to make war upon Antigonus, as general of the forces in Cappadocia, and empowering him out of the treasure at Quinda to take five hundred talents, compensation for his own losses, and to levy as much as he thought necessary to carry on the war. They wrote also to the same effect to Antigenes and Teutamus, the chief officers of the Argyraspids; who, on receiving these letters, treated Eumenes with a show of respect and kindness; but it was apparent enough they were full of envy and emulation, disdaining to give place to him. Their envy Eumenes moderated, by refusing to accept the money, as if he had not needed it; and their ambition and emulation, who were neither able to govern, nor willing to obey, he conquered by help of superstition. For he told them that Alexander had appeared to him in a dream, and showed him a regal pavilion richly furnished, with a throne in it; and told him if they would sit in council there, he himself would be present, and prosper all the consultations and actions upon which they should enter in his name. Antigenes and Teutamus were easily prevailed upon to believe this, being as little willing to come and consult Eumenes, as he himself was to be seen waiting at other men's doors. Accordingly, they erected a tent royal, and a throne, called Alexander's, and there they met to consult upon all affairs of moment.

Afterwards they advanced into the interior of

Asia, and in their march met with Peucestes,[7] who was friendly to them, and with the other satraps, who joined forces with them, and greatly encouraged the Macedonians with the number and appearance of their men. But they themselves, having since Alexander's decease become imperious and ungoverned in their tempers, and luxurious in their daily habits, imagining themselves great princes, and pampered in their conceit by the flattery of the barbarians, when all these conflicting pretensions now came together, were soon found to be exacting and quarrelsome one with another, while all alike unmeasurably flattered the Macedonians, giving them money for revels and sacrifices, till in a short time they brought the camp to be a dissolute place of entertainment, and the army a mere multitude of voters, canvassed as in a democracy for the election of this or that commander. Eumenes, perceiving they despised one another, and all of them feared him, and sought an opportunity to kill him, pretended to be in want of money, and borrowed many talents, of those especially who most hated him, to make them at once confide in him, and forbear all violence to him for fear of losing their own money. Thus his enemies' estates were the guard of his person, and by receiving money he purchased safety, for which it is more common to give it.

The Macedonians, also, while there was no show of danger, allowed themselves to be corrupted, and made all their court to those who gave them presents, who had their body-guards, and affected to appear as generals-in-chief. But when Antigonus came upon them with a great army, and their affairs themselves

[7] The satrap or governor of Persia; the other satraps are also all of the eastern provinces, in which the action continues down to Eumenes's death.

seemed to call out for a true general, then not only the common soldiers cast their eyes upon Eumenes, these men, who had appeared so great in a peaceful time of ease, submitted all of them to him, and quietly posted themselves severally as he appointed them. And when Antigonus attempted to pass the river Pasitigris, all the rest that were appointed to guard the passes were not so much as aware of his march; only Eumenes met and encountered him, slew many of his men, and filled the river with the dead, and took four thousand prisoners. But it was most particularly when Eumenes was sick, that the Macedonians let it be seen how in their judgment, while others could feast them handsomely and make entertainments, he alone knew how to fight and lead an army. For Peucestes, having made a splendid entertainment in Persia, and given each of the soldiers a sheep to sacrifice with, made himself sure of being commander-in-chief. Some few days after, the army was to march, and Eumenes, having been dangerously ill, was carried in a litter apart from the body of the army, that any rest he got might not be disturbed. But when they were a little advanced, unexpectedly they had a view of the enemy, who had passed the hills that lay between them, and was marching down into the plain. At the sight of the golden armor glittering in the sun as they marched down in their order, the elephants with their castles on their backs, and the men in their purple, as their manner was when they were going to give battle, the front stopped their march, and called out for Eumenes, for they would not advance a step but under his conduct; and fixing their arms in the ground, gave the word among themselves to stand, requiring their officers also not to stir or engage or hazard themselves without Eumenes. News of this being brought to Eumenes, he hastened those that carried his litter, and drawing back the curtains on both sides, joyfully put forth his right hand. As soon as the soldiers saw him, they saluted him in their Macedonian dialect, and took up their shields, and striking them with their pikes, gave a great shout; inviting the enemy to come on, for now they had a leader.

Antigonus understanding by some prisoners he had taken that Eumenes was out of health, to that degree that he was carried in a litter, presumed it would be no hard matter to crush the rest of them, since he was ill. He therefore made the greater haste to come up with them and engage. But being come so near as to discover how the enemy was drawn up and appointed, he was astonished, and paused for some time; at last he saw the litter carrying from one wing of the army to the other, and, as his manner was, laughing aloud, he said to his friends, "That litter there, it seems, is the thing that offers us battle;" and immediately wheeled about, retired with all his army, and pitched his camp. The men on the other side, finding a little respite, returned to their former habits, and allowing themselves to be flattered, and making the most of the indulgence of their generals, took up their winter quarters near the whole country of the Gabeni,[8] so that the front was quartered nearly a thousand furlongs from the rear; which Antigonus understanding, marched suddenly towards them, taking the most difficult road through a country that wanted water; but the way was short though uneven; hoping, if he should surprise them thus scattered in their winter quarters, the soldiers would not easily be able to come up time enough, and join with their officers. But having to pass through a country uninhab-

---

[8] Gabene, or Gabiene.

ited, where he met with violent winds and severe frosts, he was much checked in his march, and his men suffered exceedingly. The only possible relief was making numerous fires, by which his enemies got notice of his coming. For the barbarians who dwelt on the mountains overlooking the desert, amazed at the multitude of fires they saw, sent messengers upon dromedaries to acquaint Peucestes. He being astonished and almost out of his senses with the news, and finding the rest in no less disorder, resolved to fly, and collect what men he could by the way. But Eumenes relieved him from his fear and trouble, undertaking so to stop the enemy's advance, that he should arrive three days later than he was expected. Having persuaded them, he immediately despatched expresses to all the officers to draw the men out of their winter quarters, and muster them with all speed. He himself with some of the chief officers rode out, and chose an elevated tract within view, at a distance, of such as travelled the desert; this he occupied and quartered out, and commanded many fires to be made in it, as the custom is in a camp. This done, and the enemies seeing the fire upon the mountains, Antigonus was filled with vexation and despondency, supposing that his enemies had been long since advertised of his march, and were prepared to receive him. Therefore, lest his army, now tired and wearied out with their march, should be forced immediately to encounter with fresh men, who had wintered well, and were ready for him, quitting the near way, he marched slowly through the towns and villages to refresh his men. But meeting with no such skirmishes as are usual when two armies lie near one another, and being assured by the people of the country that no army had been seen, but only continual fires in that place, he concluded he had been outwitted by a stratagem of

Eumenes, and much troubled, advanced to give open battle.

By this time, the greatest part of the forces were come together to Eumenes, and admiring his sagacity, declared him alone commander-in-chief of the whole army; upon with Antigenes and Teutamus, the commanders of the Argyraspids, being very much offended, and envying Eumenes, formed a conspiracy against him; and assembling the greater part of the satraps and officers, consulted when and how to cut him off. When they had unanimously agreed, first to use his service in the next battle, and then to take an occasion to destroy him, Eudamus, the master of the elephants, and Phædimus, gave Eumenes private advice of this design, not out of kindness or good-will to him, but lest they should lose the money they had lent him. Eumenes, having commended them, retired to his tent, and telling his friends he lived amnog a herd of wild beasts, made his will, and tore up all his letters, lest his correspondents after his death should be questioned or punished on account of anything in his secret papers. Having thus disposed of his affairs, he thought of letting the enemy win the field, or of flying through Media and Armenia and seizing Cappadocia, but came to no resolution while his friends stayed with him. After turning to many expedients in his mind, which his changeable fortune had made versatile, he at last put his men in array, and encouraged the Greeks and barbarians; as for the phalanx and the Argyraspids, they encouraged him, and bade him be of good heart, for the enemy would never be able to stand them. For indeed they were the oldest of Philip's and Alexander's soldiers, tried men, that had long made war their exercise, that had never been beaten or foiled; most of them seventy, none less than sixty years old. And so when they charged Antigonus's men, they cried out, "You fight against your fathers, you rascals," and furiously falling on, routed the whole phalanx at once, nobody being able to stand them, and the greatest part dying by their hands. So that Antigonus's foot were routed, but his horse got the better, and he became master of the baggage, through the cowardice of Peucestes, who behaved himself negligently and basely; while Antigonus used his judgment calmly in the danger, being aided moreover by the ground. For the place where they fought was a large plain, neither deep, nor hard under foot, but, like the sea-shore, covered with a fine soft sand, which the treading of so many men and horses, in the time of the battle, reduced to a small white dust, that like a cloud of lime darkened the air, so that one could not see clearly at any distance, and so made it easy for Antigonus to take the baggage unperceived.

After the battle, Teutamus sent a message to Antigonus to demand the baggage. He made answer, he would not only restore it to the Argyaspids, but serve them further in other things if they would but deliver up Eumenes. Upon which the Argyraspids took a villanous resolution to deliver him up alive into the hands of his enemies. So they came to wait upon him, being unsuspected by him, but watching their opportunity, some lamenting the loss of the baggage, some encouraging him as if he had been victor, some accusing the other commanders, till at last they all fell upon him, and seizing his sword, bound his hands behind him with his own girdle. When Antigonus had sent Nicanor to receive him, he begged he might be led through the body of the Macedonians, and have liberty to speak to them, neither to request, nor deprecate any thing, but only to advise them what would be for their interest. A silence being made, as he stood upon a rising ground, he stretched out his hands bound, and said, "What trophy, O ye basest of all the Macedonians, could Antigonus have wished for so great as you yourselves have erected for him, in delivering up your general captive into his hands? You are not ashamed, when you are conquerors, to own yourselves conquered, for the sake only of your baggage, as if it were wealth, not arms, wherein victory consisted; nay, you deliver up your general to redeem your stuff. As for me, I am unvanquished, though a captive, conqueror of my enemies, and betrayed by my fellow soldiers. For you, I adjure you by Jupiter, the protector of arms, and by all the gods that are the avengers of perjury, to kill me here with your own hands; for it is all one; and if I am murdered yonder, it will be esteemed your act, nor will Antigonus complain, for he desires not Eumenes alive, but dead. Or if you withhold your own hands, release but one of mine, it shall suffice to do the work; and if you dare not trust me with a sword, throw me bound as I am under the feet of the wild beasts. This if you do I shall freely acquit you from the guilt of my death, as the most just and kind of men to their general."

While Eumenes was thus speaking, the rest of the soldiers wept for grief, but the Argyraspids shouted out to lead him on, and give no attention to his trifling. For it was no such great matter if this Chersonesian pest should meet his death, who in thousands of battles had annoyed and wasted the Macedonians; it would be a much more grievous thing for the choicest of Philip's and Alexander's soldiers to be defrauded of the fruits of so long service, and in their old age to come to beg their bread, and to leave their wives three nights in the power of their enemies. So they hurried him on with violence. But Antigonus, fearing the multitude, for nobody was left in the camp, sent ten of his strongest elephants with divers of his Mede and Parthian lances to keep off the press. Then he could not endure to have Eumenes brought into his presence, by reason of their former intimacy and friendship; but when they that had taken him inquired how he would have him kept, "As I would," said he, "an elephant or a lion." A little after, being moved with compassion, he commanded the heaviest of his irons to be knocked off, one of his servants to be admitted to anoint him, and that any of his friends that were willing should have liberty to visit him, and bring him what he wanted. Long time he deliberated what to do with him, sometimes inclining to the advice and promises of Nearchus of Crete, and Demetrius his son, who were very earnest to preserve Eumenes, whilst all the rest were unanimously instant and importunate to have him taken off. It is related that Eumenes inquired of Onomarchus, his keeper, why Antigonus now he had his enemy in his hands, would not either forthwith dispatch or generously release him? And that Onomarchus contumeliously answered him, that the field had been a more proper place than this to show his contempt of death. To whom Eumenes replied, "And by heavens, I showed it there; ask the men else that engaged me, but I could never meet a man that was my superior." "Therefore," rejoined Onomarchus, "now you have found such a man, why don't you submit quietly to his pleasure?"

When Antigonus resolved to kill Eumenes, he commanded to keep his food from him, and so with two or three days' fasting he began to draw near his end; but the camp being on a sudden to remove, an executioner was sent to dispatch him. Antigonus granted his body to his friends, permitted them to burn it, and having gathered his ashes into a silver urn, to send them to his wife and children.

Eumenes was thus taken off; and Divine Providence assigned to no other man the chastisement of the commanders and soldiers that had betrayed him; but Antigonus himself, abominating the Argyraspids as wicked and inhuman villains, delivered them up to Sibyrtius, the governor of Arachosia, commanding him by all ways and means to destroy and exterminate them, so that not a man of them might ever come to Macedon, or so much as within sight of the Greek sea.

COMPARISON OF SERTORIUS WITH EUMENES

THESE are the most remarkable passages that are come to our knowledge concerning Eumenes and Sertorius. In comparing their lives, we may observe that this was common to them both; that being aliens, strangers and banished men, they came to be commanders of powerful forces, and had the leading of numerous and warlike armies, made up of divers nations. This was peculiar to Sertorius, that the chief command was, by his whole party, freely yielded to him, as to the person of the greatest merit and renown, whereas Eumenes had many who contested the office with him, and only by his actions obtained the superiority. They followed the one honestly, out of desire to be commanded by him; they submitted themselves to the other for their own security, because they could not command themselves. The one, being a Roman, was the general of the Spaniards and Lusitanians, who for many years had been under the subjection of Rome; and the other, a Chersonesian, was chief commander of the Macedonians, who were the great conquerors of mankind, and were at that time subduing the world. Sertorius, being already in high esteem for his former services in the wars, and his abilities in the senate, was advanced to the dignity of a general; whereas Eumenes obtained this honor from the office of a writer, or secretary, in which he had been despised. Nor did he only at first rise from inferior opportunities, but afterwards, also, met with greater impediments in the progress of his authority, and that not only from those who publicly resisted him, but from many others that privately conspired against him. It was much otherwise with Sertorius, not one of whose party publicly opposed him, only late in life and secretly a few of his acquaintance entered into a conspiracy against him. Sertorius put an end to his dangers as often as he was victorious in the field, whereas the victories of Eumenes were the beginning of his perils, through the malice of those that envied him.

Their deeds in war were equal and parallel, but their general inclinations different. Eumenes naturally loved war and contention, but Sertorius esteemed peace and tranquillity; when Eumenes might have lived in safety, with honor, if he would have quietly retired out of their way, he persisted in a dangerous contest with the greatest of the Macedonian leaders; but Sertorius, who was unwilling to trouble himself with any public disturbances, was forced, for the safety of his person, to make war against those who would not suffer him to live in peace. If Eumenes could have contented himself with the second place, Antigonus, freed from his competition for the first, would have used him well, and shown him favor, whereas Pompey's friends would never permit Sertorius so much as to live in quiet. The one made war of his own accord, out of a desire for command; and the other was constrained to accept of command, to defend himself from war that was made against him. Eumenes was certainly a true lover of war, for he preferred his covetous ambition before his own security; but Sertorius was truly warlike, who procured his own safety by the success of his arms.

As to the manner of their deaths, it happened to one without the least thought or surmise of it; but to the other when he suspected it daily; which in the first, argues an equitable temper, and a noble mind, not to distrust his friends; but in the other, it showed some infirmity of spirit, for Eumenes intended to fly and was taken. The death of Sertorius dishonored not his life; he suffered that from his companions which none of his enemies were ever able to perform. The other, not being able to deliver himself before his imprisonment, being willing also to live in captivity, did neither prevent nor expect his fate with honor or bravery; for by meanly supplicating and petitioning, he made his enemy, that pretended only to have power over his body, to be lord and master of his body and mind.